ECONOMIC AND SOCIAL RIGHTS UNDER THE EU CHARTER OF FUNDAMENTAL RIGHTS— A LEGAL PERSPECTIVE

The Charter of Fundamental Rights of the European Union includes, in addition to the traditional 'civil and political rights', a large number of rights of an economic or social nature. This collection of essays by leading scholars in this field considers the significance of the inclusion of such rights within the EU Charter, in terms of protection of individual and collective social and economic interests within and between the EU and its Member States. What differences might it make to EU law and policy (both in terms of its substance, and in terms of the processes by which it is formed), that certain economic and social rights are proclaimed in the EU Charter?

Economic and Social Rights under the EU Charter of Fundamental Rights—A Legal Perspective

Edited by
TAMARA K HERVEY AND JEFF KENNER
University of Nottingham

·HART·
PUBLISHING

OXFORD – PORTLAND OREGON
2003

Published in North America (US and Canada) by
Hart Publishing
c/o International Specialized Book Services
5804 NE Hassalo Street
Portland, Oregon
97213-3644
USA

Hart Publishing is a specialist legal publisher based in Oxford, England.
To order further copies of this book or to request a list of other
publications please write to:

Hart Publishing, Salter's Boatyard, Folly Bridge,
Abingdon Road, Oxford OX1 4LB
Telephone: +44 (0)1865 245533 or Fax: +44 (0)1865 794882
e-mail: mail@hartpub.co.uk
WEBSITE: http//:www.hartpub.co.uk

British Library Cataloguing in Publication Data
Data Available
ISBN 1–84113–095–8 (hardback)

Typeset by Hope Services (Abingdon) Ltd.
Printed and bound in Great Britain by
Biddles Ltd, *www.biddles.co.uk*

Contents

Introduction

The Charter of Fundamental Rights of the European Union, solemnly proclaimed at Nice in December 2000, brings together 'modern' economic and social rights with 'traditional' and more widely recognised civil and political rights in a single text that boldly aims to make visible the 'common values' of European Union (EU) citizens. Fundamental rights proclaimed in the Charter are drawn from a variety of international and national sources including human rights instruments of the United Nations, the Council of Europe and the European Community's own Charter of the Fundamental Social Rights of Workers of 1989. Additional sources include the European Community Treaty, Community legislation and case law of both the European Court of Justice and the European Court of Human Rights. This edited collection explores, from a legal perspective, the significance of the elevation of economic and social rights in the Charter, the content of those rights and their relationship with civil, political and cultural rights, both as expressed in the Charter and elsewhere in international and national human rights law.

The publication of this collection is intended to coincide with the final stages of the work of the Convention on the Future of the European Union which has, as part of its mandate, the task of debating the legal status of the Charter and its place in a putative 'Constitution for European citizens'.[1] The uncertainty as to the legal status of the Charter[2] may be compounded, with respect to economic and social rights found in the Charter, by the uncertainty as to the legal effectiveness of such rights more generally. The Charter is addressed to the institutions and bodies of the EU and to its Member States 'only when they are implementing Union law'.[3] In the context of economic and social rights, the obligations in the Charter range from negative obligations not to interfere in the exercise of a particular right, through more positive obligations to protect and ensure effective exercise of a right, to obligations to promote rights of a programmatic or aspirational nature. Economic and social rights are traditionally conceptualised as falling into the latter category. However, even rights in the

---

[1] Laeken Declaration on the 'The Future of European Union', 15 December 2001. Available at: <http://europa.eu.int/futurum/documents>.

[2] The Charter is not formally binding in the sense of having full legislative scope. However, as Advocate General Tizzano has stated, in the context of the right to annual paid leave in Art 31(2) EUCFR, that, 'in proceedings concerned with the nature and scope of a fundamental right, the relevant statements of the Charter cannot be ignored' (Case C–173/99 *R v Secretary of State for Trade and Industry, ex parte BECTU* [2001] ECR I–4881, Opinion of 8 February 2001, para 28).

[3] Art 51(1) EUCFR.

latter sense may impose enforceable obligations, for instance an obligation not to retract from rights once given.[4]

The papers in this collection engage with a number of inter-related research questions, with respect to the status of economic and social rights within the Charter, in the contexts of international human rights law and the place of the Charter within the EU's unique legal order. Research questions include: the extent to which the rights set out in the Charter merely codify or represent a development of existing provisions of Community or EU law; whether strategic litigation based on economic and social rights in the Charter might be conceived; what are the relationships between the 'economic' and 'social' rights in the Charter and those contained in international or national constitutional instruments; how problems with social rights in a market legal order might be resolved; and the relationship between social rights in the Charter and the EU's emerging constitutional order, new modes of governance and juridical constitutionalism.

The publication of this collection follows a workshop entitled *Economic and Social Rights under the EU Charter of Fundamental Rights: a legal perspective*, held at the School of Law, University of Nottingham, on 28–29 June 2002. All the papers in this collection were presented and fully debated at the workshop attended by both the paper givers and invited discussants. The mix of expertise among the participants (comprising EU, human rights, international and labour lawyers, from both civil and common law traditions) made for a lively debate and exchange of different perspectives, drawing together links and contradictions between the different papers. These different perspectives, and also the different legal methodologies brought by the various contributors, are reflected in this collection.

As we were holding our workshop in June 2002, Frank Vandenbroucke, the Belgian minister for social affairs, sketched his vision for the EU's involvement in the development of social policy. He took the view that the social protection agenda in the EU 'remains politically and institutionally fragile'. One of our over-arching research questions in this collection has been to consider the extent to which the Charter might affect that position. In the context of globalisation, post-Fordism and other challenges and changes to the post-war European labour law and welfare settlement, could the expression of economic and social rights in the Charter actually make a difference in terms of embedding values of community and solidarity within the EU's legal order? To what extent could the Charter *improve upon* or go beyond that 1950s labour and welfare settlement— for instance, by encompassing different gender roles in the workplace and family, or taking account of the multi-cultural nature of European societies? Ultimately the values of community and solidarity proceed from the basis of judging a society in terms of its treatment of the least privileged within it—or even its treatment of those who are 'outsiders'. Traditionally, one way of

---

[4] See Art 53 EUCFR on the level of protection.

expressing these values is to adopt the terminology of human rights, with all its 'normative cachet'. Rights inhere in individuals by virtue of their humanity, not their status, and therefore by definition encompass the least privileged, the 'excluded' and the 'outsider'. Extending the concept of 'rights' to labour law rights and social or welfare rights and principles may constitute one mechanism for shoring up values of community and solidarity. While legal mechanisms, including 'rights', are of course inherently limited in terms of their ability to alter power relationships in society, they do represent one potent institutional force that at least potentially may have that effect. Ultimately, then, if they are to survive, the values of community and solidarity need to find expression (perhaps as rights) within all the global over-lapping legal orders or discourses. These would of course include national constitutional legal orders and traditional international human rights fora, but also trade-related legal orders such as that of the World Trade Organisation and the EU. Does the inclusion of economic and social rights in the Charter therefore signal a change of status of these values within the EU's legal order?

Looking at the contributions overall, responses to this question have been mixed. Some contributors (Barbera, Costello) have pointed to the potential that the Charter may have for protecting social values and engendering a more deliberative and dynamic form of European constitutionalism (Poiares Maduro). In this light, some have pointed to the significance of the inclusion of economic and social rights (and also cultural rights) in the same document as civil and political rights (Bell, Deakin & Browne, Wallace & Shaw, Kenner); to the possibility of using the Charter to shore up the positions of the less-privileged, for instance within internal market or competition law litigation (Hunt, Ryan, Hervey); or in the law and policy-making processes of the EU institutions and Member States (Poiares Maduro, Bernard, Bell, Barbera, Tooze). In the specific context of litigation, contributors have discussed the potential for courts to use the Charter in their armoury against dominant positions represented by capital rather than labour, but the limited scope for the EU courts to invoke the Charter has also been recognised (Bernard, Poiares Maduro). Several contributors have highlighted negative features of the Charter, such as gaps in coverage (Bell, Hervey), hierarchies of rights and principles (Hunt, Kenner); inconsistencies with what has already been achieved, through either national, EU or international fora (Tooze), and to the extent that the Charter expresses rights as inhering in individuals, it may also be fundamentally problematic in terms of essentially collective values such as community and solidarity (Ryan).

A further set of research questions considered in this collection focuses on the models or assumptions that underpin the provisions found in the Charter. For instance, what model or models of equality does the Charter express (Bell, Costello, Wallace & Shaw)? What notions—in terms of representativity, legitimacy, democracy and accountability—underpin the Charter's provisions on collective activity in the labour law field (Ryan, Bernard)? How far is the Charter compatible with the capability approach whereby social rights can help to shape the mobilisation of labour and resources at local level and act as a bridge between the welfare state and the market (Deakin & Browne)?

Finally, the collection engages with a set of research questions relating to the relationship between economic and social rights in the Charter and the EU's methods of governance. This is particularly significant given the application of the EU's 'new governance' processes to many of the main 'sites' of economic and social rights in the revised EC Treaty post-Nice: in particular, labour law, employment promotion and social exclusion. Will these 'new governance' methods extend the reach of the Charter to national social and cultural policies (Bernard, Wallace & Shaw)? Does the true significance of the Charter lie in the *process* by which it was reached—a process perhaps endowing the Charter with greater legitimacy than the EU's 'ordinary' intergovernmental settlements, as a 'constitutional moment' of true importance (Poiares Maduro)? If the Charter is the start of a dialogic process, rather than the expression of some sort of human rights nirvana, can we hope for a more enriched dialogue, given the rich traditions the Charter has called upon (Wallace & Shaw, Costello, Bell, Bernard, Kenner, Tooze)? This may be one of the most significant elements of the Charter, if it can be seen as part of a historical process of articulating—through various dialogues—economic and social rights as part of an ongoing process of deliberative constitutionalism (Poiares Maduro).

The collection begins with an overview of the history of economic and social rights in the EU's legal order, in the context of an analysis of whether the Charter's apparent commitment to the 'indivisibility' of human rights is real or a 'mirage' (Kenner). This locates the Charter's economic and social rights within the wider international human rights discourse on 'indivisibility' of rights. The next chapter develops this theme by arguing for a conception of 'social rights' that not only recognises their equivalence with 'market rights', but also identifies them as a constitutive part of a functioning market order. In this way the market can be understood as a mechanism for the application of social rights through processes of regulatory learning and reflexive law (Deakin & Browne). There follow two chapters considering the impact or potential impact of the Charter on individual (Hunt) and collective (Ryan) labour law at both EU and national levels. Three chapters then turn to the Charter's provisions on equality and non-discrimination. Bell sets the scene, with an overview of the general equality provisions in the Charter. This is followed by a more detailed examination of the Charter's gender equality provisions, in the context of their interactions with other equality provisions (Costello), and the specific measures on 'reconciliation of work and family life' (Barbera). The emphasis of the latter, of necessity, takes the enquiry outside the labour market sphere, and chapters follow this on the provisions on social security and social assistance (Tooze) and health care (Hervey) in the Charter. The other 'social welfare' element considered in the collection is that of education, and this is discussed in the context of the Charter's contribution or potential contribution to the multi-culturalism agenda in the EU (Wallace & Shaw). One of Wallace and Shaw's conclusions is that the processes by which the Charter was negotiated may turn out to be more significant than its actual content. The collection closes with two further contributions concerned with the Charter's medium and longer-term significance for governance and constitutional processes in the EU (Bernard, Poiares Maduro). Bernard identifies the Open Method of Co-ordination as potentially the most effective mechanism for adapting the Charter to the circumstances of each Member State and providing a filter for the development of a European discourse on fundamental rights. Poiares Maduro highlights the dual nature of the Charter as both an independent and dynamic source of European constitutionalism, distinct from national constitutions, and, paradoxically, as a tool to limit the integration of Europe by raising the status of national constitutional values.

We gratefully acknowledge the funding given for the workshop from the British Academy (Award No BCG–33316) and, at the University of Nottingham, the Human Rights Law Centre and the School of Law. We would also like to thank Catherine Lovesy for her excellent administrative support for the project as a whole, particularly the organisation of the workshop, and the support given by our two graduate students, Tawhida Ahmed and Lioubov Samokhina at the workshop. Tawhida Ahmed also deserves special thanks for her editorial support for this collection.

The discussants and other participants at the workshop—Kenneth Armstrong, Catherine Barnard, David Harris, Robert McCorquodale, Clare McGlynn, Jean McHale, Tonia Novitz, Steve Peers, Joanne Scott, Phil Syrpis, Patrick Twomey, Martin Trybus, Lisa Waddington and Stephen Weatherill—were unstinting with their time and energy, and we gratefully acknowledge their contributions, comments and suggestions. Finally, we would like to thank Richard Hart, for being the most understanding publisher with whom we have ever worked.

Tamara K Hervey and Jeff Kenner
Nottingham, February 2003

List of Contributors

Marzia Barbera is Professor of Labour Law, University of Brescia.

Mark Bell is a Senior Lecturer in Law, Centre for European Law and Integration, University of Leicester.

Nicholas Bernard is a Reader in Law, Queen's University Belfast.

Jude Browne is a Research Fellow, Centre for Business Research, University of Cambridge.

Cathryn Costello is a Lecturer in European Law, University of Dublin.

Simon Deakin is Robert Monks Professor of Corporate Governance, Centre for Business Research, University of Cambridge.

Tamara K Hervey is Professor of Law, University of Nottingham.

Jo Hunt is a Lecturer in Law at Cardiff University, and an associate member of the university's Centre for Business Relationships, Accountability, Sustainability and Society (BRASS).

Jeff Kenner is a Senior Lecturer in Law, University of Nottingham.

Miguel Poiares Maduro is Professor of Law, New University of Lisbon.

Bernard Ryan is a Lecturer in Law, University of Kent.

Jo Shaw is Professor and Jean Monnet Chair of European Law, University of Manchester; and Senior Research Fellow at the Federal Trust for Education and Research, London.

Jennifer Tooze is a Home Office sponsored legal trainee. Previously, a PhD student at the University of Nottingham.

Chloë Wallace is a Lecturer in Law, Centre for the Study of Law and Policy in Europe, University of Leeds.

Table of Cases

European Court of Justice and Court of First Instance
(Alphabetical)

Table of Legislation

COUNCIL OF EUROPE

NATIONAL

Belgium

Table of Abbreviations

CFI	Court of First Instance
the Charter	Charter of Fundamental Rights of the European Union, 2000
the Community Social Charter	Community Charter of the Fundamental Social Rights of Workers, 1989
CRC	UN Convention on the Rights of the Child, 1989
the Court	European Court of Justice
EC	Treaty establishing the European Community
ECHR	European Convention on Human Rights, 1950
ESC	European Social Charter, 1961
EUCFR	Charter of Fundamental Rights of the European Union, 2000
Explanatory Document	Explanations relating to the complete text of the Charter
ICCPR	International Covenant on Civil and Political Rights, 1966
ICESCR	International Covenant on Economic, Social and Cultural Rights, 1966
ILO	International Labour Organisation
OMC	Open Method of Co-ordination
RevESC	Revised European Social Charter, 1996
(Rev)ESC	Consolidated version of the European Social Charter (as revised)
TEU	Treaty on European Union
UN	United Nations

1

Economic and Social Rights in the EU Legal Order: The Mirage of Indivisibility

JEFF KENNER*

INTRODUCTION

All human rights are universal, indivisible and interdependent and interrelated. The international community must treat human rights globally in a fair and equal manner, on the same footing, and with the same emphasis.
(UN Vienna Declaration and Programme of Action, 25 June 1993)[1]

Conscious of its spiritual and moral heritage, the Union is founded on the indivisible, universal values of human dignity, freedom, equality and solidarity . . .
(Charter of Fundamental Rights of the European Union, 7 December 2000)[2]

WHEN JUXTAPOSED THESE statements—both of which stem from the Universal Declaration of Human Rights (UDHR)[3]—allude to a seamless, non-hierarchical affirmation of inalienable rights and shared societal values that are at once intertwined and capable of promotion and protection in equal measure without reference to crude and artificial categorisations.

However, the language of indivisibility, although frequently utilised, cloaks the reality of a 50-year long schism between 'classic' civil and political rights and freedoms, the foundations of which were laid in the eighteenth century,[4] and 'modern' or 'second generation' economic and social rights and principles, associated with the twentieth century welfare state and the introduction of international labour standards.[5] In February 1952, at the height of the Cold

---

* School of Law, University of Nottingham. The author would like to thank Stephen Weatherill, Tamara Hervey, Kenneth Armstrong, David Harris, Robert McCorquodale, Patrick Twomey, Martin Trybus and other contributors to the Workshop for their helpful comments and suggestions.

[1] World Conference on Human Rights, A/CONF. 157/23, point 5.

[2] OJ 2000 C364/1, second para of the preamble.

[3] Adopted by UN General Assembly resolution 217 A (III) of 10 December 1948.

[4] In particular, the American Declaration of Independence, 1776, and the French Declaration of the Rights of Man and the Citizen, 1789.

[5] Following the establishment of the International Labour Organisation (ILO), after the signing of the Treaty of Versailles in 1919, in order to establish 'fair and humane conditions of

War,[6] the UN General Assembly passed a resolution to divide the rights and aspirations proclaimed in the UDHR into two separate covenants,[7] one concerning civil and political rights,[8] the other addressing economic, social and cultural rights,[9] each legally binding under international law. These developments were mirrored at regional level where the newly established Council of Europe drafted two separate treaties, the European Convention on Human Rights 1950 (ECHR)[10] and the European Social Charter 1961 (ESC),[11] prioritising the former over the latter and establishing different mechanisms for enforcement and monitoring.

In the ensuing period, at both a theoretical and practical level, civil and political rights have received broad support and recognition in liberal democracies, whereas economic and social rights tend to have a subordinate status and remain highly contested.[12] To an extent this can be understood as an inevitable consequence of disagreements about the framework of 'rights' and 'citizenship'[13] and the almost overwhelming desire of political leaders to reach constitutional settlements based on 'the right to have rights'.[14]

These disagreements all too often lead to decisions to downgrade or exclude economic and social rights, often on the basis of highly contentious assumptions about the overriding importance of liberalism, individualism and the sanctity of

labour'. These post-war developments coincided with the codification of economic and social rights at national level, most notably, the Mexican Constitution, 1917, the Constitution of the Soviet Union, 1918, and the Constitution of Weimar, 1919. See further, L Betten & N Grief, *EU Law and Human Rights* (Harlow, Longman, 1998) pp 4–5.

[6]   The United States, which had been initially supportive of economic and social rights, following President Roosevelt's avowal of 'freedom from want' in 1941, reversed its position, fearing that the expansion of state obligations associated with the realisation of these rights would lead to growth in communism and Soviet influence.

[7]   General Assembly resolution 543 (VI) of 5 February 1952, overturning General Assembly resolution 421 (V) of 4 December 1950. See further, A Eide & A Rosas, 'Economic, Social and Cultural Rights: A Universal Challenge' in A Eide, C Krause & A Rosas (eds), *Economic, Social and Cultural Rights: A Textbook* (Dordrecht, Martinus Nijhoff, 1995) 15–19.

[8]   International Covenant on Civil and Political Rights (ICCPR), adopted by General Assembly resolution 2200A (XXI), 16 December 1966. The ICCPR entered into legal force on 23 March 1976.

[9]   International Covenant on Economic, Social and Cultural Rights (ICESCR), adopted by General Assembly resolution 2200A (XXI), 16 December 1966. The ICESR entered into legal force on 3 January 1976. For analysis, see M Craven, *The International Covenant on Economic, Social and Cultural Rights* (Oxford, Clarendon Press, 1995).

[10]   Adopted in 1950, 87 UNTS 103. The ECHR entered into force in 1953. See further, D Harris, M O'Boyle & C Warbrick, *Law of the European Convention on Human Rights* (London, Butterworths, 1995).

[11]   Adopted in 1961, 529 UNTS 89. The ESC entered into force in 1965. For analysis, see D Harris, *The European Social Charter*, 8th edn (Charlottesville, University of Virginia Press, 1984), O Kahn-Freund, 'The European Social Charter' in F Jacobs (ed), *European Law and the Individual* (North-Holland, Amsterdam, 1976) 181–211.

[12]   See Eide & Rosas, above n 7 at 15.

[13]   See J Waldron, *Law and Disagreement* (Oxford, OUP, 1999) 107–18.

[14]   This phrase has been widely attributed to Hannah Arendt. For discussion see, C Lefort, *Democracy and Political Theory* (Cambridge, Polity Press, 1988) at 37; and R Bellamy, 'Constitutive Citizenship versus Constitutional Rights: Republican Reflections on the EU Charter and the Human Rights Act' in T Campbell, K Ewing and A Tomkins (eds), *Sceptical Essays on Human Rights* (Oxford, OUP, 2001) 15–39 at 15.

property ownership.[15] In essence, core civil and political rights, such as the right to life and freedom of expression, are regarded as 'absolute' and therefore directly enforceable or justiciable. Such rights are viewed as truly 'fundamental' in the sense that they connote the inherent rights of the individual and, as such, often traverse conventional political boundaries. The state's obligation is one of non-interference rather than positive action. By contrast, many economic and social rights, such as rights to housing or social assistance, are often not regarded as 'rights' at all,[16] or at least not *fundamental rights*, but rather as mere policies or programmes capable of progressive realisation[17] and non-justiciable in the sense that they are deemed incapable of being invoked in a court of law or applied by judges.[18] Moreover, international labour rights, such as the right to work or organise, which are understood by some as essential for the practical realisation of human dignity, are regarded by others as ideologically driven because they create positive obligations on states to intervene and, it is argued, may undermine the enjoyment of individual freedom and distort the functioning of free markets.[19] On a more practical level the hierarchy of rights has been reinforced by the inescapable fact that while many civil and political rights are relatively cost free,[20] the full realisation of economic and social rights requires a substantial investment of resources, the establishment of an effective infrastructure and progressive taxation over a sustained period.

Many of these arguments are oversimplified and fallacious. Categories of rights cannot logically or practically be separated or compartmentalised and indeed are mutually dependent.[21] For example, the right to freedom of association, generally regarded as a civil and political right,[22] is contingent upon the right to organise and bargain collectively, usually labelled as an economic and social right,[23] and vice versa.[24] Furthermore, the role of the state, in respect of civil and political liberties, such as the general right to equality, is not merely

---

[15] For a summary, see the annotations on the Text of the Draft International Covenants on Human Rights, UN Doc A/2929 (1955) p 7. See further, P Alston & H Steiner, *International Human Rights in Context: Law, Politics, Morals: Text and Materials*, 2nd edn (Oxford, OUP, 2000) pp 237–45, and A Eide, 'Economic, Social and Cultural Rights as Human Rights' in Eide *et al*, above n 7 at 21–40.

[16] See M Cranston, *What are Human Rights?* (London, Bodley Head, 1973).

[17] For example, see the obligation on states under Art 2(1) of the ICESR. For further discussion in the context of the rights to social security and social assistance, see J Tooze, in this collection; in the context of the right to health, see T Hervey, in this collection.

[18] For a critique, see M Scheinin, 'Economic and Social Rights as Legal Rights' in Eide *et al*, above n 7 at 41–62.

[19] Alston & Steiner, above n 15 at 237.

[20] See Eide, above n 15 at 22.

[21] See Alston & Steiner, above n 15 at 247; Hervey, in this collection at p 195. On this point, see also the views of the European Court of Human Rights in *Airey v Ireland* Series A No 32 (1979) 2 EHRR 305, para 26.

[22] See Art 22 ICCPR and Art 11 ECHR.

[23] See Art 8 ICESR and Arts 5 and 6 ESC.

[24] As demonstrated by ILO Convention 87 on Freedom of Association and the Protection of the Right to Organise (1948). See B Ryan, in this collection, sections on freedom of assembly, pp 69–72 and 74–76.

negative or defensive because active steps are required to ensure meaningful participation in society and equal opportunities for all.[25] In addition, economic and social rights, such as those contained in the ESC, are often envisaged as justiciable[26] and can be formulated in such a way as to be capable of protection through systems of adjudication.[27] Indeed, despite the formal separation between the ECHR and the ESC, a series of attempts have been made in recent years to render economic and social rights more legally effective.[28] Nevertheless, despite the strength of the case, achieving change has been a complex and difficult process.

The proclamation of the Charter of Fundamental Rights of the European Union (the Charter) as a unified, composite text can be understood as part of a much broader fundamental rights dialogue that seeks to transcend the artificial and somewhat arid debate about the labelling of 'rights' and places emphasis on the institutional duties of states and international bodies to respect and protect core rights and values as a matter of obligation. With much fanfare it has been proclaimed, on behalf of the 'peoples of Europe', that 'in creating an ever closer union among them', they 'are resolved to share a peaceful future based on *common values*'.[29] Hence, the Charter has been imbued with immense iconographic significance for a Europe of peoples as distinct from markets.[30] Put simply, the objective is to make the process of European integration more open and legitimate by furnishing it with a layer of rights embodying values with which, intrinsically, most people can readily identify.

Undoubtedly the Charter carries with it a deep political desire to give resonance to the values that it propounds and yet it has been widely recognised that European integrationists have long been ambivalent about fundamental rights

---

[25] See M Weiss, 'The Politics of the EU Charter of Fundamental Rights' in B Hepple (ed) *Social and Labour Rights in a Global Context* (Cambridge, CUP, 2002) 73–94; M Bell and C Costello, in this collection.

[26] For example, see the 'Limburg Principles' of 1986 enunciated by a group of experts examining the implementation of the ICESR, UN doc. E/CN.4/1987/17. See further, J Tooze, in this collection, p 163, fn 5 and the literature cited therein.

[27] See further, F Jacobs, 'The Extension of the European Convention on Human Rights to Include Economic, Social and Cultural Rights' (1978) 3 *Human Rights Review* 166, and A Berenstein, 'Economic and Social Rights: Their Inclusion in the European Convention on Human Rights, Problems of Formulation and Interpretation' (1981) 2 *Human Rights Law Journal* 257. For full analysis, see B Bercusson, 'Fundamental Social and Economic Rights in the European Community' in A Cassese, A Clapham & J Weiler (eds) *Human Rights and the European Community: Methods of Protection* (Baden-Baden, Nomos, 1991) 195–291 at 198–201.

[28] See Scheinin, above n 18 at 56–58. For example under the ESC, following the 1991 Amending Protocol, a more effective European Committee of Social Rights (ECSR) has replaced the Committee of Independent Experts. The amended provisions are now contained in the RevESC 1996. For discussion, see N Casey, 'The European Social Charter and Revised European Social Charter' in C Costello (ed), *Fundamental Social Rights: Current Legal Protection and the Challenge of the EU Charter of Fundamental Rights* (Dublin, Irish Centre for European Law, 2001) 55–75, and T Novitz, 'Remedies for Violation of Social Rights within the Council of Europe' in C Kilpatrick, T Novitz & P Skidmore (eds), *The Future of Remedies in Europe* (Oxford, Hart, 2000) 231–51.

[29] First recital of the preamble of the Charter. Emphasis added.

[30] On this point, see J Weiler, 'Editorial: Does the European Union Truly Need a Charter of Rights?' (2000) 6 *European Law Journal* 95 at 95.

in general and economic and social rights in particular.[31] The institutions of the EU, including the European Court of Justice, have utilised the language of rights cautiously and selectively where necessary for the purposes of furthering the integration process and enhancing its legitimacy.[32] Although the Charter offers the prospect of a more comprehensive approach to the legitimation of rights within a complex, multi-level transnational polity, this chapter, by tracing the evolution of economic and social rights within the European Union, will aim to show how it is also reflective of the 'dynamic ambiguity'[33] of a European integration project that oscillates between centralising and decentralising axes.[34]

ECONOMIC AND SOCIAL RIGHTS AND THE INTEGRATION PROCESS

Market Integration—No Room for Economic and Social Rights?

When the foreign ministers of the European Coal and Steel Community gathered at Messina in 1955 to launch the process of European economic integration their primary concern was to establish a common market and a functional apparatus to support it. Any other considerations, moral or social, were secondary[35] and would have been seen as a diversion from the immediate task. The Community's founders formed the view that there was no need to duplicate the work of other international institutions that were well established and best placed to formulate and monitor the observance of transnational standards for fundamental rights.[36] Moreover, by differentiating economic integration from fundamental rights, the fledgling Community would be able to prioritise market building while minimising interference with well-established and jealously guarded national systems of social protection, labour law and industrial relations. It followed that, from the perspective of the late 1950s, the social provisions in the EEC Treaty,[37] including the commitment to equal pay between men and women,[38] amounted to no more than a network of policies and programmes rather than an enforceable set of legal principles.[39]

---

[31] On the EU's 'ambivalent constitutionalism' see G de Búrca, 'The Drafting of the European Union Charter of Fundamental Rights' (2001) 26 *European Law Review* 126 at 126–28.

[32] See esp, G de Búrca, 'The Language of Rights and European Integration' in J Shaw & G More, *New Legal Dynamics of European Union* (Oxford, Clarendon Press, 1995) 29–54 at 39–43.

[33] I would like to thank Stephen Weatherill for suggesting this phrase.

[34] See M Poiares Maduro, in this collection.

[35] See de Búrca in Shaw & More, above n 32 at 29.

[36] See A Clapham, 'A Human Rights Policy for the EC' (1990) 10 *Yearbook of European Law* 291.

[37] Arts 117–122 EEC.

[38] Art 119 EEC.

[39] For a classic exposition, see O Kahn-Freund, 'Labour Law and Social Security' in E Stein & T Nicholson (eds), *American Enterprise in the European Common Market: A Legal Profile, Vol 1* (Ann Arbor, University of Michigan Press, 1960) 297–458 at 298–361.

Within the Community sphere, economic and social rights were to be subsumed by the market imperative. There was a consensus that the establishment
of the common market would lead to rapid improvements in productivity and,
axiomatically, social standards. Furthermore, the effect of an integrated market
would be benign, for two reasons. First, the interests of workers would be taken
into account because trade unions in the Member States were strong and
second, there was a general desire among governments of the Member States to
meet broad social aspirations.[40]

Satisfied with these convenient assumptions, and respectful of the demarcation lines between international institutions, the Community did not directly
address the issue of fundamental rights until the 1970s when a vision began to
emerge of a politically integrated Europe capable of transcending economic
integration and addressing the social rights deficit.[41] Europe's 'political imagination'[42] now embraced a formative notion of citizenship based on the recognition and protection of rights, including economic and social rights, through the
political objectives of a 'Union'.[43]

In 1979 the European Commission sought to give meaning to the idea of
political union by publishing a memorandum urging the Council to discuss the
prospect of the Community's accession to the ECHR.[44] Whilst the
Commission's memorandum was little more than a kite flying exercise, it provoked a debate about the visibility of rights in the Community based on the simple but novel assertion that the 'European Citizen' has a 'legitimate interest in
having his rights *vis-à-vis* the Community laid down in advance'.[45] Once the
Commission had aired the issue no legislative proposal ensued. The
Commission's non-decision can partly be explained by a degree of uncertainty
over the Community's competence to accede to the ECHR,[46] but it also reflected

[40] See the 'Ohlin Report' on the *Social Aspects of European Integration* (1956) 74 *International
Labour Review* 99; and the 'Spaak Report', *Rapport des chefs de délégation aux ministres des
affaires étrangères* (Brussels), 21 April 1956. For discussion, see S Deakin, 'Labour Law as Market
Regulation: the Economic Foundations of European Social Policy' in P Davies, A Lyon-Caen,
S Sciarra & S Simitis (eds), *European Community Labour Law: Principles and Perspectives* (Oxford,
Clarendon Press, 1996) 62–93, and J Kenner, *EU Employment Law: From Rome to Amsterdam and
Beyond* (Oxford, Hart, 2003) pp 1–21.

[41] See M Poiares Maduro, 'Striking the Elusive Balance Between Economic Freedom and Social
Rights in the EU', in P Alston (ed), *The EU and Human Rights* (Oxford, OUP, 1999) 449–72 at 466.
See also, Lord Wedderburn, 'European Community Law and Workers' Rights: Fact or Fake in
1992?' (1991) 13 *Dublin University Law Journal* 1.

[42] On the search for a European political philosophy see, I Ward, 'Beyond Constitutionalism:
The Search for a European Political Imagination' (2001) 7 *European Law Journal* 24.

[43] The 'Tindemans Report', COM(75) 481, Bull EC Supp 1/76, p 26. See also, European
Parliament Resolution of 10 July 1975 on a 'Charter of the Rights of the Peoples of the European
Community', OJ 1975 C179/28.

[44] See Commission Memorandum of 4 April 1979, EC Bull Supp 2/79, p 5. Discussed by
K Economides & J Weiler, 'Accession of the Communities to the European Convention on Human
Rights: Commission Memorandum' (1979) 42 *Modern Law Review* 683.

[45] *Ibid* p 686.

[46] The Commission had good reason for caution. Fifteen years later the Court advised that the
Community did not possess competence to accede to the ECHR in *Opinion 2/94* [1996] ECR I–1759.
The Court's judgment was based on the notion of conferred powers and the duty of the Community

a certain ambiguity about both the Community's identity as a human rights actor and its relationship with other international institutions operating in this arena. These factors have led to sensitivity and caution whenever proposals have been put forward to incorporate rights or obligations derived from other international sources of law. Indeed, a prime motivation for adopting the Charter some 20 years later was to offer an alternative to EU accession to the ECHR.

Following the publication of the Internal Market 'White Paper' in 1985,[47] there was widespread concern about the possible negative effects of the internal market on social conditions in the Member States arising from, first, a shift in market share to countries with lower production costs and, second, downward pressure on wages and social standards generally because of the demands of competition.[48] The demand for a 'social dimension' to counteract the dangers of a deregulatory 'race to the bottom' was pressing.[49] However, in the absence of a consensus among the Member States for an increase in the Community's competence to introduce minimum standards in the area of social policy,[50] the Community began to explore the possibilities of an alternative approach based on identifying a catalogue of 'fundamental social rights' to be observed by the Member States and to act as a spur for legislative and programmatic activity at both Community and national levels.

The Community Social Charter—Social Citizenship Denied?

The first indication of a new approach can be found in the third recital of the preamble of the Single European Act of 1986, where it was declared that the Community was:

to act within those powers under Art 5 EC. Although Art 5 was added to the Treaty at the time of the TEU, the notion of conferred powers can be derived directly from Art 308 EC, which only permits action to further 'one of the objectives of the Community'. The Court concluded, 'no Treaty provision confers on the Community institutions any general powers to enact rules on human rights or to conclude international conventions in this field' (para 27).

[47] COM(85) 310.

[48] See *The Social Dimension of the Internal Market*, reproduced by the Commission in *Social Europe*, Special Ed (Luxembourg, European Communities, 1988).

[49] The 'race to the bottom' or 'meltdown' theory arises in a deregulatory federal system where states are allowed to unilaterally lower their social standards in order to undercut other states. Businesses relocate in response and the other states respond by lowering their standards in order to compete. See further, C Barnard, 'Social dumping and the race to the bottom: Some Lessons for the European Union from Delaware?' (2000) 25 *European Law Review* 57 at 57–63.

[50] At the insistence of the United Kingdom a rider was attached to Art 100a [now 95] EC whereby, under para 2, approximation measures concerning the establishment and functioning of the internal market did not apply to provisions 'relating to the rights and interests of employed persons'. Unanimity would be required for social policy measures in all policy areas except measures concerning 'the working environment, as regards the health and safety of workers' under Art 118a [now 137] EC. On the scope of these provisions, see Case C–84/94 *United Kingdom v Council (Working Time Directive)* [1996] ECR I–5755. See further, J Kenner, 'A Distinctive Legal Base for Social Policy?—The Court of Justice Answers a "Delicate Question"' (1997) 22 *European Law Review* 579.

> Determined to work together to promote democracy on the basis of fundamental rights recognised in the constitutions and laws of the Member States, in the Convention for the Protection of Human Rights and Fundamental Freedoms and the European Social Charter, notably freedom, equality and social justice.

Undoubtedly this statement was designed to be little more than diplomatic plumage, but it provided a foundation, albeit a shallow one, for a bold proposal from the Economic and Social Committee[51] for a framework directive setting out 'inalienable basic social rights' inspired by ILO conventions, the ECHR and the ESC.[52] The Committee's aim was to offer a Community guarantee of basic social rights 'immune to competitive pressures'.[53] In a subsequent Opinion, the Committee rejected the idea of a separate Community Social Charter and recommended instead that such a guarantee should be aimed not at establishing new rules but as a means of taking account of existing rules already agreed in other transnational fora.[54]

In the event the Commission decided to press ahead with its own proposal for a 'Social Charter'.[55] Seeking to reaffirm the concept of a distinctive 'European Social Model', while drawing inspiration from international human rights law, the Commission offered its own categorisation of fundamental social rights for *citizens*.[56] For example, under its proposals, all 'citizens', irrespective of their employment status, were to have rights to adequate social protection, an income in retirement, education and training.[57] The Commission's proposals were designed to be socially inclusive, with no attempt to limit citizenship to nationals of the Member States. Indeed the breadth of this approach was consonant with the views of some commentators who envisioned the emergence of a European 'social state' (*Sozialstaat*)[58] founded on a 'European sphere of entitlements to a decent livelihood'.[59]

The Commission's bold attempt to promote a vision of European social citizenship was premature for three reasons. First, the immediate priority of the Member States was to respond to the demands of trade unions for workers' rights and greater involvement of the 'social partners'. Second, there was no competence for the Community to act, independently of the market integration

---

[51] Doc CES 1069/87, 19 November 1987. Based on a discussion of an earlier report, Doc CES 225/87, 17 September 1987.

[52] *Ibid* para 2.1.

[53] *Ibid* para 1.6.

[54] Doc CES 270/89, 22 February 1989.

[55] COM (89) 248, reproduced in *Social Europe* 1/90. For analysis of the Social Charter and the background to its adoption, see Kenner (2003) above n 40 at 109–52.

[56] *Ibid* para 5 of the draft preamble.

[57] *Ibid* Title I, draft points 9, 13 and 22.

[58] See S Leibfried & P Pierson, 'Prospects for Social Europe' (1992) 20 *Politics & Society* 333 at 336, and B Hepple, 'The Implementation of the Community Charter of Fundamental Social Rights' (1990) 53 *Modern Law Review* 643, who explains, at 653, that the notion of a *Sozialstaat* is derived from the German public law principle of 'social government based on the rule of law'. In essence, the *Sozialstaat* requires the state to create a just social order.

[59] See Leibfried & Pierson, *ibid*.

process, in areas such as education, health and social welfare. Whereas 'workers' had a clearly established status in Community law as 'market citizens', the 'European citizen' had yet to be conceived.[60] Third, the Charter was to be addressed to the Member States for whom any notion of a European *Sozialstaat* was anathema. The idea of the Community seeking to override the priorities of national social assistance and social protection systems was simply untenable. The Member States would have been extremely wary of the concept of 'social citizenship' because it carries with it ideas of entitlements and guarantees.[61]

Hence, although a second Commission draft had reinforced references to the social rights of citizens,[62] the French Presidency presented a drastically revised draft that formed the basis for the final text. Most significantly, the title of the document had been changed to the 'Community Charter of the Fundamental Social Rights *of Workers*'.[63] All references in the draft to 'citizens' had been deleted and replaced with 'workers' or 'persons'. Whereas the original text had placed emphasis on the need to address the concerns of the unemployed and socially excluded, the 'Workers' Charter'[64] excised and diluted these references.[65] Provisions concerning social protection,[66] and the rights of the disabled and elderly persons[67] remained in place but only on the basis that these were areas where the Community would have influence but, in accordance with the principle of subsidiarity,[68] would not be able to dictate policy to the Member States who alone would be responsible for the implementation of the Community Social Charter. The vision of a Community Social Charter had been narrowed to the extent that it now promoted health protection and safety at work,[69] but not public health;[70] and a minimum age of employment for children,[71] but not education.[72] Paradoxically, the Community Social

[60] See M Everson, 'The Legacy of the Market Citizen', in Shaw & More, above n 32 at 73–90. For comment, see Poiares Maduro, above n 41 at 462.

[61] See Everson, above n 60, at 82–83.

[62] COM (89) 471.

[63] For a very useful comparison between the draft and the final text, see Annex 1 of the Fourth Report of the Employment Committee of the House of Commons Session 1990–91, *The European Community Social Charter* (London, HMSO, 1991).

[64] On this point, see L Betten, 'The EU Charter on Fundamental Rights: a Trojan Horse or a Mouse?' (2001) 17 *International Journal of Comparative Labour Law and Industrial Relations* 151.

[65] The reference to unemployment in para 3 of the draft preamble was excised altogether. Moreover, para 7 of the draft preamble referred to the need to combat 'every form of social exclusion'. The final text merely stated that 'it is important to combat social exclusion', para 8.

[66] Point 10.

[67] Points 24–26.

[68] See the fifteenth recital of the preamble and point 27 of the Community Social Charter. For discussion, see J Shaw, 'The Scope and Content of European Community Social Law: A Review of Progress and a Bibliographical Note' (1992) 14 *Journal of Social Welfare and Family Law* 71 at 74–75.

[69] Point 19 of the Community Social Charter.

[70] See M Kleinman and D Piachaud, 'European Social Policy: Conceptions and Choices' (1993) 3 *Journal of European Social Policy* 1 at 3.

[71] Point 20.

[72] Kleinman and Piachaud, above n 70 at 3. The European Parliament had earlier proposed that these areas should be included in the Charter: EP Doc. A2–399/88.

Charter protects workers who are not citizens but not citizens who are not workers.[73]

On the one hand, by limiting the scope of the Community Social Charter to workers, the majority of Member States[74] were seeking to resist any attempt to extend the Community's limited competence in the area of social policy under the guise of fundamental rights while, on the other hand, deploying the discourse of rights to legitimise Community action to protect and lay down minimum standards in the workplace and combat the threat of social dumping. In this way, targeted programmatic legislative and non-legislative measures could be pursued but there would be no prospect of a 'spill-over' from social-market rights for workers to social rights for citizens.[75]

Nevertheless, in the intervening years, the Community Social Charter has been remarkably influential for several reasons. Firstly, notwithstanding the fact that the Community Social Charter itself has no legal effect,[76] it still has legal consequences. As a high level declaration of intent, it has provided a dynamic for Community action programmes and legislation. During the 1990s, the Community Social Charter was referred to 43 times in Community legal instruments[77] often serving to reinforce an otherwise shaky legal foundation. For example, the trinity of directives on pregnancy and maternity, the organisation of working time and young workers—all based on the health and safety imperative in Article 118a (now 137) EC—each contain references in their preambles to the Community Social Charter as a source of inspiration.[78] Once such a reference is made in the preamble of a directive it may be used for interpretative purposes by the EU courts.[79] Thus, when the European Court of Justice (the Court) upheld the validity of the Working Time Directive,[80] it was able to draw upon references in its preamble to the Community Social Charter[81] to support a broad interpretation of the concepts of 'health and safety' and the 'working environment'.

---

[73] House of Commons Report, above n 63 at paras 52–54. There are several references in the Community Social Charter to rights extending to 'every worker of the European Community' (points 1, 8, 9, 10, 11, 15 and 24). There is no apparent restriction concerning nationality or citizenship. Indeed, the preamble explicitly provides for equal treatment of workers who are legally resident nationals of non-member countries and members of their families (para 9).

[74] The United Kingdom refused to sign the final text which was adopted as a non-binding 'solemn declaration at the Strasbourg European Council of December 1989. The text of the Community Social Charter is reproduced in ch 2 of *Social Europe 1/90.*

[75] See W Streeck, 'Neo-Voluntarism: A New European Social Policy Regime?' (1995) 1 *European Law Journal* 31 at 45.

[76] See the introduction to the Commission's second annual report on the application of the Community Social Charter, COM (92) 562.

[77] See Betten (2001) above n 64 at 158.

[78] Respectively, Directive 92/85/EEC, OJ 1992 L348/1, fifth recital (point 19 of the Charter); Directive 93/104/EC, OJ 1993 L307/18, fourth recital (points 7,8 and 19); and Directive 94/33/EC, OJ 1993 L216/12, third recital (points 20 and 22).

[79] See Case C–292/99 *R v The Immigration Appeal Tribunal, ex parte Antonissen* [1991] ECR I–745 at 778.

[80] Case C–84/94 *United Kingdom v Council* [1996] ECR I–5755.

[81] Para 76.

Secondly, the Community Social Charter has provided a platform for Treaty amendments and, in turn, a review of the Court's case law on fundamental rights. When the Treaty on European Union (TEU) annexed the Agreement on Social Policy to the EC Treaty,[82] its explicit purpose was to 'implement' the Community Social Charter on the basis of the *acquis communautaire*.[83] Now that the Agreement on Social Policy has been fully incorporated into the EC Treaty, following the Treaty of Amsterdam,[84] the revised Article 136 EC[85] refers to 'fundamental social rights' derived from the Community Social Charter and the ESC as the basis for its social policy activities. Although this reference is merely declaratory, it signifies the autonomy of an emerging social policy rooted in the concept of rights.

In February 2000, the significance of this evolution was recognised by the Court in *Schröder*[86] and related cases[87] concerning the exclusion of part-time workers from occupational pension schemes contrary to the principle of equal pay between men and women under Article 119 [now 141] EC. In its previous jurisprudence, the Court had observed that economic rather than social factors were the motivating force behind this obligation,[88] which it was later to recognise as a 'fundamental right' that forms part of the principle of non-discrimination on grounds of sex.[89] Drawing on this case law, the Court was prepared to authorise a decision by Germany to backdate pensions for the affected workers, notwithstanding any negative economic consequences, on the basis that the economic aim pursued by ex-Article 119 EC, and consequently the revised Article 141 EC, must now be regarded as secondary to the social aim pursued by the same provision, which constitutes the expression of a fundamental human right.[90] Although the facts of the cases predated the Treaty of Amsterdam, the judgment reveals an acute awareness on the part of the Court of the autonomy of the social provisions now contained in Articles 136–145 EC.[91]

---

[82] Effective from 2 November 1993.

[83] This commitment was contained in the preamble of the Agreement, annexed to Protocol 14 on Social Policy. The Protocol provided that the Agreement applied to all Member States except the United Kingdom.

[84] Effective from 1 May 1999.

[85] Ex-Art 117 EEC.

[86] Case C–50/96 *Deutsche Telekom AG v Schröder* [2000] ECR I–743. Discussed by Kenner (2003) above n 40 at 458–65.

[87] Cases C–234–235/96 *Deutsche Telekom AG v Vick and Conze* [2000] ECR I–799, and Cases 270–271/97 *Deutsche Post AG v Sievers and Schrage* [2000] ECR I–929.

[88] Case 43/75 *Defrenne v Sabena II* [1976] ECR 455, paras 9–12.

[89] Case 149/77 *Defrenne v Sabena III* [1978] ECR 1365, paras 26–27, Cases 75/82 and 117/82 *Razzouk and Beydoun v Commission* [1984] ECR 1509, para 16, and Case C–13/94 *P v S and Cornwall CC* [1996] ECR I–2143, para 19.

[90] Para 57.

[91] This also helps to explain the Court's approach in Case C–67/96 *Albany International BV v Stichting Bedrijfspensioenfonds Textielindustrie* [1999] ECR I–5751, where the Court upheld the Dutch system of compulsory pension funds because of the social task that they perform by protecting all workers, notwithstanding the fact that the operation of such funds might violate Community competition law.

Thirdly, the Community Social Charter has indirectly elevated the status of the ESC in the EU's legal order. Many of the economic and social rights contained in the ESC were replicated in the Community Social Charter including, for example, the right of workers to safe and healthy working conditions,[92] to a fair remuneration, and to bargain collectively.[93] While the ESC creates positive legal obligations on the contracting parties in international law, its provisions are not self-executing or directly effective. Without incorporation into domestic law it has, at most, a 'reflex effect'[94] as a source of law in the Member States and also, more importantly for our purposes, the EU. Where the rights contained in the ESC are regarded as 'fundamental' by the Court they can be invoked as part of the general principles of law the observance of which the Court is bound to protect under Article 220 EC,[95] providing that the issue at stake is within the framework of the structure and objectives of the Community.[96] Thus, in cases such as *Rutili*,[97] *Johnston*,[98] *Wachauf*[99] and *P v S*,[100] the Court has been able to identify Community provisions as specific manifestations of more general principles enshrined in the ECHR and national constitutions[101] and therefore reflective of common values,[102] an approach now formally recognised in Article 6(2) TEU. On rare occasions the Court has referred directly to the ESC and ILO conventions,[103] but all too often, provisions in international law concerning economic and social rights have been interpreted through the prism of the ECHR, reflecting a tendency to give greater credence to civil and political rights.

For example, in *Albany International*, Advocate General Jacobs drew on an extensive range of international law when seeking to determine whether the Community recognised the right to bargain collectively. The Advocate General noted that, although Article 11 ECHR has been held to safeguard the freedom of trade unions to protect the occupational interests of their members,[104] this

---

[92] Art 3 ESC, Point 19 of the Community Social Charter.

[93] Art 6 ESC, Point 12 of the Community Social Charter.

[94] See, generally, R Rogowski & T Wilthagen (eds) *Reflexive Labour Law* (Deventer, Kluwer, 1994).

[95] Art 220 EC states that: 'The Court of Justice shall ensure that in the interpretation and application of the Treaty *the law* is observed' (emphasis added).

[96] Case 11/70 *Internationale Handelsgesellschaft v Einfuhr-und Vorrasstelle Getreide* [1970] ECR 1125, para 4. See generally, B de Witte, 'The Past and Future Role of the European Court of Justice in the Protection of Human Rights' in Alston, above n 41 859–97, and P Craig & G de Búrca, *EU Law—Text, Cases and Materials*, 3rd edn (Oxford, OUP, 2002) 317–70.

[97] Case 36/75 *Rutili v Minister for the Interior* [1975] ECR 1219, para 32.

[98] Case 222/84 *Johnston v Chief Constable of the RUC* [1986] ECR 1651, para 18.

[99] Case 5/88 *Wachauf v Germany* [1989] ECR 2609, para 19.

[100] Case C–13/94 *P v S and Cornwall County Council* [1996] ECR I–2143, para 18.

[101] See Case 44/79 *Hauer v Land Rheinland-Pfalz* [1979] ECR 3727, paras 14–16.

[102] See Craig & de Búrca, above n 96 p 324.

[103] See Case 149/77 *Defrenne v Sabena III* [1978] ECR 1365; and Case 24/86 *Blaizot v University of Liège* [1988] ECR 379.

[104] See Case 67/96 *Albany International BV v Stichting Bedrijfspensioenfonds Textielindustrie* [1999] ECR I–5751 above n 91. On this point see *National Union of Belgian Police v Belgium* Series A No 20 (1975) 1 EHRR 578 para 40.

only protects a core of specific activities.[105] It does not include any right for a trade union to be consulted by the state,[106] nor an obligation on the state to conclude collective agreements.[107] There is no direct reference in the case law of the European Court of Human Rights to a right to bargain collectively.[108] In the view of Advocate General Jacobs, Article 6 ESC, and other international instruments upon which the Member States had collaborated,[109] were not sufficiently strong to create a fundamental right to collective bargaining.[110] In the absence of such a clear-cut right in international law it was, by implication, inappropriate for the Court to move at a faster pace than the European Court of Human Rights when interpreting the scope of corresponding rights recognised by the Community.

Thus, although the Community Social Charter has been remarkably effective as a soft law tool, acting as an impulse for change, its effectiveness has ultimately been constrained by its limited vision of social citizenship and its place at the periphery of the integration process. What was now required, in the wake of the 'legitimacy crisis' of the mid-1990s,[111] was a more all-embracing approach to provide the EU with a human rights foundation with economic and social rights at its core.

THE EU CHARTER OF FUNDAMENTAL RIGHTS—TOWARDS INDIVISIBILITY?

In 1996 the report of an ad hoc *Comité des Sages*[112] called for a 'bill of rights' encompassing both civic and social rights. Although this was not acted upon at the time of the Treaty of Amsterdam, the baton was soon seized by a group of legal experts appointed by the Commission who published a report on affirming fundamental rights in the EU.[113] The experts called for full recognition of

---

[105] See paras 143–45 of the opinion. In fact the only right expressly recognised by the Court has been to be heard by the State, *ibid* para 39, and *Swedish Engine Drivers' Union v Sweden* Series A No 20 (1976) 1 EHRR 617 para 40.

[106] *Belgian Police*, above n 104 at para 38

[107] *Swedish Engine Drivers*, above n 105 at para 39.

[108] In para 148 the Advocate General cites the *Swedish Engine Drivers* case, (above n 105) where the majority of the Commission of Human Rights had argued in favour of interpreting Art 11 ECHR to include a right of trade unions to engage in collective bargaining. The Court, however, held that it did not have to give a ruling on that question since, it said, such a right was not at issue and was granted to the applicant union under national law.

[109] ILO Convention Nos 87 & 98; Art 22 ICCPR, and Art 8 ICESR.

[110] Paras 146–47. In para 149 the Advocate General points to the restrictive interpretation of Art 6 ESC in the cases concerning the *Belgian Police*, above n 104 at para 38; and *Swedish Engine Drivers*, above n 105, para 39. In both cases the European Court of Human Rights commented upon the meaning of Art 6(1) ESC in the course of interpreting Art 11 ECHR. For further discussion of *Albany*, see B Ryan, in this collection, at p 75.

[111] See further, G de Búrca, 'The Quest for Legitimacy in the European Union' (1996) 59 *Modern Law Review* 349.

[112] *For a Europe of Civic and Social Rights* (Luxembourg, European Communities, 1996).

[113] *Affirming Fundamental Rights in the European Union Time to Act* (Brussels, European Commission, 1999). Available at: <http://europa.eu.int/comm/justice_home/unit/charte/index_en.html>.

economic and social rights contained in the ECHR, the ESC and ILO conventions, and concluded that all rights should be set out in a single text to be inserted into the Treaties.[114] The publication of the report coincided with the 50th anniversary of the UDHR and a separate report calling for the establishment of a EU centre for monitoring human rights.[115] In addition, the adoption of the Revised ESC (RevESC) in 1996, and the launch of the ILO's Declaration on Fundamental Principles and Rights at Work in 1998,[116] increased the visibility of economic and social rights on the international stage. In response to these developments, the Cologne European Council of June 1999 decided to establish a Charter of Fundamental Rights in order to make their overriding importance and relevance *more visible* to the Union's citizens.[117] Significantly, the European Council referred to a specific 'citizens' guarantee' of economic and social rights in Article 136 EC derived from the Community Social Charter and the ESC.[118]

The stage was now set for a unique drafting process involving a novel EU body composed of representatives of governments, the Commission, the European Parliament and national parliaments. The body, which renamed itself the 'Convention', was designed to furnish the process with legitimacy although in practice it lacked a formal mechanism for involving 'civil society' in its work.[119] Moreover, national governments steered the process to ensure that discussions were 'not about minting new rights but rather an exercise in increasing the visibility of existing rights'.[120] They also ensured that the Charter of Fundamental Rights of the European Union would be directed at the EU institutions rather than the Member States, who are bound as sovereign governments under international law. By the conclusion of the negotiations it was clear that the Charter would be issued as a non-binding political declaration and, although drafted on the basis that it would eventually have 'mandatory legal force',[121] the question of its legal status would be deferred.[122] Nevertheless, the Charter's legal status will be revisited in 2004[123] and, in the meantime, its unan-

---

[114] *Affirming Fundamental Rights in the European Union Time to Act* p 17.

[115] *Leading by Example: A Human Rights Agenda for the European Union for the Year 2000* (Florence, EUI, 2000).

[116] Available at: <www.ilo.org>. For discussion see J Bellace, 'The ILO Declaration of Fundamental Principles and Rights at Work' (2001) 17 *International Journal of Comparative Labour Law and Industrial Relations* 269.

[117] Cologne Presidency Conclusions, Annex IV, para 1. Emphasis added.

[118] *Ibid* para 2.

[119] See de Búrca (2001) above n 31 at 126.

[120] See Lord Goldsmith, 'A Charter of Rights, Freedoms and Principles' (2001) 38 *Common Market Law Review* 1201 at 1207.

[121] See COM(2000) 559 final, para 3.

[122] Both the Commission and the European Parliament called for a legally binding Charter. See COM(2000) 644, para 11, and European Parliament resolutions A5–0064/2000 and B5–767/2000.

[123] This will be the task of the Convention on the Future of Europe established by the European Council in December 2001. The new Convention has been closely modelled on the Convention formed to draft the Charter.

imous endorsement in the form of a joint institutional proclamation[124] and the legitimacy bestowed on the drafting process, will ensure that it is taken into account by each of the institutions when proposing or adopting legislation or performing any executive or judicial functions.

For the purposes of this chapter, I will seek to explore the Charter's assertion of indivisibility by evaluating a selection of the rights in Chapter IV on Solidarity, Articles 27–38 EUCFR, which contains most but not all of the economic and social rights in the Charter.[125] Several of the recitals in the preamble of the Charter help us to understand both the boldness of this commitment and also its limitations.

For example, the Charter's proclamation of indivisible values and its express reference to solidarity alongside dignity, equality and freedom,[126] sends a clear message that the EU institutions, when carrying out their obligations, will be bound to take note of the more elevated position that economic and social rights now occupy. Therefore, the Charter's social values are capable of having a mainstreaming effect[127] applying to all EU legislative and programmatic action, and serving as a point of reference for judicial interpretation of EU law within the scope of application of the Treaties. Also, it is equally important that, by contrast with the Community Social Charter, the 'common values' in the Charter are recognised as universally applicable[128] and, in most cases, contain an explicit guarantee to 'everyone' or 'every worker'.[129] Hence, the Charter seeks to address concerns about legitimacy by promoting inclusiveness, extending its coverage to third-country nationals, without altering the parameters of binding EU social law.[130]

The fifth and seventh recitals of the preamble to the Charter send out further ambiguous messages. In the fifth recital, rights derived from the common constitutional traditions of the Member States, the Treaties and international law are reaffirmed, including, explicitly, the two 'Social Charters' (the Community Social Charter and the ESC), subject to the 'powers and tasks of the Community and the Union' in accordance with the principle of subsidiarity.[131] Thus the Charter signifies a deepening of the process of political integration within a framework of decentralisation and strictly limited EU competence. In the seventh recital, there is a seemingly innocuous reference to the 50 'vertical'

---

[124] For the full text of the Charter with explanatory notes produced on behalf of the Convention, see CHARTE 4473/00, CONVENT 49; Council, *Explanations Relating to the complete text of the Charter* (Luxembourg, Office for Official Publications of the European Communities, 2001) accessible from http://www.europa.eu.int/ (the Explanatory Document).

[125] See further Kenner (2003) above n 40 at 511–45.

[126] First recital.

[127] See M Gijzen, 'The Charter: A Milestone for Social Protection in Europe?' (2001) 8 *Maastricht Journal* 33 at 42.

[128] First recital.

[129] See C Costello, 'The Legal Status and Legal Effect of the Charter of Fundamental Rights of the European Union' in Costello, above n 28, 127–50 at 144.

[130] See Gijzen, above n 127 at 38.

[131] Fifth recital.

provisions of the Charter as a collection of 'rights, freedoms and principles'.[132] Whilst the language used is strictly neutral, is it possible to distinguish between specific enforceable rights and freedoms and general unenforceable principles[133] that do not equate with rights and are not truly 'fundamental'? According to Lord Goldsmith, who was the United Kingdom Government's representative on the Convention,[134] such an interpretation is implicit because, he suggests, the economic and social rights contained in the Charter are merely 'principles' that will only be realised as exercisable rights 'to the extent that they are implemented by national law or, in those areas where there is such competence, by Community law'.[135] Goldsmith asserts that economic and social rights are different and, by implication, less important than civil and political rights because they are 'usually not justiciable' and are recognised and given effect to in different ways in the Member States who have primary competence in most of these areas.[136] For Goldsmith, the Charter conveys a hierarchy of rights backed up by a hierarchy of laws, a double blow to the notion of indivisible enforceable rights. Goldsmith's analysis is based on a number of challengeable assumptions about the non-justiciability of economic and social rights discussed in the first part of this chapter, but how far, if at all, does the substance of the Charter support his case?

Chapter IV of the Charter, entitled 'Solidarity', Articles 27–38 EUCFR, contains the following core labour rights:

- information and consultation within the undertaking (Article 27);
- collective bargaining and action (Article 28);
- protection in the event of unjustified dismissal (Article 30);
- fair and just working conditions (Article 31);
- prohibition of child labour and protection of young people at work (Article 32);
- protection from dismissal for a reason connected with maternity and the right to paid maternity leave and parental leave (Article 33(2)).

In addition the Solidarity Chapter recognises the right of the family to legal, economic and social protection,[137] 'recognises and respects' the entitlement to social security,[138] and the right to social and housing assistance.[139]

---

[132] Seventh recital.

[133] See A Heringa & L Verhey, 'The EU Charter: Text and Structure' (2001) 8 *Maastricht Journal* 11 at 14.

[134] Goldsmith, above n 120 at 1212. Lord Goldsmith's article was written in a personal capacity prior to his appointment as the Attorney General in the United Kingdom Government.

[135] *Ibid* at 1213. Some of the contributors to this collection take issue with Goldsmith's interpretation; see, J Tooze, in this collection, at p 164; T Hervey in this collection, at p 203.

[136] *Ibid* at 1212.

[137] Art 33(1) EUCFR, based on Art 16 ESC. For further discussion, see M Barbera, in this collection.

[138] Art 34(1) EUCFR, which is sourced from Arts 137 and 140 EC, Art 12 ESC and point 10 of the Community Social Charter. For further discussion, see J Tooze, in this collection.

[139] Art 34(3) EUCFR, which draws on Arts 30–31 ESC and point 10 of the Community Social Charter. For further discussion, see J Tooze, in this collection.

Miscellaneous rights include access to a free placement service for job seekers,[140] health care,[141] and a 'high level' of environmental and consumer protection. It should be noted that certain rights that may come under the broad penumbra of 'fundamental social rights' are found elsewhere in the Charter. Examples include: the prohibition of forced or compulsory labour;[142] the right to education;[143] freedom to choose an occupation and engage in work;[144] equality between men and women;[145] rights of the child;[146] and rights of the elderly.[147]

Even if we include these provisions, it is apparent that the Charter provides a less than comprehensive catalogue of economic and social rights. Moreover, as we shall see below, several of the labour rights are so heavily qualified that it is questionable whether they can be described as rights at all.[148] Despite the explicit reference to the 'visibility' of the ESC and the Community Social Charter in the Cologne mandate, the drafting Convention was highly selective in its approach to these texts. Key omissions include the right to work,[149] the right to a fair remuneration[150] and the right to housing.[151] It is perhaps not coincidental that these rights fall in areas that touch most closely upon national sovereignty and have significant resource implications.

Goldsmith justifies these exclusions on the basis that, in his view, economic and social rights are not justiciable in the same way as other rights.[152] It is undoubtedly the case that certain social rights, such as the right to social assistance or housing, concern positive social entitlements provided by governments, but that does not mean that they are inherently non-justiciable.[153] As the South African Constitutional Court has shown in *Grootboom*, the right of access to housing can create both positive and negative obligations for the state when

[140] Art 29 EUCFR, based on Art 1(3) ESC and point 13 of the Community Social Charter.

[141] Art 35 EUCFR, derived from Art 12 ESC and point 10 of the Community Social Charter. For further discussion, see T Hervey, in this collection.

[142] Art 5(2) EUCFR, based on Art 4(2) ECHR.

[143] Derived from the common constitutional traditions of the Member States and Art 2 of the Protocol to the ECHR. The right to education also includes vocational and continuing training—Art 10 ESC and point 15 of the Community Social Charter. For further discussion, see C Wallace and J Shaw, in this collection.

[144] Drawn from Art 1(2) ESC and the case law of the Court—eg Case 44/79 *Hauer v Land Rheinland-Pfalz* [1979] ECR 3727.

[145] Based on Arts 2, 3(2) and 141 EC. Other sources are Art 20 RevESC and point 16 of the Community Social Charter. For further discussion, see C Costello, in this collection.

[146] Based on the New York Convention on the Rights of the Child of 20 November 1989. For further discussion, see M Bell, in this collection.

[147] Drawn from Art 23 RevESC and points 24–25 of the Community Social Charter. For further discussion, see M Bell, in this collection.

[148] See C McCrudden, *The Future of the EU Charter of Fundamental Rights*, UACES On-line Reflection Papers, No 1, February 2002, www.uaces.org, p 17.

[149] Art 1 ESC.

[150] Art 4 ESC and point 5 of the Community Social Charter.

[151] Art 31 of the Revised ESC.

[152] Goldsmith, above n 120 at 1212.

[153] See M Craven, 'A View from Elsewhere: Social Rights, the International Covenant and the EU Charter of Fundamental Rights' in Costello, above n 28, 77–93 at 87.

fulfilling its constitutional duties.[154] The state has to balance these obligations whilst recognising that the purpose of the Constitution is to transform society into a more just and equitable place where people can fulfil their potential as human beings.[155] The Charter does not easily equate with the South African Constitution because it does not have a similar transformative constitutional dynamic, but neither is it a static document that merely purports to uphold the economic and social status quo. Hence, although it would be difficult to provide for a right to an adequate level of housing in a legal text,[156] that should not absolve the EU and the Member States from a general duty to formulate policies and programmes in a manner consistent with international guidance.[157]

The exclusion of these rights suggests that, from the perspective of the EU, certain economic and social rights are insufficiently fundamental to warrant visibility. If we accept Goldsmith's explanation that these 'rights' have been excluded because they are non-justiciable, what then is the status of the remaining provisions in the Solidarity Chapter? Upon detailed examination what emerges is a mix of individual rights, guiding principles that the EU recognises and respects, and pure objectives.[158] The distinction between 'rights' and 'principles' is far from clear.

For example, Article 30 EUCFR recognises the right of 'every worker' to protection against unjustified dismissal in accordance with Community law and 'national laws and practices'. During the negotiations the United Kingdom had to 'fight very hard'[159] to add this rider. This was an important consideration because under the United Kingdom's employment legislation workers who are in the first year of their employment contract are excluded from protection against unjustified dismissal.[160] Moreover, Article 137(2) EC, which allows for the adoption of binding Community directives concerning the 'protection of workers where their employment contract is terminated' is subject to a requirement of unanimity among the Member States when voting in the Council of the EU. Let us suppose that the Commission, at a future date, publishes a draft directive under Article 137(2) EC to protect all workers against dismissal from the first day of their employment in order to give full effect to the clearly expressed right in the Charter. In those circumstances what would be the legal effect of the rider if and/or when the Charter enters into legal force?

---

[154] *Government of the Republic of South Africa v Grootboom* [2001] (1) SA 46 CC, paras 20 and 34. For discussion see, P De Vos, '*Grootboom*, the Right of Access to Housing and Substantive Equality as Contextual Fairness' (2001) 17 *South African Journal of Human Rights* 258; and S Liebenberg, 'The Right to Social Assistance: the Implications of *Grootboom* for Policy Reform in South Africa' (2001) 17 *South African Journal of Human Rights* 232.

[155] De Vos, *ibid* at 260.

[156] Goldsmith, above n 120 at 1212.

[157] Craven, above n 153 at 89.

[158] See B Hepple, 'The EU Charter of Fundamental Rights' (2001) 30 *Industrial Law Journal* 225 at 228.

[159] Goldsmith, above n 120 at 1213.

[160] See Betten (2001) above n 64 at 163.

In seeking to answer this question it is necessary to refer to the 'horizontal' provisions in Articles 51–54 EUCFR that are designed, in part, to have a constraining effect on its interpretation and scope.[161] Under Article 51(1), the Charter is addressed to the 'institutions and bodies' of the EU 'with due regard to the principle of subsidiarity' and to the Member States 'only when they are implementing Union law'. In accordance with their respective powers they shall 'respect the rights, observe the principles and promote the application' of the Charter. This might suggest that the Commission is now obliged to bring forward this hypothetical proposal. However, Article 51(2) EUCFR states that the Charter 'does not establish any new power or task for the Community or the Union, or modify powers and tasks defined by the Treaties'. The purpose of this clause is to close down the perceived danger of the Charter being used as a 'Trojan horse' to extend the Community's powers in the event of it entering into legal force.[162] In addition, Article 52(2) EUCFR, concerning the scope of guaranteed rights, declares that rights recognised by the Charter, which are based on the Treaties, 'shall be exercised under the conditions and within the limits defined by the Treaties'.

Therefore, although the wording of the Charter appears to create an institutional imperative on the Commission to bring forward a legislative proposal under Article 137(2) EC, it only creates a moral duty on the individual members of the Council to act. Notwithstanding the fact that the United Kingdom's service qualification denies many workers the 'right' promised in the Charter, it would be perfectly entitled to exercise its veto or to seek to secure an amendment that would enable it to continue to exclude the most vulnerable workers from protection against unjustified dismissal. The United Kingdom, and indeed any other Member State in a similar position, would be able to rest certain in the knowledge that, as the Charter is addressed to the institutions of the EU, it is assumed that Member States are already adhering to their international obligations.

Articles 27 and 28 EUCFR, which are concerned with collective labour rights, contain a similar rider, reflecting the sensitivity of Member States in this area and the limitations of Community competence. However, whereas the right to protection against unfair dismissal in Article 30 EUCFR is clearly *expressed* as a fundamental right, Article 27 EUCFR, concerning workers' right to information and consultation within the undertaking appears to blur the rights/principles distinction. Article 27 EUCFR declares that workers or their representatives at the appropriate levels are 'guaranteed' the right to information and consultation within the undertaking in good time 'in the cases and under the conditions provided for by Community law and national laws and practices'.[163]

---

[161] For analysis see Kenner (2003) above n 40 at 528–43.

[162] See Betten, above n 64 at 151. But see M Barbera, in this collection, text at p 152.

[163] Art 27 EUCFR is consistent with Art 21 RevESC and points 17–18 of the Community Social Charter. It also incorporates the notion of social dialogue contained in Arts 138 and 139 [ex 118b] EC.

Hence, although Article 27 EUCFR reinforces the Community's general obligation to act to promote worker involvement in corporate decision-making processes, it offers no more than a qualified guarantee to the individual, leaving scope for local and national actors to determine the levels at which information and consultation takes place and the precise conditions under which the guarantee will operate.[164] Moreover, the guarantee in the Charter falls short of the right of workers to take part in the determination and improvement of working conditions and the working environment, an important feature of the RevESC.[165]

Article 27 EUCFR highlights the difficulty, and perhaps the undesirability, of seeking to draw up a uniform set of rights and principles in a pluralistic legal order in which rights are recognised as 'fundamental' at multiple levels.[166] There is no single model of employee involvement in the decision-making structures of companies in the European Union and attempts by the Commission to impose one in the 1970s were firmly resisted by a combination of several Member States and national trade unions and employers' organisations.[167] As the ILO noted in a report on workers' participation in 1981, this is an issue where the 'diversity of methods is as great as the diversity of aims'.[168] Article 27 EUCFR is indicative of a more differentiated approach to rights that seeks to promote a degree of political autonomy in the workplace without imposing what one critic of the Charter has described as 'a unitary conception of constitutionalism whereby all must abide by a uniform set of standards'.[169] Directive 2002/14/EC on establishing a general framework for informing and consulting employees in the European Community[170] is consistent with the pluralistic approach of the Charter, providing for mandatory information and consultation of workers in larger companies while allowing for diversity in national and sectoral systems. Article 27 EUCFR is a masterful compromise but it also reveals the limitations of the concept of 'Solidarity' at the level of the European Union because ultimately it fails to address the central issue of the inequality of the employment relationship that is, after all, the very foundation of labour law.[171]

Our discussion of Articles 27 and 30 EUCFR has focused on the limitations of the Charter in areas that fall within the legislative scope of Article 137 EC. Article 28 EUCFR, concerning the right of collective bargaining and action, is an example of a Charter provision that seeks to guarantee collective rights that may be regarded as outside Community competence altogether or, at the very

---

[164]   See Hepple (2001) above n 158 at 228–29.
[165]   Art 22 RevESC.
[166]   See further, N Walker, 'Human Rights in a Postnational Order: Reconciling Political and Constitutional Pluralism' in Campbell *et al*, above n 14, 119–41; and D Chalmers, 'Post-nationalism and the Quest for Constitutional Substitutes' (2000) 27 *Journal of Law and Society* 178
[167]   See Kenner (2003) above n 40 pp 62–69.
[168]   *Workers' Participation in Decisions within Undertakings* (Geneva, ILO, 1981) p 21.
[169]   See Bellamy, above n 14 at 16.
[170]   Directive 2002/14/EC, OJ 2002 L80/29.
[171]   See B Hepple, 'Social Values and European Law' [1995] *Current Legal Problems* 39 at 52.

least, outside the social provisions. Article 137(5) EC excludes pay, the right of association, the right to strike and the right to impose lock outs from the legislative remit of that Article. Notwithstanding this exclusion Article 28 EUCFR purports to grant workers, *inter alia*, the right 'in cases of conflicts of interest, to take collective action to defend their interests, including strike action' in accordance with Community law and national law and practices. However, if the Charter enters into legal force, far from guaranteeing the right to strike it may, paradoxically, subvert it. Any proposal to legislate to harmonise national laws on the right to strike at EU level[172] would conflict not only with the exclusion in Article 137(5) EC but also with Article 52(2) EUCFR which, according to the Explanatory Document,[173] preserves the system of rights and conditions conferred by the Treaties and Community legislation. Even if the proposal were to be based on the need to approximate the common market under Article 94 EC, to prevent social dumping,[174] Article 51(2) EUCFR might inhibit the Community from exercising its powers in this respect, making it difficult to justify the need to legislate. The combined effect of these provisions renders the Charter's proclamation of a right to take collective action nugatory.

By contrast, Article 31(2) EUCFR, which grants 'every worker' the right to limit their maximum working hours, to daily and weekly rest and an annual period of paid leave, is not fettered by any reference to national laws or practices. Each element contains a right that is *per se* justiciable. Moreover, the immediate source of each of these rights is a Community Directive on the Organisation of Working Time.[175] The unconditional nature of Article 31(2) EUCFR calls into question the status of Article 18(1)(b)(i) of the Directive which permits Member States—in practice only the United Kingdom—the option of introducing a voluntary opt-out for individual workers from the average 48-hour maximum working week.[176] Although any worker unwilling to work longer hours must not be subjected to any detriment by the employer, this safeguard only provides limited protection against coercive practices in sectors where low pay and long, often unsociable, hours are the norm. This clause is due to be reviewed by November 2003 and it is difficult to see how it can be reconciled with Article 31(2) EUCFR.[177]

---

[172] See further, P Germanotta & T Novitz, 'Globalisation and the Right to Strike: The Case for European-Level Protection of Secondary Action' (2002) 18 *International Journal of Comparative Labour Law and Industrial Relations* 67.

[173] The Explanatory Document; CHARTE 4473/00, CONVENT 49, p 48.

[174] On the basis that this would prevent distortions of competition and help to establish the 'common market' in accordance with Art 2 EC. Utilisation of Art 94 EC in this regard would be possible notwithstanding the limited scope of the narrower 'internal market' concept in Art 14 EC and its distinct legal base for approximation measures in Art 95 EC. On this point see Kenner (2003) above n 40 pp 86–87.

[175] Directive 93/104/EC, OJ 1993 L 307/18.

[176] Art 6 of the Directive.

[177] On 21 March 2002 the Commission issued the United Kingdom with an initial warning letter regarding, inter alia, the way in which 'voluntary' working time is measured. This letter marks the first stage in possible infringement proceedings under Art 226 EC.

Article 31(2) EUCFR was raised in pleadings in *BECTU*,[178] a trade union challenge to the validity of a United Kingdom law that denied employees the right to accrue paid leave until after 13 weeks of their employment. BECTU argued that this rule was incompatible with the Charter right as expressed in Article 7(1) of the Directive which grants 'every worker' the right to paid leave. In practice many workers in the entertainment industry were unable to exercise their right to paid leave because they were employed for shorter periods. The United Kingdom countered this argument by referring to a rider attached to the provision in the Directive where it is stated that it applies 'in accordance with the conditions for entitlement . . . laid down by national legislation and/or practice'. Although the wording in the Directive is almost identical to similar limitations contained in Articles 27–28 and 30 EUCFR, discussed above, no such restriction can be found in Article 31(2) EUCFR.

In his opinion Advocate General Tizzano drew from the Charter 'as a substantive point of reference'[179] and placed the rider in the Directive in context. The reference in the Directive to national laws and practices concerning the 'conditions for entitlement' means that, although Member States have some latitude in defining the arrangements for the enjoyment of paid leave, it does not permit national rules that negate that entitlement[180] or affect its scope.[181] The Charter is not, in itself, legally binding but, by reaffirming rights in other instruments, it provides 'the most reliable and definitive confirmation of the fact that the right to paid annual leave constitutes a fundamental right'.[182] It follows that the right to paid leave in the Directive is 'an automatic and unconditional right granted to every worker'.[183] The Court was able to reach the same conclusion without making a direct reference to the Charter. It was implicit that the Charter merely reaffirmed the fundamental right to paid leave contained in the Directive.

BECTU demonstrates the potential of the Charter to reinforce rights derived primarily from the Treaties and Community legislation. By contrast, *Bowden*,[184] another case from the United Kingdom concerning the right to paid leave in the Directive, reveals its limitations. *Bowden* concerned the rights of a group of 'non-mobile' workers in the transport sector who were excluded from the scope of the Directive.[185] No reference to the Charter was made in either the opinion or the judgment, even though the legislative exclusion denied the workers in question the 'fundamental right' of 'every worker' to paid annual leave that had been deemed 'automatic and unconditional' by the same Advocate

---

[178] Case C–173/99 *R v Secretary of State for Trade and Industry, ex parte BECTU* [2001] ECR I–4881.

[179] Opinion, para 28. Emphasis added.

[180] Paras 34–35.

[181] Paras 39–45.

[182] Opinion, para 28. Emphasis added.

[183] Paras 29–30.

[184] Case C–133/00 *Bowden and others v Tuffnells Parcels Express Ltd* [2001] ECR I–7031.

[185] Art 1(3) of Directive 93/104/EC.

General in *BECTU*. The workers in question fell outside the scope of the Directive and were unable to rely on the right to paid leave.

In part this ruling can be understood as an act of deference to the Community legislature that had recently adopted a Directive that would extend the scope of the Directive to cover 'non-mobile' transport workers such as the workers in question.[186] More compellingly, even though Article 31(2) EUCFR is expressed in unconditional terms, unlike other provisions in the Solidarity Chapter, it is trumped by the horizontal clause in Article 52(2) EUCFR that effectively precludes the Court from applying the Charter in these circumstances because it can only be 'exercised under the conditions and within the limits' defined by the Treaties. Therefore even if the Charter had been legally binding the Court would have been unable to uphold the apparently unconditional right in Article 31(2) EUCFR deemed a fundamental right by the Advocate General in *BECTU* on the basis of the same Directive.

Article 31(2) EUCFR can be compared with Article 34 EUCFR under which the EU 'recognises and respects' a range of entitlements to social security benefits and social services[187] and the right to social and housing assistance 'so as to ensure a decent existence for all those who lack sufficient resources' in order to combat social exclusion and poverty.[188] These are perhaps the clearest examples of rights expressed as mere principles. As the entitlements referred to in Article 34 EUCFR are entirely matters of national competence, this statement may be understand as only a moral obligation. It is clearly not intended to be justiciable and, although it covers areas not included in the Community Social Charter, it does not alter the status quo. Hence, the purpose of this Article is to reaffirm the European model of social protection while respecting national competences.

One question that is central to the debate over the indivisibility of the rights enunciated in the Charter concerns the approach of the Court to the interpretation of provisions derived from the ESC and the RevESC. Hitherto the Court and its Advocates General have tended to refer primarily to the ECHR and to underplay the status and autonomy of both the ESC and the authority of the legal experts on the European Committee of Social Rights that oversees its operation.[189] The approach of Advocate General Jacobs in *Albany International*, discussed above, provides a vivid example of this trend. Does the inclusion in the Charter of rights drawn selectively from each of these texts serve to elevate their

---

[186] Directive 2000/34/EC, OJ 2000 L 195/41.

[187] Based on Arts 137(3) and 140 EC, Art 12 ESC and point 10 of the Community Social Charter.

[188] Derived from Arts 30–31 RevESC and point 10 of the Community Social Charter. For a discussion of the possible implications of these provisions, see J Tooze, in this collection.

[189] The ECSR consists of nine experts assisted by an observer from the ILO. Under the Amending Protocol of 1991 its functions are to examine the national reports and make a legal assessment of the states' observance of their legal obligations. For further discussion, see Casey, above n 28 at 56; and Novitz, above n 28 who notes, at 250, attempts by the Parliamentary Assembly of the Council of Europe to establish either a 'parallel European Court of Social Rights' or the absorption of the ESC within the ECHR 'in order to create the basis for strict legal observance': *Recommendation No 1354 on the Future of the European Social Charter* (1998) para 18.

status within the EU legal order? The evidence suggests that the present hierarchical approach will be maintained. Most importantly, unlike the European Court of Human Rights, the European Committee of Social Rights does not have the status of a fully functioning court and is not regarded as an equivalent body by the Court, which prefers to engage in intra-judicial dialogue.[190] This is problematic because the European Court of Human Rights is concerned only with the interplay between the ESC/RevESC and the ECHR when interpreting and applying the rights protected by the latter. The European Committee of Social Rights alone has the expertise and responsibility to produce a regular, coherent overview of these texts. In carrying out its institutional responsibilities under the Charter, the Court must address the requirement of indivisibility by placing greater weight on the findings of the ESCR, and yet the Charter itself reinforces this hierarchy of adjudication in Article 52(3) EUCFR. Under this horizontal provision, where rights correspond with those guaranteed by the ECHR 'the meaning and scope of those rights shall be the same as those laid down by the said convention'. According to the Explanatory Document this is intended to ensure consistency between the ECHR and the Charter as determined both by the text of the ECHR and the case law of the European Court of Human Rights.[191] The Charter is silent on the status of the European Committee of Social Rights and its adjudications. By implying the superiority of the ECHR and its Court, the Charter appears to be reaffirming the 'second generation' status of economic and social rights.

CONCLUSION

Labour lawyers have traditionally been sceptical about human rights[192] and there is little in the Charter of Fundamental Rights of the European Union to assuage their distrust. The Charter, whatever its ultimate legal status, offers the 'peoples of Europe' only tantalising glimpses of 'rights' that are, at once, visible and yet unattainable. In particular, a detailed evaluation of the Solidarity chapter reveals that the Charter's bold affirmation of indivisible rights is a mirage. The Charter contains a highly selective and incomplete list of 'fundamental social rights' that distinguishes between enforceable rights, many of which are conditional, and recognition of vague principles.[193] For the EU institutions, the Charter creates an obligation to promote each of the enumerated rights but denies them the capacity to extend their powers or tasks to secure its objectives.

---

[190] See B Fitzpatrick, 'European Union Law and the Council of Europe Conventions' in Costello, above n 28, 95–108 at 101.

[191] The Explanatory Document; CHARTE 4473/00, CONVENT 49 p 48.

[192] For a stimulating discussion see S Fredman, 'Scepticism under Scrutiny: Labour Law and Human Rights' in Campbell *et al*, above n 14 197–213.

[193] See 'Editorial Comments: The EU Charter of Fundamental Rights still under discussion' (2001) 38 *Common Market Law Review* 1 at 3.

For individuals, the Charter may be visible, as with any other official document available under the transparency principle, but it neither directly affects workers' and/or citizens' social rights, nor does it guarantee basic social entitlements. For EU Member States, the Charter is a reminder of their international human rights commitments but, other than at the point of implementing EU law, it adds no new obligations even in areas that are outside the scope of the Treaties and, therefore, beyond the remit of the EU institutions to whom it is primarily directed.

Despite these misgivings, and perhaps because of them, the Charter may yet serve to raise the status of economic and social rights in the EU's legal order. Indeed the very ambiguity of the Charter derives from the fact that it preserves the status quo and yet simultaneously signifies the onset of deeper integration as part of a grand design that places fundamental rights at the pinnacle of the process of constitutionalisation of the EU.[194] It is in this context that the positioning of civil, political, cultural, social and economic rights in a single unified text must be understood. For the Charter marks what Hunt has described elsewhere in this collection as a 'shift in ethic'[195] whereby the value of economic and social rights are recognised and transformed within both the legal and political spheres.[196]

As part of this process of recognition and transformation, the EU institutions now have a duty to address gaps in the content of the Charter and limitations on its effectiveness. Lessons can be learned from the experience of the Community Social Charter which, as this chapter has shown, has provided an inspiration for Community social legislation and judicial interpretation notwithstanding its non-binding status. Moreover, the Charter projects a much wider conception of social citizenship than the Community Social Charter and has a far more elevated status in the integration process from which to influence events. As a living instrument, the Charter's influence will lie with its capacity to energise and give direction to legislative and programmatic action at EU and national level. For the Court the challenge is to translate the Charter's vision of indivisible rights and draw upon its sources to give full effect to the wide range of economic and social rights, many of which are potentially justiciable, in so far as interpretation of those rights falls within its jurisdiction. Most importantly of all, the Charter, by acting as a beacon of fundamental social values, can form part of the construction of a pluralistic 'European social constitution' that would seek to guarantee, over time, a more effective system of protection of economic and social rights within the EU's multi-level legal order.

---

[194] For further discussion, see M Poiares Maduro, in this collection.
[195] See J Hunt, in this collection, p 45.
[196] See the conclusions of B Ryan, in this collection, on pp 89–90.

2

Social Rights and Market Order: Adapting the Capability Approach

SIMON DEAKIN and JUDE BROWNE*

INTRODUCTION

THE CHARTER OF Fundamental Rights of the European Union (the Charter) contains detailed and extensive provisions on social rights, in particular in Chapter Three, on Equality, and Chapter Four, on Solidarity. In the view of many commentators, these provisions are not as strong as they might be; many of them were indeed watered down in the process leading to agreement on the text of the Charter. In one respect, though, the Charter marks a significant step in the constitutional recognition of social rights. There is no attempt to subordinate social rights to civil, political and economic rights, or to hive them off into a separate and inferior text as in the case of the European Social Charter 1961 (ESC). In this regard, the Charter is following a practice which can be traced back to the case law of the European Court of Justice (the Court). In decisions relating to equal pay,[1] health and safety,[2] transfers of undertakings[3] and the competition law implications of collective bargaining,[4] the Court has consistently emphasised that the social goals of the EC Treaty do not have to yield to the economic objective of an integrated internal market. As a result, the European market order can be said to incorporate a set of core social rights. At

* Centre for Business Research, University of Cambridge. We are grateful to Ingrid Robeyns, Patrick Twomey and the editors for comments on an earlier draft. We are solely responsible for the views expressed in the paper and for any remaining errors or omissions.
    [1] Case 43/75 *Defrenne v Sabena (No. 2)* [1976] ECR 455; Joined Cases C–270/97 and C–271/97 *Deustsche Post v Sievers and Schrage* [2000] ECR 2267
    [2] Case C–84/94 *United Kingdom v Council (Working Time)* [1996] ECR–I 5755.
    [3] C–51/00 *Temco Service Industries SA v Imzilyn and others* [2002] ECR I–969. Rejecting the view of Advocate-General Geelhoed that extending the protection of the Acquired Rights Directive to employees whose jobs had been subcontracted would give excessive weight to employment protection over considerations of freedom of contract and the competitiveness of enterprises; see A Garde, 'Recent Developments in the Law Relating to Transfers of Undertakings' (2002) 39 *Common Market Law Review* 523 at 532–4.
    [4] Case C–67/96 *Albany International v Stichting Bedrijfspensioenfonds Textielindustrie* [1999] ECR–I 5751; see also Joined Cases C–180/98 to C–184/98 *Pavel Pavlov v Stichting Pensioenfonds Medische Specialisten* [2000] ECR–I 6451; Case C–222/98 *van der Woude v Stichting Beatrixoord* [2000] ECR–I 7111.

least on the face of it this represents a striking difference from the constitutional law and practice of, for example, the United States.

The idea that social rights should have equivalent constitutional status to civil, political and economic rights is far from problem-free. Two sets of issues arise here. First, do we need to talk about social *rights* at all in this context? National level welfare states have tended to operate through a combination of social *provision* (often in the form of services provided directly by governmental bodies) and social *regulation* (in forms which include legislation and collective bargaining). How do social rights relate to these other types of intervention? Secondly, what is the link between the various instruments of social policy (including social rights) on the one hand, and the mechanisms of the market on the other? Because social policy interventions involve redistribution and regulation, they are often seen as the antithesis of market freedoms such as freedom of contract and the right to enjoy property. The same point can be made in relation to economic rights such as those arising from freedom of establishment or the free movement of goods. To place social rights on an equal footing with these civil, political and economic rights is, in the eyes of some, to risk at best incoherence, at worst a fundamental contradiction in the legal-constitutional system.

In addressing these questions, this chapter will argue for a particular conception of social rights which sees them as having a central, constitutive relationship to the market. The historical function of social rights is to reconcile the traditional mechanisms of social policy with the mechanisms of a market order. It is not difficult to find examples of welfare state regimes in which, notwithstanding extensive social provision, social rights are weakly articulated (such as Britain in the 1940s and 1950s), just as it is possible to think of market-orientated economies in which the values of social solidarity do not find strong expression in any form (such as the present day USA). Therefore this is not an argument that social rights are the *sine qua non* of either the welfare state or the market system. Rather, it is a claim that the welfare state and the market function well together in a context where social rights are effectively recognised, a key aspect of which is their constitutional parity with economic rights.

The argument is developed as follows. The next section discusses a number of possible meanings of the term 'social rights'. TH Marshall's three-fold distinction between civil, political and social rights is examined against the background of the post-1945 welfare state system. This is then contrasted with FA Hayek's critical account of social legislation. It is argued that both accounts place undue emphasis on the 'market correcting' function of social policy mechanisms, that is, their role in correcting for the undesirable effects of markets, and fail to notice their 'market constituting' or 'market creating' role. The next section argues that social rights can be seen to be at the foundation of a market order, building here on the 'capability approach' of Amartya Sen, and giving examples from contemporary EU social law. Then the issue of the link between social rights and other social policy interventions—social provision and social regulation—is addressed. Here, it is suggested that in translating abstract social rights into concrete forms of intervention, market mechanisms—in particular competition and reputation—have a crucial role to play. Just as social rights are at the foundation of the market, the market provides the means for the application at micro level of social rights. Again, examples are given from contemporary EU practice. The final section reflects on the significance of the arguments made in the preceding sections for the future of the Charter.

CONTRASTING CONCEPTIONS OF THE 'SOCIAL': MARSHALL AND HAYEK

In Marshall's classic and still influential formulation in his 1949 Cambridge lectures, *Citizenship and Social Class*,[5] social rights were distinguished from 'civil' and 'political' rights. Civil rights were 'rights necessary for the individual freedom–liberty of the person, freedom of speech, thought and faith, the right to own property and to conclude valid contracts, and the right to justice'. Political rights were characterised in terms of 'the right to participate in the exercise of political power, as a member of a body invested with political authority or as an elector of the members of such a body'. Social rights were loosely defined, but according to Marshall covered a wide range of entitlements:

> from the right to a modicum of economic welfare and security to the right to share to the full in the social heritage and to live the life of a civilised being according to the standards prevailing in society.[6]

Two conclusions followed from this characterisation. The first was that social rights operate in tension with the market order. Civil rights, Marshall thought, were 'intensely individual, and that is why they harmonized with the individualistic phase of capitalism'.[7] The social rights of the twentieth century, by contrast, displaced the market, at least to a certain degree: the process of 'incorporating social rights in the status of citizenship' involved 'creating a universal right to real income which is not proportionate to the market value of the claimant'.[8] This gave rise to what Marshall called 'a basic conflict between social rights and market value'.[9]

Yet Marshall was also aware that social rights can be viewed in a different sense, as part of the market order:

> Social rights in their modern form imply an invasion of contract by status, the subordination of market price to social justice, the replacement of the free bargain by the declaration of rights. But are these principles quite foreign to the practice of the

---

[5] Reprinted London, Pluto, 1992 (subsequent references are to this edition).
[6] Above, n 5 at 8.
[7] Above, n 5 at 26.
[8] Above, n 5 at 28.
[9] Above, n 5 at 42.

market today, or are they there already, entrenched within the contract system itself? I think it is clear that they are.[10]

In *Citizenship and Social Class*, this claim was followed by a discussion of the evolution of collective bargaining, which stressed its dual nature as 'a normal peaceful market operation', which gives expression to 'the right of the citizen to a minimum standard of civilized living'. However, Marshall later concluded that whatever else the post-war welfare state settlement had achieved, 'the basic conflict between social rights and market value has not been resolved'.[11]

The second conclusion Marshall drew was that the legal form of social rights differed from that of civil and political rights. More precisely, they lacked a clear juridical status; it seems that Marshall did not expect the courts to play a prominent role in articulating social claims. The institutions Marshall associated most closely with social rights were 'the educational system and the social services'.[12] He also suggested that in relation to the receipt of welfare services,

> the rights of the citizen cannot be precisely defined . . . A modicum of legally enforceable rights may be granted, but what matters to the citizen is the superstructure of legitimate expectations.[13]

This was in contrast to civil rights which he saw as 'an eighteenth century achievement . . . in large measure the work of the courts'. In this respect, Marshall reflected the emphases of his own time: in the post-war British welfare state of the 1940s, against the backdrop of which *Citizenship and Social Class* was written, social rights were almost invariably seen as the product of legislative action and, increasingly, of bureaucratic provision, leaving the courts on the margins.

Hayek's theory of spontaneous order, outlined in the course of the 1970s in the three volume work *Law, Legislation and Liberty*,[14] took up the same theme of the conflict between social policy and the market, but sought to resolve it by reasserting the sphere of private law at the expense of social legislation. Hayek's account, while highly critical of the welfare state, was nevertheless not based on a denial of the importance of law in shaping social institutions. Hayek believed that economic behaviour presupposes the existence of a body of social and legal norms, which serve to coordinate the expectations of individual agents. His 'market order' rests on rules of a particular kind, the 'abstract rules of just conduct', which Hayek associated with private law. Private law and the market are mutually supportive elements of a 'spontaneous order' which is both the

---

[10] Above, n 5 at 40.

[11] Above, n 5 at 42.

[12] Above, n 5 at 8.

[13] Above, n 5 at 34.

[14] *Law, Legislation and Liberty. A New Statement of the Liberal Principles of Justice and Political Economy* (London, Routledge, 1980). This 1980 edn collects the three vols previously published: *Rules and Order* (London, Routledge, 1973), *The Mirage of Social Justice* (London, Routledge, 1976) and *The Political Order of a Free People* (London, Routledge, 1979); subsequent references are to the relevant individual volume.

foundation of a society's well being and also the necessary condition for the freedom of its individual members. Social legislation, by contrast, interferes with the abstract rules of just conduct in a way which undermines personal autonomy and the well being of society.

The principal features of the rules of just conduct are firstly, that they are purpose-independent; secondly, that they apply generally across a large range of cases and situations whose nature cannot be known in advance; and thirdly, that 'by defining a protected domain of each, [they] enable an order of actions to form itself wherein the individuals can make feasible plans'.[15] By contrast, the rules of organisation are concerned with the internal ordering of governmental and similar bodies; they are 'designed to achieve particular ends, to supplement positive orders that something should be done or that particular results should be achieved, and to set up for these purposes the various agencies through which government operates'.[16] Here 'the distinction between the rules of just conduct and the rules of organisation is closely related to, and sometimes explicitly equated with, the distinction between private and public law'.[17]

This distinction is important because in Hayek's view, public law cannot substitute for private law as the basis for a spontaneous order; nor can the two forms be combined. This is because private law respects, where public law does not, the autonomy and capacity for action of individuals:

> It would . . . seem that wherever a Great Society has arisen, it has been made possible by a system of rules of just conduct which included what David Hume called 'the three fundamental laws of nature', *that of stability of possession, of its transference by consent*, and *of the performance of promises*, or . . . the essential content of all contemporary systems of private law.[18]

Although he does not undertake a detailed examination of juridical structures, Hayek implies that the relationship between contract, property and tort is determined by their respective roles in defining and protecting the autonomy of individual agents. Private law is the precondition of the market order in the sense that without it, individuals would not be free to use their own information and knowledge for their own purposes. Although market transactions may be supported by conventions or social norms which are the consequence of interaction between individuals, these norms are not sufficient for the preservation of the spontaneous order of the market 'in most circumstances the organisation which we call government becomes indispensable to assure that those rules are obeyed'.[19] Hence the exercise of 'coercion' or legal enforcement of norms is justified within a spontaneous order 'where this is necessary to secure the private domain of the individual against interference by others'.[20] While a given

---

[15] *Rules and Order*, above n 14 at 85–86.
[16] *Rules and Order*, above n 14 at 125.
[17] *Rules and Order*, above n 14 at 132.
[18] *The Mirage of Social Justice*, above n 14 at 140.
[19] *Rules and Order*, above n 14 at 47.
[20] *Rules and Order*, above n 14 at 57.

rule of just conduct almost certainly has a spontaneous origin, in the sense that 'individuals followed rules which had not been deliberately made but had arisen spontaneously',[21] such rules do not lose their essential character merely by virtue of being systematised:

> [t]he spontaneous character of the resulting order must therefore be distinguished from the spontaneous origin of the rules on which it rests, and it is possible that an order which would still have to be described as spontaneous rests on rules which are entirely the result of deliberate design.[22]

Public or regulatory law, by contrast, is understood to consist of specific commands and directions which, in aiming at certain substantive redistributions of resources, undermine the autonomy of economic agents. What is illegitimate and counter-productive, in Hayek's view, is not legal ordering of the market as such—this is essential at the level of the rules of private law—but rather the application of public law to the regulation of the market, understood as a spontaneous order. The law can most appropriately support economic progress by protecting private property rights and by ensuring that returns accrue to those who make investments in the process of discovery. This is so even though certain gains may accrue by chance, leaving some agents with 'undeserved disappointments'.[23] Ex-post redistribution of resources blunts incentives for individuals to invest in their own skills and efforts.

Hayek did not suggest that legal intervention, for example for the enforcement of property and contract rights, is necessarily illegitimate. On the contrary, he accepted the occasionally 'coercive' character of private law. Nor did he claim that the techniques of public law could never be legitimately deployed. Nor, even, are all forms of legislative intervention in market activity deemed to be inappropriate. Hayek excluded from condemnation legislation which involved 'the removal of discriminations by law which had crept in as a result of the greater influence that certain groups like landlords, employers, creditors, etc., had had on the law';[24] he also accepted a role for 'the provision by government of certain services which are of special importance to some unfortunate minorities, the weak or those unable to provide for themselves'.[25] But he drew the line at a 'third kind of "social" legislation', whose aim is 'to direct private activity towards particular ends and to the benefit of particular groups', and referred in this context to the UK Trade Disputes Act 1906 and to US New Deal legislation supporting the growth of collective bargaining. Here, it was precisely the 'progressive replacement of private law by public law' which was the source of difficulty.[26]

---

[21] *Rules and Order*, above n 14 at 45.
[22] *Rules and Order*, above n 14 at 45–46.
[23] *The Mirage of Social Justice*, above n 14 at 127.
[24] *Rules and Order*, above n 14 at 141.
[25] *Rules and Order*, above n 14 at 141–42.
[26] *Rules and Order*, above n 14 at 142–43.

Social Rights as the Foundation of the Market: Adapting Sen's 'Capability Approach'

Thus in Hayek's account of the role of law in market ordering, it is the institutions of private law—in particular, property and contract—which guarantee to individuals the conditions for their effective participation in the market. However, this conception is inadequate to the task of explaining the persistence of inequalities whose effects on markets, and the labour market in particular, cannot simply be dismissed as 'undeserved disappointments'. It is possible to argue from within the theory of spontaneous order, as Robert Sugden has done, that for the market to generate social well being it is necessary not simply to have a system of property rights, but for individuals to have *endowments* in the sense of items of value which are tradable,

> the market has a strong tendency to supply each person with those things he wants, *provided that he owns things that other people want, and provided that the things he wants are things that other people own.*[27]

Another way of putting this is to say that the market has no inbuilt tendency to satisfy the wants of those who do not have things that other people want.

Extremes of inequality have the effect of excluding certain groups from the market altogether. The result is not just that these individuals no longer have access to the goods which the market can supply; the rest of society also suffers a loss from their inability to take part in the system of exchange. Resources which could have been mobilised for the benefit of society as a whole will, instead, remain unutilised. The logic of this position, as Sugden makes clear,[28] is that redistribution is needed not to reverse the unpleasant results of the market, but rather to provide the preconditions for the market working in the first place. Although Sugden does not put it in such terms, one implication of his argument is that many of the redistributive and protective rules of labour law and the welfare state have a market-creating function. The tension between social rights and the market cannot be resolved by simply reducing the scope of the former in favour of the latter.

A market-creating role for social rights is one possible implication of the 'capability approach' developed by Amartya Sen in a series of works including *Commodities and Capabilities*[29] and *Development as Freedom*.[30] Sen describes individual well-being in terms of a person's ability to achieve a given set of functionings. In this context,

---

[27] R Sugden, 'Spontaneous Order', in P Newman (ed) *The New Palgrave Dictionary of Economics and the Law* Volume III (London, Macmillan, 1998) 485–95 at 492.

[28] Above n 27 at 493.

[29] (Deventer, North Holland, 1985).

[30] (Oxford, OUP, 1999).

the 'concept of 'functionings' . . . reflects the various things a person may value doing or being. The valued functionings may vary from elementary ones, such as being adequately nourished and being free from avoidable disease, to very complex activities or personal states, such as being able to take part in the life of the community and having self-respect . . . A 'capability' [is] a kind of freedom: the substantive freedom to achieve alternative functioning combinations.[31]

An individual's capability is to some degree a consequence of their entitlements, that is, their ability to possess, control and extract benefits from a particular commodity. An individual's feasible set of utilisation functions is therefore constrained by the limits upon their own resources. However, there are also non-choice factors affecting functioning, for example, an individual's metabolic rate which is a consequence of their physical state. The state of an individual's knowledge may also be a non-choice factor, although this can be improved by education. In this case, the element of choice may lie elsewhere, at the collective or societal level, that is to say, with policy makers, government officials, and judges. The same questions arise in the choice of commodities. Apart from the resources available to an individual, their capability to make use of a commodity may depend at a fundamental level upon access to a legal system which recognises and guarantees protection of contract and property rights, but also upon access to health care, education and other resources which equip them to enter into relations of exchange with others.

Crucial to Sen's 'capability approach' is the idea of *conversion factors*. These are the characteristics of an individual's *person*, their *society* and their *environment* which together determine their capability to achieve a given range of functionings. *Personal characteristics*, in this sense could include an individual's metabolism, or their biological sex; *societal characteristics* would include social norms, legal rules and public policies (such as norms which result in social discrimination or gender stereotyping, or legal interventions to offset these phenomena); and *environmental characteristics* could refer to climate, physical surroundings, technological infrastructure and legal-political institutions.

Sen's work does not address the issue of the juridical foundations of the capability approach in the way that Hayek explicitly considered the question of the legal foundations of the market. However, the capability approach has clear implications for the way in which social rights are conceived. Specifically, social rights may be understood as part of the process of 'institutionalising capabilities', that is to say, as providing mechanisms for extending the range of choice of alternative functionings on the part of individuals. In using capabilities in this way to re-orient the rationale of social rights, we may also come closer to achieving the resolution between social rights and the market order which was left unresolved by Marshall. If capabilities are a consequence not simply of the endowments and motivations of individuals but also of the access they have to the processes of socialisation, education and training which enable them to

---

[31] As above, n 30 at 75.

exploit their resource endowments, then by providing the conditions under which access to these processes is made generally available, mechanisms of redistribution such as progressive taxation, wage regulation and the provision of social security benefits may be not just compatible with, but become a pre-condition to, the operation of the labour market. In this way social rights, which underpin mechanisms of distribution and serve to ensure that they are recog-nised in the legal and constitutional sphere, may play a pivotal role in providing an institutional foundation for individual capabilities.

This point may be illustrated by considering laws against sex discrimination. A conventional economic view of laws which protect women against dismissal on the grounds of pregnancy would be as follows. From the viewpoint of enterprises which would otherwise dismiss pregnant employees once they become unable to carry on working as normally, such laws impose a private cost. These enterprises may respond by declining to hire women of child-bearing age who will, as a result, find it more difficult to get jobs. If this happens, there may be an overall loss to society in terms of efficiency, because resources are misallocated and under-utilised, as well as a disadvantage to the women who are unemployed as a result.

An alternative way of thinking about discrimination against pregnant work-ers is as follows. In the absence of legal protection against this type of discrimi-nation, women of child-bearing age will not expect to continue in employment once (or shortly after) they become pregnant. It is not necessary for all market participants to make a precise calculation along these lines; rather, a norm or convention will emerge, according to which pregnant women expect to lose their jobs and their employers expect to be able to dismiss them without any harm attaching to their reputation. The overall effect is that investments in skills and training are not undertaken, making society worse off as a result. Women workers will have an incentive not to make relation-specific investments in the jobs which they undertake. In an extreme situation, they may withdraw from active participation in the labour market altogether, and norms may encourage this too—as in the case of the 'marriage bar' norm, according to which any woman who married was expected thereupon to resign her position. This norm was widely observed, for example, in the British public sector up to the 1950s and, in the case of some local authorities, was enshrined in regulations.[32]

What is the effect of the introduction of a prohibition on the dismissal of pregnant women under these circumstances? In addition to remedying the injus-tice which would otherwise affect individuals who are dismissed for this reason, a law of this kind has the potential to alter incentive structures in such a way as to encourage women employees to seek out, and employers to provide training for, jobs involving relation-specific skills. The demonstration effect of damages awards against employers may over time lead to a situation in which the norm

---

[32] On the marriage bar, see S Walby, *Patriarchy at Work: Patriarchal and Capitalist Relations in Employment* (Cambridge, Polity Press, 1986).

of automatic dismissal is replaced by its opposite. Stigma attaches to those employers who flout the law. As more employers observe the new norm as a matter of course, it will tend to become self-enforcing, in a way which is independent of the law itself. Conversely, more women will expect, as a matter of course, to carry on working while raising families, in a way which may have a wider destabilising effect on the set of conventions which together make up the 'traditional' household division of labour between men and women.

Pregnancy protection laws of the kind mandated by several Community Directives[33] can therefore be seen as a form of institutional support for individual capabilities. In other words, they provide the conditions under which, for women workers, the freedom to enter the labour market becomes more than merely formal; it becomes a substantive freedom. This effect is not confined to laws in the area of equality of treatment. Consider laws which set minimum wages or which otherwise establish legally-binding wage floors, such as the principle known as 'inderogability' in Italian labour law and observed in some form in most continental labour law systems, although not well represented in the British labour law tradition.[34] These laws have been the subject of severe criticisms from economic and legal commentators.[35] The objection made against them is that they artificially raise wages above the market clearing level, thereby reducing demand for labour and excluding the less able from access to the labour market. By doing so, they potentially infringe the basic constitutional right to work in systems which recognise that concept.

This argument assumes that a 'free' labour market more or less accurately allocates wages to workers according to their relative productivity. However, there are spontaneous (non-state) forces at work in the labour market which make this unlikely. In an unregulated or 'free' labour market without effective labour standards, wage rates are only weakly linked, at best, to the comparative productivity of workers.[36] By removing protective legislation which has a general or 'universal' effect, protecting all labour market entrants, deregulation directly undermines the capabilities of those individuals who are at most risk of social exclusion through discrimination and the undervaluation of their labour. The de-motivation of those who find themselves excluded from access to pro-

---

[33] In particular, Dir 92/85/EEC on measures to encourage improvements in the safety and health of pregnant workers and workers who have recently given birth or are breastfeeding, OJ 1992 L 348/1; see also relevant case law of the Court under Dir 76/207/EEC, OJ 1976 L 39/40, including Case C–177/88 *Dekker v VJV Centrum* [1991] ECR I–3941, and Case C–32/93 *Webb v EMO Air Cargo Ltd* [1994] ECR I–3567.

[34] The concept of 'inderogability' refers to the binding effect of labour standards which cannot be adversely modified by contracting. See Lord Wedderburn, 'Inderogability, Collective Agreements and Community law' (1992) 21 *Industrial Law Journal* 245.

[35] A Ichino and P Ichino, (1998) 'A chi serve il diritto del lavoro? Riflessioni interdisciplinari sulla funzione economica e la giustificazione costituzionale dell'inderogabilitá delle norme giuslavoristiche', in A Amendola (ed) *Istituzione e mercato del lavoro* (Rome, Edizione Scientifiche Italiane, 1998).

[36] C Craig, J Rubery, R Tarling, and F Wilkinson *Labour Market Structure, Industrial Organisation and Low Pay* (Cambridge, Cambridge University Press, 1982).

ductive employment is met by ever-increasing pressure on them to take jobs at any cost. This takes the form of measures within social security law which discipline the 'voluntarily' unemployed by, for example, withdrawing benefits from individuals who refuse to accept jobs offering low-standard terms and conditions of employment. On the demand side, employers are encouraged to take on the unemployed by subsidy schemes which top up low wages. This exacerbates the effect of removing the incentives for training and investment in human capital which flow from a legal requirement for employers to pay a minimum wage. All these developments are well documented in the case of the British experience of deregulation which reached its high point in the early 1990s.[37]

By contrast, legislation setting a floor to wages and terms and conditions of employment in effect requires firms to adopt strategies based on enhancing the quality of labour inputs through improvements to health and safety protection, training and skills development. This form of labour regulation may therefore be expected to have a positive impact on incentives for training. Minimum wage laws are therefore another means of enhancing capabilities, in the sense of improving the substantive labour market freedoms of workers. The support given by Community law to the notion of an 'equitable wage'[38] and the recognition by the Court that collective bargaining gives rise to considerations of social rights[39] are highly relevant in this context.

THE MARKET AS A MECHANISM FOR THE APPLICATION OF SOCIAL RIGHTS:
REGULATORY LEARNING AND REFLEXIVE LAW IN THE EU

Sen's capability approach offers a new way of assessing and evaluating legal, social, political and economic interactions.[40] Individuals' well-being and substantive freedoms are analysed through an examination of their capability sets, understood as their ability to maximise their potential functionings. Nevertheless, the capability approach is not a full theory of justice; Sen states that '[i]t is not clear that there is any royal road to evaluation of economic or social policies'.[41] Rather, it can be used as an evaluative tool or space in which to assess individuals' freedoms or potential. Sen's insistence that there is no universally-applicable, prescriptive list of functionings and capabilities means that

---

[37] S Deakin and F Wilkinson, 'Labour Law, Social Security and Economic Inequality' (1991) 15 *Cambridge Journal of Economics* 125.

[38] See the Commission Opinion on an Equitable Wage, COM(93) 388 final, OJ 1993 C 248/7, which, while advisory only, is not entirely without significance as a first step in the recognition of this principle within the Community's legal order.

[39] Case C–67/96 *Albany International v Stichting Bedrijfspensioenfonds Textielindustrie* [1999] ECR–I 5751.

[40] R Salais, 'Libertés du travail et capacités: une perspective pour une construction européenne?' [1999] *Droit Social* 467.

[41] *Development as Freedom*, above n 30 at 84.

attention is focused instead on social choice procedures by which the content of capability sets can be collectively and democratically determined in particular contexts. The implication of this approach is that a procedure which aims at the expansion of capability sets should focus on the conversion factors which, in a given society, determine the translation of impersonal and transferable resources, such as human and physical capital, into functionings and capabilities. The capability approach therefore offers (among other things) a normative framework for judging particular institutional forms and policy proposals.

This helps to clarify the juridical form of social rights, and their relationship both to social provision and to social regulation. According to Lo Faro,

> the notion of social rights can refer to a series of predominantly, but not exclusively, financial benefits bestowed by the public machinery within the context of social policies of the redistributive type.[42]

The problem with this idea, as he notes, is that many of the 'rights' in question depend, for their realisation, on certain economic and political conditions which are independent of the legal form of the relevant benefits or claims. The idea of the 'right to work' can be cited as one example of this problem; its effective realisation appears to depend upon external economic conditions or, perhaps, on various kinds of government action, which the legal system is more or less powerless to affect.

Lo Faro's critique should not be taken to justify a clear-cut division between social rights on the one hand and civil, political and economic rights on the other. The enforcement of civil rights also depends on the existence of a legal infrastructure, in the form of courts and enforcement agencies, which at a fundamental level requires government intervention. More generally, it rests upon the widespread recognition within a society of conventions of property and contract, which are taken for granted at the level of everyday economic interaction. While there is a complex link between formal institutions, on the one hand, and the emergence of these tacit conventions on the other, it is not feasible to suppose that the latter can exist wholly without reference to the former. This is a basic observation of the process of industrial development which is now widely acknowledged in debates concerning the appropriate legal framework for economic growth.

Lo Faro's observations are orientated towards a different issue, namely the appropriate balance between substantive and procedural norms. The 'substantive' version of social rights may be contrasted, Lo Faro suggests, with a 'procedural' version which has the two-fold merit of avoiding the neoliberal association of social rights with economic 'costs', and stressing the links between social rights and participative democracy. This version takes, as its concrete form, constitutional guarantees of freedom of association and collec-

---

[42] A Lo Faro, *Regulating Social Europe. Reality and Myth of Collective Bargaining in the EC Legal Order* (Oxford, Hart, 2000) at 152.

tive representation. There is an important connection here to the idea of a social choice procedure of the kind which Sen sees as providing the most appropriate basis for the enhancement of capability sets. In Sen's approach, to argue for capabilities is to make a case for particular democratic processes by which capabilities may be enhanced. When considering the question of social rights in this vein, we should, similarly, be less concerned with bringing about particular distributions of resources, than with ensuring that the processes by which particular claims are asserted and settled are legitimate from a capability perspective. In the particular context which we are considering here, namely the contemporary process of European integration, the crucial issue is how to locate social rights within the logic of market integration which drives the European project. This takes us back to our starting point, namely the view (found in both Marshall and Hayek) that social rights 'block' market processes. How does the capability approach provide a way around this apparent contradiction?

There are several ways in which the capability approach might be helpful in this regard. In thinking about social rights in a manner influenced by Sen, we may discern two categories of such rights: (1) social rights as immediate claims to *resources* (financial benefits such as welfare payments) and (2) social rights as particular forms of *procedural* or institutionalised interaction (such as rules governing workplace relations, collective bargaining and corporate governance). In relating to the first of these categories, we can think of social rights as claims to commodities which can then be converted by individuals into functionings or potential functionings (capabilities). The provision of sick pay, maternity pay, or social welfare benefits give rise to social rights in a quite traditional, well recognised sense. The second category of social rights links to Sen's distinctive idea of 'social conversion factors'. Sen suggests that social or institutional settings shape individuals' possibilities of achieving their goals. Social rights, seen in this way as procedural rights, are the means by which to shape these institutional environments, so as to ensure that a wider range of individuals are able to convert their assets—skills, capital—into their desired functionings.

Given that social rights can work in this variety of ways, they can be viewed as providing a central normative goal—the enhancement of capability sets—which can then be seen to structure a range of discourses about social and economic policy, *without presupposing* any particular substantive economic model or policy programme. This leaves open to further argument the particular form of social rights and social regulation recommended by the capability approach. The capability approach is not in itself prescriptive about the mechanisms that should be employed to realise its goal and thus can be sympathetically disposed to a variety of *means* of enhancing individual well-being from the capability perspective, including direct state provision of resources, compulsory reshaping of institutions, or voluntary action to refashion widely held norms. It can also operate through market mechanisms including competition and reputation (the latter playing a particularly important role in the transmission of information to market participants). In each case, outcomes arise through a context-dependent process of social learning.

The translation of social rights, expressed in an abstract form in the core 'constitutional' (Treaty-based) and legislative texts of the EU, into concrete forms of social provision and social regulation at the level of the Member States, is very much a process of learning in this sense. Health and safety law provides one example among many of this effect. The principle of the 'humanisation of work' which originates in German labour law is expressed in the 1989 Framework Directive on Health and Safety in terms of:

> adapting the work to the individual, especially as regards the design of work places, the choice of work equipment and the choice of working time and production methods, with a view, in particular, to alleviating monotonous work and work at a predetermined work rate and to reducing their effect on health.[43]

Similarly, in the Directive on the Organisation of Working Time, it is provided that Member States are required to take the steps necessary to ensure that an employer 'who intends to organise work according to a certain pattern' takes account of the principle, 'especially as regards breaks during working time'.[44] Because of the derogations contained in the Directive, the implementation of the standards it lays down in relation to working time limits, breaks and shift patterns is left to a surprisingly large extent to collective bargaining or forms of joint decision-making between the social partners at various levels (and, in one exceptional and perhaps dubious case, to individual agents at enterprise level).[45] Local-level solutions to the organisation of working time are thereby encouraged. However, the principle of the humanisation of work remains a key interpretive point of reference in examining the legitimacy of particular derogations.

The Framework Health and Safety Directive and Organisation of Working Time Directive use the technique of 'reflexive law', that is to say, law which aims to achieve its intended goal indirectly, through 'second order effects' on the part of autonomous agents. These agents might be individual actors in a market setting, or the social partners in the context of collective dialogue or negotiation. By definition, the precise outcome of the application of the law cannot be known in advance. It depends upon the nature of the local context in which the 'second order effects' operate. However, in setting the context for this interaction, the legal system aims to 'steer' the outcome in a particular direction. In this sense, social rights create the spaces within which local solutions are sought; they determine the parameters of legitimate action.

A further illustration of this process is provided by the EU Green Paper[46] and Resolution[47] on corporate social responsibility. Here, a range of mechanisms

---

[43] Directive 89/391/EEC, OJ 1989 L 183/1, Art 6(2)(d).

[44] Directive 93/104/EC, OJ 1993 L 307/18, Art 13.

[45] *Ibid*, Art 18(1)(b)(i).

[46] *Promoting a European Framework for Corporate Social Responsibility*, COM(2001) 366. For further discussion see J Hunt, in this collection at p 59.

[47] OJ 2002 C 86/03.

within corporate governance are seen as providing the basis for advancing social policy goals. These include shareholder activism based on the aims of 'socially responsible investment' (SRI), stakeholder engagement with management, and reputational harm to companies failing to comply with relevant standards. Thus

> European market indices identifying companies with the strongest social and environmental performance will become increasingly necessary as a basis for launching SRI funds and as a performance benchmark for SRI.

But

> [t]o ensure the quality and objectivity of these indices, the assessment of the social and environmental performance of companies listed in them should be done on the basis of the information submitted by the management *but also by the stakeholders.*

More generally, 'the involvement of stakeholders, including trade unions and NGOs, could improve the quality of verification' of company reporting on the 'triple bottom line' of social, economic and ethical performance.[48] At the same time, this is seen as a process shaped by the presence of fundamental rights and by certain inderogable legal standards: 'corporate social responsibility should not be seen as a substitute to regulation or legislation concerning social rights or environmental standards'.[49] The aim is to link 'a high level of social cohesion, environmental protection and respect for fundamental rights' with the aim of 'improving competitiveness in all types of business, from small and medium-sized enterprises to multinationals, and in all sectors of activity'.[50] In using market mechanisms to bring about social policy goals, the policy aims to make complete the reconciliation of social rights and the market.[51]

But while certain mechanisms are ruled in by this approach, others are ruled out. Thus, for example, the single market rules cannot be used to undermine collective bargaining. This is the effect of *Albany*,[52] where the Court declined to accept an argument (which Advocate General Jacobs had approved) according to which arrangements for multi-employer collective bargaining could be subjected to scrutiny under a version of the 'rule of reason' where they could be shown to have an anti-competitive effect under Article 81 (ex 85) EC. The Court declined to go down this route because of the recognition granted to rights in relation to collective bargaining and social dialogue in Articles 137 and 138 EC (the relevant parts of which were formerly contained in Articles 118 and 118a EC). Here, social rights contained in the nearest thing which the EU has to a core

---

[48] *Green Paper*, above n 46 at 19.

[49] *Green Paper*, above n 46 at 5.

[50] Resolution, above n 47, Art 11.

[51] For further discussion of the approach of the Green Paper in the context of gender equality in the UK, see J Browne, S Deakin and F Wilkinson, 'Capabilities, Social Rights and European Market Integration' Centre for Business Research Working Paper No 253, 2002, University of Cambridge.

[52] Case C–67/96 *Albany International v Stichting Bedrijfspensioenfonds Textielindustrie* [1999] ECR–I 5751. Judgment of the Court, at para 60; cf the Opinion of the AG, at paras 186–94, proposing a limited immunity for collective bargaining which would be subject to a number of conditions being satisfied.

constitutional text were used to place limits on the reach of the single market principle. A similar 'blocking' technique was deployed in the *Working Time* case,[53] in which the Court rejected the United Kingdom's argument that the Organisation of Working Time Directive lacked a proper jurisdictional base under the EC Treaty. Here the Court was influenced by the need to acknowledge 'a broad interpretation of the powers which Article 118a EC [now part of Article 137 EC] confers upon the Council for the protection of the health and safety of workers'.[54] Again, the presence of social rights qualifies the reach of the economic provisions of the core Treaty texts, which (in this context) cannot be invoked to constrain mechanisms of social regulation.

In one respect, the decisions in *Working Time* and *Albany* did not go far enough. The Court could have based its ruling on the argument that social and labour standards have a pro-competitive effect, in the sense of encouraging enterprises to invest in human capital and avoiding the destructive social effects of low-wage competition. Such measures have a clear capability-enhancing effect, by widening the opportunities for training and improvement of job quality. The 'blocking' technique simply asserts that social and economic rights stand on an equal but separate footing, without directly addressing the neoliberal argument that the former undermine the latter. In the final analysis, the Court may not be able to avoid that argument. The best answer to it is that implied by the Resolution on Corporate Social Responsibility, namely that social cohesion and the competitiveness of enterprise are two sides of the same coin.

The Capability Approach and the Charter

This Chapter has considered whether an adequate rationale exists for the parity of social and economic rights which is characteristic of the Charter. It was argued that social rights can be understood as mechanisms for enhancing the substantive economic freedoms of individuals to achieve a wide range of functionings. In that sense, a case for social rights may be derived from the 'capability approach' of Sen. Social rights are the foundation of a market order which is based on the most extensive mobilisation of resources and the widest division of labour which are compatible with a given society's initial endowments in terms of human and physical resources. In turn, a market order is one which offers a welfare state regime an extensive set of mechanisms for the application of social rights, ranging from collective bargaining to shareholder pressure, inter-firm competition and reputational effects.

The aim of this Chapter has been to lay out a particular way of conceptualising social rights as a bridge between the welfare state and the market. It has not

---

[53] Case C–84/94 *United Kingdom v Council (Working Time)* [1996] ECR–I 5755.
[54] Para 15.

undertaken the task of identifying what the content of particular social rights at particular levels might be if this approach is followed. Nor has it undertaken an analysis of existing social law systems, at EU level or otherwise, to see whether they are completely compatible with the capability approach as described here. The current content of EU social law is evidently lop-sided, the result of contingent historical and political factors which have dictated that while the law on some areas is rich and detailed (gender equality), on others it is sparse (termination of the individual employment relationship). The provisions of Chapters Three and Four of the Charter are more comprehensive in the sense of at least covering the core of most national labour law systems,[55] but the substance of these Charter rights leaves much to be desired. However, these issues of the scope and content of the existing law are in a sense beside the point. The point is that those social rights which are contained in the Charter and in the Treaties should be understood as shaping the process through which local-level solutions to questions of the scope and content of the law emerge. This would be compatible with a capability approach which avoids prescriptive, a priori solutions in favour of one based on diversity and regulatory learning.

---

[55] See the contributions by J Kenner, B Ryan and J Hunt in this collection.

3

Fair and Just Working Conditions

JO HUNT*

INTRODUCTION

FROM ITS INCEPTION, the EC has had a stated commitment to improving working conditions. Qualitatively, this commitment may be seen as having been taken a stage further with the inclusion of Articles 30 and 31 in the Charter of Fundamental Rights of the European Union (the Charter), which recognise workers' fundamental rights to fair and just working conditions and protection against unfair dismissal. The articulation of such rights at this point in time is particularly significant, given the impact that the quest for flexibility in the labour market may have on workers' security. Of course, in its present form, as a non-binding proclamation, the Charter itself remains unenforceable by individuals. However, to the extent that the process of creating the Charter may stimulate the development of a human rights-based approach in this area, the Charter could become an effective counterweight to the threat of a reduction in the levels of protection granted to workers within the Member States, as states come under increasing pressure to respond to the multiple demands of further economic integration. The effectiveness of this counterweight will depend on how the Community courts and legislature respond to this invitation to take these social rights seriously.

For advocates of a stronger social dimension, EU social policy has been slow in breaking free of the straight jacket of the economic imperative, of the market making rationale for EU involvement in this area.[1] To the extent that the Charter may 'herald and concretise a shift in the normative underpinnings of the EU as a polity',[2] the terms of engagement for EU intervention in the area of rights at work may be reconceived. With a shift in ethic towards one in which social rights are recognised as inherently valuable, social rights would be granted as ends not means, and with it, on a macro level would come a recasting of the constitutional balance between economic rights and social rights.[3]

* Cardiff Law School, Cardiff University. I would like to thank the convenors and participants at the Nottingham workshop, and especially Phil Syrpis, the discussant.

[1] On this point, see the contribution of S Deakin and J Browne in this collection.

[2] G de Burca, 'Human Rights: The Charter and Beyond' in *Europe 2004 Le Grand Debat : Setting the Agenda and Outlining the Options*, Proceedings of European Commission Symposium (Brussels, European Commission, 2001).

[3] See further, the chapter by M Poiares Maduro in this collection.

At the very least, the Charter, as with the Community Charter of the Fundamental Social Rights of Workers 1989 (Community Social Charter) before it, may stimulate legislative intervention in the area of rights at work. Already, aspects of the 'rights' contained in Articles 30 and 31 EUCFR have found expression through Community legislation, and conceptually, scope exists for more standard setting on the part of the EU in the form of the adoption of legally enforceable rights. However, the use of rights-based legislation has been increasingly sidelined over recent years with a general move towards the use of governance mechanisms which offer alternatives to enforceable substantive rights-based approaches.[4] These alternatives include more procedural forms of governance, as well as the increasing privatisation of the labour relationship through the development of self-regulatory mechanisms such as corporate social responsibility. These contrasting policy approaches will be examined in section two of this Chapter, where consideration will be given to the prospects for the development of a rights-based approach to the issue of fair and just working conditions, and of a reconceptualisation of the rationales for EU involvement.

Where rights are enforceable then of course they open up opportunities for the involvement of the courts. Whilst the Charter's provisions are not (as yet) themselves directly justiciable, their overlap with existing provisions may afford the possibility for the meaning and scope of Community legislation to be reassessed through the prism of fundamental rights. Such possibilities will be explored in section three, along with the issue of the position of social rights in the context of litigation in the areas of free movement. In considering the potential presented by Articles 30 and 31 EUCFR, attention will be paid to the respective rights contained in the Council of Europe's European Social Charter 1961 (ESC) and the Revised European Social Charter 1996 (RevESC), from which both articles are, at least in part drawn. The relevant ESC rights will be detailed in the first section, in the context of a broader examination of the status of rights to fair and just working conditions and protection against dismissal under international human rights law. Having placed the EU level developments against the backdrop of the multiple instruments and mechanisms for the protection of social rights, the Chapter concludes with a consideration of whether the EU may yet seek to become the ultimate guarantor of social rights for its Member States.

RIGHTS TO FAIR AND JUST WORKING CONDITIONS AS FUNDAMENTAL RIGHTS

Social Rights as 'Second Class' Fundamental Rights

According to popular convention, human rights are often categorised into 'generations' with the 'first generation' of civil and political rights being followed by

---

[4] See the discussion of governance methods in the Chapter by N Bernard in this collection.

the second of economic, social and cultural, with the newest, third generation of rights—group rights—most recently emerging. Not all accept this 'generational' approach to human rights[5] or the distinctions between the different categories of rights. Nevertheless, second generation rights are generally depicted as being positive (requiring state expenditure for their realisation), programmatic (merely specifying goals or objectives to be achieved) and non-justiciable (not amenable to being involved by individuals as the basis of claims before courts), in contrast with the essentially negative and justiciable first generation rights.

Convincing attempts have been made to highlight the artificiality of these distinctions as part of an exercise in enhancing the status of second generation rights on both the international and domestic plane.[6] Of course, within the EU constitutional order, the status of certain second generation rights appears already assured. It could be argued that rights such as those relating to freedom to conduct a business, and the right to property, and, of course the rights to free movement for economic purposes, are more deeply entrenched and afforded greater legal protection under Community law than other categories of human rights, of whatever generation. These rights could be positioned at the core of a body of 'economic' rights, and are afforded a particularly privileged place in the EU legal order in comparison to that of 'social' rights more generally, which I take to refer to a broad category of rights and freedoms which cover rights *at* work, rights to health care and to education, to food and housing, as well as to rights which are more directly linked to enabling market participation, and which are often also depicted as economic rights, such as the right *to* work, and rights to social assistance.[7]

The apparent 'second class' status of such social rights is felt at national and international levels. At the national level, social rights are often absent from the rights set out in a state's basic constitutional documents.[8] On the international level, whilst social rights may be quantitatively well represented in the form of various declarations, charters, covenants and conventions, the machinery for the enforcement of social rights is generally limited to more or less effective systems of state supervision and monitoring, and does not extend to allowing

---

[5] See, for example, the critique in A Eide and A Rosas, 'Economic, Social and Cultural Rights: A Universal Challenge' in A Eide, C Krause, and A Rosas (eds) *Economic, Social and Cultural Rights: A Textbook*, 2nd edn (The Hague, Kluwer Law International, 2001) 3–8, at 4–5.

[6] See M Schenin, 'Economic and Social Rights as Legal Rights' in Eide, Kraus and Rosas, *ibid*, 29–54, and A Lyon-Caen, 'The Legal Efficacy and Significance of Fundamental Social Rights: Lessons from the European Experience' in B Hepple (ed) *Social and Labour Rights in a Global Context* (Cambridge, CUP, 2002) 182–91.

[7] See for example the categorisation of rights by A Eide, 'Economic, Social and Cultural Rights as Human Rights' in Eide, Krause and Rosas, *ibid*, 9–28 at 18.

[8] The constitutions of Finland and Portugal are exceptions. For details of the coverage of social rights in the constitutions of the EU Member States and the accession countries, see European Parliament Working Paper *Fundamental Social Rights in Europe*, 1999, SOCI 104 EN, PE 168.629. For post 1999 developments, there is a very useful collection of constitutions at <http://www.uni-wuerzburg.de/law/>

individuals to submit complaints under the instruments when their social rights are being violated.[9] As a matter of international law then, the mechanisms for ensuring that social rights are taken seriously are weak indeed in comparison with those for the protection of civil rights.[10]

Nevertheless, some apparent 'social' rights have been rendered individually justiciable through their 'related interdependence'[11] with civil and political rights. More directly, certain 'social' rights are equally categorised as civil and political rights, and thus enjoy an enhanced status as compared with the other social rights in this way—for example, the right of association and to join trade unions is expressly provided for under certain civil and political human rights instruments—though the rights to fair and just working conditions are not. In terms of the legal protection that is afforded under international human rights instruments some social rights may appear better protected than others.[12]

The Constitutional Status of Social Rights: Some Fundamental Social Rights are More Fundamental than Others?

Setting the justiciability issue aside, it is also the case that certain social rights may be perceived as being more worthy of protection as fundamental human rights than others. For example, whilst continuing its work in other areas, the International Labour Organisation (ILO) has concentrated its efforts in ensuring respect for four core 'Fundamental Principles and Rights at Work',[13] namely, (a) freedom of association and the effective recognition of the right to collective bargaining, (b) the elimination of all forms of forced or compulsory labour, (c) the effective abolition of child labour, and (d) the elimination of discrimination in respect of employment and occupation.

This identification of a set of particular social rights as core rights, with the pressures for their protection more immediately acute than for others reinforces the idea that some social rights are more fundamental than others—that arguments for the constitutional protection of social rights are more persuasive in respect of a hard core of rights. These arguments were particularly apparent in the process of drafting the Charter, with comments to the effect that the inclu-

---

[9] A collective complaints procedure, with standing granted to trade unions, employers associations and NGOs came into force in respect of the ESC in 1998. For a critical assessment of this new procedure, see T Novitz, 'Are Social Rights Necessarily Collective Rights? A Critical Analysis of the Collective Complaints Protocol to the European Social Charter' (2002) *European Human Rights Law Review* 50.

[10] It is recognised that in some states, primarily by virtue of their monist system, certain rights contained in such instruments as the ESC and ILO conventions are directly applicable and may be invoked by individuals before national courts.

[11] C Scott, 'The Interdependence and Permeability of Human Rights Norms: Towards a Partial Fusion of the International Covenants on Human Rights' (1989) 27 *Osgoode Hall Law Journal* 769.

[12] See J Kenner in this collection.

[13] See *Declaration on Fundamental Principles and Rights at Work*, done at 86th Session, Geneva, June 1998.

sion of such rights as the right to fair and just working conditions, and rights against unfair dismissal amounted to something of an inflation of the importance of these rights, on the grounds that such matters are more regularly protected through legislation (and/or collective bargaining) at national level, rather than through constitutional guarantee.[14]

Indeed, for some, the constitutional entrenchment of social rights (either as individually enforceable rights, or as expressions of values to be respected and attained) is a step that should be opposed. Jowell for example has argued that 'it is not the function of the constitution to predetermine the allocation of resources of the distribution or redistribution of wealth, or the proper place of the market'.[15] Thus the absence of constitutional guarantees for social rights provides room for manoeuvre for the elected government of the day to determine its redistributive and regulatory social policies, and can allow for dynamic, responsive regulation in the face of rapidly changing economic and social contexts. For others, however, the protection of social rights through legislation alone is a cause for concern. Liebenberg for example warns that

> legislation may be amended through simple parliamentary majorities whereas constitutional rights are usually entrenched. This provides a safeguard against the withdrawal of social rights for reasons of political expediency.[16]

To the extent that constitutions may be defined as the expression of the way in which 'a community wishes to be governed',[17] then the enumeration of social rights in constitutional documents presents a powerful symbol of the values which that community holds. Within the EU, many states contain fundamental social rights within their constitutions, though these are more often in terms of (not individually enforceable) goals to be attained, and are of the nature of mechanisms to facilitate the participation of the individual in the economic and political life of the community. Thus the most often-occurring social rights under Member States' constitutions include the right to work, the right to education and training, and the right to social security. Very few constitutions contain references to fair and just working conditions.

Rights to Fair and Just Working Conditions under International Human Rights Instruments

Despite the limited constitutional recognition of the significance of rights to fair and just working conditions as fundamental human rights in national orders,

---

[14] See, eg, the submission by the Federation of German Industries (BDI) and the Confederation of German Employers' Associations (BDA), CHARTE 4489/00 CONTRIB 339.

[15] J Jowell, 'Is Equality a Constitutional Principle?' (1994) 47 *Current Legal Problems* 1.

[16] S Liebenberg, 'The Protection of Economic and Social Rights in Domestic Legal Systems' in Eide, Krause and Rosas, above n 5 at 82.

[17] KD Ewing, 'Social Rights and Constitutional Law' (1999) *Public Law* 104 at 112.

such rights are recognised in all major international human rights instruments. By so doing, these documents would appear to go beyond conceptions of social rights as justified on the grounds of their instrumental value in ensuring a sufficient degree of security and social integration for civil and political rights to be enjoyed, and extend to a view of the inherent value of social rights in enabling true liberty, self-fulfilment and well-being to be realised. This broader view of the rationale for the status of social rights (and specifically rights at work) as fundamental rights is reflected in the first principle of the Philadelphia Declaration of the ILO,[18] namely that *labour is not a commodity*. An appreciation of this principle leads, according to Ben-Israel, to demands for measures which promote and protect worker's 'social dignity'. As Ben-Israel submits,

> . . . by treating labour as a commodity, we circumvent the moral basis on which the employer/employee relationship stands, and incorrectly make the market the sole regulator of the relationship. Accepting the worker's labour as an extension of the workers personality . . . signifies that the transaction of such an incomplete commodification as work cannot be considered only in relation to its market value. It has to be considered from a moral dimension which will reflect the freedom and dignity of the employee's personality.[19]

The very first ILO Convention in 1919 addressed working time issues in respect of the setting of maximum hours of work in industrial undertakings.[20] Since then, the ILO has sought to give practical expression to the objective of achieving social justice through the adoption of a large number of conventions and recommendations in the field of fair and just working conditions, though the incidence of ratification amongst EU Member States has been far from universal.[21]

All Member States are signatories to the UN's 1966 International Covenant on Economic, Social and Cultural Rights (ICESCR), which employs, at Article 7, a particularly wide ranging formulation of 'just and favourable conditions of work'. This includes remuneration which provides all workers with

> fair wages and equal remuneration for work of equal value without distinction of any kind . . . and a decent living for themselves and their families in accordance with the provisions of the present Covenant; safe and healthy working conditions; equal opportunity for everyone to be promoted in his employment to an appropriate higher

---

[18] The Declaration sets out the 'aims and purposes of the ILO and the principles which should inspire the policy of its Members'. The Declaration, adopted in 1944 has been incorporated into the ILO's Constitution, which dates back to 1919. For ILO documents see: <www.ilo.org>.

[19] R Ben-Israel, 'The Rise, Fall and Resurrection of Social Dignity', in R Blanpain (ed), *Labour Law, Human Rights and Social Justice: Liber Amicorum in Honour of Ruth Ben-Israel* (The Hague, Kluwer Law International, 2001) 1–8 at 4, following JK Ingram, *Address on Work and the Workman*, delivered to the 1880 British Trades Union Congress. Excerpts of that address are contained in P O'Higgins, 'Labour is Not a Commodity'—an Irish Contribution to International Labour Law' (1997) 29 *Industrial Law Journal* 225.

[20] ILO Convention 1, Hours of Work (Industry).

[21] See generally A Neal (ed), *Fundamental Social Rights at Work in the European Community* (Aldershot, Ashgate, 1999) 47.

level, subject to no considerations other than those of seniority and competence; and rest, leisure and reasonable limitation of working hours and periodic holidays with pay, as well as remuneration for public holidays.

At the regional level, fair and just working conditions receive extensive attention in the ESC and RevESC.[22] The RevESC resulted out of attempts to revitalise the protection of social rights under the Council of Europe system. As part of this process, closer attention has been paid to the interrelationship between the ESC and the EU systems, with some of the new RevESC rights clearly being modelled on existing EU measures.[23] Other new rights were reportedly included with a view to the RevESC providing 'a model for future legislation for Europe, including the European Union'.[24] With the explanatory memorandum to the Charter identifying rights under the ESC and RevESC as the source of certain of the Charter rights (including aspects of Articles 30 and 31 EUCFR), there would appear to be quite active cross-fertilisation of norms between these two orders. Some appreciation of the scope and meaning of rights to fair and just working conditions in the ESC and RevESC is therefore warranted, though with the observation that the context within which the rights have emerged and developed in the Council of Europe legal order, is of course, very different to that of the market-led EU.

At first sight, it may appear that the ESC's formulation of 'just conditions at work' appears somewhat narrower than that employed in the ICESCR, as it concerns specifically the issue of working time and annual leave. According to Article 2(1), States undertake

> to provide for reasonable daily and weekly working hours, the working week to be progressively reduced to the extent that the increase in productivity and other relevant factors permit.[25]

The reasoning behind the inclusion of this right touches on a number of related issues, however, including first and foremost, health and safety considerations, as well as respect for the private and family life of workers.[26] The ESC itself provides no stipulation as to maximum hourly and weekly working hours, a decision which was taken, according to Harris, on the grounds that any specified level could in time 'prove unduly modest'.[27] State compliance with this

---

[22] To date, the following EU Member States have ratified the RevESC: Finland, France, Ireland, Italy, Portugal and Sweden: <http://conventions.coe.int/Treaty/EC/CadreListeTraites.htm>.

[23] Eg Art 25 RevESC, 'All workers have the right to protection of their claims in the event of the insolvency of their employer'.

[24] F Vandamme, 'The Revision of the European Social Charter' (1994) 133 *International Labour Review* 635 at 642.

[25] States party to the ESC commit to accepting a minimum number of rights (or numbered paragraphs), which must contain certain core rights, so designated not by reason of them being any more fundamental than others, but so as to cover a broad range of issues. Not all EU states have accepted the rights discussed here. Art 2(1) for example, is not accepted as binding by Austria, Denmark, Sweden or the UK.

[26] Council of Europe, *Conditions of Employment in the European Social Charter, Human Rights Social Charter Monographs No 6*, 2nd edn (Strasbourg, Council of Europe, 2000) p 16.

[27] D Harris, *The European Social Charter* (Charlottesville, University Press of Virginia, 1984). The level under discussion at the time the Charter was drafted was a 40 hour maximum working week.

provision requires them to show that 'reasonable' hours of work are being guaranteed 'through law, collective agreement, or any other obligatory means involving supervision by an appropriate authority'.[28] Rather than seeking to impose a Europe-wide minimum standard of working hours, the ESC instead focuses on ensuring that there are efficient procedural guarantees at national level to guard against 'unreasonable' demands on workers. The issue of reasonable hours is considered on a case by case basis in the light of a range of factors, including unemployment rates.

The rest of Article 2 ESC concerns paid holidays (raised from a minimum of two to four weeks under the RevESC), additional compensatory breaks for workers engaged in dangerous or unhealthy occupations (though the RevESC now makes the obligation of reducing the risk factors at work, rather than simply compensating for them, paramount), and weekly rest periods, 'which shall, as far as possible coincide with the day recognised by custom or tradition in the country or region concerned as a day of rest'. Article 2 RevESC as a whole is subject to the application of Article 33 RevESC, which provides that obligations will have been met as long as 'the great majority' (deemed to be at least 80 per cent) of workers are protected.

Article 3 ESC is concerned specifically with health and safety at work, and applies to all workers, including the self employed.[29] States are required to take action to enable the effective exercise of the right to health and safety at work, and such action should include the adoption and enforcement of health and safety regulations, and consultation with employers' and workers' associations on measures intended to improve industrial safety and health. The RevESC now stipulates that all aspects of state action as regards health and safety should be undertaken in consultation with workers and employers organisations, and under Article 3(1) RevESC states are required to 'formulate, implement and periodically review a coherent national policy on occupational safety, occupational health and the working environment'.

Perhaps surprisingly, the ESC made no mention of rights against unfair dismissal, although it is included in new Article 24 RevESC. Article 4(4) of the original ESC did however place an obligation on states to recognise the right of all workers to a reasonable period of notice for termination of employment (save in cases of dismissal for a serious offence). This provision is included in the Article on the right to fair remuneration, which the Committee of Independent Experts (CIE)[30] has recognised as 'an essential corollary of the first three rights . . . which . . . would stand in danger of losing much of their meaning without an effective guarantee of the right to fair remuneration'.[31] According to the CIE, it was included so as to ensure that workers are guaranteed wages for a reasonable

[28] ESC Committee of Independent Experts, Conclusions I, p 169.
[29] Art 33 does not apply to the health and safety provisions, that is, all workers not just 'the great majority' must receive protection.
[30] Now renamed the European Committee of Social Rights.
[31] ESC Committee of Independent Experts, Conclusions I, p 25.

period whilst looking for another job. Article 24 RevESC now provides that states are to recognise the rights of workers not to have their employment terminated without a valid reason connected to their capacity, conduct, or the operational requirements of the undertaking, to a right to compensation where unjustified dismissal has occurred, and to a right to appeal to an impartial body. According to the appendix to the RevESC, however, states are permitted to exclude certain categories of the workforce from this protection, including those on fixed term contracts, and those undertaking a qualifying period of employment, 'provided this is determined in advance and is of a reasonable duration'.[32]

Finally, Article 26 RevESC concerns the right of all workers to dignity at work, and places states under an obligation to 'promote awareness, information and prevention' of sexual harassment, as well as 'recurrent reprehensible or distinctly negative and offensive action directed against individual workers', and to take all appropriate measures to protect workers from such conduct. Compliance with this obligation, according to the appendix to the RevESC, will not require the enactment of legislation by states.

Fair and Just Working Conditions under the Charter

It was against this background of international and regional human rights instruments that the EU Charter of Fundamental Rights was drafted. The resulting provisions on fair and just working conditions and unfair dismissal reflect a somewhat idiosyncratic pick and mix from some of the fundamental social rights recognised in the human rights instruments discussed above. Article 30 EUCFR, on protection in the event of unjustified dismissal is perhaps a surprising inclusion,[33] (albeit that it is to operate 'in accordance with Community law and national laws and practices') given its only very recent appearance in the RevESC,[34] and its absence from the ICESCR and, indeed, the Community Social Charter. The Community Social Charter was never of itself intended to give rise to directly justiciable rights, but instead was to provide an indication of core values and principles which would require further legislative implementation either through supranational action or through action at Member State level alone. Recognition of the fundamental nature of rights to health and safety, and limitations to working hours contained in the Community Social Charter are repeated in the Charter, with Article 31 EUCFR ranging over workers' rights to

---

[32] Explanatory Report, para 86. The Explanatory Report is available at <http://conventions. coe.int/Treaty/en/Reports/Html/163.htm>. The provisions of Art 24 (Rev)ESC are in large measure modelled on ILO Convention 158 on the termination of the employment contract at the initiative of the employer.

[33] ILO Convention 158 has been ratified by only six current EU Member States: Spain, Finland, France, Portugal, Sweden and Luxembourg.

[34] Art 30 EUCFR is stated in the Explanatory Document to draw on Art 24 RevESC.

health and safety,[35] the right to limitation of maximum working hours, to daily and weekly rest periods, to an annual period of paid leave,[36] as well as dignity at work.[37]

A number of the rights contained within Articles 30 and 31 EUCFR are of course already reflected in existing Community legislation. Most obviously, maximum working time, daily and weekly rest periods and an annual period of paid leave are provided for under the Working Time Directive; the Framework Directive on Safety and Health at Work places employers under an obligation to 'to ensure the safety and health of workers in every aspect related to the work', and this Directive is further supplemented by a detailed and extensive body of related measures.[38] Specific protection against unfair dismissal is provided for under the Acquired Rights Directive[39] (and of course, under the general equality directives). Furthermore, a set of directives, (both adopted and proposed) in relation to atypical workers (fixed term,[40] part-time[41] and temporary workers[42]) are designed to ensure that such workers are entitled to equivalent working conditions to those of permanent and full-time workers.

Perhaps most notably absent from the Charter's provisions on fair and just working conditions is any declaration of a right to fair remuneration, a right recognised under the ESC as an essential right without which other rights at work would lose their meaning, and furthermore one which had been included in the Community Social Charter. Whilst making an early appearance on the Convention's work programme,[43] this right was to slip swiftly from the agenda. The inclusion of this right was most often attacked on the grounds that it is a matter that falls strictly within Member States' exclusive competence, and that it is very much of the nature of a political aspiration, rather than an enforceable right. The inclusion of rights which 'merely establish objectives for action' in the catalogue of Charter rights was in principle ruled out by the 1999 Cologne European Council. Although the existence of national minimum wage legislation may defeat the argument that rights to fair remuneration are not justiciable, the fear of competence creep of such sensitive issues onto the EU's legislative agenda presumably played a key role in keeping such a fundamental right out of the Charter. In short, the Charter rights in respect of fair and just working conditions reflect less the core rights of workers regarded as fundamental under

---

[35] Which is stated in the Explanatory Document to be drawn from Art 3 ESC, point 19 of the Community Social Charter, and Dir 89/391/EEC Framework Directive on Safety and Health of Workers at Work, OJ 1989 L183/1.

[36] Stated to be based on Art 2 ESC, point 8 of the Community Social Charter, and Dir 93/104/EC Working Time Directive OJ 1993 L307/18.

[37] Drawing from Art 26 RevESC.

[38] For more detail see C Barnard, *EC Employment Law* 2nd edn (Oxford, OUP, 2000) Chapter 6.

[39] Dir 77/187, revised by Dir 98/50, now consolidated by Dir 2001/23/EC OJ 2001 L 82/16.

[40] Dir 99/70/EC, OJ 1999 L 175/43.

[41] Dir 98/23/EC OJ 1998 L 131/10.

[42] Proposal, COM(2002) 149.

[43] Note from the Praesidium, Proposals for Social Rights, CONVENT 18, CHARTE 4192/00, Brussels, 27 March 2000.

international human rights instruments, and more a cataloguing of the EU's legislative achievements to date.

Protection of Fundamental Rights through Community Secondary Legislation?

The 'fundamental' rights contained in the Charter are thus not meant to be statements of mere political aspiration, but are to be, potentially at least, exercisable rights amenable to judicial protection. It may be argued that, to a very great extent, these rights are already protected and respected in the EU legal order through the various pieces of Community secondary legislation which have been adopted in the field of fair and just working conditions. However, whilst these rights expressed through the secondary legislation could be described as 'fundamental' in terms of their moral importance and as expressions of the principle of social dignity, the rights as contained in Community legislation are not fundamental if we are to consider this to mean unequivocal, and universal. Of course, in any legal order one can expect conditionalities to be attached to the exercise of any human right. However, the expression of the fundamental social rights to fair and just working conditions through secondary legislation is notably partial and incomplete, and limited in both material and personal scope.

In terms of the limitation of the personal scope, for example, Community secondary legislation in the field of working conditions often applies to only certain categories of workers. Even in relation to the particularly well developed field of health and safety at work, the Framework Health and Safety Directive and the directives based on it would appear to apply only to workers, and not the self employed, a distinction which has not been permitted under the ESC system. The protection of the Working Time Directive was originally restricted to certain sections of the workforce,[44] and, with its extensive opt-outs and derogations, it has been attacked as 'difficult to conceptualise as a vehicle for individual rights and actually detracts from the working time and health and safety rights in the [Community Social Charter]'.[45] In short, as the Confederation of British Industry (CBI) stated in its submission to the drafting Convention, arguing against the inclusion of rights on working conditions to be included in the Charter,[46] such rights under Community law exist as 'heavily qualified legislative rights which apply in only specific circumstances'.

---

[44] Although further legislation and sectoral agreements on extending protection to excluded sectors and activities has been enacted, see Dir 2000/34/EC OJ 2000 L 180/22.

[45] J Murray, *Transnational Labour Regulation: The ILO and EC Compared* (The Hague, Kluwer Law International, 2001) at 206.

[46] Second submission by the CBI, CHARTE 4298/00, CONTRIB 170.

Social Rights as Ends or Means?

That Community legislation in respect of what are now referred to as fundamental social rights provides only a partial and incomplete expression of these
rights, is of course perfectly understandable given the institutional, procedural
and normative context within which this legislation has been made. Simply,
when legislating in the field of working conditions, the dominant rationale for
action has been one under which the granting of social rights is viewed as
contingent on some other purpose. Very crudely, as a rule, social aims have
by necessity had to be tied to other, economic aims and objectives in order for
measures granting social rights to be adopted. Thus the early employment
protection directives of the 1970s were introduced under the 'market making'
former Article 100 EEC [now Article 94 EC], with social rights granted to the
extent that a case could be made for their contribution to the establishment and
functioning of the common market, often in terms of creating a level playing
field and equalising costs for employers.[47] The contingent, supporting role
played by social considerations can still be seen today, for example in the
recently proposed directive on working conditions for temporary workers, (a
measure 'designed to ensure full compliance with Article 31[EUCFR]')[48] which
is justified on the grounds that it is needed

> to provide a stable framework for the development of temporary work. By guaran-
> teeing minimum rights for temporary workers, the proposal will make the sector seem
> more attractive and enhance its reputation. The greater attractiveness of agency work
> will give more choice to firms and allow them to better meet their needs for flexibility,
> since they will have access to a larger pool of applicants.[49]

Thus, in the EU context, the view persists that social rights, at least in relation
to working conditions, are granted to workers as means, and not ends in themselves. It is the case that over the past three decades there has been something of
a shift in the arguments presented to justify social interventions in relation to
working conditions on the part of the EU, in the move from equalisation of
costs, or 'level-playing field' arguments, to arguments which present social policy 'as a productive factor'.[50] Under the latter conception, EU intervention in the
field of social policy is countenanced in so far as it contributes to promoting and
protecting 'the social values of solidarity and justice whilst improving economic
performance'.[51] Arguably, neither view fits with a fundamental social rights dis-

---

[47] Although this approach has dominated the policy discourse, many have argued that it is based
on a misapprehension of the impact of different national standards on productivity and competition. See for a consideration of the rationales for EU involvement, P Syrpis, 'The Integrationist
Rationale for EU Social Policy' in J Shaw (ed), *Social Law and Policy in an Evolving European Union*
(Oxford, Hart Publishing, 2000) 17–30.

[48] Preamble, COM(2002) 149 final.

[49] COM(2002) 149 final at 10.

[50] *Social Policy Agenda*, COM (2000) 379 at 6.

[51] *Ibid.*

course, which suggests that social rights, as human rights, are accorded because of their inherent value, and not because of the consequential impact that they may have in achieving some other end. Whilst the EC Treaty now affords the EU institutions dedicated legal bases in the area of working conditions,[52] and reminds the institutions and Member States that they should have in mind fundamental social rights when acting under these bases,[53] the incidences of social rights having been granted 'for their own sake', rather than because of the contribution they can make to the achievement of some other, more 'legitimate' EU goal are few and far between. Where the EU does attempt to legislate in furtherance of a dominant social rationale (as perhaps with the mooted legislation on anti-harassment and dignity at work)[54] it faces particular opposition on the grounds that the case for EU level intervention cannot be made out, that such action is unwarranted, and fails to pass the subsidiarity test. Whilst the Community may legislate on social matters, the accepted role and rationale for EU intervention in this field remains rather different to the primary rationale underpinning the work of the ILO and the Council of Europe. Simply, there is no general acceptance that the EU has an overriding duty from the perspective of social justice (rather than from a conception of market integration, or stimulation of economic growth) to ensure that all workers across the EU are invested with certain fundamental rights.

Social Rights and the Third Way

The identification of dominant 'economic' and 'social' rationales for EU intervention, and the construction of a potential antagonism between the two is of course very much out of step with 'third way' approaches which currently hold sway, and which are presented as providing opportunities for the reconciliation of competing rationales and ideologies. The 'social policy as a productive factor' rationale for intervention, constructed around the 'positive and dynamic interaction of economic, employment and social policies'[55] reflects well attempts to reconcile apparently opposing objectives. Within the policy documents emerging from the Commission, social policy is presented as theoretically co-equal with employment and economic policy, the three fields forming a heterarchical, mutually interdependent relationship.

However, some have had cause to doubt whether social policy has in fact gained an equal status with economic and employment policy in this 'virtuous circle'.[56] For example, Ball has argued that in the light of the 'policy prescriptions'

---

[52] Art 137 EC.

[53] Art 136 EC.

[54] See Commission Communication, *Adapting to Change in Work and Society: a New Community Strategy on Health and Safety at Work 2002–2006*, COM (2002) 118.

[55] Above n 50. See also Deakin and Browne in this collection.

[56] E Szyszczak, 'The New Paradigm for Social Policy: A Virtuous Circle?' (2001) 38 *Common Market Law Review* 1125.

of the European Employment Strategy (EES), the prospects for social policy—particularly in relation to working conditions—may not be good.[57] The focus of the EES she says has been on quantity, not quality of work. Ultimately, according to Ball,

> the focus on 'more' jobs within the EES presents a risk that the objective of 'better' jobs or decent work may be sacrificed. The onus is on the EU itself to ensure that it continues to pursue a vital and proactive policy of rights-based legislation to counter the risk.[58]

Since Ball's observations were made, there have been a number of developments, which are suggestive of the emergence of a counterweight to the risk of more over better jobs. The achievement of 'quality in work' has become an explicit EU policy objective, with a framework for taking forward the commitment in the Social Policy Agenda to attaining quality in work having been developed.[59] The goal of quality in work is also now a general horizontal objective in the EES,[60] and of course, the inclusion of certain fundamental social rights at work in the Charter may also be seen as contributing weight to the bolstering of the 'better work' agenda. The pursuit of the goal of quality in work may involve the adoption of new legislation at Community level, and a case could be made for EU intervention in respect of those fundamental rights at work recognised in the Charter, but not yet the subject of existing legislation (such as dignity at work and individual dismissals). It remains to be seen whether the fundamental social rights discourse relating to these rights and in circulation within the EU system will result in such matters being addressed from a human rights perspective, suggestive of minimum non-derogable legislative standards covering all workers, or whether such legislation will be subject to the now familiar opt-outs, derogations and conditions.

It could also be the case that the issue of working conditions comes to be addressed not through further substantive legislation at all, but through other mechanisms and policy tools of the sort which are associated with third way approaches,[61] and with which may prove themselves more politically acceptable in the current climate. Much has been written on the 'new approaches to governance',[62] particularly in relation to their application in the field of social policy,

---

[57] S Ball, 'The European Employment Strategy: The Will But Not the Way?' (2001) 30 *Industrial Law Journal* 353.

[58] *Ibid* at 355.

[59] Commission Communication, *Employment and Social Policies: A Framework for Investing in Quality*, COM (2001) 313. For discussion see J Kenner, *EU Employment Law: From Rome to Amsterdam and Beyond* (Oxford, Hart, 2003) pp 467–509.

[60] Council Decision of 18 February 2002 on Guidelines for Member States employment policies for the year 2002, 2002/177/EC, OJ 2002 L 60/60.

[61] See on the 'third way' in the context of EU employment law and policy, J Kenner, 'The EC Employment Title and the 'Third Way': Making Soft Law Work' (1999) 15 *International Journal of Comparative Labour Law and Industrial Relations* 33.

[62] On the 'new governance' agenda see N Bernard in this collection; O de Schutter, N Lebessis and J Paterson (eds), *Governance in the European Union* (Luxembourg, OOPEC, 2001); and the special edition on 'new governance' edited by J Scott and D Trubeck (2002) 8 *European Law Journal* 1.

which has provided something of a test bed for approaches which are based on mechanisms other than substantive, rights-granting legislation. Examples include the application of the open method of co-ordination, and of course policy formulation and implementation by the social partners (at multiple levels).[63] In addition, the EU has also declared its commitment to the use of Corporate Social Responsibility as a policy technique—an approach that relies on companies themselves to undertake voluntarily to promote best practices in their relationships with their internal and external stakeholders.[64] Areas such as health and safety at work, work organisation, and change management (including dismissals for economic reasons) have all been targeted as key areas for the use of this approach, which is to be monitored through benchmarking and public reporting systems.[65] Whilst the EU institutions have been anxious to ensure that Corporate Social Responsibility is presented as a complement to, rather than a replacement for legislation,[66] it may well be that, should political agreement on legislation on working conditions legislation prove unattainable, Corporate Social Responsibility becomes an increasingly important, pragmatic solution to remedy what may otherwise appear a social deficit on the part of the EU.

Are we to be concerned by the emergence of such new approaches to governance? Arguably, such alternatives to traditional legislation may appear more responsive, dynamic, and possibly more legitimate. National and sub-national diversity may be better captured and accommodated. Social rights should still be seen as having a role to play in this new context, though the rights one would expect to see guaranteed are procedural rights to participation in the substantive standard setting process. In this regard, the contribution of EU law, including the Charter, is clearly deficient. Further, to the extent that increasingly, alternatives other than legislation granting substantive rights substantive rights may be employed, and increasing reliance is placed on private actors in formulating and implementing EU social policy, the extent to which the Charter rights may be regarded as a minimum safety net is seriously impeded in that it is addressed to the EU institutions and the Member States only when implementing EU law,[67] a formulation which arguably fails to capture the range of actors who should be held to respect its provisions.

---

[63] C Barnard, 'The Social Partners and the Governance Agenda' (2002) 8 *European Law Journal* 80.

[64] See J Hunt, 'The European Union: Promoting a Framework for Corporate Social Responsibility?' in F Macmillan (ed), *International Corporate Law: Vol 2* (Oxford, Hart Publishing, 2003, forthcoming). See also S Deakin and J Browne in this collection at pp 40–41.

[65] Commission Green Paper on Corporate Social Responsibility COM(2001) 366 final; *Corporate Social Responsibility: A Business Contribution to Sustainable Development*, COM (2002) 347 final; and Health and Safety Strategy, above n 54.

[66] Commission Green Paper and COM(2002) 347 *ibid*; Council Resolution OJ 2002 C 86/03. Though according to Commissioner Diamantopoulou 'globalisation and advances in communications technology are making it increasingly hard for legislators to address social problems with the necessary lightness of touch. I suspect that . . . corporate social responsibility . . . will come to be seen as the preferred solution'. Speech to the American Chamber of Commerce, Brussels, 30 October 2000, available at: <http://europa.eu.int/comm/dgs/employment_social/speeches/001030ad.pdf>.

[67] Art 51(1) EUCFR. For full analysis see the chapter by M Poiares Maduro in this collection.

RIGHTS TO FAIR AND JUST WORKING CONDITIONS BEFORE THE COURTS

Re-interpreting Legislative Commitments through the Prism of Fundamental Social Rights

Whether or not the Charter gives rise to further legislation in respect of working conditions, it certainly provides an opportunity for existing legislation in this field to be reassessed in the light of the fundamental social rights that are now expressed as underpinning them. The Charter presents fundamental social rights in the field of working conditions as broad statements of principle, rather than detailed legislative regulations. The Charter itself, for example, does not set any minimum—or maximum—requirements as to what is demanded in terms of measures which respect workers' 'health, safety and dignity', nor does it indicate what fair and just weekly working hours should be. Existing legislation can be seen as having a crucial role to play in filling in the detail, reflecting what is currently considered within European society as 'fair and just'. However, the Charter and the fundamental social rights discourse it stimulates, may bring into play a dynamic which ensures that its rights are not 'trapped' in existing legislative settlements. For example, whilst Member States may currently take advantage of the various opt outs and derogations contained in secondary legislation (such as the Working Time Directive) they may find that the developing discourse of fundamental social rights may feed into the normative frame within which the Courts operate, leading to a more extensive interpretation of existing measures, and a corresponding closing down of States' room for manoeuvre.

The applicants in *BECTU*,[68] a British trade union, were clearly hopeful that such a human rights-inspired re-reading of Community legislation would be undertaken by the Court, in the context of the challenge they had made to the conformity of national legislation with Community legislation on the organisation of working time. In accepting the union's challenge to the UK's legislation which required a 13-week qualification period to be worked with the same employer before the right to annual leave under Article 7(1) of the Directive could be exercised, Advocate General Tizzano read the relevant provisions in the light of the status of the right to annual leave as a fundamental social right. According to the Advocate General, 'the most reliable and definitive confirmation'[69] of this status came in the form of Article 31 EUCFR. Against this backdrop, the Advocate General reasoned that Article 7(1) of the Directive, which provides that Member States are to ensure entitlement to paid annual leave 'in accordance with the conditions for entitlement to, and granting of such leave laid down by national legislation and/or practice' did not allow the imposition

---

[68] Case C–173/99 *R v Secretary of Trade for Industry, ex parte BECTU* [2001] ECR I–4881.
[69] Opinion, para 28.

of qualifying periods which 'ultimately negate such a right entirely'.[70] Famously of course, the Advocate General also declared that

in proceedings concerned with the nature and scope of a fundamental right, the relevant statements of the Charter cannot be ignored; in particular we cannot ignore its clear purpose of serving, where its provisions allow, as a substantive point of reference for all those involved—Member States, institutions, natural and legal persons—in the Community context.[71]

The Court was somewhat more cautious in its approach, and whilst agreeing that the Directive does not allow legislative qualifications such as that imposed by the UK, it shied away from the language of fundamental rights, preferring instead to characterise the right to paid annual leave as 'a particularly important principle of Community social law', albeit one 'from which there can be no derogations'.[72] Significantly, in rejecting the UK Government's contention that the qualification period 'strikes a fair balance between the objective of the Directive . . . and the need to avoid imposing excessive constraints on small and medium-sized undertakings',[73] the Court reaffirmed the principle in the preamble of the Directive that 'the improvement of workers' safety, hygiene and health at work . . . should not be subordinated to purely economic considerations'.[74] However, no mention of the Charter is made in the Court's ruling, though reference is made to relevant provisions of the Community Social Charter,[75] which is cited in the Working Time Directive's preamble. Whilst cautious and pragmatic, *BECTU* may suggest that the Court is prepared to take social rights seriously, and extend their scope and coverage beyond the current requirements of international human rights instruments such as the RevESC.[76]

However, Advocate General Tizzano's bold, purposive approach to the impact of fundamental social rights in *BECTU* was less in evidence in his opinion in the *Bowden* case.[77] Denied annual paid leave by their employer, the applicants, office workers employed in the road transport sector, found that the national implementing legislation did not assist them as the road transport sector is one of the areas excluded from the protective scope of the legislation. This exclusion was explicitly permitted under Article 1(3) of the Working Time Directive.[78] The referring court was not, however, content with this literal

---

[70] Opinion, para 36.

[71] Opinion, para 28.

[72] Judgment, para 43.

[73] Judgment, para 57.

[74] Judgment, para 59.

[75] Judgment, para 39.

[76] In addition to the operation of the 80% rule in this area, the Committee has appeared to suggest that imposition of qualifying periods (of even up to one year) may be permissible. See European Social Charter, European Committee of Social Rights, Conclusions XIV–2 (1998), at p 702 (Sweden).

[77] Case C–133/00 *Bowden and others v Tuffnells Parcels Express Ltd* [2001] ECR I–7031.

[78] The exclusion of 'non-mobile' workers in the transport sector has now been removed by Dir 2000/34/EC, OJ 2000 L 180/22.

interpretation of the provisions, and sought the Court's approval to apply a 'just and purposive construction' of the Directive, seeking to give effect to the fundamental right of every worker to annual paid leave, and avoid the 'significantly destructive' effect of the exemption. The opportunity to extend judicially the scope of the Directive was rejected by both Advocate General Tizzano and the Court. Far from being 'universal and automatic', the right to paid annual leave was limited by a narrow reading of the scope of Community legislation.

As was suggested by Advocate General Tizzano in *Bowden*, challenges to the legality of the Directive itself may lie on the grounds that the EU institutions failed to respect the fundamental right of all workers to paid annual leave by excluding certain sectors from the protection of the Directive. The Advocate General was doubtful whether such a challenge would be successful in relation to the exclusions on the grounds that they

> might be accounted for by the difficulty of propounding clear criteria to distinguish between activities carried on within those sectors and the need not to delay the introduction of rules for that reason.

Nevertheless such justifications may be less convincing in relation to the individual opt out from the maximum working week,[79] at least in so far as a case may be made that the procedural safeguards contained in the Directive are inadequate to ensure that overall workers are entitled to reasonable limitations on their working hours. National implementation and enforcement of procedural safeguards may also be called into question on this basis.[80]

Immediately, the impact of the Charter rights would appear to be most apparent in relation to the working time related provisions in Article 31 EUCFR. As regards Article 30 EUCFR, it is well known that the UK was intent on incorporating the rider that rights to unfair dismissal would operate in accordance with Community and national law, as it believed that this would thereby insulate the one year qualification period for unfair dismissal claims from potential challenge.[81] However, the UK also believed that its 13-week qualification period for annual leave was justified under the terms of 7(1) of the Working Time Directive in *BECTU*, although the Court saw fit to subject the national 'conditions for entitlement to, and granting of such leave' to a reasonableness test in the light of the fundamental nature of the right to annual leave. Could not such a review also be possible in relation to the fundamental right to protection against unfair

---

[79] Art 18(1)(b)(i) of the Directive. The option of the opt-out (taken up only by the UK) is under review by the Commission and is due to be reported on in the latter part of 2003. Meanwhile, the Commission issued a formal letter to the UK in March 2002, outlining concerns it had with the UK's implementation of the Directive, including the absence of any requirement for employers to keep records of voluntary overtime worked by employees.

[80] The Commission letter has also highlighted concern over the fact that national law does not place employers under an obligation to ensure that workers take the breaks to which they are entitled.

[81] See further J Kenner in this collection at pp 18–19.

dismissal? Even assuming such an action could find its way before the Court,[82] the fact that the right appears less well established under international human rights law than those on working time may provide an escape route for the Court, as may reference to the RevESC's acceptance of 'reasonable' qualification periods for access to this right.

Despite its currently non-legally binding status, the Charter may at the very least provide the Court with the impetus towards a more extensive interpretation of current rights. The extent to which it may do so hinges critically of course on the opportunities it is presented with, and perhaps, on the signals it receives from other institutions. It is perhaps not insignificant that the Court's decisions in both *BECTU* and *Bowden* appear in line with the observations made by the Commission in those cases. It would not be the first time that the Court has appeared to use the Commission as a bellwether when faced with legally and politically controversial questions.[83]

Fundamental Economic Freedoms and Fundamental Social Rights

As Poiares Maduro reminds us, the constitutional balance between economic freedoms and social rights in the EU order has, to a very significant extent, been moulded by courts and litigants, with litigation having traditionally been dominated by those seeking to curtail social rights.[84] The Court has been faced many times with challenges to national measures concerning just working conditions on the grounds that they constitute a hindrance to the exercise of economic freedoms. National legislative and collectively bargained rules on pay,[85] annual leave entitlement,[86] and working hours[87] have all been subject to such challenges. Whilst Lenaerts and Foubert suggest that the Court has 'developed a coherent theory of social rights, which defines the limits of European economic integration much more than the EC legislation in force would suggest',[88] others

---

[82] One possible route before the Court could come from a reference from a national court faced with the question of whether the one-year qualifying period which applies before (certain) unfair dismissal actions can be brought gives full effect to the requirements set out in the Acquired Rights Directive (above n 39), according to which Member States are to ensure that all employees who consider themselves wronged by failure to comply with the Directive are able to pursue their claims by judicial process.

[83] J Hunt, 'The Court of Justice as a Policy Actor: The Case of the Acquired Rights Directive' (1998) 18 *Legal Studies* 336.

[84] M Poiares Maduro, 'Striking the Elusive Balance Between Economic Freedom and Social Rights in the EU' in P Alston (ed), *The EU and Human Rights* (Oxford, OUP, 1999)449–72.

[85] Eg Joined Cases 62/81 and 63/81 *Seco v EVI* [1982] ECR 223; Case C–165/98 *Mazzoleni v ISA* [2001] ECR I–2189.

[86] Joined Cases C–49,50,52–54,68–71/98, *Finalarte* [2001] ECR I–7831.

[87] Eg Case 155/80 *Oebel* [1981] ECR 1993; C–145/88 *Torfaen BC v B & Q Plc* [1989] ECR 3851; Joined Cases C–69 and 258/93 *Punto Casa and PPV* [1994] ECR I–2355.

[88] K Lenaerts and P Foubert, 'Social Rights in the Case Law of the European Court of Justice' (2001) 28 *Legal Issues of Economic Integration* 267 at 272.

are less satisfied with the balance that has been struck by the Court, or at least, with the opaque terms it has struck.[89]

Certainly, the Court has not extended the language of 'fundamental rights', which it has accorded to economic rights and freedoms, to the social provisions with which such rights may conflict. Nevertheless, the 'protection of workers' has been recognised as one of the overriding reasons relating to the public interest, which may pose a justifiable restriction on free movement,[90] and now, with rights to fair and just working conditions so publicly designated 'fundamental' rights, might it be the case that the Court will be inspired to reconsider the line it takes when economic and social rights collide, and offer further protection to working conditions? Would, for example, the existence of the Charter make any difference to the approach taken by the Court in cases such as *Finalarte*,[91] which concerned the lawfulness of German rules imposing requirements for service providers established outside Germany to pay into a holiday fund for their workers posted in Germany. The system had been described by the referring court as one which had been introduced explicitly to protect the German construction industry, by combating 'the allegedly unfair practice of European business engaged in low-pay competition'.[92] Characterised as such, the system would be contrary to EC law, in that a restriction on free movement was imposed for economic reasons.[93] Instead, however, the Court suggested that the system should be approached as one for the promotion of the protection of posted workers[94]—in essence, though not explicitly articulated as such, the promotion of workers' rights to fair and just working conditions.

This, though, is only the first stage in the Court's assessment of whether the social right should trump the economic freedom. In turn the Court directs the national court to examine whether the rules in the host state provide 'a genuine benefit on the workers concerned which significantly adds to their social protection'[95] as compared with protection in the home state. However, just when it appears that the Court is apparently opening a space for the highest levels of protection to be safeguarded (holiday entitlement above minimum levels in the Working Time Directive, with a higher daily allowance than under home state rules), the test of proportionality is introduced, requiring the national court to balance on the one hand the administrative and economic burdens that the rules impose on service providers and, on the other, the increased social protection they confer on workers compared with that guaranteed by the law of the service

---

[89] P Davies 'Market Integration and Social Policy in the Court of Justice' (1995) 24 *Industrial Law Journal* 49.

[90] See N Bernard in this collection at pp 249–52.

[91] Above n 86.

[92] *Ibid*, para 38.

[93] *Ibid*, para 39, citing Cases C–352/85 *Bond van Adverteerders* [1998] ECR 2085 and C–398/95 *SETTG* [1997] ECR I–3091.

[94] *Ibid*, para 41.

[95] *Ibid*, para 42.

providers' home state.[96] Ultimately, the Court avoids answering the question of which values and objectives—those of reducing the costs borne by economic actors, or increasing the social protection of workers—are to be prioritised in the Community legal order. Whilst the proclamation of the Charter, with its recognition of a set of social rights could be seen as providing space for a more robust protection and promotion of rights at work by the Court, now that both economic and social rights are regarded as 'fundamental', there is little to guide it in balancing these rights. Nonetheless the Charter does at least mark a further, and significant step onwards for the conceptualisation of the place of labour under the Treaty. From the starting point in the original Treaty of Rome, where labour, as one of the four factors of production, was very much perceived as a 'commodity', the Charter, with its human rights based focus to the rights of workers, brings home very clearly the message that labour is not a commodity.

CONCLUSIONS

Whilst not explicitly setting a legislative agenda, nor creating legally enforceable rights, the process of drafting and proclaiming the Charter may stimulate activity in both the legislative and judicial spheres in connection with working conditions and rights at work. However, in relation to action within both of these spheres, and given the traditional and generally accepted mandate of the EU, intervention designed to promote and protect the rights of workers is regarded as legitimate where it clearly contributes to attaining an economic goal of the EU. Without tying social rights to an economic rationale, support for the case for *EU* intervention remains weak. Any stronger role, independent of such rationales, is suggestive of the EU making a claim for itself as the primary source and guarantor of social rights and the social conscience for the countries of the EU. This is a role which the Member States, with varying degrees of commitment, have been prepared to afford the relatively toothless Council of Europe, and they are unlikely to be prepared for it to be reassigned to the EU.

However, with the rights now proclaimed, and with the (albeit as yet not legally enforceable) obligation on Member States to ensure that they are respected when implementing EU law, the Charter is arguably leading the EU in this direction. The Charter and the rights it contains may come to act as a bulwark against the possible rolling back of the levels of worker protection at national level as the Member States come under increasing pressure through their obligations in other policy spheres. The 'minimum standards' agreed upon in Community social legislation may come to impose a higher level of protection than initially assumed when interpreted in the light of their fundamental social right status, and perhaps, a higher level of protection than demanded by the ESC.

---

[96] *Ibid*, paras 49–50.

4

The Charter
and Collective Labour Law

BERNARD RYAN*

INTRODUCTION

O NCE THE COLOGNE European Council had decided that the catalogue of
fundamental rights of the EU should include social rights, it was probable
that there would be implications for collective labour law. Collective labour
rights have a central place in the Council of Europe Social Charter 1961 (ESC)
and the Community Charter of Fundamental Social Rights 1989 (Community
Social Charter)—the two instruments which the Cologne decision indicated as
the starting-point for the identification of social rights.[1] Collective labour rights
had also featured prominently in the *Comité des Sages* and Simitis Reports
which preceded the Cologne decision, and which had argued that the recognition of fundamental rights at the EU level should include social rights.[2] In the
event, three provisions of the Charter are directly relevant to collective labour
law: Article 12 EUCFR on the freedom of assembly and association, which
specifically refers to trade unions; Article 27 EUCFR on the right to information
and consultation in employment; and Article 28 EUCFR on the rights to collective bargaining and collective action.

This generous provision made for collective labour rights in the Charter is
quite ironic, given the historical weakness of collective labour law at the EU
level. Among the rights now recognised in Articles 12, 27 and 28 EUCFR, only
that to information and consultation has been the subject of meaningful
Community legislation. Worse, the power to legislate in two of the areas
covered by the Articles 12, 27 and 28 EUCFR—the right of association and
collective action—is excluded from the Community's social policy competence

---

* Lecturer in Law, University of Kent. I am grateful to Tonia Novitz, the editors and the par-
ticipants at the Nottingham workshop for their comments on earlier versions of the paper.
    [1] European Council decision on the drawing up of a Charter of Fundamental Rights of the
European Union, *Bulletin of the European Union* 6–1999, Presidency Conclusions, Annex 4.
    [2] The *Comité des Sages* report, *For a Europe of Civic and Social Rights* (European Commission,
Brussels, 1996), pp 47–51 and the Simitis Report, *Affirming Fundamental Rights in the European
Union: Time to Act* (Brussels, European Commission, 1999) p16, each proposed recognition of the
collective labour rights which eventually appeared in the Charter.

in Article 137 EC.[3] The failure to provide at the EU level for trade union association, collective bargaining and industrial action has long been a subject of criticism and of calls for reform by commentators on the field.[4]

Against that background, the question addressed here is whether the Charter will make a difference to the recognition given to collective labour rights in Community law. The analysis here starts with an examination of the text of Articles 12, 27 and 28 EUCFR and of the account of their origins contained in the *Explanations Relating to the Complete Text of the Charter* (the Explanatory Document).[5] It will be shown that, while Articles 12, 27 and 28 EUCFR recognise the most important collective labour rights, the drafters of the Charter were cautious in important respects, both in the content of these rights, and in the choice of international instruments cited in support of them. In the second part of the essay, a number of examples will then be given—drawn from the law of the single market and EU institutional law—of circumstances in which these provisions of the Charter may have effects upon EU law. The general conclusion is that, while it is plausible to anticipate that Articles 12, 27 and 28 of the Charter will have an impact upon EU law, this is largely because of the limited extent of the recognition it gives to collective labour rights.

COLLECTIVE LABOUR RIGHTS IN THE CHARTER

The collective labour rights set out in the Charter have their origins in previous instruments. The Explanatory Document makes clear that Articles 12, 27 and 28 EUCFR draw in particular upon the European Convention on Human Rights (ECHR), the ESC, together with the Revised European Social Charter 1996 (RevESC), and the Community Social Charter. The reliance upon those instruments is in line with the Treaties—Article 6(2) EU refers to the ECHR, while Article 136 EC refers to the ESC and to the Community Social Charter. The analysis here of Articles 12, 27 and 28 EUCFR considers in each case their origins, their relationship with the previous case law of the Community courts, and possible criticisms of the text of the Article in question.

---

[3] See Art 137(6) EC, which became Art 137(5) EC on the entry into force of the Treaty of Nice on 1 February 2003.

[4] For an early example, see A Jacobs, 'Towards Community Action on Strike Law?' (1978) 15 *Common Market Law Review* 133. More recent examples are *A Legal Framework for European Industrial Relations* (Brussels, European Trade Union Institute, 1999) and P Germanotta and T Novitz, 'Globalisation and the Right to Strike: The Case for European-Level Protection of Secondary Action' (2002) 18 *International Journal of Comparative Labour Law and Industrial Relations* 67.

[5] Luxembourg, European Communities, 2001. The Explanatory Document was prepared by the Praesidium of the Convention which drafted the Charter, but it is stated at p 3 that the explanations are not legally binding.

Article 12 EUCFR: Freedom of Assembly and Association

The first paragraph of Article 12 EUCFR states that

Everyone has the right to freedom of peaceful assembly and to freedom of association at all levels, in particular in political, trade union and civic matters, which implies the right of everyone to form and to join trade unions for the protection of his or her interests.

According to the Explanatory Document, Article 12(1) EUCFR 'corresponds to' Article 11 ECHR.[6] The main textual differences are that Article 11 ECHR does not provide that the right of association is recognised 'at all levels', does not make specific reference to political and civic association, and refers to trade unions in relation to the right of association, but not the right of assembly. Article 11 ECHR also permits rights of assembly and association to be limited in the case of members of the armed forces, the police and the civil service, even though no such limitation appears in Article 12 EUCFR. The Explanatory Document goes on to state that Article 12(1) EUCFR is 'based on' Article 11 of the Community Social Charter. This more cautious formulation perhaps reflects the differences between the two texts: the Community Social Charter extends the right of association to employers and to professional organisations and specifically protects the 'freedom to join or not to join' such associations 'without any personal or occupational damage being thereby suffered', but it does not expressly recognise a right of assembly.

Article 12 EUCFR is in line with the Community courts' previous case law on the freedom of association. In *Bosman* in 1995, the Court of Justice recognised, in the context of a sporting association, that the freedom of association set out in Article 11 ECHR is a fundamental principle which EU law respects.[7] That approach was followed in subsequent cases involving companies and a proposed political grouping in the European Parliament.[8] The implications of freedom of association for collective labour law were considered at length in the Opinion of Advocate General Jacobs in the *Albany* cases in 1999,[9] when he

---

[6] Explanatory Document, p 30.

[7] Case C–415/93 *URBFSA v Bosman* [1995] ECR I–4521 para 79, where the argument was unsuccessfully invoked to resist the application of Art 39 EC to sporting associations. The possibility that the principle of freedom of association might in certain circumstances protect the decisions of sporting associations was allowed by AG Alber in his Opinion in Case C–176/96 *Lehtonen v FRBSB* [2000] ECR I–2681 para 69, but that suggestion was not taken up by the Court.

[8] In Case C–235/92P *Montecatini v Commission* [1999] ECR I–4539, para 137, an attempt to use the principle to challenge the Commission's findings of a concerted practice was unsuccessful. So too was the attempt to use Art 11 ECHR in Cases T–222/99, T–327/99 and T–329/99, *Martinez and others v European Parliament* [2001] ECR II–0283 (Court of First Instance) para 231, to overturn an internal decision of the European Parliament not to permit the formation of a political grouping. That judgment is under appeal at the time of writing as Cases C–486/01P and C–488/01P.

[9] Case C–67/96 *Albany International* [1999] ECR I–5751, Joined Cases C–115/97, C–116/97 and C–117/97 *Brentjens* [1999] ECR I–6025, and Case C–219/97 *Drijvende Bokken* [1999] ECR I–6121. See also the contributions of J Kenner, S Deakin & J Browne and N Bernard in this collection at pp 12–13, 41–42 and 251–2.

sought to determine whether concepts of fundamental rights might protect trade unions and their action from the prohibition on anti-competitive agreements in Article 81 EC.[10] Citing *Bosman* in particular, he too concluded that the Community legal order recognised a fundamental right to freedom of association, as set out in Article 11 ECHR.[11]

Given the centrality of Article 11 ECHR to the Community courts and to Article 12 EUCFR, it is significant that it has to date had only mixed implications for trade unions. Article 11 ECHR has in particular been held to require respect for both the 'positive' right of individuals to choose to join a trade union and the 'negative' right to refuse to join, notwithstanding that the Convention's *travaux préparatoires* show that the latter was deliberately omitted from its text.[12] The effect of this recognition of a right of non-association has been to preclude the law's support for, or tolerance of, compulsory union membership, even though that was a traditional method of union recruitment and protection of collective bargaining in some EU Member States.[13] That negative consequence for trade unions has only partly been offset by their reliance upon the negative right of association in order to deny an individual's claim to join the union of their choice.[14] Nor is it affected by the limits to the right of non-association which emerged in subsequent case law—that it does not prohibit incentives for workers to join trade unions which fall short of compulsion,[15] or pressure on an employer to participate in a collective agreement.[16]

A similarly mixed pattern has been seen in the Article 11 ECHR case law on the treatment of trade unions. While the European Court of Human Rights has insisted that Article 11 ECHR upholds the 'freedom to protect the occupational interests of trade union members by trade union action,' it has nevertheless allowed states a choice as to the means by which trade unionism is supported.[17]

---

[10] See para 139 of AG Jacobs's opinion in *Albany International*.

[11] AG Jacobs also referred to the judgments in two staff cases—Case 175/73 *Union Syndicale, Massa and Kortner* [1974] ECR 917 and Cases 193/87 and 194/87 *Maurissen v Court of Auditors* [1990] ECR I–95—in support of the recognition of freedom of association as a fundamental principle in the context of labour relations. These cases were however concerned with the interpretation of the freedom of trade union activity recognised in Art 24a of the Community's Staff Regulations. While the judgment in *Massa and Kortner* referred (at para 14) to the 'general principles of labour law', neither there nor in other staff cases have the Community courts referred to Art 11 ECHR or to a general principle of freedom of association.

[12] See *Young, James and Webster v United Kingdom* Series A no 44 (1982) EHRR 38, and in particular para 51. The negative right of association has been applied in two non-trade union cases: *Sigurjonsson v Iceland* Series A no 264 (1993) 16 EHRR 422 and *Chassagnou v France* (2000) EHRR 615. The European Court of Human Rights has however reserved its position as to whether the 'negative right of association . . . is to be considered on an equal footing with the positive right': para 35 of the judgment in *Sigurjonsson*.

[13] See M Forde, 'The "Closed Shop" Case' (1982) 11 *Industrial Law Journal* 1 at 12–14.

[14] Decision of the European Commission of Human Rights in *Cheall v United Kingdom* (1985) 42 DR 178.

[15] *Sibson v United Kingdom* Series A no 258-A (1993) 17 EHRR 193.

[16] *Gustafsson v Sweden* (1996) 22 EHRR 409.

[17] Each of these propositions was first set out in *National Union of Belgian Police v Belgium* Series A no 9 (1979–80) 1 EHRR 578, para 39 (decided in 1975).

Claims by minority unions to be consulted with, or to participate in collective bargaining, have as a result been unsuccessful.[18] So too have been attempts to use Article 11 ECHR to challenge limits to the legal right to strike.[19] Indeed, the judgment in *Wilson* in July 2002 was the first occasion on which Article 11 ECHR was used by the European Court of Human Rights to find that a state had failed to guarantee trade union representation.[20] In that case, the possibility in British law for an employer to offer inducements to employees to accept the termination of collective bargaining was held to contravene Article 11 ECHR, since the employer could thereby 'effectively . . . undermine or frustrate a trade union's ability to strive for the protection of its members' interests.'[21] It remains to be seen whether the judgment in *Wilson* was simply a response to an extreme example of failure to support trade unionism, or instead reflects a greater willingness on the part of the European Court of Human Rights to use Article 11 ECHR to the advantage of trade unions.

These limits to the protection offered by Article 11 ECHR mean that it is all the more problematic that the Explanatory Document does not cite other international instruments in support of the freedom of association. In particular, there is no reference to ILO Convention 87 on the Freedom of Association and Protection of the Right to Organise[22] or to Article 5 ESC, even though these have been fully accepted by 15 and 13 Member States, respectively.[23] The omission of reference to these instruments separates the interpretation of freedom of assembly and association under the Charter from the elaboration of these principles by the supervisory bodies of the ILO and the ESC.[24] The ILO supervisory bodies in particular have given a different answer to two of the key questions addressed by the European Court of Human Rights: ILO Convention 87 does not require protection of the negative right of association, but does give extensive protection to

---

[18] See *National Union of Belgian Police v Belgium* and *Swedish Engine Drivers' Union v Sweden* Series A no 20 (1979–80) 1 EHRR 617 (decided in 1976), respectively.

[19] See the judgment in *Schmidt and Dahlstrom v Sweden* Series A no 21 (1979–80) 1 EHRR 632 (decided in 1976), the decision of inadmissibility in *National Association of Teachers in Further and Higher Education v United Kingdom* (1998) 93 DR 63, and the decision of inadmissibility in *UNISON v United Kingdom*, Application 53574/99 (10 January 2002).

[20] *Wilson and the National Union of Journalists and others*, Applications 30668/96, 30671/96 and 30678/96 (2 July 2002).

[21] *Ibid*, para 48.

[22] In fact, the Explanatory Document nowhere refers to ILO instruments, despite their potential relevance to social rights. Other non-European instruments are cited however: the Universal Declaration of Human Rights (Art 1), the Statute of the International Criminal Court (Art 3), the Geneva Convention on the Status of Refugees (Art 18) and the New York Convention on the Rights of the Child (Art 24).

[23] Greece has a general reservation in relation to Art 5 ESC, while Spain has a reservation to the extent that Art 5 ESC is inconsistent with provisions of its Constitution concerning the armed forces, public officials and essential services.

[24] On the interpretation of ILO Convention 87, see L Swepston, 'Human Rights Law and Freedom of Association: Development through ILO Supervision' (1998) 137 *International Labour Review* 169. For an account of the approach of the European Committee of Social Rights to Art 5 of the Social Charter, see NA Casey, *The Right to Organise and Bargain Collectively: Protection within the European Social Charter* (Strasbourg, Council of Europe, 1996) pp 11–45.

the right to strike.[25] A more specific example of the difference between the interpretation of Article 11 ECHR and that of the other instruments has concerned the ineligibility of certain non-EU citizens for election to Austrian works councils. Where the ILO and ESC supervisory bodies found a breach of the principle of freedom of association,[26] the European Court of Human Rights concluded in *Karakurt* that works councils were statutory bodies to which the guarantee of freedom of association in Article 11 ECHR did not apply.[27]

Article 27 EUCFR: The Right to Information and Consultation

Article 27 EUCFR states that:

> Workers or their representatives must, at the appropriate levels, be guaranteed information and consultation in good time in the cases and under the conditions provided for by Community law and national laws and practices.

As authority for Article 27 EUCFR, the Explanatory Document refers to Article 21 RevESC and to points 17 and 18 of the Community Social Charter. One respect in which Article 27 EUCFR goes further than earlier instruments is that only eight Member States had previously agreed to the principle in the context of the ESC.[28] Article 27 EUCFR also appears stronger than its predecessors in the language it uses to characterise the obligation upon participating states. Its statement that information and consultation 'must . . . be guaranteed' may be contrasted with the terminology of Article 21 RevESC—'the parties undertake to adopt or encourage measures enabling workers or their representatives' to be informed and consulted—and of point 17 of the Community Social Charter—'information, consultation and participation for workers must be developed along appropriate lines.'

The recognition given to a right to information and consultation in Article 27 EUCFR goes beyond previous case law of the Community courts, which does not appear to have addressed the possible existence of such a 'fundamental'

---

[25] See Swepston, *ibid* pp 183–84 and 186–90.

[26] The Austrian law has been found contrary to Art 5 of the Social Charter: see Recommendation RChS (99) 1 by the Council of Europe Committee of Ministers. The ILO Committee of Experts too has concluded that it is contrary to Art 3 of Convention 87, most recently in CEACR 72nd session (2001).

[27] The European Court of Human Rights' decision on admissibility was *Karakurt v Austria*, Application 32441/96 [2001] EHRR CD 273. Note that in two cases before the Court of Justice at the time of writing it is alleged that Austrian law on employee representation is contrary to the principle of equal treatment of workers on grounds of nationality: Case C–171/01 *Gemeinsam Zajedno* (OJ 2001 C 173/30) and Case C–465/01 *Commission v Austria* (OJ 2002 C 84/43).

[28] The right of information and consultation was first set out in Art 2 of the 1988 Additional Protocol to the ESC, which seven EU Member States had ratified by the end of 2000 (Denmark, Finland, Greece, Italy, Netherlands, Spain and Sweden). The right was then included as Art 26 RevESC in 1996. This had been ratified by four EU Member States by the end of 2000—two of whom (Italy and Sweden) had already ratified the 1988 Protocol, and two of whom (France and Ireland) had not. Ireland did not however agree to be bound by Art 26 RevESC.

right. An argument along these lines was advanced in a challenge to the Commission's approval of the Nestlé/Perrier merger in 1992 by a trade union and works councils representing Perrier workers. One of their claims was that 'By authorizing the notified concentration without safeguarding fundamental social rights such as the right to information and prior consultation in all cases where jobs are in jeopardy, the Commission infringed the fundamental social principles of Community law'.[29] The Court of First Instance (CFI) did not however rule on the existence of a fundamental right to information and consultation. Neither has the European Court of Justice (the Court) considered whether there might be a 'fundamental' right to information and consultation in the leading cases in which it has interpreted legislation on the subject.[30]

The text of Article 27 EUCFR is nevertheless open to criticism in a number of respects. One general weakness is that Article 27 EUCFR is silent as regards 'participation', even though that is also covered by points 17 and 18 of the Community Social Charter, as well as by the Simitis Report.[31] A second criticism concerns the bearers of the entitlement to information and consultation. Article 27 EUCFR guarantees workers *or* their representatives information and consultation, suggesting that these are alternatives. That approach is consistent with the RevESC, which has the same formulation, and with the Community Social Charter, which refers ambiguously to 'information, consultation and participation for workers'. It may be contrasted however with the title of Article 27 EUCFR, which refers to 'workers' right to information and consultation', and also with earlier drafts of the Article, which provided for information and consultation both of workers *and* their representatives.[32] Thirdly, Article 27 EUCFR requires information and consultation only 'in the cases and under the conditions provided for by Community law and national laws and practices'. This suggests that the content of Article 27 EUCFR depends *entirely* upon EU level and national action.[33] That approach is to be contrasted with the two earlier instruments, which while allowing national practice to limit entitlement to information and consultation,[34] attempted to give detail to the requirement

---

[29] When the trade union and works councils sought interim relief before the CFI, see Case T–96/92R *CCE de la Société Générale des Grandes Sources and others v Commission* [1992] ECR II–2579 para 14.

[30] See Case C–383/92, *Commission v United Kingdom* [1994] ECR I–2479 (Collective Redundancies Directive), the related Case C–382/92, *Commission v United Kingdom* [1994] ECR I–2435 (Transfer of Undertakings Directive) and Case C–62/99 *Bofrost* [2001] ECR I–2579 (European Works Council Directive, OJ 1994 L 254/64).

[31] See *Affirming Fundamental Rights* (above n 2) p 16.

[32] For this point, see B Bercusson, 'A European Agenda?' in K Ewing (ed) *Employment Rights at Work* (London, Institute of Employment Rights, 2001) 159–87 at 168. The formulation 'workers and their representatives' appears in CONVENT 18 (27 March 2000) and CONVENT 45 (28 July 2000), but had been changed to 'workers or their representatives' in CONVENT 47 (14 September 2000).

[33] See Bercusson, *ibid*, p 168.

[34] The RevESC also permits the right of information and consultation to be excluded in the case of undertakings employing less than a defined number of workers: see its Appendix, Arts 21 and 22, point 6.

of information and consultation. Article 21 RevESC provides for information 'regularly or at the appropriate time and in a comprehensible way about the economic and financial situation of the undertaking' and for consultation 'in good time on proposed decisions which could substantially affect the interests of workers, particularly on those decisions which could have an important impact on the employment situation in the undertaking.'[35] Similarly, point 18 of the Community Social Charter provides for information, consultation and participation 'particularly' in specified cases: when technological changes, or the restructuring of undertakings have employment implications, in the case of collective redundancies, and when 'transfrontier workers in particular are affected by employment policies pursued by the undertaking'.

Article 28 EUCFR: The Right of Collective Bargaining and Action

Article 28 EUCFR provides that:

> Workers and employers, or their respective organisations, have, in accordance with Community law and national laws, the right to negotiate and conclude collective agreements at the appropriate levels and, in cases of conflicts of interest, to take collective action to defend their interests, including strike action.

The account of Article 28 EUCFR given in the Explanatory Document is remarkable for its inexactitude.[36] The Explanatory Document firstly cites Article 6 ESC in support, even though six Member States have entered reservations with respect to it.[37] The Explanatory Document also states that Article 28 EUCFR is based on points 12 to 14 of the Community Social Charter. This is uncomplicated in the case of points 12 and 13 of the Community Social Charter, which set out rights to collective bargaining and collective action, respectively. Its point 14 is however a limiting clause, according to which Member States are left to determine the extent to which rights of association, collective bargaining and collective action apply to the armed forces, the police and the civil service. Just as with Article 11(2) ECHR, this is a limitation that does not appear on the face of the Charter. Finally, the Explanatory Document states that 'The right of collective action was recognised by the European Court of Human Rights as one

---

[35] In addition, Art 29 RevESC, to which the *Explanations* do not refer, provides for employers to inform and consult workers' representatives prior to collective redundancies.

[36] Explanatory Document, p 46.

[37] Greece has a general reservation in relation to Art 6 ESC, while Spain has a reservation to the extent that Art 6 ESC conflicts with provisions of its Constitution concerning the armed forces, public officials and essential services. Germany has a reservation in relation to the guarantees of collective bargaining in Art 6(2) ESC and collective action in Art 6(4) ESC in relation to pensionable civil servants, judges and soldiers. Austria and Luxembourg have general reservations in relation to Art 6(4) ESC, and it has been excluded by the Netherlands in relation to civil servants alone. In addition to these cases of states which have sought to limit rights of collective action, Portugal has a reservation to the effect that Art 6(4) ESC may not qualify the prohibition on lockouts contained in Art 57(3) of its Constitution.

of the elements of trade union rights laid down by Article 11 ECHR.' This is something of an exaggeration, however, since (as we have seen) the European Court of Human Rights merely takes the view that the right to strike is one possible method of enabling trade unions to protect the interests of their members.

In articulating fundamental rights to collective bargaining and collective action, Article 28 EUCFR nevertheless goes well beyond the rights which had previously been recognised in Community law. This can be seen in particular by a comparison of Article 28 EUCFR with the Opinion of Advocate General Jacobs in the *Albany* cases.[38] Basing himself upon Article 11 ECHR, his conclusion was that Community law protected 'the right to form and join trade unions' and 'the right to take collective action in order to protect occupational interests in so far as it is indispensable for the enjoyment of freedom of association.'[39] In other respects, however, his interpretation was that collective labour law fell outside the fundamental rights recognised by Community law. In particular, there was not 'sufficient convergence of national legal orders and international legal instruments on the recognition of a specific fundamental right to bargain collectively.'[40] In order to reach this restricted conclusion, Advocate General Jacobs specifically rejected the possibility of reliance upon Article 6 ESC:

> the mere fact that a right is included in the Charter does not mean that it is generally recognised as a fundamental right. The structure of the Charter is such that the rights set out represent policy goals rather than enforceable rights, and the states parties to it are required only to select which of the rights specified they undertake to protect.[41]

He also rejected the attempt to rely upon provisions of the Community Social Charter relating to trade unions and collective bargaining (points 11 and 12), principally because

> the Charter has very limited legal effects. It is not a legal act of the Community but a solemn political declaration adopted by Heads of State or Government of 11 of the then 12 Member States, and it has not been published in the Official Journal.[42]

Yet Article 6 ESC and point 12 of the Community Social Charter are precisely the provisions which the Explanatory Document now indicates as the basis for the right to collective bargaining.

Here too, some criticism of the text of the Charter may be made. There is firstly a lack of detail as to the implications of the rights recognised by the

---

[38] See n 9 above. The discussion of fundamental rights is at paras 132–63 of the joined opinion in the cases, reported at [1999] ECR I–5751.

[39] *Ibid* paras 158 and 159.

[40] *Ibid* para 160.

[41] *Ibid* para 146.

[42] *Ibid* para 137. It should be observed however that with the coming into force of the Treaty on European Union in 1993, the Community Social Charter had been formally recognised by all the Member States other than the United Kingdom in the Preamble to the annexed Agreement on Social Policy.

Charter. While the language of Article 28 EUCFR is borrowed from the Community Social Charter, the latter also specifies that

> in order to facilitate the settlement of industrial disputes the establishment and utilisation at the appropriate levels of conciliation, mediation and arbitration procedures shall be encouraged.

A similar provision is contained in Article 6 ESC, which moreover obliges contracting parties to promote 'joint consultation' and (crucially) 'machinery for voluntary negotiations . . . with a view to the regulation of terms and conditions of employment by means of collective agreements.' The consequence of the brevity of Article 28 EUCFR is that it is not certain that these various implications follow from it. A second weakness, parallel to that in Article 27 EUCFR, concerns the bearers of the rights of collective bargaining and action. Bercusson has highlighted the fact that Article 28 EUCFR states that 'workers and employers, or their respective organisations' have these rights. This may make sense in the case of collective bargaining, but has the negative implication that the right of *workers* to engage in collective action is not specifically affirmed. It is to be contrasted with Article 6 ESC, which refers to the rights of employers and workers, without reference to their organisations. That approach was also the one adopted earlier in the drafting of the Charter.[43]

Finally, it is significant that here—as in relation to Article 12 EUCFR—the Explanatory Document fails to refer to ILO instruments in the field. The right to collective bargaining is protected by ILO Convention 98 on the Right to Organise and Collective Bargaining while the right to strike has been found to be covered by ILO Convention 87. Each of these Conventions has been ratified by all Member States, and the absence of any reference to them divorces the Charter from the extensive interpretation of the rights of collective bargaining and action by ILO supervisory bodies.[44] The wariness of the Charter's drafters in relation to the ILO may reflect its supervisory bodies' willingness to uphold the rights of trade unions and the autonomy of industrial relations. The ILO bodies answer to the question of the bearers of the right to take collective action offers an example: unlike the European instruments referred to, under ILO Convention 87 it is established that 'the right to strike is a fundamental right of workers and their representatives.'[45]

---

[43] For these points, see Bercusson above n 32 at 170. In particular, CONVENT 45 (28 July 2000) referred to rights of collective bargaining and action of 'employers and workers' alone. That had changed in CONVENT 47 (14 September 2000) with the addition of 'or their respective organisations'.

[44] See B Gernigon, A Odero and H Guido, 'ILO Principles Concerning Collective Bargaining' (2000) 139 *International Labour Review* 33, and B Gernigon, A Odero and H Guido, 'ILO Principles Concerning the Right to Strike' (1998) 137 *International Labour Review* 441, respectively.

[45] Gernigon, Odero and Guido, 1998, *ibid* at 442.

THE INFLUENCE OF THE CHARTER

Articles 12, 27 and 28 EUCFR can therefore be characterised as generous by comparison with the previous jurisprudence of the Community courts, but imperfect by comparison with alternatives. The starting-point for analysis of the possible influence of these Articles upon EU law is Article 51(1) EUCFR, according to which the Charter is 'addressed to the institutions and bodies of the Union'. Article 51(1) EUCFR has encouraged speculation that the Charter would be treated by the Community courts as an authoritative statement of the fundamental rights which are recognised in the Community legal order.[46] Those suggestions have been borne out by a number of decisions of the CFI which have referred to the right to good administration in Article 41 EUCFR and the right to an effective legal remedy in its Article 47.[47] The Court has, however, refused to follow the CFI's lead—most notably in *UPA v Council*, where it made no reference to Article 47 when reiterating its established approach to the standing of individuals under Article 230(4) EC.[48]

If the Charter is taken as an authoritative guide to the fundamental rights recognised in the EU legal order, then its most immediate effect in the context of EU labour law is likely to be in the interpretation of labour legislation. This possibility has already been seen in *BECTU*, which concerned the Working Time Directive.[49] In that case, Advocate-General Tizzano relied upon Article 31 EUCFR, among other sources, to conclude that Community law recognised a fundamental right to paid annual leave.[50] It is true that the Court of Justice in *BECTU* did not follow the Advocate General's line of argument, and neither referred to the Charter nor found a 'fundamental social right' to annual leave. The Court preferred instead the more cautious formulation that the 'entitlement to paid annual leave' was 'a particularly important principle of Community social law.' What is significant however is that, because the Community Social Charter had been referred to in the preamble of the Directive, the court felt free to rely upon the provision for annual leave in point 8 of the Community Social

---

[46] For example, K Lenearts and E de Smijter, 'A "Bill of Rights" for the European Union' (2001) 273 *Common Market Law Review* 273 at 298–9. For discussion in this volume, see especially M Poiares Maduro and M Bell.

[47] Case T–54/99 *max.mobil v Commission*, [2002] II–ECR 313, paras 48 and 57 (Arts 41 and 47 EUCFR), Case T–198/01R *Technische Glaswerke*, order of 4 April 2002, para 85 (Art 41 EUCFR), Case T–177/01 *Jégo-Quéré et Cie v Commission*, [2002] ECR II–2365, para 47 (Art 47 EUCFR) and Case T–211/02 *Tideland Signal v Commission*, CFI judgment of 27 September 2002, para 37 (Art 41 EUCFR).

[48] Case C–50/00 [2002] ECR I–6677.

[49] Case C–173/99 *R v Secretary of State for Trade and Industry, ex parte BECTU* [2001] ECR I–4881. For the Directive see OJ 1993 L 307/18. For further discussion see J Kenner and J Hunt in this collection at pp 22 and 60–63.

[50] Paras 26–28 of the Opinion. See too the characterisation of the right to annual leave as a 'fundamental social right' by AG Tizzano in Case C–133/00 *Bowden v Tufnells Parcels Express Ltd* [2001] ECR I–7031, para 27.

Charter in support of its conclusion.[51] *BECTU* suggests that the Charter's provisions in the field of labour law may well encourage the Community courts to recognise fundamental social rights, even if the language used, and the instruments referred to, may vary.[52]

For the time being, the limits to EU action in the field of collective labour law mean that the possibility of fundamental rights being used in the interpretation of legislation refers only to the right to information and consultation in Article 27 EUCFR. In that context, it may be significant that, of the six distinct directives concerning information and consultation, four make reference to point 17 of the Community Social Charter in their preambles. These are the directives providing for consultation prior to collective redundancies,[53] on information and consultation prior to transfers of undertakings,[54] on the establishment of a European Works Council or information and consultation procedures in EU multinationals,[55] and on a general framework for information and consultation of employees.[56] It is conceivable that, in the interpretation of these Directives, Article 27 EUCFR will either be invoked outright or will have the effect of inducing the Community courts to rely upon point 17 of the Community Social Charter. A similar conclusion is possible in the case of Directive 89/391/EEC, which provides among other things for the information, consultation and participation of workers in relation to workplace health and safety,[57] as it was adopted prior to the Community Social Charter and so might be thought to give recognition to a right of information and consultation *avant la lettre*. The more difficult case is the 2001 Directive on the involvement of employees in the European Company.[58] This, though plainly within the field, refers to neither the Community Charter nor the Charter, and the case for relying upon a presumed right to information and consultation in its interpretation is correspondingly weaker.

A number of examples are now offered of circumstances in which Articles 12, 27 and 28 EUCFR may also come to influence the interpretation of provisions of the EC Treaty. Two of the issues examined draw on recent cases in which collective action and the legal requirements relating to the single market have been in conflict—the duty on Member States to uphold the free movement of economic factors, and the application of competition law to collective bargaining. A consideration of two further examples then suggests that Articles 12, 27 and

---

[51] Judgment in *BECTU*, paras 39 and 43.

[52] But see the discussion of *Bowden* by J Kenner and J Hunt at pp 22–23 and 61–63.

[53] Dir 98/59/EC on collective redundancies, OJ 1998 L 225/16, sixth recital and Art 2.

[54] Dir 2001/23/EC on transfers of undertakings, OJ 2001 L 82/16, fifth recital and Art 7.

[55] Dir 94/45/EC on the establishment of a European works council, OJ 1994 L 254/ 64, fourth recital.

[56] Dir 2002/14/EC establishing a general framework for informing and consulting employees, OJ 2002 L80/ 29, second recital.

[57] Arts 10 and 11 of Dir 89/391/EEC on the safety and health of workers at work, OJ 1989 L 183/1.

[58] Dir 2001/86/EC supplementing the statute of a European company with regard to the involvement of employees, OJ 2001 L 294/22.

28 EUCFR might also have a role in remedying deficiencies in the EU institutional framework: the limited competence of the Community in relation to collective labour law and the doubts over the conversion of framework agreements into Community legislation.

Ensuring Free Movement

One possible role for the collective labour rights recognised in the Charter is in limiting the obligations upon Member States to prevent private action which disrupts the single market.[59] The starting-point here is the judgment in *Commission v France* in 1997, in which the Court stated for the first time that Member States were under a duty,

> not merely themselves to abstain from adopting measures or engaging in conduct liable to constitute an obstacle to trade but also . . . to take all necessary and appropriate measures to ensure that that fundamental freedom is respected in their territory.

In that case, the French authorities were found to have failed over a long period to take adequate steps to prevent damage to and threats against agricultural imports from other Member States. As a result, France was found to have breached the prohibition in Article 28 EC on quantitative restrictions on imports and measures equivalent to them, read in conjunction with the duty of co-operation in Article 10 EC.[60]

There is no doubt that the principle set out in *Commission v France* is of potential application to industrial action—certainly in the transport sector and in ports, but also in other industries.[61] There is however a great deal of uncertainty as to the scope of the duty to ensure free movement. It presumably applies where private action impedes either the import or the export of goods, and there seems little reason why it should not extend to private action which frustrates the movement of economic factors other than goods—particularly, workers and services. What remains unclear is *which* private action gives rise to the duty to intervene.[62] In *Commission v France* the private conduct in question was criminal in nature, involved a physical threat to imports and was prolonged in duration. But what of breaches of contract, torts and indeed lawful action? What of behaviour which frustrates movement without physically threatening or impeding it? And, how long must the behaviour last, or be expected to last, before the duty to intervene arises? All of these questions are directly relevant in the case of industrial action: even if it tends to frustrate the single market, it may not

---

[59] See also N Bernard in this collection.

[60] Case C–265/95 *Commission v France* [1997] ECR I–6959, para 32.

[61] See generally G Orlandini, 'The Free Movement of Goods as a Possible 'Community' Limitation on Industrial Conflict' (2000) 6 *European Law Journal* 341.

[62] For a discussion, see K Muylle, 'Angry Farmers and Passive Policemen: Private Conduct and the Free Movement of Goods' (1998) 23 *European Law Review* 467 at 471.

involve unlawful conduct, may involve no physical obstruction to the movement of economic factors, and may be relatively short in duration.[63]

The potential conflict between a Member State's duty to ensure free movement and the right to take industrial action has already been reflected in EU law. In the wake of the judgment in *Commission v France*, Council Regulation 2679/98/EC introduced an intervention mechanism under which the Commission can require a Member State to secure the free movement of goods within five days.[64] After criticism that the proposed new mechanism would lead to intervention in labour disputes, Article 2 of the Regulation states that

> This Regulation may not be interpreted as affecting in any way the exercise of fundamental rights as recognised in Member States, including the right or freedom to strike. These rights may include the right or freedom to take other actions covered by the specific industrial relations systems in Member States.[65]

In so far as it relates to industrial action, Article 2 of the Regulation is scarcely a model of clarity. The main problem is with the statement in its first sentence that the protection of the right to strike is based upon 'fundamental rights as recognised in Member States'. It is unclear whether this phrase refers to the fundamental rights recognised in the Member State in question, or if instead there is a common standard based on the recognition given to the right to strike in Member States as a whole. The protection given by the second sentence of Article 2 of the Regulation to other forms of industrial action permitted in particular Member States does perhaps suggest that the latter interpretation is the correct one. Otherwise, it would have been possible to have a single sentence protecting 'fundamental rights as recognised in Member States, including the right or freedom *to take industrial action*'. But if the latter interpretation *is* correct, the consequence is that unlawful strike action in some states is protected from the intervention mechanism of Regulation 1679/98, while lawful action in others is not.

The uncertainty concerning both the scope of the *Commission v France* principle and the exception to Regulation 2679/98/EC suggest a potential role for Article 28 EUCFR—together perhaps with the guarantees of freedom of expres-

---

[63] Some of these questions are likely to be answered in Case C–112/00 *Schmidberger*, which concerns the permission given by the Austrian authorities to an environmental demonstration which obstructed traffic in the Brenner pass for a 28 hour period. In his Opinion of 11 July 2002, AG Jacobs concluded that even a short obstruction by private parties could give rise to a breach of a Member State's duty to ensure the free movement of goods. He went on to find that the permission given in this case was justified: the demonstration involved the exercise of fundamental freedoms which were recognised in national law and were acceptable to EC law, and it did not have disproportionate effects upon the free movement of goods.

[64] OJ 1998 L 337/8. A provision for recourse to the Court where a Member State fails to comply had been included in the Commission's original proposal (see Art 4(1) of the proposal at OJ 1998 C 10/14), but was removed from the text by the Council of Ministers.

[65] Art 2 was inserted by the Council of Ministers when it amended the proposal in June 1998. For a summary of the legislative history, see the Report of the European Parliament's Committee on Economic and Monetary Affairs and Industrial Policy, 28 October 1998 (A4–0385/98).

sion and freedom of assembly in Articles 11 and 12 EUCFR.[66] Article 28 EUCFR gives recognition to lawful industrial action arising out of a conflict of interest between workers and employers. It might therefore be invoked to argue that *lawful* industrial action cannot give rise to a Member State duty to uphold the free movement of economic factors or to a Commission power under Regulation 2679/98/EC to instruct it so to do. At the same time, however, the text of Article 28 EUCFR leaves little scope to protect *unlawful* action in the context of an industrial dispute against the duty to intervene or the application of Regulation 2679/98/EC. The requirement of a conflict of interest might also pose problems to the application of Article 28 EUCFR in the case of secondary action or industrial action of a political nature.

Competition Law

A second point of tension between the law of the single market and collective labour law in recent years has concerned the application of Community competition law to collective agreements.[67] In the *Albany*[68] cases, a number of employers had objected to their compulsory affiliation to sectoral pension funds, which had come about by a ministerial order after a joint request from employers and trade unions in the sectors in question. One of the main arguments against compulsory affiliation was that the ministerial order amounted to state support for an anti-competitive agreement, contrary to the combination of Articles 10 and 81 EC. The Court sided with the pensions funds, and in so doing created an immunity for collective agreements from Article 81 EC. Its starting point was that the EC Treaty provided in various places for a social policy to improve living standards and recognised the legitimacy of social dialogue and of agreements between employers and unions. In its view, it was

> beyond question that certain restrictions of competition are inherent in collective agreements between organisations representing employers and workers. However, the social policy objectives pursued by such agreements would be seriously undermined if management and labour were subject to Article [81(1)] of the Treaty when seeking jointly to adopt measures to improve conditions of work and employment.

It followed that 'agreements concluded in the context of collective negotiations between management and labour in pursuit of such objectives must, by virtue of their nature and purpose, be regarded as falling outside the scope of Article [81(1)] of the Treaty.'[69]

---

[66] Arts 11 and 12 EUCFR were referred to in the context of an environmental demonstration by AG Jacobs in his Opinion in *Schmidberger*, n 63 above, para 101.

[67] See N Bernard in this collection at pp 249–52.

[68] See n 9 above.

[69] See paras 59 and 60 of the judgment in *Albany*, paras 56 and 57 of the judgment in *Brentjens*, and paras 46 and 47 of the judgment in *Drijvende Bokken*. The Court's conclusion was broadly consistent both with AG Jacobs's Opinion in the *Albany* cases and with the earlier observation of

We have already seen that in the *Albany* cases Advocate General Jacobs considered, but rejected, the possibility that there was a fundamental right to collective bargaining recognised in Community law. The Court for its part remained silent on this point. It is therefore worth considering the potential impact of the recognition of a right to collective bargaining in Article 28 EUCFR upon the issue in those cases.

One possibility is that Article 28 EUCFR will provide a sounder basis for the exception for collective agreements than the arguments given by the Court in its *Albany* judgments.[70] The court referred in particular to the Treaty provisions requiring the Commission to promote social dialogue between management and labour (now Article 138 EC) and permitting agreements between them (now Article 139 EC). The difficulty with that argument however was that these provisions contemplated such dialogue and agreement at the EU level alone. The court also relied upon the statement in the old Article 118 EC that 'the Commission shall have the task of promoting close co-operation between Member States in the social field', including in relation to 'freedom of association and collective bargaining'. But that statement, although giving recognition to collective bargaining at the national level, did not survive the reorganisation of the social policy provisions in the EC Treaty by the Treaty of Amsterdam. One clear benefit of Article 28 EUCFR is to provide a more convincing explanation for the special treatment of national level collective bargaining within Community competition law.

Secondly, Article 28 EUCFR might influence the Community courts' appreciation of the legitimate *content* of collective agreements for the purposes of the *Albany* immunity. As described there, only collective agreements whose purpose concerned social policy objectives could benefit from the immunity.[71] The 'purpose' test was satisfied in those cases because the agreements related to the provision of pensions to workers, and thereby 'contribute[d] directly to improving one of their working conditions, namely their remuneration.'[72] Similarly, in *Van der Woude*, the Court held that a collective agreement providing for employee health insurance benefited from the immunity, as it helped improve working conditions by ensuring that employees could meet medical

AG Lenz in *Bosman* (above, n 7), that 'in order to guarantee the collective bargaining autonomy of employers and trade unions, it may be necessary to exclude collective agreements from competition law where that is necessary for that purpose' (para 274). *Bosman* did not however concern a collective agreement, and the Court anyway decided the case without considering Art 81 EC.

[70] See paras 54–58 of the judgment in *Albany*, paras 51–55 of that in *Brentjens* and paras 41–45 of that in *Drijvende Bokken*. For detailed criticism of this part of the *Albany* judgments, see S Vousden, 'Albany, Market Law and Social Exclusion' (2000) 29 *Industrial Law Journal* 181 at 186.

[71] The immunity also applies only to arrangements whose 'nature' is that of a collective agreement, but the recognition given to collective bargaining in Article 28 EUCFR does not seem to affect this requirement. For an example of where the *Albany* immunity did not arise because an agreement did not result from collective bargaining, see Cases C–180/98 to C–184/98 *Pavlov and others* [2000] ECR I–6451.

[72] Para 63 of the judgment in *Albany*, para 60 of that in *Brentjens* and para 50 of that in *Drijvende Bokken*.

expenses, and by reducing the costs of insurance.[73] Collective agreements which are not concerned with 'social policy' or employment conditions presumably therefore fall outside of the immunity. Examples might include agreements which affect third parties—such as where employers agree not to hire non-union or unqualified labour, or not to deal with non-union or under-cutting firms.[74] There might also be difficulties with collective agreements which attempt to further public policy—for example in relation to parenting, vocational training or employment creation.[75] There is also the possibility suggested by Advocate General Fennelly in *Van der Woude*, that a principle of necessity might limit the agreements which fall within the *Albany* immunity. As he put it:

> as an exception to the general field of application of Article [81] of the EC Treaty, the scope of the Albany exception must be narrowly construed. Those allegedly harmed by such anti-competitive restrictions . . . may always challenge them on the basis that the agreement does not pursue a genuine social objective because the restrictions from it, or from its application, go beyond what is required by the pursuit of its objective.[76]

It is possible that Article 28 EUCFR might persuade the Community courts to resist attempts on these—or other—grounds to limits the range of collective agreements, which can benefit from the *Albany* immunity.

A final possibility is that the Charter might influence the interpretation of the term 'undertaking' for competition law purposes. The *Albany* judgments did not indicate which 'undertakings' were thought to be potentially in breach of the prohibition in Article 81(1) EC on anti-competitive agreements. This question was less problematic in those cases, as they concerned multi-employer agreements, which arguably involved an agreement between the employer undertakings.[77] The question that remains is whether a trade union might be classed as an 'undertaking' for the purposes of competition law. If it were, single-employer agreements and inter-union agreements would be within the scope of Article 81 EC, and indeed trade unions would be open to allegations of abuse of a dominant position under Article 82 EC. Even before the Charter, Advocate General Jacobs may well have been correct to conclude in the *Albany* cases that trade unions were not undertakings where they acted as representatives of

---

[73] Case C–222/98 *Van der Woude* [2000] ECR I–7111, para 25.

[74] In *Albany*, AG Jacobs proposed that a collective agreement should be immune from Art 81 EC only where it 'deal[t] with core subjects of collective bargaining such as wages and working conditions and . . . [did] not directly affect third parties or markets'. He went on to suggest that 'relations between employers and third parties, such as clients, suppliers, competing employers, or consumers' were examples of third party effects which would preclude the immunity (para 193 of the Opinion). While this 'third party' test was not adopted by the Court of Justice, its approach in *Albany* is not inconsistent with it.

[75] See Vousden, pp 189–90.

[76] Para 32 of the Opinion.

[77] For a discussion of this point with reference to those judgments, see S Evju, 'Collective Agreements and Competition Law. The *Albany* puzzle and *Van der Woude*' (2001) 17 *International Journal of Comparative Labour Law and Industrial Relations* 165 at 174–76.

employees.[78] Nevertheless, the recognition given to trade unions in Article 12 EUCFR and that given to collective bargaining in Article 28 EUCFR suggest that trade unions are a special kind of organisation which should not be covered by competition law at all, or at least not where they act in a representative capacity. The multi-employer case would then be the only circumstance in which the *Albany* immunity was necessary.

Competence

The potential for the recognition of collective labour rights by the Charter to influence EU law extends beyond the law of the single market to institutional law. A particularly important question is whether Articles 12, 27 and 28 EUCFR might affect the competence of the EU institutions in relation to collective labour law. The possibility for that to occur might be precluded by Article 51(2) EUCFR, which states that 'The Charter does not establish any new power or task for the Community of the Union, or modify powers and tasks as defined by the Treaties.' Article 51(2) EUCFR plainly excludes the use of the Charter either as a source of EU or Community competence in its own right or as a basis for the modification of the competences set out in the Treaties.[79] It is arguable nevertheless that the Charter could be invoked in the interpretation of existing competences, as that would not involve 'modification' in the sense of Article 51(2) EUCFR. On that basis, the discussion here attempts to identify areas of uncertainty in relation to the extent of Community competence in relation to collective labour law, where the Charter's recognition of collective labour rights may have a role to play.[80]

The root of the difficulties in relation to Community competence over collective labour law is that the principal internal legislative power applicable to social policy, Article 137 EC, contains within it the limiting paragraph 5 (formerly paragraph 6), according to which 'The provisions of this Article shall not apply to . . . the rights of association, the right to strike or the right to impose lock-out.' Article 137(5) EC prevents the Community's social policy power from being used to lay down minimum standards for national labour laws on rights of association and strike action in order to preclude strategies of 'competitive deregulation' by Member States. It also precludes legislation under Article 137 EC on the formation of transnational trade unions and on transnational indus-

---

[78] Paras 218–27 and 237–44 of the Opinion. The point was not addressed by the Court of Justice in its *Albany* judgments.

[79] See further, the contribution of M Poiares Maduro in this collection.

[80] The general possibility that the Charter may affect the interpretation of competences has also been identified in G de Búrca, 'Human Rights: The Charter and Beyond' *Jean Monnet Working Papers* 10/01 (2001), with the tension between the right to take collective action in Article 28 EUCFR and Article 137(5) EC offered as an example.

trial action, even though the Community is self-evidently the appropriate level for legislation of that kind.[81]

In relation to the Community's internal competence over collective labour law, the key question is whether the reference in Article 137(5) EC to 'this Article' means that other Treaty provisions can instead be used to legislate on the right of association and the right to strike. The main possible alternatives are the power to adopt harmonising directives in Article 94 EC and the residual power in Article 308 EC. In the wake of the *Tobacco Advertising* judgment in 2000, there are however two obstacles to reliance upon these Articles. Firstly, that judgment suggests that Article 94 EC can only be used to adopt legislation which 'actually contributes' to the elimination either of obstacles to cross-border trade or of an 'appreciable' distortion of competition.[82] Legislation on the freedom of association and right to strike, whether at the national or the transnational level, seems unlikely to meet this test. It would be unconcerned with the facilitation of cross-border trade, and any distortion of competition due to differences in the law on these subjects in the Member States might be thought too 'remote and indirect' to give rise to competence under Article 94 EC.[83] Secondly, the *Tobacco Advertising* judgment stated in relation to the EC Treaty provisions on public health that 'other articles of the Treaty may not . . . be used as a legal basis in order to circumvent the express exclusion of harmonisation laid down in Article [152(4)].'[84] The implication is that Article 94 EC and Article 308 EC cannot be used in order to circumvent a limitation on a more specific power elsewhere in the Treaty.

There is therefore a good deal of uncertainty as to whether the limits in Article 137(5) EC can be avoided by recourse to Articles 94 or 308 EC. Might the recognition of the right to form trade unions in Article 12 EUCFR and of the right to take collective action in Article 28 EUCFR make a difference to the answer? The argument for this proposition is that, since the Charter recognises these rights as fundamental, a way should if possible be found to ensure that there is competence to enact legislation on them. If so, then there would be room to argue either for a more benign reading of Article 94 EC than is implied by

---

[81] Greater detail on the case for (internal) EU action in relation to rights of association and industrial action is in B Ryan, 'Pay, Trade Union Rights and European Community Law' (1997) 13 *International Journal of Comparative Labour Law and Industrial Relations* 305 at 317–24.

[82] Case C–376/98 *Germany v Parliament and Council* [2000] ECR I–8419, especially paras 84, 94 and 106–8. The judgment there was concerned with the scope of what is now Art 95 EC, which is inapplicable to labour law. It seems reasonable however to assume that the analysis of the power to legislate to further the 'internal market' is also applicable to the Art 94 power to further the 'common market'. For a discussion of this point, see the note on *Tobacco Advertising* by J Usher, (2001) 38 *Common Market Law Review* 1519, pp 1528–30. An alternative view, according to which the 'common market' is a broader concept, is also possible: see J Kenner, *EU Employment Law: From Rome to Amsterdam and Beyond* (Oxford, Hart, 2003) p 84.

[83] For this terminology, see *Germany v Parliament and Council*, para 109.

[84] *Germany v Parliament and Council*, para 79. In this, the Court of Justice echoed its earlier statement in Opinion 2/94 that Article 308 EC 'cannot serve as a basis for widening the scope of Community powers beyond the general framework created by the provisions of the Treaty as a whole': *Opinion 2/94* (Accession to the ECHR) [1996] ECR I–1763 para 30.

Tobacco Advertising or—perhaps more plausibly—for the inapplicability in this context of the principle that Articles 94 and 308 EC cannot be used to overcome the limits to more specific Community competences.

A second area of uncertainty in relation to competence over collective labour law concerns international action.[85] The extent of the Community's external competence over collective labour law has acquired greater significance in recent years as a result of the renewed debate over international labour standards since the agreement to establish the World Trade Organisation (WTO) in 1994[86] and the inclusion of 'freedom of association and the effective recognition of the right to collective bargaining' among the core labour standards identified by the ILO in 1998.[87] Three areas of possible international action by the EU can be identified, in each of which the potential contribution of Articles 12 and 28 EUCFR may again be assessed.

International agreements on development co-operation are a first area of action. EU policy is to include a requirement of respect for core labour standards—including those concerning collective labour rights—within development co-operation agreements.[88] These agreements are based upon the express power in Article 177 EC, paragraph 2 of which states that EU development co-operation 'shall contribute to the general objective of . . . respecting human rights and fundamental freedoms.' Articles 12 and 28 EUCFR have an obvious role here. The recognition given to rights of association and collective bargaining by the Charter might be thought to overcome any doubt as to whether respect for those rights falls within the notion of 'human rights and fundamental freedoms' in Article 177(2) EC.

EU participation in the (so far, hypothetical) enforcement of core labour standards within the WTO legal framework is a second possibility to consider.[89] For that to occur, it would be necessary to rely upon the express power in Article 133 EC to enter international agreements in pursuance of a common commercial policy. The case law to date is helpful, as it shows that Article 133 EC agreements can have subsidiary elements, including respect for certain labour conditions,[90] provided that the agreement in question is 'principally'

---

[85] I am indebted to Tonia Novitz for her guidance on this general question. Her assessment can be found in ' "A Human Face" for the Union or More Cosmetic Surgery? EU Competence in Global Social Governance and Promotion of Core Labour Standards' (2002) 9 *Maastricht Journal of European and Comparative Law* 231.

[86] See C McCrudden and A Davies 'A Perspective on Trade and Labour Rights' (2000) 3 *Journal of International Economic Law* 43 esp at 44–48.

[87] Available at http://www.ilo.org/public/english/standards/decl/declaration/index.htm and in (1998) 137 *International Labour Review* 253.

[88] See Art 50 of the EC-ACP Cotonou Agreement, OJ 2000 L317/3 and more generally European Commission, 'Promoting Core Labour Standards and Improving Social Governance in the Context of Globalisation' COM(2001) 416 pp 11–12.

[89] For discussion of this possibility, see Y Moorman 'Integration of ILO Core Standards into the WTO' (2001) 39 *Columbia Journal of Transnational Law* 555 and K Addo, 'The Correlation between Labour Standards and International Trade: Which Way Forward' (2002) 36 *Journal of World Trade* 285.

[90] See *Opinion 1/78 (Natural Rubber Agreement)* [1979] ECR 2971, para 56.

concerned with the regulation of international trade.[91] Were respect for collective labour standards to be incorporated within the WTO legal framework, the Charter's provisions on collective labour rights might well contribute to the conclusion that these tests had been satisfied. The difficulty however is that the Treaty of Nice has included a new paragraph 6 within Article 133 EC, according to which

> An agreement may not be concluded . . . if it includes provisions which go beyond the Community's internal powers, in particular by leading to a harmonisation of the laws or regulations of the Member States in an area for which this Treaty rules out such harmonisation.

The point of the new Article 133(6) EC is to reinforce the principle of parallelism between the Community's internal and external trade policies.[92] Once the exclusion in Article 137(5) EC is taken into account, the new paragraph makes it difficult for Article 133 EC to be used by the EU in order to protect rights of association and industrial action within the WTO legal framework. For it to have power to do so, Articles 94 and 308 EC would have to be available internally for the same purposes. While Articles 12 and 28 EUCFR may affect the possibility of recourse to those internal competences, it is hard to see, however, that they can make any difference to the requirement of parallelism.

Reliance by the EU upon an implied power in the social policy domain in order to participate in ILO Conventions 87 and 98 alongside the Member States is a third possibility. Here too, however, the requirement of parallelism is a major difficulty. In *Opinion 2/91* the Court indicated that in the area of social policy, where there was internal competence, external competence would follow.[93] While this means that there is external competence in relation to rights of information and consultation and collective bargaining, because of Article 137(5) EC, the Community's social policy does not appear to include an implied power to enter ILO agreements on the freedom of association and industrial action. Here too, external competence in relation to those matters exists only if Articles 94 and 308 EC can be used internally. As with Article 133 EC however, while Articles 12 and 28 EUCFR may influence the applicability of Articles 94 and 308 EC to collective labour, it is unlikely that they can affect the principle of parallelism itself.

Framework Agreements

A second institutional question which may be examined concerns legislation adopted under Article 137 EC in order to implement framework agreements

---

[91] For this test, see Opinion 2/00 *(Biosafety Protocol)* [2001] ECR I–9713, para 25.

[92] Discussed in C Herrmann, 'Common Commercial Policy after Nice: Sisyphus Would Have Done a Better Job' (2002) 39 *Common Market Law Review* 7 at 21–22.

[93] Opinion 2/91, [1993] ECR I–1061, especially para 17. The Opinion concerned ILO Convention 170 on the safe use of chemicals at work.

concluded by employers' and workers' organisations under Article 139 EC. In *UEAPME* the CFI expressed reservations about this mechanism:

> The participation of the two institutions in question has the effect . . . of endowing an agreement concluded between management and labour with a Community foundation of a legislative character, without recourse to the classic procedures provided for under the Treaty for the preparation of legislation, which entail the participation of the European Parliament . . . [T]he principle of democracy on which the Union is founded requires in the absence of the participation of the European Parliament in the legislative process—that the participation of the people be otherwise assured, in this instance through the parties representative of management and labour who concluded the agreement.[94]

Based on this premise, the CFI held that, before agreeing to convert a framework agreement into legislation, the Commission and Council were obliged to 'ascertain whether, having regard to the content of the agreement in question, the signatories, taken together, are sufficiently representative.'[95]

The approach of the CFI in *UEAPME* was consistent with criticism of the framework agreement route to legislation by academic writers,[96] and undoubtedly had merit in formal democratic terms.[97] It has however been argued by Bercusson that the approach of the CFI misunderstood the nature of Article 139 EC agreements. In his view, the possibility of such legislation

> has its conceptual roots *not* exclusively in the political legal traditions of constitutional arrangements, but also, indeed mainly, in those of industrial relations. Specifically, the EU social dialogue is perceived as akin to another level, transnational, of collective bargaining super-imposed on national systems.

Viewed in this light, the possibility of framework agreements under Article 139 EC was no longer a suspect source of EC legislation, but rather the route to ensuring *erga omnes* effect for EU-level collective agreements.[98] The existence of alternative conceptions of Article 139 EC agreements suggests a possible role for the recognition given to collective bargaining in Article 28 EUCFR. The fact that it provides for the right to negotiate and conclude collective agreements 'at

---

[94] Case T–135/96 *Union Européene de l'Artisanat et des Petites et Moyennes Entreprises (UEAPME) v EU Council and EC Commission* [1998] ECR II–2235, paras 88 and 89.

[95] *Ibid* para 90.

[96] See L Betten, 'The Democratic Deficit of Participatory Democracy in Community Social Policy' (1998) 23 *European Law Review* 20 at 28–36, and S Fredman, 'Social Law in the European Union: The Impact of the Lawmaking Process' in P Craig and C Harlow (eds), *Lawmaking in the European Union* (Deventer, Kluwer, 1998) pp 405–11.

[97] One may wonder though if employer and labour organisations could *ever* ensure sufficient participation by 'the people' in order to meet the democratic criticism outlined by the CFI.

[98] B Bercusson, 'Democratic Legitimacy and European Labour Law' (1999) 28 *Industrial Law Journal* 153, p 164 (emphasis in original). For a discussion, see N Bernard, 'Legitimising EU Law: Is the Social Dialogue the Way Forward? Some Reflections around the UEAPME Case' in J Shaw (ed) *Social Law and Policy in an Evolving European Union* (Hart, Oxford, 2000) and P Syrpis, 'Social Democracy and Judicial Review in the Community Order' in C Kilpatrick, T Novitz and P Skidmore (eds), *The Future of Remedies in Europe* (Hart, Oxford, 2000).

the appropriate levels' is of particular significance. In the light of Article 28 EUCFR, Article 139 EC can be re-interpreted as one of the principal means by which the fundamental right to engage in collective bargaining is recognised at the EU level. It might therefore be argued that Article 28 EUCFR strengthens the capacity of the Commission and Council to extend framework agreements without undue concern for the representativity of the parties.

FUNDAMENTAL RIGHTS, COLLECTIVE LABOUR LAW AND THE EUROPEAN UNION

The potential to rely upon concepts of fundamental rights to strengthen collective labour rights is a subject upon which different opinions are possible. Among labour law writers, the dominant contemporary view is that protection for collective labour rights can be achieved through the recognition of fundamental rights, provided that category is understood to includes social rights.[99] This is a view which the analysis here tends to support. It has been shown that there are a number of important contexts in which Articles 12, 27 and 28 EUCFR may enhance the place of collective labour rights within EU law—in the interpretation of labour legislation, in protecting collective action from the full force of the law of the single market, and in strengthening legislative powers in the labour law field. By extension, the analysis here also supports the view that the strengthening of the status of the Charter would be advantageous to the development of Community labour law.[100] If its status were strengthened, that would at the very least enhance the potential role of the Articles 12, 27 and 28 EUCFR in the interpretation of Community law in the ways suggested here.

In addition to these potential legal effects, Articles 12, 27 and 28 EUCFR may also have effects in the political sphere. Indeed, an awareness of this possibility arguably played a part in the drafting of these provisions. The Praesidium's initial draft of the social rights clauses proposed to state that 'employers and workers have the right to associate freely, including at the European Union level' and that 'workers and employers have the right in cases of conflicts of interest to take collective action at the European Union level should the occasion arise, including the right to strike.'[101] These specific references to the EU level had however been removed by the time of the final version of the Charter. It is hard to resist the conclusion that this was done to avoid calling attention to the lack of both competence and legislation in relation to transnational trade

---

[99] See for example K Ewing, 'Social Rights and Human Rights: Britain and the Social Charter— the Conservative Legacy' [2000] *European Human Rights Law Review* 91 and N Valticos, 'International Labour Standards and Human Rights: Approaching the Year 2000' (1998) 137 *International Labour Review* 135.

[100] In support of the incorporation of the Charter, see for example the European Trade Union Confederation, 'The Future of Europe (Laeken): ETUC Proposals' Resolution of 10–11 October 2001 and K Ewing, *The EU Charter of Fundamental Rights: Waste of Time or Wasted Opportunity?* (London, Institute of Employment Rights, 2002) pp 31–36.

[101] See CONVENT 18 (27 March 2000).

unionism and industrial action. But even as the Charter stands, Articles 12 and 28 EUCFR still point to the inadequacy of the existing provision in relation to the national and transnational aspects of rights of association, collective bargaining and the right to strike. The failure to provide for these matters may be thought objectionable if the purpose of EU labour law is understood to be the guaranteeing of fair competition and provision for transnational action. Once these matters are thought to engage fundamental rights, the failure to provide for them at the Community level appears quite incoherent.[102]

That said, it should be appreciated that it is the underdevelopment of collective labour law within the EU, which leaves such room for the Charter to have an impact in the legal and political spheres. These possible effects of the Charter do not preclude doubts as to the adequacy of notions of fundamental rights as a basis for the development of collective labour law, whether in the EU or elsewhere.[103] Collective labour rights may have to give way to other economic rights with which they collide, and which are now recognised in the Charter: the freedom to choose an occupation and the right to work (Article 15 EUCFR), the freedom to conduct a business (Article 16 EUCFR) and the right to property (Article 17 EUCFR). More generally, a potential difficulty emerges in the political sphere when notions of fundamental rights prove incomplete as a guarantee of legal rights in the field of collective labour law. The danger is that an overemphasis on the protection of fundamental rights may obscure, or even undermine, alternative arguments for the extensive recognition of collective labour rights, deriving from inequality of income and social power.

---

[102] For an account of these different rationales for EU intervention in labour law, see B Ryan, 'The Private Enforcement of European Union Labour Laws' in Kilpatrick, Novitz and Skidmore (eds), above n 98 at 142–47.

[103] For doubts in the Canadian context see J Fudge, 'Lessons from Canada: the Impact of the Charter of Rights and Freedoms on Labour and Employment Law' in K Ewing (ed), *Human Rights at Work* (London, Institute of Employment Rights, 2000).

5

The Right to Equality
and Non-Discrimination

MARK BELL*

EQUALITY AND NON-DISCRIMINATION are well-established fundamental rights in EU law.[1] A combination of Treaty provisions, secondary legislation and case law has demonstrated the importance attached by the EU to equality and non-discrimination, both as general concepts[2] and in respect of specific situations.[3] Therefore, it might be considered that the Charter's provisions in this area simply represent the codification of a familiar *status quo* and contain none of the novelty surrounding some other provisions. Nonetheless, the Charter reveals a degree of imagination and innovation in the section devoted to 'Equality'. Indeed, the branding of Chapter Three of the Charter as 'Equality' immediately promises a shift from the existing paradigm, away from a focus on negative rights not to be treated differently without justification, towards a positive right to equal opportunity and status.

'Equality' and 'non-discrimination' are contested notions with many different interpretations.[4] The first section of this chapter examines in more detail the alternative visions of equality that exist in academic commentary. Three main poles of analysis are identified: equality as non-discrimination; substantive equality; and equality as diversity. The second and third parts of this chapter turn to the provisions of the Equality Chapter in the Charter. The articles therein can be easily separated into two types: first, the horizontal, general guarantees to equality and non-discrimination; second, the vertical provisions on specific forms of inequality and discrimination. These vertical provisions are

---

* Senior Lecturer in Law, Centre for European Law and Integration, University of Leicester. I would like to thank Catherine Barnard, Tamara Hervey, Jeff Kenner and Lisa Waddington for valuable and constructive comments on an earlier draft of this chapter.
[1] See G More, 'The Principle of Equal Treatment: From Market Unifier to Fundamental Right?' in P Craig and G de Búrca (eds), *The Evolution of EU Law* (Oxford, Oxford University Press, 1999); G de Búrca, 'The Role of Equality in European Community Law' in A Dashwood and S O'Leary (eds), *The Principle of Equal Treatment in European Community Law* (London, Sweet and Maxwell, 1997).

[2] N Bernard, 'What are the Purposes of EC Discrimination Law?' in J Dine and B Watt (eds), *Discrimination Law—Concepts, Limitations, and Justifications* (London, Longman, 1996).

[3] For example, the body of law on gender equality in employment. See further, C Barnard, *EC Employment law* (Oxford, Oxford University Press, 2000).

[4] S Fredman, *Discrimination Law* (Oxford, Clarendon Press, 2002) ch 1.

addressed to the situation of women and men, children, older people, people with disabilities and, more vaguely, issues relating to 'cultural, religious and linguistic diversity'. As shall be discussed, the vertical provisions differ considerably in their form and substance. Using the framework identified in section one, both the horizontal and vertical provisions are analysed to discover what impressions they give of the EU's vision of equality.

VISIONS OF EQUALITY

Equality is an open-textured concept, with alternative and competing visions of what it should entail. Many legal systems seem to contain a mix of different ideas on what equality involves, a variety that increases over time with new legislative interventions being layered on top of what already exists.[5] The most well-established dichotomy surrounds the choice between individual and group justice strategies—the former focusing heavily on individual litigation to enforce equality laws, and the latter turning in the direction of positive action measures to compensate for past and present disadvantages experienced on a collective basis.[6] The stage has become more crowded in recent years, most notably as a consequence of the mainstreaming approach.[7] From within this picture, three principal perspectives will be highlighted and deployed as a framework for the rest of this chapter.

Equality as Non-Discrimination

The starting point for equality is frequently its legal articulation through the right to non-discrimination. This views inequality as a product of using irrelevant criteria in resource allocation.[8] In order for everyone to be treated equally, it is simply necessary that the irrelevant characteristics, such as gender or race, be removed from the decision-making process.[9] This type of strict rationality

---

[5] For example, D Schiek, 'Torn Between Arithmetic and Substantive Equality? Perspectives on Equality in German Labour Law' (2002) 18 *International Journal of Comparative Labour Law and Industrial Relations* 149.

[6] J Blom, B Fitzpatrick, J Gregory, R Knegt and U O'Hare, *The Utilisation of Sex Equality Litigation in the Member States of the European Community*, V/782/96-EN (Report to the Equal Opportunities Unit of DG V, 1995) 2.

[7] F Beveridge, S Nott and K Stephen, 'Addressing Gender in National and Community Law and Policy-Making' in J Shaw (ed), *Social Law and Policy in an Evolving Union* (Oxford, Hart Publishing, 2000) 140.

[8] C McCrudden, 'International and European Norms Regarding National Legal Remedies for Racial Inequality' in S Fredman (ed), *Discrimination and Human Rights—The Case of Racism* (Oxford, Oxford University Press, 2001) 253.

[9] K Wentholt, 'Formal and Substantive Equal Treatment: the Limitations and Potential of the Legal Concept of Equality' in T Loenen and P Rodrigues (eds), *Non-Discrimination Law: Comparative Perspectives* (The Hague, Kluwer, 1999) 54.

has the advantage of being widely applicable. Once a given characteristic is deemed to be inappropriate/irrelevant, then the non-discrimination norm can be extended accordingly. The list of suspect classifications can be open-ended, as this will evolve over time, reflecting changing societal consensus on permissible grounds for different treatment. The very openness of this notion of equality leads to accusations that it is an empty vessel—differences of treatment are only discriminatory if the ground for the differential treatment is regarded as irrelevant, but this is a constantly shifting and expanding list.[10]

The flexibility of the non-discrimination principle also depends largely upon the justifications allowed. Yet, there is no settled view on what constitutes a permissible justification for differential treatment. Moreover, this is the area where cracks emerge in the initial equivalence of all grounds of discrimination. For example, the European Court of Human Rights regards differential treatment on grounds such as sex[11] or nationality[12] as particularly difficult to justify.

The non-discrimination principle is commonly located in constitutional equality guarantees and various international human rights instruments. Article 14 ECHR is an excellent representation of this approach.[13] There is a non-exhaustive list of discriminatory grounds, which has been expanded through case law from the European Court of Human Rights.[14] That Court's definition of discrimination is highly malleable:

> A difference of treatment is discriminatory if it has no objective and reasonable justification, that is if it does not pursue a legitimate aim or if there is not a reasonable relationship of proportionality between the means employed and the aim sought to be realised.[15]

The focus on non-discrimination is also evident within EU law, most manifestly as a general principle applied by the European Court of Justice. Its approach emphasises the need for a comparative evaluation to discover if the treatment was discriminatory:

> the principle of equal treatment is breached when two categories of persons whose factual and legal circumstances disclose no essential difference are treated differently or where situations which are different are treated in an identical manner.[16]

---

[10] L Betten, 'New Equality Provisions in European Law: Some Thoughts on the Fundamental Value of Equality as a Legal Principle' in K Economides, L Betten, J Bridge, A Tettenborn and V Shrubsall (eds), *Fundamental Values* (Oxford, Hart Publishing, 2000) 73.

[11] *Abdulaziz, Cabales and Balkandali v UK* Series A No 94 (1985) 7 EHRR 471 at 501.

[12] *Gaygusuz v Austria* [1996] 23 EHRR 364 Reports 1996–IV at 381.

[13] Art 14 ECHR: 'The enjoyment of the rights and freedoms set forth in this Convention shall be secured without discrimination on any ground such as sex, race, colour, language, religion, political or other opinion, national or social origin, association with a national minority, property, birth or other status.'

[14] See further, G Moon, 'The Draft Discrimination Protocol to the European Convention on Human Rights: A Progress Report' (2000) *European Human Rights Law Review* 49 at 52.

[15] Opinion of the European Court of Human Rights on draft Protocol 12 to the European Convention on Human Rights, Doc 8606, 5 January 2000, para 5.

[16] Case T–10/93 *A v Commission* [1994] ECR II–179, para 42.

This definition of discrimination also permeates EC anti-discrimination legislation.[17]

Nonetheless, the non-discrimination approach has been criticised for being too limited and failing to confront the entrenched nature of inequality.[18] Where a web of disadvantage systematically excludes persons with certain characteristics, then equal treatment alone may not be sufficient.[19] This has become most obvious within EU law in the context of gender equality. Treating women in exactly the same way as men does not take into account the additional hurdles to participation in the labour market that women disproportionately experience; childcare and other family responsibilities are the most obvious examples.[20] Alternatively, in order to make equality a reality for many people with disabilities, it is not enough to accord them identical treatment to that received by people without disabilities; on the contrary, it may be necessary to make adjustments to the way in which work, education or services are currently organised in order to facilitate equal participation.[21]

Substantive Equality

The shortcoming of the non-discrimination model has resulted in greater emphasis on securing 'full equality in practice'.[22] This implies the adoption of strategies designed to deal with the underlying barriers to equal participation, such as the unequal distribution of childcare responsibilities. This is often expressed in the language of 'equality of opportunity', yet even this concept has multiple meanings.[23] On one level, it can be a focus on the equalisation of starting points—that is, the identification of the obstacles to individuals and groups competing on the same terms as others, leading to the removal of such barriers, or at least compensatory measures designed to neutralise their impact.[24] For example, if educational facilities for people with learning difficulties have been historically poor, then it may be necessary to develop targeted training opportunities as a means to address this legacy. In moving towards group-specific solutions, the substantive equality model abandons the strict neutrality of the non-discrimination approach.

[17] B Hepple and C Barnard, 'Substantive Equality' (2000) 59 *Cambridge Law Journal* 562.

[18] S Fredman, 'Combating Racism with Human Rights: the Right to Equality' in S Fredman (ed) *Discrimination and Human Rights—the Case of Racism* (Oxford, Oxford University Press, 2001) 20.

[19] McCrudden, above n 8, at 255.

[20] Wentholt, above n 9, at 57.

[21] L Waddington, 'Evolving Disability Policies: From Social Welfare to Human Rights—an International Trend from a European Perspective' (2001) 19 *Netherlands Quarterly of Human Rights* 141.

[22] Art 141(4) EC.

[23] S Fredman, *Discrimination Law* (Oxford, Clarenden Press, 2002) pp 14–15.

[24] S Fredman, 'Affirmative Action and the Court of Justice: A Critical Analysis' in J Shaw (ed), *Social Law and Policy in an Evolving European Union* (Oxford, Hart Publishing, 2000) 175.

More proactive interventions may place the stress on ensuring equality of results. This requires a determination of what constitutes fair (proportionate) participation and then taking positive actions to realise this goal.[25] For example, in Northern Ireland historically there has been a low representation of Catholics in the police. In order to produce a swift reversal in this trend, a quota system has been introduced that requires the appointment of one Catholic person for every person of another religion awarded a post.[26] This could result in individual unfairness for unsuccessful non-Catholic applicants, who may be better qualified than some successful Catholic candidates.[27] Yet, the substantive equality model, in this guise, places greater emphasis on the need to provide fair participation for all relevant groups.

EU law contains a number of elements reflecting the influence of the substantive equality model. First, it is possible to highlight the prominent location of indirect discrimination in EU anti-discrimination law instruments.[28] Indirect discrimination shifts the focus from formal equal treatment towards an examination of the effects in practice of rules/procedures on different groups. This represents an emphasis on securing substantive equality, as well as challenging the unquestioned structures that perpetuate inequality.[29] In addition, the EC Treaty provides specific legal protection for positive action schemes on gender equality[30] and similar provisions have been inserted in the Race Equality Directive[31] and the Framework Employment Directive.[32] Yet, positive action remains supplementary to the dominant focus on non-discrimination. This has proven problematic in case law with the Court striking a delicate balance between permitting positive action for women prior to and at the point of selection for employment, but not where this results in an automatic preference for members of the under-represented sex.[33]

[25] C Barnard, 'The Changing Scope of the Fundamental Principle of Equality?' (2001) 46 *McGill Law Journal* 955 at 976.

[26] S 46(1) Police (Northern Ireland) Act 2000.

[27] An initial legal challenge from an unsuccessful Protestant applicant failed: *Irish Independent*, 24 July 2002, 'Protestant loses police "equal rights" case'.

[28] Indirect discrimination is explicitly forbidden in EU gender equality law (Art 2(2), Dir 97/80/EC [1998] OJ L 14/6), as well as in the Race Equality Directive (Art 2(2)(b), Dir 2000/43/EC [2000] OJ L 180/22) and the Framework Employment Directive (Art 2(2)(b) Dir 2000/78/EC [2000] OJ L 303/16).

[29] T Loenen, 'Indirect Discrimination: Oscillating Between Containment and Revolution' in T Loenen and P Rodrigues (eds), *Non-discrimination Law: Comparative Perspectives* (The Hague, Kluwer, 1999) 198.

[30] Art 141(4) EC.

[31] Art 5, Dir 2000/43/EC [2000] OJ L 180/22.

[32] Art 7, Dir 2000/78/EC [2000] OJ L303/16.

[33] See, *inter alia*, Case C–158/97 *Badeck* [2000] ECR I–1875, Case C–407/98 *Abrahamsson and Anderson v Fogelqvist* [2000] ECR I–5539. See further C Costello, in this collection.

Equality as Diversity

Since 1999, the equality agenda of the EU has broadened considerably as a consequence of the addition to the EC Treaty of a new legal competence 'to combat discrimination based on sex, racial or ethnic origin, religion or belief, disability, age or sexual orientation' (Article 13 EC). This presents greater challenges surrounding how the EU manages diversity within its body of equality law. Tensions can be found between different grounds of discrimination, such as religion or sexual orientation. Respect for religious diversity might imply wide autonomy for faith-based schools, but this could conflict with equal treatment irrespective of sexual orientation if (for example) a school sought to exclude lesbian and gay teachers.[34] Moreover, it is clear that the priority issues for different groups will vary. The treatment of third country nationals is closely related to combating racial discrimination, whereas sexual orientation discrimination demands attention to the treatment of unmarried couples.

Accommodating diversity within equality law implies greater differentiation in policy responses. Moreover, diversity reinforces the need for equality to be taken into account in all areas of policy-making. The traditional labour market focus of EU equality law does not provide an adequate response to the needs of older persons who have already left employment voluntarily, or alternatively people with severe disabilities who have a highly reduced capacity to work. Yet, dealing with various expressions of inequality across many different policy areas presents a daunting agenda for public institutions. A pragmatic response in Northern Ireland and, to a lesser degree, Great Britain has been to place considerable emphasis on the participation of affected communities in auditing policies and practices, and the negotiation of change.[35] This results in a process that is clearly more flexible than the substantive equality model, which implies a single aim (be it equal opportunities or equal results) for all forms of discrimination. McCrudden suggests that each group negotiates its own version of equality, with the implication that equality will be an inherently varied concept.[36] This model provides a muddy image of equality law, one that lacks consistency and shifts over time, but where this flexibility is regarded as a desirable quality.

In recent years, EU equality law has come to reflect the patchwork of models presented above. Different levels of legal protection exist for different grounds of discrimination and divergence can be found on the material scope of the discrimination prohibition, enforcement mechanisms and the permissible justi-

---

[34] See further C Wallace and J Shaw, in this collection, at p 228–31; C Costello, in this collection at fn 119. Also D Schiek, 'Elements of a New Framework for the Principle of Equal Treatment of Persons' (2002) 8 *European Law Journal* 290 at 311.

[35] S Fredman, 'Equality: a new generation?' (2001) 30 *Industrial Law Journal* 145 at 165–66.

[36] C McCrudden, 'Theorizing European Equality Law and the Role of Mainstreaming', Paper for Irish Centre for European Law/Equality Authority Conference on Equality Law, Dublin, 30 June 2001.

fications for discrimination.[37] However, the participative role for civil society in negotiating this diversity framework remains vague. Some specific organisations have become well-established interlocutors of the EU institutions,[38] but an overall mechanism for mainstreaming, consultation and participation by all 'excluded' groups remains absent.

Having established this framework of three alternative conceptions of equality, the subsequent sections of this chapter consider the extent to which each is reflected in the Equality Chapter of the Charter. This analysis is divided into two parts, representing the principal elements of the Equality Chapter. Hence, there is first an examination of the horizontal provisions on non-discrimination, followed by scrutiny of the vertical provisions, the latter being more clearly linked to issues of substantive equality and managing diversity.

HORIZONTAL PROVISIONS: NON-DISCRIMINATION

The Concept of Discrimination in the Charter

The non-discrimination model is very clearly reflected in the opening articles of the Equality Chapter. Article 20 EUCFR declares that 'everyone is equal before the law'. Article 21 EUCFR provides the corollary to this principle. Paragraph 1 states:

> Any discrimination based on any ground such as sex, race, colour, ethnic or social origin, genetic features, language, religion or belief, political or other opinion, membership of a national minority, property, birth, disability, age or sexual orientation shall be prohibited.

Although 'discrimination' is not defined explicitly, Article 21 EUCFR must be read in conjunction with Article 52(1) EUCFR, which stipulates that:

> subject to the principle of proportionality, limitations may be made only if they are necessary and genuinely meet objectives of general interest recognised by the Union or the need to protect the rights and freedoms of others.

This indicates that the underlying concept of discrimination bears a great similarity to Article 14 ECHR. Differential treatment will only be discriminatory if it cannot be objectively justified.

In contrast, the EU's anti-discrimination Directives create a central dichotomy between direct and indirect discrimination. Whereas direct discrimination can be justified only by reference to the express derogations provided elsewhere in the Directive, indirect discrimination remains open to objective

---

[37] L Waddington and M Bell, 'More Equal than Others: Distinguishing European Union Equality Directives' (2001) 38 *Common Market Law Review* 587.

[38] Mazey argues this is true for the European Women's Lobby: S Mazey, 'The Development of EU Gender Policies: Towards the Recognition of Difference' (2002) 15 *EUSA Review* 3.

justification.[39] This balance ensures that the most overt forms of discrimination remain permissible in a very narrow range of predetermined circumstances, whilst the broader scope of indirect discrimination is balanced by the possibility for this to be justified by reasons of business necessity or competing policy objectives, such as the management of public expenditure.[40] The Charter could be criticised for setting a lower benchmark than the Directives, because even direct discrimination is always capable of being justified. Yet, it is crucial to distinguish the role of anti-discrimination legislation from the role of the Charter. Legislation provides a space in which detailed situations can be confronted and specific exceptions inserted. It addresses a limited material scope and operates in relation to a closed list of discriminatory grounds. In contrast, the Charter applies to all areas of EU law and the list of prohibited grounds is non-exhaustive. The experience of Article 14 ECHR demonstrates that new grounds are likely to emerge over time, produced by changes in society or even science.[41] The appropriate exceptions to these prospective grounds cannot be predicted, therefore, a flexible framework is essential in order to leave room for the Court (or other courts applying Community law) to mould the non-discrimination principle in line with wider social developments.

In the light of this flexibility, it is difficult to understand the justification for the second paragraph of Article 21 EUCFR, which regulates a specific ground of discrimination: nationality. Whilst most of the grounds found in Article 14 ECHR are simply replicated in Article 21(1) EUCFR, 'national origin' has been carefully stripped away. Instead, a second paragraph has been added to Article 21:

> Within the scope of application of the Treaty establishing the European Community and of the Treaty on European Union, and without prejudice to the special provisions of those Treaties, any discrimination on grounds of nationality shall be prohibited.

The explanatory memorandum clarifies further that this 'corresponds to Article 12 of the EC Treaty and must be applied in compliance with the Treaty'.[42] Although Article 12 EC uses suggestively ambiguous language ('any discrimination on grounds of nationality shall be prohibited'), in practice this has been interpreted as extending only to discrimination between EU nationals.[43] Therefore, Article 21(2) EUCFR essentially amounts to a restatement of Article 12 EC, as currently interpreted, with the clarification that the principle of non-

---

[39] Age discrimination is an exception to this trend because both direct and indirect forms of age discrimination are open to objective justification according to Art 6 of the Framework Directive (2000/78/EC [2000] OJ L 303/16). See C Costello, in this collection, at pp 117–18.

[40] Case C–226/98 *Jørgensen* [2000] ECR I–2447. See further, Loenen, above n 29 at 203.

[41] The inclusion of 'genetic features' in Art 21(1) of the Charter is an example of the impact of scientific developments on discrimination law.

[42] Praesidium, 'Text of the explanations relating to the complete text of the Charter as set out in CHARTE 4487/00 CONVENT 50' CHARTE 4473/00 CONVENT 49, Brussels, 11 October 2000, p 23.

[43] See further Opinion of AG Jacobs in Cases C–95/99 to C–98/99 and C–180/99 *Khalil and others* [2001] ECR I–7413.

discrimination on grounds of nationality extends throughout the EU Treaty. The reticence of the Member States to make any commitment to non-discrimination for third country nationals places the Charter in a poor light when compared with Article 14 ECHR. The inclusion of national origin in Article 14 ECHR has not provoked major difficulties. As discussed above, the approach of the European Court of Human Rights has been to treat as discrimination any differential treatment without objective justification.[44] This ensures that many differences of treatment based on nationality remain capable of justification, but that such distinctions are at least subject to judicial oversight.

Article 21 EUCFR and Article 13 EC

Although a distinction must be drawn between the functions of the Charter and secondary legislation, a more difficult relationship is that between the Charter and other provisions of the founding Treaties. In part, this flows from the uncertain legal status of the Charter and the ongoing debate on whether to incorporate it within the founding EU or EC Treaties. For a number of reasons explored below, Article 21 EUCFR is a useful complement to Article 13 EC; however, the combination produces certain internal contradictions that remain to be explained.

The primary added value conferred by the Charter lies in one of the main weaknesses of Article 13 EC—its entirely facilitative character and the absence of any directly effective rights to non-discrimination. Although the Charter's capacity to act as a general non-discrimination guarantee remains qualified by its non-binding legal status, it seems likely that the Court will eventually treat the Charter as being effectively binding, in a similar manner to its use of the ECHR.[45] Indeed, the Court of First Instance already seems to be adopting this strategy.[46] In this way, Article 21(1) EUCFR could generate similar legal effects to the powerful prohibition on nationality discrimination found in Article 12 EC.

Admittedly, non-discrimination as a general principle of Community law was already available to protect individuals from discrimination by the EU's bodies and institutions. Nevertheless, Article 21 EUCFR provides a valuable source of clarification as to the full range of protected grounds. The Court has previously had the opportunity through cases involving the employees of the EU to specify that discrimination on grounds such as sex[47] or religion[48] is contrary to the general principles of Community law. Yet, for other, less well recognised, grounds

---

[44] *Gaygusuz v Austria* [1996] 23 EHRR 364 Report 1996–IV at 381.

[45] See further, B de Witte, 'The Legal Status of the Charter: Vital Question or Non-Issue?' (2001) 8 *Maastricht Journal of European and Comparative Law* 81.

[46] Case T–54/99 *max.mobil Telekommunikation Service GmbH v Commission* [2002] ECR II–313. See M Poiares Maduro, in this collection, at pp 282–3; B Ryan, in this collection, at p 77.

[47] Case 20/71 *Sabbatini* [1972] ECR 345.

[48] Case 130/75 *Prais v Council* [1976] ECR 1589.

of discrimination the Charter provides practical assistance in resolving any doubts over the extent of the non-discrimination principle. For example, the Charter placed further pressure on the institutions to reconsider recruitment practices that discriminate on grounds of age. It may be no coincidence that the Commission and Parliament subsequently agreed to end the use of upper age limits in their recruitment policies in May 2002.[49]

At the same time as acknowledging the potential for litigants to make reference to Article 21(1) EUCFR in support of challenges to discriminatory practices, it must also be considered that the other Charter provisions could be invoked in a challenge to aspects of existing anti-discrimination legislation. For example, the Framework Directive strikes a complex and delicate balance between the right to non-discrimination and the freedom of religious organisations to choose employees who share their beliefs.[50] It is only to be expected that a party unsuccessful under the terms of the Directive (whether an individual refused employment or a religious organisation held to have committed unlawful discrimination) will invoke the fundamental rights protected by the Charter[51] as a higher source of law.

Lenaerts and de Smijter argue that such arguments will fail due to Article 52(2) EUCFR.[52] This states:

> Rights recognised by this Charter which are based on the Community Treaties or the Treaty on European Union shall be exercised under the conditions and within the limits defined by those Treaties.

Certainly, this would appear to exclude the possibility of the EU courts using the Charter to interpret differently the right to equal pay or the scope for positive action for women, because these are specifically provided for in Article 141 EC. However, the situation is different as regards the example given in the previous paragraph. Article 13 EC does not confer any substantive rights, but simply the opportunity for the Community to take further action to combat discrimination on grounds of sex, racial or ethnic origin, religion or belief, disability, age or sexual orientation. Therefore, it would be difficult to treat Article 21 EUCFR as merely recognising rights based on Article 13 EC. Moreover, unlike Article 141 EC, the conditions and limits to any rights based on Article 13 EC are not found in the Treaties, but in secondary legislation, whereas Article 52(2) EUCFR only refers to conditions and limits 'defined by those Treaties'. Naturally, the EU courts can be expected to tread carefully in questioning the controversial and sensitive balance of rights struck within secondary legislation like the Framework Directive. Nonetheless, the Charter is likely to make a significant contribution in determining the resolution of conflicts of rights disputes.

---

[49] This followed pressure from the European Ombudsman: Commission (UK Office), *The Week in Europe*, 10 May 2002.

[50] Art 4(2), Dir 2000/78/EC [2000] OJ L 303/16.

[51] Article 10(1) EUCFR guarantees 'freedom of thought, conscience and religion'.

[52] K Lenaerts and E de Smijter, 'A "Bill of Rights" for the European Union' (2001) 38 *Common Market Law Review* 273 at 285.

Even if the Charter principles are not considered to conflict directly with any legislation already adopted under Article 13 EC, the different content of Article 21 EUCFR provokes a number of questions surrounding their underlying compatibility. In particular, if it is appropriate that all the forms of discrimination mentioned in Article 21(1) EUCFR should be forbidden within the scope of EU law, then why should the EU only have the power to take further supporting steps in respect of an inner circle of grounds? It is interesting that social origin, included in the initial drafts of Article 13 EC, but ultimately deleted,[53] has now found its way back into EU law via the Charter. There seems to be a hierarchy emerging between grounds of discrimination that should be subject to the soft, flexible non-discrimination requirement found in Article 21 EUCFR, and others that are suitable for detailed regulation. Moreover, whereas the Charter grounds only enjoy protection in respect of the actions of EU institutions, bodies and Member States (when implementing EU law), the Article 13 EC grounds can be protected more generally against the actions of national authorities, as well as private actors, such as employers and service-providers. Whilst not suggesting that all grounds found in the Charter are appropriate for detailed implementing legislation, it is not evident on what basis grounds have been selected for inclusion in Article 21 EUCFR following their earlier exclusion from Article 13 EC.

In summary, it is clear that the horizontal provisions of the Charter closely reflect a vision of equality as non-discrimination. All grounds of discrimination, with the exception of nationality, are treated in the same fashion and there is no provision for positive action. If and when the EU courts interpret this part of the Charter, they will find a wide space for determining the meaning of the non-discrimination norm and in particular when differential treatment is permissible. This contrasts with Article 13 EC and its Directives. Although these are also largely shaped by the vision of equality as non-discrimination, they reflect a more detailed and rigorous approach to which forms of discrimination are contrary to the law.

VERTICAL PROVISIONS: SUBSTANTIVE EQUALITY AND MANAGING DIVERSITY

Articles 20 and 21 EUCFR take a horizontal character, applying to all forms of potential discrimination. In contrast, the remaining provisions of the Equality Chapter adopt a vertical character, dealing individually with specific forms of discrimination and disadvantage. Whilst Articles 20 and 21 EUCFR remained essentially unchanged between the July draft of the Charter[54] and the final text

[53] L Flynn, 'The Implications of Article 13 EC—After Amsterdam, Will Some Forms of Discrimination be More Equal than Others?' (1999) 36 *Common Market Law Review* 1127. Flynn argues that this ground of discrimination could be important in ensuring full protection against discrimination for travelling communities and descendants thereof (at 1132).

[54] Praesidium, 'Draft Charter of Fundamental Rights of the European Union' CHARTE 4422/00 CONVENT 45, 28 July 2000.

declared in December 2000, the other part of the Equality Chapter underwent significant mutation. Whereas specific provisions were already foreseen on gender equality, children and persons with disabilities, to these were added provisions on 'cultural, religious and linguistic diversity' and the 'rights of the elderly'. Questions remain concerning the coherence and rationale of these vertical provisions. Some take the form of enforceable rights, whereas others appear to be more in the nature of principles to guide policy orientation—a dichotomy found more generally in the social provisions of the Charter.[55] This distinction seems to map out the different visions of equality being used in this part of the Charter. Whereas the provisions on gender equality, people with disabilities and children contain elements of the substantive equality model, the provisions on diversity and the elderly seem limited to a rather vague form of mainstreaming. Each is examined in more detail below.

Gender Equality

Cathryn Costello discusses Article 23 EUCFR on equality between men and women in detail elsewhere in this collection. Interestingly, it reflects all aspects of the equality framework identified earlier in this essay. Article 21(1) EUCFR requires non-discrimination on the ground of sex. The integration of gender equality objectives throughout law and policy is then mandated by the first sentence of Article 23 EUCFR: 'equality between men and women must be ensured in all areas, including employment, work and pay'. In the second part of Article 23 EUCFR, there is explicit recognition of the substantive equality model and the need for positive action: 'the principle of equality shall not prevent the maintenance or adoption of measures providing for specific advantages in favour of the under-represented sex'. In essence, this pattern reproduces that already existing in the EC Treaty.[56] Whilst not without its weaknesses,[57] it provides a template against which other aspects of the Equality Chapter can be compared.

People with Disabilities

Waddington highlights the shift that has taken place in recent years away from a protective approach to people with disabilities, in favour of a rights-based

---

[55] M Gijzen, 'The Charter: A Milestone for Social Protection in Europe?' (2001) 8 *Maastricht Journal of European and Comparative Law* 33; J Kenner, in this collection, at pp 55–6. Cf L Betten, 'The EU Charter on Fundamental Rights: a Trojan Horse or a Mouse?' (2001) 17 *International Journal of Comparative Labour Law and Industrial Relations* 15 at 156.

[56] See Arts 3(2), 13 and 141 EC.

[57] The European Women's Lobby had requested additional provisions on matters such as gender parity in democracy and gender related violence: Contribution by the European Women's Lobby, CHARTE 4439/00, CONTRIB 293.

strategy.[58] This is linked to the changing perception of disability; instead of pathologising disability as a medically defined impairment, there is greater emphasis on its social construction. In particular, the source of disablement often arises from the way in which work and society are organised, rendering them inaccessible and exclusionary for people with different abilities.[59] Older human rights instruments reflect the former concepts and approaches—for example, the European Social Charter 1961 (ESC) places considerable emphasis on access of 'physically and mentally disabled persons' to 'specialised institutions' and 'sheltered employment'.[60] In contrast, the Revised European Social Charter 1996 (RevESC) states that rights are accorded to people 'irrespective of age and the nature and origin of their disabilities'.[61] Training should be within 'general schemes wherever possible' and 'sheltered employment' becomes a last resort option. Instead, there is a duty to 'adjust the working conditions to the needs of the disabled'.[62]

The Charter cautiously adopts the language of rights in Article 26 EUCFR:

> The Union recognises and respects the *right* of persons with disabilities to benefit from measures designed to ensure their independence, social and occupational integration and participation in the life of the community.[63]

The strength of this provision lies in the implicit mandate for positive actions to assist the integration of disabled people. In this respect, Article 26 EUCFR reflects the substantive equality model. Moreover, the protection thereby conferred for targeted measures forms constructive support for the Framework Directive, which extends a wider legal space for positive action in relation to disability, than that allowed in respect of the other grounds of discrimination in Article 13 EC.[64] Article 26 EUCFR may also assist in resolving any future challenge to the legality of the reasonable accommodation obligation placed on employers by the Framework Directive. In Ireland, the Supreme Court held a similar obligation to violate the property rights of employers,[65] and it cannot be ignored that Article 17 EUCFR contains a lengthy protection of the right to property. Article 26 EUCFR provides evidence that the reasonable accommodation obligation is a restriction on the use of property in the general interest and hence compatible with Article 17 EUCFR.

In contrast, the commitment to mainstreaming disability issues into all areas of law and policy is quite ambiguous, especially when compared to the crisp text

---

[58] Waddington, above n 21.

[59] Para 5, Introduction, UN Standard Rules on the Equalization of Opportunities for Persons with Disabilities, Resolution 48/96 of the General Assembly, 20 December 1993.

[60] Art 15 ESC.

[61] Art 15 RevESC.

[62] *Ibid.*

[63] Author's emphasis.

[64] Art 7(2), see Waddington and Bell, above n 37 at 603.

[65] In the matter of Article 26 of the Constitution and in the matter of the Employment Equality Bill 1996 (S.C. No. 118 of 1997) 2 *Irish Reports* 321.

in relation to gender mainstreaming. The reference to *respecting* the rights of persons with disabilities could be read as implying a positive duty on the EU to take a diversity of abilities into account; indeed, this approach would fit well with the vision of equality as diversity. Yet, 'respect' can also be interpreted in a more neutral fashion as simply not infringing people's rights. As a minimum, Article 26 EUCFR would support a mainstreaming approach, even if the precise obligations it imposes on the EU are not very clear.

Children's Rights

The location of children's rights within the Equality Chapter is a rather novel approach when compared with other international human rights texts. Children's rights have been often rendered invisible in general human rights instruments, with the main reference point being the dedicated treatment this subject receives in the UN Convention on the Rights of the Child 1989 (CRC).[66] The Charter's approach reflects various submissions from the European Children's Network (Euronet), which argued in favour of recognition that age discrimination also operates against those of young age,[67] thereby making this an equality issue. Article 24 EUCFR states:

> 1. Children shall have the right to such protection and care as is necessary for their well-being. They may express their views freely. Such views shall be taken into consideration on matters that concern them in accordance with their age and maturity.
> 2. In all actions relating to children, whether taken by public authorities or private institutions, the child's best interests must be a primary consideration.
> 3. Every child shall have the right to maintain on a regular basis a personal relationship and direct contact with both his or her parents, unless that is contrary to his or her interests.

As the explanatory memorandum confirms, these rights largely replicate various provisions found in the CRC.[68] As with the provision on persons with disabilities, there is a shift in paradigm away from paternalistic protection of vulnerable groups, towards an empowering, rights-based philosophy.[69]

In its content, this provision appears to be quite different from the other elements of the Equality Chapter. Paragraph 1 acknowledges the need for specific actions to protect children's rights. In this respect, the substantive equality model has influenced Article 24 EUCFR. In addition, both paragraphs 1 and 2

---

[66] Contribution by Euronet, CHARTE 4240/00 CONTRIB 113, p. 10.

[67] *Ibid* p 15. See also, Contribution by Euronet, CHARTE 4442/00 CONTRIB 296.

[68] Praesidium, above n 42 at 24. McGlynn highlights some textual differences between the Charter and the UN Convention that could imply stronger rights under the Charter text: C McGlynn, 'Families and the European Union Charter of Fundamental Rights: Progressive Change or Entrenching the Status Quo?' (2001) 26 *European Law Review* 582 at 596.

[69] McGlynn, *ibid* at 594.

refer to taking into account the views and interests of children[70] and this can be equated with a form of mainstreaming. Indeed, Article 24 EUCFR is perhaps the best example in the Charter of the need to balance equality with diversity. Although the objective is to ensure children are treated equally to adults, the means of achieving this end are quite different than for other social groups. In particular, the non-discrimination norm contained within Article 21 EUCFR is less easy to apply. Young age is a criterion where direct discrimination remains common, but it is often regarded as justified for reasons relating to the protection and care of children. For example, the Young Workers' Directive[71] enshrines differential treatment of young people in the workplace through specific limits on working hours and occupational access. Nonetheless, this seems to be in the best interests of young people given the need to protect their educational opportunities. At the same time, the location of children's rights in the Equality Chapter acts as a reminder that protection can drift into detrimental discrimination. For example, when children are permitted to work, then it is not obvious why different treatment should be permitted in levels of remuneration. Therefore, the non-discrimination model is not entirely irrelevant here.

Probably, the main contribution of the Charter in this area is to combat the invisibility of children as actors in EU law. Whilst family law remains primarily a national legal competence, children's rights are being increasingly regulated by the EU.[72] This has been most evident as the EU constructs its 'Area of Freedom, Security and Justice'. On the one hand, a significant dimension to realising a European judicial area has been the establishment of common EC rules on the mutual recognition and enforcement of judgments—including judgments relating to child custody, child maintenance and the abduction of children, where the parents are located in two different EU states.[73] On the other, most measures on immigration and asylum have a direct relation to the situation of children, most especially unaccompanied migrant children.[74] The Charter asserts the need to ensure that the best interests of children are guiding objectives in the elaboration of such instruments. Whilst most other groups in society can represent and voice their own interests, children's rights need to be guaranteed by adults. Therefore, it may be appropriate to consider establishing an EU Children's Ombudsman or

---

[70] Contrast the provision in Art 14 EUCFR concerning education; see Wallace and Shaw, in this collection, at pp 236–43.

[71] Council Dir 94/33/EC of 22 June 1994 on the protection of young people at work [1994] OJ L 216/12.

[72] See further, C McGlynn, 'The Europeanisation of Family Law' (2001) 13 *Child and Family Law Quarterly* 35; H Stalford, 'The Citizenship Status of Children in European Union Law' (2000) 8 *International Journal of Children's Rights* 101.

[73] European Commission, 'Proposal for a Council Regulation Concerning Jurisdiction and the Recognition and Enforcement of Judgements in Matrimonial Matters and in Matters of Parental Responsibility Repealing Regulation 1347/2000/EC and Amending Regulation 44/2001/EC in Matters Relating to Maintenance' COM (2002) 222.

[74] A Hunter, 'Between the Domestic and the International: The Role of the European Union in Providing Protection for Unaccompanied Refugee Children in the United Kingdom' (2001) 3 *European Journal of Migration and Law* 383.

some similar institution, in order to ensure that Article 24 EUCFR is effectively woven into and throughout EU law and policy.

Older People

In contrast to the firm guarantees for children's rights, older people are dealt with in a relatively vague provision. Article 25 EUCFR states: 'The Union recognises and respects the rights of the elderly to lead a life of dignity and independence and to participate in social and cultural life.' In comparison with the gender equality article, there is no mandate for positive action and the mainstreaming obligation is ambiguous. As discussed above, the requirement placed on the EU to 'respect' the rights of older people at least implies a negative obligation not to infringe older people's interests through EU law and policy. Yet, this is much weaker than the provision on persons with disabilities, where there is also recognition of their entitlement to benefit from targeted actions to ensure their integration. Article 25 EUCFR might be described as reflecting a very diluted version of the vision of equality as diversity. Its inclusion implies that there is, in principle, an acceptance that older age raises equality issues that demand specific responses. However, there is very little guidance on how this will be implemented.

Unsurprisingly, Article 25 EUCFR fell considerably short of the demands of Eurolink-Age, one of the largest European networks of organisations concerned with ageing issues.[75] This recommended taking the relevant provisions of the RevESC as a model. This is closer to the substantive equality model. Article 23 RevESC commits signatories to 'adopt or encourage' appropriate measures to provide older persons with: 'adequate resources'; sufficient information on services and support available to them; suitable housing (including support in adapting housing); all necessary healthcare; and support when living within care institutions (including the right to participate in decisions concerning the living conditions in such places). Article 25 EUCFR lacks such a vision. It could be argued that the provisions of the RevESC are essentially programmatic policy principles, not liable to give rise to enforceable individual rights, and in this sense the Charter is no different. Nevertheless, the RevESC provides a more transparent set of guidelines against which to measure state action. Such directional principles are growing in relevance as the EU's role increases in key areas affecting older people.

Since the early 1990s, there has been a steady growth in the EU's attention to the position of older workers within the internal market. This has crystallised around the European Employment Strategy, which has identified 'active ageing' as a key objective;[76] namely, the retention of older persons within the labour mar-

---

[75] Position Paper from Eurolink-Age, CHARTE 4293/00 CONTRIB 165.
[76] For example, Council Decision of 18 February 2002 on guidelines for Member States' employment policies for the year 2002 [2002] OJ L 60/60.

ket as a means to increase employment participation rates and to enlarge the proportion of working people within the population in order to sustain public finances. The policy co-ordination process that characterises the Employment Strategy is now being extended to other policy fields, such as social inclusion[77] and pensions,[78] where challenges also result from the shifting demographic structure of the EU. The application of this 'Open Method of Co-ordination' in areas that directly impact upon older people makes it crucial that their interests are sufficiently taken into account in policy formulation. For example, the 2002 Barcelona European Council agreed to increase the average retirement age in the EU by around five years by 2010.[79] There is a risk here that older people become a labour market commodity to be managed rather than a group of people who are able to participate and shape the policy choices affecting their future. Article 25 EUCFR is a useful means of sensitising the EU as it assumes a greater role in regulating policies impacting upon older people, but it lacks substantive guarantees.

Cultural, Religious and Linguistic Diversity[80]

The most flexible element of the Equality Chapter is Article 22: 'The Union shall respect cultural, religious and linguistic diversity'. The explanatory memorandum to the Charter identifies this clause as stemming from existing provisions in the Treaties:[81] Article 6 EU, with its reference to respect for the 'national identities' of the Member States; and Article 151 EC, which mandates the Community to 'contribute to the flowering of the cultures of the Member States, while respecting their national and regional diversity'. Yet, this eclipses the driving forces behind this Article, which were essentially concerned with the protection of minority rights.[82] There were various submissions to the Convention drafting the Charter supporting explicit recognition of minority cultural and linguistic rights,[83] as well as numerous representations on religion from both traditional and less traditional religious movements.[84] France is reported to

---

[77] Commission, 'Joint report on social inclusion' COM (2001) 565.

[78] Commission, 'Supporting national strategies for safe and sustainable pensions through an integrated approach' COM (2001) 362.

[79] Para 32, Barcelona European Council conclusions, *EU-Bulletin*, 3–2002.

[80] For further discussion, see Wallace and Shaw, in this collection.

[81] Praesidium (above n 42).

[82] G Schwellnus, ' "Much Ado About Nothing?" Minority Protection and the EU Charter of Fundamental Rights' Constitutionalism Web-Papers, ConWEB No. 5/2001, http://www.qub.ac.uk/ies/onlinepapers/const.html.

[83] For example, Common statement of the Platform of European Social NGOs, CHARTE 4286/00 CONTRIB 158; Contribution by the European Bureau for Lesser Used Languages, CHARTE 4166/00 CONTRIB 50; Contribution by the Minority Rights Group International, CHARTE 4478/00 CONTRIB 329.

[84] Inter alia, Submission by the Church and Society Commission of the Conference of European Churches, CHARTE 4323/00 CONTRIB 189; Contribution of the Secretariat of the Commission of the Bishops' conference of the European Community, CHARTE 4128/00 ADD 1 CONTRIB 23; Submission of the Church of Scientology, CHARTE 4365/00 CONTRIB 228.

have ultimately blocked reference to minority rights, given that it has consistently rejected the existence of minorities under its constitutional order.[85] Nonetheless, Article 22 EUCFR represents a surrogate protection mechanism; respect for cultural diversity implicitly suggests the existence of minority cultures.

A forceful reading of Article 22 EUCFR would argue that it establishes a positive duty on the EU, which 'shall respect' diversity. This could be read as supporting a substantive equality approach, especially where formal equal treatment of different communities would in fact result in minority groups being placed at a disadvantage. For example, the principle of respect for religious diversity might have produced a different outcome in cases such as *Van Duyn*, concerning the legality of restrictions on the movement of community citizens working for the Church of Scientology.[86] A more contemporary example of the challenges posed by cultural diversity can be found within the proposed Family Reunion Directive and its treatment of polygamous marriages. The Commission is proposing that only one spouse may be admitted, unless this conflicts with children's rights pursuant to the CRC. Whilst this may reflect the stronger terms of the Charter's provisions on children's rights, there is little analysis of whether this complies with the duty to respect cultural diversity.[87]

The absence of reference to ethnic diversity within Article 22 EUCFR confirms the EU's mixed messages in this area. There is no apparent protection for positive action on grounds of race or ethnicity, although this is mandated by the UN Convention on the Elimination of All Forms of Racial Discrimination[88] and included within the Race Equality Directive.[89] Moreover, the Charter compares unfavourably with other international instruments that acknowledge the need for minority groups to enjoy specific rights in order to realise substantive equality. For example, the International Covenant on Civil and Political Rights 1966 provides that:

> in those states in which ethnic, religious or linguistic minorities exist, persons belonging to such minorities shall not be denied the right, in community with other members of the group, to enjoy their own culture, to profess and practice their own religion, or to use their own language.[90]

---

[85] Schwellnus (above n 82) 10.

[86] Van Duyn was a Dutch national refused entry to the UK in 1973 in order to work at a Scientology establishment, a decision subsequently upheld by the Court of Justice given that the UK deemed the Church to be 'socially harmful': Case 41/74 *Van Duyn v Home Office* [1974] ECR 1337, 1350.

[87] European Commission, 'Amended Proposal for a Council Directive on the Right to Family Reunification' COM (2002) 225, Art 4(4).

[88] Art 2(2) CERD.

[89] Art 5, Dir 2000/78/EC [2000] OJ L 303/16.

[90] Art 27, ICCPR.

A FOGGY VISION OR THE LOGIC OF DIVERSITY?

It is probably rather trite to conclude that there is no single vision of equality in the Charter, but rather a muddled combination of perspectives. The core rests on the traditional non-discrimination model. As a general constitutional principle, formal equal treatment appears to appeal to courts and legislators,[91] not least because of its clarity and flexibility. This aspect of the Charter fits comfortably with the existing case law of the Court and the central dimensions of EU equality legislation. It is, however, significant that there has been an attempt to move beyond this familiar framework and to experiment with provisions that variously reflect goals of substantive equality and the accommodation of diversity.

The vertical provisions of the Charter can be easily criticised for the qualitative differences between the different articles and the rather ad hoc nature in which the various groups came to receive specific protection. Yet, there may be an implicit recognition that the non-discrimination model is not sufficient to deliver equality and that a symmetrical approach is not always appropriate. The Charter accepts that people with disabilities, children and older people have particular needs beyond being treated the same as those without disabilities or those who are neither young, nor old. Similarly, the provision on gender equality foresees the justification for positive actions in order to secure substantive equality, although it refers more neutrally to 'the under-represented sex'. The failure to provide any comparable protection for specific measures in favour of minority ethnic communities is disappointing and out of tune with the stronger message in the Race Equality Directive.

If the Charter equivocates on the substantive equality model, the need to integrate diversity into law and policy-making might be described as a sub-text running throughout the vertical provisions. The duty to 'respect' diversity in terms of culture, religion, language, age and ability will require the EU institutions to devote greater consideration to how these issues are currently dealt with in law and policy. Importantly, the provisions on age and disability also refer to participation rights. Certainly, the Charter itself provides an example of how civil society can be involved in the elaboration of norms on equality and discrimination. The numerous submissions to the Convention reveal how diversity does indeed produce different equality agendas and priorities. Taking seriously these different voices and demands will of necessity produce a messy framework sometimes lacking in consistency. The diversity model suggests that this should not be always regarded as problematic, but may have beneficial aspects. The Charter shares these features, however, the different provisions do not always

---

[91] Cf, M Rodríguez-Piñero Bravo-Ferrer and M Rodríguez-Piñero Royo, 'The Principle of Equality in the Labour Market—Reflections in the Spanish Model' (2002) 18 *International Journal of Comparative Labour Law and Industrial Relations* 169.

reflect the alternative agendas of civil society organisations, but rather the shadowy bargaining and drafting process.

Overall, the Charter marks another stage in the development of EU equality law. The legislation emerging from Article 13 EC set various priorities and strayed away from the idea of a single equality law. Instead, diverse norms have emerged with some common elements, but also considerable variations.[92] The Charter can be seen as muddying the water yet further or as an expression of the EU's positive engagement with diversity. Whichever view is preferred, it confirms that the EU does not view equality as requiring uniformity.

---

[92] See also, Directive 2000/73/EC of the European Parliament and Council of 23 September 2002 amending Council Directive 76/207/EEC on the implementation of the principle of equal treatment for men and women as regards access to employment, vocational training and promotion, and working conditions, OJ 2002 L 269/15.

6

Gender Equalities and the Charter of Fundamental Rights of the European Union

CATHRYN COSTELLO*

INTRODUCTION

GENDER EQUALITY IS the most robust and highly developed aspect of European Union social policy.[1] While other areas of social policy are characterised by shared competences and flexibility of instruments, gender equality has been described as 'federalism encapsulated',[2] long based on an ethos of enforceable individual rights, invocable against Member States and private individuals.[3] Indeed, the enforcement of EU gender equality provisions has been the locus for the development of seminal principles in relation to effective enforcement.[4] It has also been acknowledged that gender equality is not only a central matter of social policy, but also a fundamental right.[5] As early as 1978 in *Defrenne III*,[6] the European Court of Justice (the Court) stated that the 'fundamental personal human rights' guaranteed in the Community legal order included the 'elimination of discrimination based on sex.' Moreover, since the

* BCL, LLM, BL; Lecturer in European Law, University of Dublin; Director, Irish Centre for European Law. Many thanks to Tamara Hervey and Martin Trybus for helpful and insightful comments on the draft and indeed to all the participants at the Nottingham Workshop: *Economic and Social Rights under the EU Charter of Fundamental Rights: A Legal Perspective*, June 2002. In addition, many thanks to John Lister for his research assistance at University of San Francisco School of Law during the summer of 2002 and to my colleague Oran Doyle for his comments.

[1] For a general overview, see C Barnard, 'Gender Equality in the EU: A Balance Sheet' in P Alston (ed), *The European Union and Human Rights* (Oxford, OUP, 1999) 215.

[2] W Streeck, 'Neo-Voluntarism: A New European Social Policy Regime' (1995) 1 *European Law Journal* 31 at 44. But see, the response by C Hoskyns, 'Encapsulating Feminism' (1996) 2 *European Law Journal* 1.

[3] See eg Case 43/75 *Defrenne v SABENA* [1976] ECR 455.

[4] See eg Case 14/83 *Von Colson v Kamann v Land Nordrhein-Westfalen* [1984] ECR 1891; Case C–177/88 *Dekker v Stichting voor Jong Volwassenen (VJV) Plus* [1990] ECR I–3941; Case C–208/90 *Emott v Minister for Social Welfare* [1991] ECR I–4269; Case C–271/91 *Marshall v Southhampton and South West Area Health Authority II* [1993] ECR I–4376.

[5] For an overview, see C Docksey, 'The Principle of Equality between Women and Men as a Fundamental Right under Community Law' (1991) 20 *Industrial Law Journal* 258.

[6] Case 149/77 *Defrenne v Sabena (Defrenne III)* [1978] ECR 1378.

Treaty of Amsterdam, the achievement of gender equality has been elevated to a general objective of the Community under Article 2 EC and a transversal consideration under Article 3(2) EC. The Community gender equality *acquis* is thus highly developed, comprising recently revised Treaty provisions,[7] including those of the Social Policy Agreement, a range of legislative measures,[8] an array of soft law[9] and extensive jurisprudence.[10]

In this context, this chapter addresses what the Charter could possibly add to the existing *acquis*. The drafting of the Charter was ostensibly a codificatory exercise. The Cologne Mandate was concerned with 'making rights more visible.'[11] The visibility aim could be conceived of in a limited sense as simply creating a 'showcase of existing rights.'[12] As we now know, the drafting Convention went beyond this original objective. The creation of a new legal instrument without novel legal effects was inevitably beyond the legal expertise

[7] Art 141 (ex Art 119) EC, Art 13 EC, Art 2 EC and Art 3(2) EC.

[8] Council Dir 75/117/EEC of 10 February 1975 on the approximation of the laws of the Member States relating to the application of the principle of equal pay for men and women OJ 1975 L 45/198; Council Dir 76/207/EEC of 9 February 1976 on the implementation of the principle of equal treatment for men and women as regards access to employment, vocational training and promotion, and working conditions OJ 1976 L 39/40 ('the Equal Treatment Directive' (ETD)); Council Dir 79/7/EEC of 19 December 1978 on the progressive implementation of the principle of equal treatment for men and women in matters of social security OJ 1979 L 6/24; Council Dir 86/378/EEC of 24 July 1986 on the implementation of the principle of equal treatment for men and women in occupational social security schemes OJ 1986 L 225/40; Council Dir 86/613/EEC of 11 December 1986 on the application of the principle of equal treatment between men and women engaged in an activity, including agriculture, in a self-employed capacity, and on the protection of self-employed women during pregnancy and motherhood OJ 1986 L 359/56; Council Dir 92/85/EEC of 19 October 1992 on the introduction of measures to encourage improvements in the safety and health at work of pregnant workers who have recently given birth or are breastfeeding OJ 1992 L 348/1; Council Dir 96/34/EC of 3 June 1996 on the framework agreement on parental leave concluded by UNICE, CEEP and the ETUC OJ 1996 L 145/11, eventually agreed to by the United Kingdom in Council Dir 97/75/EC of 15 December 1997 amending and extending, to the United Kingdom of Great Britain and Northern Ireland, Dir 96/34/EEC on the framework agreement on parental leave concluded by UNICE, CEEP and the ETUC OJ 1997 L 10/24; Council Dir 97/80/EC of 15 December 1997 on the burden of proof in cases of discrimination based on sex OJ 1998 L 14/6, eventually accepted by the United Kingdom in Council Dir 98/52/EC of 13 July 1998 on the extension of Directive 97/80/EC on the burden of proof in cases of discrimination based on sex to the United Kingdom of Great Britain and Northern Ireland OJ 1998 L 205/66.

[9] Commission Communication on the consultation of management and labour on the prevention of sexual harassment at work COM (1996) 378; Council Resolution of 27 March 1995 on the balanced participation of men and women in decision-making OJ 1995 L168; Council Recommendation of December 2 1996 on the balanced participation of men and women in the decision-making process OJ 1996 L 319/11; Council Recommendation 84/635 on the promotion of positive action for women OJ 1984 L 331/34.

[10] For a complete listing and brief account of the jurisprudence of the Court on the interpretation of the prohibitions on gender discrimination in Community law up to July 1998, see European Commission, *Handbook on Equal Treatment for Women and Men in the European Union* 2nd edn (Brussels, Office of Official Publications, 1999).

[11] Cologne European Council Conclusions, Annex IV, para 37 (June 1999).

[12] To employ the metaphor of UK Minister Keith Vaz as noted in the House of Lords Select Committee of European Affairs, Eighth Report, *The EU Charter of Fundamental Rights*, para 55 (16 May 2002). Alternatively it may indeed have a more substantial meaning. Visibility of rights could also relate to the visibility of their exercise and enforcement—visibility requiring vigilance for new subtle forms of infringements and in vulnerable groups.

of the drafters and beyond the limits of self-restraint of the legal epistemic community who interpret the instrument.[13] The Preamble to the Charter recites more ambitious aims including strengthening the protection of fundamental rights 'in the light of changes in society, social progress and scientific and social development.' Thus, it is apparent that through its synthesis of existing protections, and breadth of application, the Charter has introduced gender equality provisions that may have novel effects.

There are at least three different ways in which the Charter may have an impact on the gender equality *acquis*. First, it may anchor gender equality's fundamental rights orientation and help overcome one of the key shortcomings in EU gender equality policy, namely its market orientation.[14] Second, the Charter may reinforce weaker aspects of the *acquis*. Third, the Charter may transform the equality *acquis*, by placing gender equality into the broader equality context, that is, by contextualising gender equality. It is primarily with this third transformative possibility that this chapter is concerned. Until recently, EU gender equality policy was characterised not only by its peculiarly elevated status in Community law, but also by its splendid isolation from other issues of equality, diversity and fundamental rights. This is, of course, explicable not by any particular adherence to gender equality as a particular human value, but rather has its origin in economic concerns.[15] The Community only became competent to deal with other types of discrimination on the entry into force of the Treaty of Amsterdam. In contrast, the Charter deals with a comprehensive range of grounds of discrimination[16] and the entire gamut of civil, political, economic and social rights. In highlighting these other areas, the Charter will lay the foundations to re-shape or even undermine the current parameters of the gender equality *acquis*.

The transformative potential of the Charter is explored in this chapter in two areas, positive action and gender/multiculturalism. The first of these has been the subject of a litigation saga before the Court.[17] The second is novel in the EU

---

[13] Including the organisers and participants in the workshop preceding this collection.

[14] G More, 'Equality of Treatment in European Community Law: the Limits of Market Equality' in A Bottomley (ed), *Feminist Perspectives on the Foundational Subjects of Law* (London, Cavendish, 1996) 261 and 'The Principle of Equal Treatment: From Market Unifier to Fundamental Right' in P Craig and G de Búrca (eds), *The Evolution of EU Law* (Oxford, OUP, 1999) 517; T Hervey & J Shaw, 'Women, Work and Care: Women's Dual Role and Double Burden in EC Sex Equality Law' (1998) 8 *Journal of European Social Policy* 43.

[15] See C Barnard, 'The Economic Origins of Article 119 EEC' in T Hervey & D O'Keeffe (eds), *Sex Equality Law in the European Union* (Chichester, Wiley, 1996) pp 321–34.

[16] Indeed Art 21(1) EUCFR is not limited to the grounds specified therein, which are illustrative only. It states 'Any discrimination based on any ground *such as* sex, race, colour, ethnic or social origin, genetic features, language, religion or belief, political or any other opinion, membership of a national minority, property, birth, disability, age or sexual orientation shall be prohibited.' (emphasis added).

[17] Cases discussed herein are Case C–450/93 *Kalanke v Freie Hansestadt Bremen* [1995] ECR I–3051, Case C–409/95 *Marschall (Hellmut) v Land Nordrhein Westfalen* [1997] ECR I–6363, Case C–158/97 *Badeck and Others* [2000] ECR I–1875, Case C–407/98 *Abrahamsson & Anderson v Fogelqvist* [2000] ECR I–5539, Case C–476/99 *Lommers v Minister van Landbouw, Natuurbeheer en Visserij* [2002] ECR I–2891.

context, but in light of other changes in Community law,[18] is likely to come to the forefront of future legal controversy. What unites these areas is that they throw several key issues in equality law into sharp relief, namely the concept of equality itself, the proper function of equality law, the nature of identity and the interaction between equality and meritocracy.

APPROACHING THE CHARTER

General Interpretative Considerations

A number of case studies are examined in this chapter, in order to explore the difference the Charter would make in resolving key disputes in the gender equality arena. When approaching bills of rights, the indeterminacy of constitutional language must be acknowledged. Typically constitutional bills of rights are 'short and dark'—characterised by terse opaque provisions. Some of the Charter's provisions share these characteristics, making any speculative effort more of a normative than descriptive exercise. However, the Charter's interpretative context is particularly dense, distinguishing it from typical constitutional documents.

The interpretative context includes the Charter's General Provisions, which purport to clarify the scope and effects of the instrument. It should be noted that these are not fixed in stone, and the Convention on the Future of Europe has deliberated on these articles.[19] Nonetheless, an outline of the current provisions is necessary in order to elucidate the synthetic nature of the Charter. A key provision is Article 51(2) EUCFR, which provides that 'the Charter does not establish any new power or task for the Community or Union, or modify powers and tasks defined by the Treaties.' The provisions of Article 52 EUCFR are also relevant, in particular Article 52(2) which provides:

> Rights recognised by this Charter which are based on the Community Treaties or on the Treaty on European Union shall be exercised under the conditions and within the limits defined by those Treaties.

Much turns on the interpretation of 'based on' and whether it requires textual identity with the EC/EU Treaty provisions or whether similarity in purpose is all that is required. The official interpretative notes to the Charter provisions (the

[18] In particular, the inclusion of Art 13 in the post-Amsterdam EC Treaty and two Dirs adopted thereunder, namely Council Dir 2000/43/EC of 29 June 2000 implementing the principle of equal treatment between persons irrespective of racial or ethnic origin OJ 2000 L 180/22 ('the Race and Ethnicity Directive') and Council Dir 2000/78/EC of 27 November 2000 establishing a general framework for equal treatment in employment and occupation OJ 2000 L 303/16 ('the Framework Directive').

[19] See Report to the Convention on the Future of Europe of the Working Group *Incorporation of the Charter/ accession to the ECHR*, CONV 354/02 WG II 16, Brussels, 22 October 2002, available at http://register.consilium.eu.int/pdf/en/02/cv00/00354en2.pdf.

Explanatory Document) purport to clarify this issue by distinguishing between the provisions on which the Charter articles are 'based' and those from which they have merely been 'drawn'. These notes do not, however, purport to have any 'legal value and are simply intended to clarify the provisions'.[20] In addition to attempting to ensure normative coherence with the EU *acquis*, the Charter also attempts to maintain parallelism with the ECHR. Article 52(3) EUCFR provides:

> In so far as the Charter contains rights which correspond to rights guaranteed by the [ECHR], the meaning and scope of those rights shall be the same as those laid down by the [ECHR].

Again, questions arise as to the requisite degree of 'correspondence' between ECHR and Charter provisions.

The drafting history may also provide interpretative guidance. Whether this is desirable has been doubted by one commentator, who has gone so far as to suggest that the Charter would restrict the ability of the judges of the Court to

> use the legal system of each of the Member States as an organic and living laboratory of human rights protection which then, case by case, can be adapted and adopted for the needs of the EU by the Court in dialogue with its national counterparts. A charter may not thwart this process, but it runs the risk of inducing a more inward looking jurisprudence and chilling the constitutional dialogue.[21]

Reference to the *travaux preparatoires* had already been made in the judicial references to the Charter, in particular in *D & Sweden*, in a manner that suggests that the restrictive impact of the *travaux* will be realised.[22]

As well as this dense interpretative context, the development of the Charter is bedevilled by its uncertain status and an uncertain future. It remains to be seen whether the Charter will become legally binding and be integrated into the Treaties.[23] Nevertheless, regardless of whether the Charter becomes part of the

---

[20] This is noted on the contents page of the official version of the Charter: *Charter of Fundamental Rights of the European Union: Explanations relating to the complete text of the Charter* (Brussels, Office for Official Publications of the European Communities, 2001).

[21] JHH Weiler, 'Does the European Union Really Need a Charter of Rights?' (2000) 6 *European Law Journal* 95.

[22] Cases C–122 and C–125/99 P *D & Sweden v Council* [2001] ECR I–4319. In this case, the claimant argued that legally registered same-sex partnerships should be regarded as 'marriages' in the context of the EC Staff Regulations, as failure to do so would amount to a violation of dignity and sexual orientation discrimination. The Court rejected this argument, inter alia, on the basis that it was clear from the drafting history of the Charter that the drafters did not intend that the concept of the right to marry under Art 9 EUCFR entailed a protection for same-sex partnerships.

[23] For a discussion, see S Fredman, C McCrudden & M Freedland, 'An EU Charter of Fundamental Rights' [2000] *Public Law* 178; C McCrudden, Jean Monnet Working Paper No.10/01 'The Future of the EU Charter of Fundamental Rights'; A von Bogdandy, 'The European Union as a Human Rights Organisation? Human Rights and the Core of the European Union' (2000) 37 *Common Market Law Review* 1307; T Eicke, 'The European Charter of Fundamental Rights— Unique Opportunity or Unwelcome Distraction' [2000] *European Human Rights Law Review* 280; I Ward, 'Tempted by Rights: The European Union and its New Charter of Fundamental Rights' (2000–2001) *Constitutional Forum* 112.

Treaties, its unique method of drafting[24] and purported synthetic nature have guaranteed that its provisions will have a continuing resonance in political and legal discourse. The process of norm articulation in the EU is characterised by a tight nexus between legal and political fora and a highly institutionalised and politicised interlocution between the Court and those who plead before it and national judges who refer questions to it.[25] The Charter, if anything, will amplify those tendencies, by providing new ammunition for legal challenges. This is all the more likely as the EU policies take shape in new areas, particularly in creating the 'area of freedom, security and justice' consecrated by the Treaty of Amsterdam. As the broad equality competence under Article 13 EC takes shape, and the common immigration and asylum policies under Title IV EC, the Charter's promise of a strong human rights orientation for the EU may lead to many legal challenges.

The Structure of the Charter/The Structure of the *Acquis*—Normative Dissonance

The Charter contains an entire Chapter entitled 'Equality'. Its key provisions guarantee equality before the law (Article 20); non-discrimination generally (Article 21); cultural, religious and linguistic diversity (Article 22); equality between men and women (Article 23); the rights of the child (Article 24); the rights of the elderly (Article 25) and the integration of persons with disabilities. (Article 26). The Charter does not define equality or discrimination, and indeed enshrines something of a differentiated vision of equality when the Charter is viewed as a whole.[26] Admittedly, the existing *acquis* is also characterised by incoherence as to its underlying vision of equality.[27] The Charter, if anything, amplifies these modulations.[28] What is clear is that the Charter purports to reflect a key feature of the equality *acquis*, namely that equality (which is 'to be ensured') is not captured by any one of its several legal embodiments, be it non-discrimination, equal treatment or equal opportunity. Rather, each of these is an aspect of equality, the latter being a broad multi-faceted guarantee. Indeed, Article 23 EUCFR may be conceived of as embodying a mainstreaming commitment.[29] The language 'must be guaranteed' is tantalising in this regard.

[24] For a discussion of which, see G de Búrca, 'The Drafting of the EU Charter of Fundamental Rights' (2001) 26 *European Law Review* 126.

[25] See eg S Sciarra (ed), *Labour Law in the Courts: National Judges and the European Court of Justice* (Oxford, Hart Publishing, 2001).

[26] See further, M Bell, in this collection.

[27] See C McCrudden, 'Theorising European Equality Law' in C Costello & E Barry (eds) *Equality in Diversity: The New EC Equality Directives* (Dublin, Irish Centre for European Law, 2003, forthcoming) 1.

[28] See further, M Bell, in this collection.

[29] Gender mainstreaming may be understood as: 'The (re)organisation, improvement, development and evaluation of policy processes so that a gender equality perspective is incorporated in all policies at all levels and at all stages, by the actors normally involved in policy making.' Council of

Discrimination, in contrast, has some stable features in the *acquis*, encompassing the now familiar tripartite division of direct and indirect discrimination[30] and harassment.[31] While these are also in likelihood embodied in the Charter, there is a dissonance between the structure of the Charter and the structure of the existing equality *acquis*, which may open up space to reexamine some existing precepts. Articles 21 and 22 EUCFR do not provide for explicit exemptions. On a literal reading, this would exclude the usual exemptions allowed under Community law for gender specific employment,[32] or in order to facilitate pregnancy and childbirth.[33] Traditionally, under Community law any overt differentiation on grounds of sex is treated as direct discrimination, and hence justifiable only on the basis of a specific exemption. This contrasts with indirect discrimination, which may be objectively justified on the basis of a range of policy grounds.[34] Thus, under the Equal Treatment Directive derogations to direct discrimination are limited to an exhaustive list of exemptions.[35] As derogations to the general rule of non-discrimination, the

---

Europe, *Gender Mainstreaming: Conceptual Framework, Methodology and Presentation of Good Practices: Final Report of Activities of the Group of Specialists on Mainstreaming* (EG-S-MS (98)) (Strasbourg, Council of Europe, 1998). For a general discussion, see F Beveridge, S Nott, and K Stephens (eds), *Making Women Count: Integrating Gender into Law and Policy-Making* (Aldershot, Ashgate, 2000).

[30] Case 170/84 *Bilka-Kaufhaus GmbH v Karin Weber von Hartz* [1986] ECR 1607; Case C–127/92 *Enderby v Frenchay Health Authority & the Secretary of State for Health* [1993] ECR I–5535. The Burden of Proof Directive defined indirect discrimination as arising 'where an apparently neutral provision, criterion or practice disadvantages a substantially higher proportion of members of one sex, unless that provision, criterion or practice is appropriate and necessary and can be justified by objective factors unrelated to sex.' Art 2(2) Dir 97/80/EC. Identifying indirect discrimination in practice may be very difficult. See for example Case C–167/97 *R v Secretary of State for Employment, ex parte Nicole Seymour-Smith and Laura Perez* [1999] ECR I–623, discussed by C Barnard and B Hepple, 'Indirect Discrimination: Interpreting *Seymour-Smith*' (1999) 58 *Cambridge Law Journal* 399 and S Moore, 'Casenote' (2000) 37 *Common Market Law Review* 157. The definition of indirect discrimination has now been revised by the 2002 amendment to the Equal Treatment Directive: Parliament and Council Dir 2002/73/EC, 23 September 2002 amending Council Dir 76/207/EEC on the implementation of the principle of equal treatment for men and women as regards access to employment, vocational training and promotion, and working conditions OJ 2002 L 269/15.

[31] As reflected in the Race Directive and the Framework Directive, above n 18, and the recent amendment to the (Gender) Equal Treatment Directive (ETD), which contains definitions of 'harassment' and 'sexual harassment'. There is no shortage of critiques of treating harassment as an equality issue, rather than a dignity issue. See, eg J Dine and B Watt, 'Sexual Harassment: Moving Away from Discrimination' (1995) 58 *Modern Law Review* 343.

[32] Art 2(2) ETD.

[33] Art 2(3) ETD.

[34] See eg, Case 96/80 *Jenkins v Kingsgate* [1981] ECR 911. T Hervey, 'Justification of Indirect Discrimination in Employment: European Community Law and United Kingdom Law Compared' (1991) 40 *International and Comparative Law Quarterly* 807 and *Justifications for Sex Discrimination in Employment* (London, Butterworths, Current European Community Legal Development Series, 1993); M Bell, in this collection, at pp 97–8.

[35] The ETD provides exemptions for sex specific employment (Art 2(2)); protective measures relating in particular to pregnancy and maternity (Art 2(3)) and positive action (Art 2(4)). Thus in Case 222/84 *Johnston v RUC* [1986] ECR 1651 the UK attempted to argue a public safety derogation to the equal treatment guarantee. This was rejected.

exemptions are to be interpreted narrowly.[36] This approach has its difficulties, not least of which is that it trades on the ambiguity of discrimination, treating every gender differentiation as discrimination, requiring justification. In the absence of explicit exemptions, difficulties arise. This is evident in relation to Article 141(1) (formerly Article 119) EC on equal pay, which appears to exclude any differentiation. The Commission suggested in *Birds Eye Walls*[37] that direct pay discrimination could be justified since 'the very concept of discrimination, whether direct or indirect, involves a difference in treatment which is unjusti-fied.'[38] The Court did not accept this argument.

According to this orthodox stance, as the Charter contains no specific exemp-tions (except for positive action under Article 22(2) EUCFR), no differentiation is permissible. The absurdity of the outcome appears to require a departure from this conceptual position. Thus any derogations must be read into the equality clause—where differential treatment is not pernicious, it need not be regarded as discriminatory. Clearly under the Charter, certain differentiations must be permissible and thus fall outside of the prohibition of discrimination altogether. Alternatively, if all differentiations are to be treated as discrimina-tory, then Article 52 EUCFR on the scope of guaranteed rights is relevant. Article 52(1) EUCFR is a general limitative clause, merely requiring that limita-tions are provided for by law, and respect the essence of those rights. This seems to allow for restrictions on all rights protected under the Convention, despite their apparent absoluteness. It may well be that claims based on other protected rights will also effectively carve out further exemptions.

While these legal niceties may seem arcane, my argument is that the restruc-turing of the gender equality guarantee opens the way for a more nuanced con-cept of discrimination, with the potential to revisit some of the inconsistencies evident in the jurisprudence under the Equal Treatment Directive. This argu-ment is illustrated in the following sections with regard to two controversial issues in the gender equality arena: first, the Court's case law on positive action, in particular its most recent ruling in *Lommers*, is re-examined. This case, at the nexus of positive action and family life reconciliation, may be re-examined in light of the Charter's Equality Chapter. Second, some tensions between gender equality and multiculturalism (as enshrined in Article 22 EUCFR) are examined. These tensions are not merely hypothetical, but may well arise in the context of the Race and Ethnicity Discrimination and Framework Directives.

---

[36] This is a general approach in Community law, in the context of market freedoms, as well as non-discrimination.

[37] Case C–132/92 [1993] ECR I–5579.

[38] *Ibid* para 15.

POSITIVE ACTION CONTROVERSIES

An Overview of the Positive Action *Acquis*

The issue of the permissible limits of positive action is one of the most fraught in Community equality law. In the leading case of *Kalanke v Freie-Hansestadt Bremen* the Court dealt what then appeared to be a significant blow to substantive equal treatment.[39] The *Kalanke* ruling was subsequently clarified in *Marschall v Land Nordrhein-Westfalen*.[40] These two cases purport to set down a settled formula to determine the legality of positive action measures in the EU, which has been reiterated in subsequent case law. The formula requires that positive action is permissible only if

it does not automatically and unconditionally give priority to women when women and men are equally qualified, and the candidatures are the subject of an objective assessment which takes account of the specific personal situations of all candidates.[41]

This was subsequently applied in *Badeck*,[42] *Abrahamsson*[43] and *Lommers*.[44] Despite the settled formula, considerable uncertainties persist, reflecting two sources of tension. First, there are deep contradictions in EU positive action jurisprudence, arising out of the failure to identify a coherent rationale for positive action. Second, the Court appears to lack the requisite constitutional gravitas to overturn national policy choices in their entirety, and at times recoils from the full implications of its earlier cases. Thus, greater deference to national policy choices is evident in the later cases in the saga, as the Court tacitly relaxes its standard of review.

Kalanke epitomised the limitations of a formal approach to equality.[45] The condemnation of the positive action measure, despite the fact that it required that candidates be equally qualified, is an example of the conflation of the distinction between discrimination in its neutral and pejorative senses.[46]

---

[39] Case C–450/93 [1995] ECR I–3051.

[40] Case C–409/95 [1997] ECR I–6363.

[41] *Ibid* para 23.

[42] Case C–158/97 [2000] ECR I–1875,

[43] Case C–407/98 *Abrahamsson & Anderson v Fogelqvist* [2000] ECR I–5539.

[44] Case C–476/99 [2002] ECR I–2891.

[45] A sample of the critical literature includes H Dieball, & D Schiek, 'Vereinbarkeit einer sog. Quotenregelung mit dem Gemeinschaftsrecht', *Informationsdienst Europäisches Arbeits- und Sozialrecht* 11/1995, 183–89; H Fenwick, 'Perpetuating Inequality in the Name of Equal Treatment' (1996) 18 *Journal of Social Welfare and Family Law*, 263–70; T Loenen & A Veldman, 'Preferential Treatment in the Labour Market after *Kalanke*: Some Comparative Perspectives' (1996) 12 *International Journal of Comparative Labour Law and Industrial Relations*, 43–53; S Moore, 'Nothing Positive from the Court of Justice' (1996) 21 *European Law Review* 156–61; U O'Hare, 'Positive Action Before the European Court of Justice' (1997) 5 *Web Journal of Current Legal Issues* (http://webjcli.ncl.ac.uk/1997/issue5/o'hare5.html).

[46] In his Opinion, AG Tesauro stated, 'I am convinced that women do not merit the attainment of numerical—and hence only formal—equality—moreover at the cost of *an incontestable violation*

Subsequently, in *Marschall*, the Court appeared to allow wider scope for positive action. However, the reasoning lacked cogency.[47] The rules in *Kalanke* and *Marschall* were virtually identical. One commentator has noted, the decision appears to be 'a persuasive attempt by the ECJ to transform one decision into its opposite'.[49] In *Badeck*[49] the Court was called upon to revisit its earlier jurisprudence. While it reiterated the formula from *Kalanke* and *Marschall*,[50] it left the assessment of the second part to the national court. The first part, relating to 'absolute and unconditional priority' appears to lose its teeth.[51] In effect, once the priority does not amount to the actual award of a position of employment, quite strong preferences may be employed. This ranges from vocational training right up to the selection of candidates for interview. However, the Court left a key issue for assessment by the national court, that is the second part of the formula, whether the candidates are subject to an objective assessment which takes account of their specific personal situations.

In *Abrahamsson*[52] the Swedish scheme of women's professorships[53] was at issue. In principle, the criteria for appointment to educational posts were merit-based. However, sufficiently qualified women could be appointed, provided that disparity between their qualification and those of the (better qualified) men, was not such as to be devoid of objectivity. Thus, the rule here allowed priority to be given even where qualifications were not equal.[54] The Court held that rule

---

of a fundamental value of every civil society: equal rights, equal treatment for all.' (emphasis added). Opinion, para 28. The male applicant, Mr Kalanke had suffered only in so far as it was his gender, rather than any of the other potential non-meritocratic criteria, which disqualified him. As Loenen and Veldman point out, to insist on equal treatment in this case implies that flipping a coin is the desired decisional mechanism. See Loenen & Veldman, *ibid*.

[47] See eg D Schiek, 'Sex Equality after Kalanke and Marschall' (1998) 4 *European Law Journal* 148–66; S Fredman, 'After Kalanke and Marschall: Affirming Affirmative Action'; U O'Hare, 'The Future of Positive Action in the European Union: The *Marschall* Case' (1998) 49 *Northern Ireland Legal Quarterly* 426; A Peters, *Women, Quotas and Constitutions: A Comparative Study of Affirmative Action for Women under American, German, European Community and International Law*, (The Hague, Kluwer Law International, 1999).

[48] L Charpentier, 'The European Court of Justice and the Rhetoric of Affirmative Action' (1998) 4 *European Law Journal* 167.

[49] Case C–158/97 *Badeck and Others* [2000] ECR I–1875.

[50] *Ibid* para 23.

[51] This was so either because it applied where candidates had equal qualifications and fixed a goal based on the number of persons who have received appropriate training or it only related to certain training places (paras 53, 54) or because the measure in question related only to call to interview, rather than appointment decisions (paras 60, 61).

[52] Case C–407/98, [2000] ECR I–5539.

[53] The background to the positive action provision is instructive. Following the realisation that achieving equal division between the sexes in education had been particularly slow, a specific law was introduced in order to foster equality in appointments as professors and research assistants. Thirty professorial positions were created as part of the programme, and positive action applied in the selection of candidates to the positions. A constitutional amendment was made to the Swedish constitution to facilitate these changes.

[54] Para 45.

amounted to an automatic priority.[55] Given the uncertain nature of the objectivity caveat, the assessment of the candidates was inadequate.

Overall, these cases reflect an attempt by the Court to walk a tightrope between individual and group conceptions of equality. Individual equality is to be ensured, and yet group-based assumptions of disadvantage are permissible. The crux of the cases, whether the measures require the requisite degree of scrutiny of individual circumstances, is ill-specified and ill-fitting.[56] The most recent case of *Lommers*[57] adds a further layer of uncertainty. At issue was the refusal of access to a subsidised nursery for the children of male civil servants. The Court effectively upheld this practice, stating that Article 2(4) of the Equal Treatment Directive (ETD) was 'specifically and exclusively designed to authorise measures which, although discriminatory in appearance' were 'in fact intended to eliminate or reduce actual instances of inequality which may exist in the reality of social life.' The Court characterised the measure as allowing women to 'pursue a career on an equal footing with men.'[58] Once the measure was proportionate (a matter again for the national court), it was justifiable.[59] One cannot but be concerned with the implications of the decision of issues of work/life balance. The case represents the coming together of the increased flexibility accorded to Member States under Article 2(4) ETD and the Court's regression on the issue of special provision for mothers under Article 2(3) ETD.[60] While a line of cases advocates equal treatment of mothers and fathers

---

[55] Para 51.

[56] The Court has failed to articulate which particular individual circumstance are relevant in this regard. In *Badeck*, AG Saggio discussed this matter in some detail. He stated, 'In my view, what the Court has described as a saving clause is of central importance in the context of the judgement: notwithstanding the requirement to give priority to female candidates, it allows other candidates to be considered and lessens the discriminatory effect of that requirement on those candidates. According to the Court, a system of quotas is sufficiently flexible and may therefore fall within the scope of Article 2(4) of the Directive if the positive action does not prevent the employer from disregarding the requirement to recruit an equally well qualified woman in the light of subjective and/or objective circumstances pertaining to the lives of the candidates, notably the male candidates. Reference to such circumstances must not however have discriminatory effects on the selection of women. Thus, for example, the criterion of length of service, which is usually taken into consideration in assessing candidates' suitability, must not be applied in a manner that discriminates against female candidates.' (Opinion, para 31).

[57] Case C–476/99 *Lommers* [2002] ECR I–2891.

[58] Judgement, para 32, citing *Kalanke,* paras 18 and 19, *Marschall,* paras 26 and 27, and *Badeck* para 19.

[59] The Court did give guidance to the national court in order to carry out the proportionality assessment. It began by noting the danger that the measure would help to perpetuate a traditional division of roles between men and women (para 41). In addition, the Court pointed out that many women in the Ministry were unable to access nursery places (para 43). Thirdly, it was noted that men could access childcare in the private sector, (para 44). This was interpreted so as to allow male officials who bring up their children by themselves to have access to the nursery scheme at issue (para 45). Fourthly, the Court referred to the emergency provision for male employees (para 46).

[60] Art 2(3) ETD provides, 'This Directive shall be without prejudice to provisions concerning the protection of women, particularly as regards pregnancy and maternity.' For discussion, see generally, C McGlynn, 'Families and the European Union Charter of Fundamental Rights: Progressive Change or Entrenching the Status Quo' (2001) 26 *European Law Review* 582.

in most instances,[61] more recent cases have heralded a shift away from this gender neutral approach.[62] *Lommers* is nonetheless extraordinary. While not explicitly based on any biological or psychological assumptions on the role of mothers, it accepts that motherhood constitutes an impediment to work which fatherhood does not.

The Impact of the Charter on Positive Action

The Charter may impact on the positive action *acquis* in three ways.

(a) The Missing Link—Standard of Review

First, the *acquis* in this area is unstable because of the failure of the Court to articulate its standard of review. Cases such as *Kalanke, Marshall* and *Lommers* represent, in all but form, the exercise of constitutional-type review by the Court. The Court in effect determines the compatibility of the national measure with the Community principle of gender equality. Comparative constitutional experience suggests that determining the appropriate standard of judicial review should be a central preoccupation in such jurisprudence.[63] However, the peculiarities of the preliminary reference procedure, the locus for most such cases,[64]

---

[61] Under Art 2(3) ETD, the Court was initially indulgent of national laws that granted special rights to mothers. See Case 184/83 *Hofmann v Barmer Ersatzkasse* [1984] ECR 3047. However, a significant change came about in Case 312/86 *Commission v France* [1986] ECR 6316, where the Court struck down various provisions of French law which included leave to care for sick children, payments for childcare expenses and additional day's holiday for each child. Although the Court there acknowledged that the exception provided for in Art 2(3) refers in particular to the situations of pregnancy and maternity, these special rights related to the protection of women in their capacity as parents, categories to which both men and women may equally belong, they could not be justified under Art 2(3). For discussion, see H Fenwick & T Hervey, 'Sex Equality in the Single Market: New Directions for the European Court of Justice' (1995) 32 *Common Market Law Review* 443. But see M Barbera, in this collection, before fn 3, who is critical of a gender-neutral approach to policies which aim to reconcile paid work and family life.

[62] Case C–218/98 *Abdoulaye and others* [1999] ECR I–5723; Case C–243/95 *Hill & Stapleton v Revenue Commissioners* [1998] ECR I–3739; Case C–333/97 *Lewen v Denda* [1999] ECR I–7243. For a discussion of Abdoulaye, see C McGlynn, 'Pregnancy, parenthood and the Court of Justice in Abdoulaye' (2000) 25 *European Law Review* 654.

[63] In constitutional jurisprudence in the USA, the appropriate degree of scrutiny for classification is the predominant focus of judicial and academic comment. See eg N Duncan, 'Croson Revisited: A Legacy of Uncertainty in the Application of Strict Scrutiny' (1995) 26 *Columbia Human Rights Law Review* 679; J Galotto, 'Strict Scrutiny for Gender, via Croson' (1993) 93 *Columbia Law Review* 508.

[64] At the outset, the Court acknowledged that the preliminary reference procedure had a role in ensuring that Member States complied with their Community law obligations. In Case 26/62 *Van Gend en Loos* [1963] ECR 1, it justified the doctrine of direct effect on the basis inter alia that, 'The vigilance of individuals concerned to protect their rights amounts to an effective supervision in addition to the supervision entrusted by Articles 169 and 170 to the diligence of the Commission and the Member States.' The preliminary reference procedure allows questions on the compatibility of national measures with Community law to be recast as questions on the interpretation of Community law. Again in the seminal case of Case 6/64 *Costa v ENEL* [1964] ECR 585, the Court stated that it 'ha[d] the power to extract from a question imperfectly formulated by the national courts those questions which alone pertain to the interpretation of the Treaty'.

are such that a legal charade is engaged in, wherein the Court purports not to examine the validity of those national measures, but rather to give abstract generalised interpretations of the Community provisions for the national court to apply. Thus no standard of review is articulated, as formally, no judicial review of national measures is undertaken. Neither will the Court define the appropriate standard of review for the national court, as this would be to impinge upon national judicial autonomy. In addition, the division of labour between the Court and the national referring court, along the interpretation/application fault-line, is a shifting one. On occasions, difficult fact-specific issues may be left to the national court to assess. On others, detailed fact-specific 'interpretative' guidance may be given, effectively determining the entire factual matrix.[65] In the positive action context, this is evident in relation to the issue of whether the candidates' assessment entails the requisite (and altogether ill-defined) degree of scrutiny of individual circumstances.

The Charter does not change the institutional mechanisms of the preliminary reference, nor does it alter the Community judicial function. Indeed, although significant changes to the Court's jurisdiction were agreed at Nice, these do not alter the basic features of the preliminary reference.[66] However, I suggest that the Charter 'lets the cat out of the bag' as to the nature of the judicial exercise in deciding on the compatibility of national practices with Community law, as the constitutional nature of the exercise becomes more explicit.[67] Advocate General Jacobs in *Marschall* opined that whether or not the policy of positive action is 'desirable or appropriate' was for the legislature, but that the Court's role was merely to 'interpret existing legislation.'[68] If the Charter is brought into the equation, it becomes more difficult for the Court to indulge in such apparent restraint. The point is not that the current approach is truly merely interpretative, but rather that by defining its judicial task in these non-contentious terms, the Court inevitably fails in its existing constitutional duties. The result is not a satisfactory jurisprudence, but rather one marred by formalist tendencies, including repeating abstract formulae,

---

[65] One of the best examples of varying approaches to the specificity of preliminary rulings arose in the context of several references from UK courts concerning the compatibility of rules prohibiting retail outlets trading on Sundays with Art 28 (ex Art 30) EC. At the time, these cases turned on whether the restriction to trade was proportionate. In the first rulings, the Court provided little guidance on the proportionality issue. Eventually the matter was re-referred in terms demanding a response to the proportionality issue. See A Arnull, 'What shall we do on Sunday' (1991) 16 *European Law Review* 112, also discussed in M Poiares Maduro, *We the Court, The European Court of Justice and the Economic Constitution* (Oxford, Hart Publishing, 1998) esp 30–34.

[66] P Craig, 'The jurisdiction of the Community Courts reconsidered' in JHH Weiler & G De Búrca (eds), *The European Court of Justice* (Oxford, OUP, 2001) 177. See also C Costello, 'The Preliminary Reference Procedure and the 2000 Intergovermental Conference' (1999) *Dublin University Law Journal* 40; and 'The Court' in *IGC 2000: Issues, Options and Implications* (Institute of European Affairs, November 2000) 78.

[67] See M Poiares Maduro, in this collection.

[68] Opinion, para 46.

failing to articulate underlying value issues, and presenting outcomes as textually determined.[69]

The Charter may thus prompt a highly desirable change in judicial mindset. Certain deference is due to national policy choices in the equality field, and yet too deferential a standard of review may render the equality provisions ethereal. It is only in expressing these tensions that a satisfactory outcome is possible. In the positive action context, given the diversity of national and regional policy choices, it may well be desirable to have a somewhat deferential standard of review.[70] This is arguably evidenced in the evolution from *Kalanke* to *Lommers*. However, as this is merely subtext, one cannot be sure. The alternative, less flattering, construction is that the Court wishes to avoid all controversy in the positive action field, so much so that it is willing to absolve any practice once it is tied to an ostensible positive action rationale. This cynical explanation is tempting particularly in relation to *Lommers*. While articulating a standard of review would not necessarily determine the outcomes of such cases, it would prevent some of the more dramatic u-turns and violent reinterpretations of the content of the purportedly 'settled formula.'

(b) The Positive Action Provisions

The Charter contains explicit provisions on positive action, which also require scrutiny. Unlike other traditional 'exemptions' to the equal treatment guarantee, the Charter does contain explicit allowance for positive action. In particular, Article 23(2) EUCFR provides that the 'principle of equality shall not prevent the maintenance or adoption of measures providing for specific advantages in favour of the under-represented sex.' This provision will not settle the law on positive action, as the tensions in the existing *acquis* derive from dissonant models of equality. The Charter fails to articulate any clear understanding of equality, displaying adherence to equality as rationality, opportunity, recognition, participation and result at once, replicating, or perhaps even exacerbating the tensions evident in the Equal Treatment Directive and Article 141(4) EC.

Article 141(4) EC provides:

> With a view to ensuring full equality in practice between men and women in working life, the principle of equal treatment shall not prevent any Member State from maintaining or adopting measures providing for specific advantages in order to make it easier for the under-represented sex to pursue vocational activity or to prevent or compensate for disadvantages in professional careers.

---

[69] For a general critique of the Court's style of reasoning, see JHH Weiler, 'Epilogue: The Judicial Après Nice' in JHH Weiler & G de Búrca (eds), *The European Court of Justice* (Oxford, OUP, 2001) 215.

[70] For a developed argument along these lines, see D Caruso, 'Limits of the Classic Method: Positive Action in the European Union after the New Equality Directives' Jean Monnet Working Paper 10/02.

Also pertinent is ex-Article 6(3) of the Agreement on Social Policy, which states:

> This Article shall not prevent any Member State from maintaining or adopting measures providing for specific advantages in order to make it easier for women to pursue a vocational activity or to prevent or compensate for disadvantages in their professional careers.

This extends to derogations from the equal pay guarantee.[71] If, as the Explanatory Document implies, Article 23 EUCFR is based on Article 141 EC, then the provisions of Article 52(2) EUCFR may be relevant. However, this is only the case if positive action is conceived of as a limitation or condition on equal treatment. This may well not be the case, since positive action is a means to achieve equality, rather than an exception to it. A textual analysis reveals that Article 23(2) EUCFR is broader than Article 141 EC.

First, as regards the conditions governing the legality of positive action, Article 141(4) EC refers to only two types of measures, namely those which make it easier to pursue vocational activity or compensate for career disadvantages. In contrast, Article 23(2) EUCFR refers simply to 'specific advantages' without specification. Tying positive action to a compensatory rationale could potentially limit its scope of permissible positive action. In the USA for example, the compensatory rationale has been employed to undermine group-based assumptions of disadvantage and ultimately to reduce the scope for positive action. Thus affirmative action measures have been struck down as insufficiently narrowly tailored, where they operate on the premise of past discrimination against groups.[72] Thus far, this difficulty has not been evident in the Court's jurisprudence post-*Marschall,* as the Court has accepted generalised assumptions in relation to women's career disadvantage.[73] Second, Article 141(4) EC refers to the achievement of equality 'in working life,' whereas Article 23(2) EUCFR contains no such limitation. Article 141(4) EC may potentially allow for measures that would facilitate equality at work, but perpetuate inequality at home.[74] Overall then, the broader, more facilitative language of the Charter may avoid some of these potential pitfalls of the Treaty provision.

---

[71] See, eg Case C–366/99 *Griesmar v Minister de l'Economie, des Finances et de l'industrie* [2001] ECR I–9383.

[72] Very often, the restrictive effects come from objections that general assumptions of disadvantage are overbroad. Eg in *City of Richmond v Croson* 448 US 448, 487 (1980), the US Supreme Court stated that 'the interest of avoiding the bureaucratic effort necessary to tailor remedial relief to those who truly have suffered the effects of prior discrimination cannot justify a rigid line drawn on the basis of a suspect classification.'

[73] Most notably in *Marschall*, the Court accepted the generalisation that 'male candidates tend to be promoted in preference to equally qualified women particularly because of prejudices or stereotypes concerning the role and capacities of women in working life'. Thus, 'the mere fact that a male candidate and a female candidate are equally qualified does not mean that they have the same chances'. (Judgment, paras 29–30.)

[74] Case C–476/99 *Lommers* [2002] ECR I–2891.

(c) Contextualisation

The third manner in which the Charter may re-orientate the positive action *acquis* is by contextualising the positive action issue, in particular as it pertains to measures which impact on childcare and work/life balance. That such measures can be conceived of and indeed justified in positive action terms is exemplified in *Lommers*. The Charter contains two provisions that bring competing rights and interests to the analysis. These are Article 24 EUCFR on the rights of the child[75] and Article 33 EUCFR on family and professional life.[76]

These provisions of Article 24 EUCFR are described as inspired by the provisions of the UN Convention on the Rights of the Child (CRC). The CRC is extraordinarily broad in its scope, covering all the traditional areas of human rights in an indivisible manner. It is also the most detailed and comprehensive of all international human rights instruments,[77] inspired by three core principles—protection, provision and participation. The provisions of Article 24(2) EUCFR mirror those of Article 3 CRC, enshrining the 'best interests of the child' as a 'primary consideration' in 'actions relating to children.'[78] This standard is familiar from family law, in particular from disputes concerning custody, adoption and maintenance of children. It is also enshrined in the Convention on the Elimination of All Forms of Discrimination against Women 1979 (CEDAW).[79] Its influence has been noted in the jurisprudence of the European Court of Human Rights.[80]

Article 24 EUCFR has an apparently all-encompassing scope covering action 'relating to' children. In contrast, the CRC applies to actions 'concerning' children. Both the employed prepositions and the reference to children (as opposed to 'the child') indicate that a broad range of policy decisions is at issue. Of course, some degree of direct impact on children is required in both instances, but the positive action decisions which affect childcare and work/life balance fall clearly within its ambit. Indeed in some UN reports it is treated as of equally broad application as the general principle of non-discrimination.

---

[75] See generally C McGlynn, 'Rights for Children?; The Potential Impact of the European Union Charter of Fundamental Rights' (2002) 8 *European Public Law* 387.

[76] See generally, C McGlynn, 'Families and the European Union Charter of Fundamental Rights: Progressive Change or Entrenching the Status Quo' (2001) 26 *European Law Review* 582.

[77] P Alston, *The Best Interests of the Child: Reconciling Culture and Human Rights* (Clarendon Press, Oxford, 1994) 2.

[78] Indeed the 'best interest' standard is reiterated throughout the CRC in relation to the separation of the child from the family setting (Art 9); parental responsibility (Art 18); adoption (Arts 20 and 21) and the police and judicial system (Arts 37 and 40).

[79] Art 5b CEDAW obliges parties to take all appropriate measures: 'To ensure that family education includes a proper understanding of maternity as a social function and the recognition of the common responsibility of men and women in the upbringing and development of their children, it being understood that the interest of the children is the primordial consideration in all cases.' Art 16(1)(d) CEDAW provides that in all matters relating to marriage and family matters 'the interests of the children shall be paramount.'

[80] U Kilkelly, *The Child and the European Convention on Human Rights* (Aldershot, Ashgate/Dartmouth, 1999).

As to the substance of the provision, while it does not specify outcomes, it does impose a generally applicable standard. However, despite its ubiquity, the 'best interests' standard has yet to acquire 'much specific content or to be the subject of any sustained analysis designed to shed light on its precise meaning.'[81] What it does require though, is that decisions are to be considered though a particular prism. That prism may be used to re-evaluate the Dutch measure in *Lommers*.

It will be recalled that Mr Lommers was denied access to subsidised childcare on grounds of his gender. He sought to have his wife taken into account, arguing that depriving him of access to subsidised childcare impeded her career development. The Court refused to examine this argument, stating that it could only examine differences in treatment between employees of the same employer. Thus the impact on Lommers's wife was immaterial. But what of baby Lommers? If Article 24 EUCFR were taken into account in this case (along with the pertinent provisions of the ETD and Article 22 EUCFR), the process of reasoning would be different. According to the Minister, the particular needs of the child were not taken into account. The primary consideration in the allocation of childcare places was the desire to enhance women's ability to progress in the workplace. The best interests of the child were not given any consideration, let alone accorded the status of 'a primary consideration'. Children were conceived of only as barriers to work.[82] If the 'best interests' of the child were factored into the decision in relation to the allocation of childcare places, it would be difficult, if not impossible, to justify allocation based on the gender of parents. The child's interests may well, for example, dictate that places are allocated according to the special needs of children, needier children requiring a child care facility in proximity to a parent. Whatever the particular outcome the allocation of places would have to be focused on the child's interests, rather than solely on the parents' gender.

Taking this analysis further, a new framework to analyse the Community's approach to work/life balance issues emerges. The Community equality *acquis* is replete with mixed messages in relation to gender-specific treatment and child-rearing.[83] Admittedly, the explicit provisions of the Charter on reconciliation of working and family life in Article 33 EUCFR appear to copperfasten the differentiation currently existing in Community legislative measures. McGlynn has described Article 33 EUCFR as:

> simply [restating] existing entitlements under the Pregnancy and Maternity Directive and the Parental Leave Directive. In particular, the omission of a reference to 'paid' parental leave is notable. Faced with a challenge to existing Community provisions on

---

[81] Alston, above n 77 at 4.

[82] Such marginalisation of children is prevalent in the Community *acquis*. See eg H Stalford, 'The Developing European Agenda on Children's Rights' (2000) 22 *Journal of Social Welfare and Family Law* 229.

[83] See n 61 and n 62 above.

reconciliation, it seems that there is little in this article which an Advocate General or the Court could use to develop and enhance the law.[84]

It contrasts sharply with an earlier draft, which provided that everyone shall have the right to reconcile their family and professional lives.[85] In light of the inert nature of Article 33 EUCFR, recourse to Articles 22 and 24 EUCFR may be more fruitful in prompting re-evaluation of that *acquis*. That re-evaluation is, in my view, highly desirable, as gender neutral policies on family life are a prerequisite so that reconciliation policies do not compound gender stereotypes and unfairly denigrate the role of fathers.[86]

THE MULTICULTURALISM WARS

The preceding section illustrates that Community law on positive action is marred by legal formalism and an incoherent vision of equality. What lies ahead in the equality field may prove even more challenging, as the scope of Community equality and human rights law extends to issues on the multiculturalism agenda.[87] This is unfamiliar terrain for the EU. While gender equality is a relatively entrenched aspect of liberal-democracy and egalitarianism, and has a particularly elevated place in EU social law, the place of multiculturalism is contested. In the past, the EU has avoided these debates by confining its equality role to gender and nationality issues, and conceiving of 'culture' as a domestic issue, of national concern and competence.[88] Thus, the protection of diversity in the Community *acquis* refers essentially to national or regional diversity. The Preamble of the Treaty on European Union refers to the desire to deepen solidarity between the peoples of Europe, 'whilst respecting their history, their culture and their traditions.' Article 6 TEU provides 'the Union shall respect the national identities of its Member States'. Article 151 EC states that the Community contributes to the 'flowering of the cultures of the Member States, while respecting national and regional diversity.' Cultural aspects should be taken into account in order to 'respect and promote the diversity of its cultures.'

The articulation of the explicit guarantee in Article 22 EUCFR is thus significant. It is characterised by mandatory language, and an all-embracing scope of application. Most significantly, it refers not to national or regional diversity, but rather cultural, religious and linguistic difference.[89] This is one of the first

---

[84] C McGlynn, 'Reclaiming a Feminist Vision: The Reconciliation of Paid Work and Family Life in European Union Law and Policy' (2001) 7 *Columbia Journal of European Law* 241 at 262.

[85] Draft Charter of Fundamental Rights of the European Union, Charter 4422/00, 28 July 2000, Art 31, available at http://db.consilium.eu.int/dfdocs/EN/04422en.pdf.

[86] But see M Barbera, in this collection, at pp 140–41.

[87] See further Wallace and Shaw, in this collection.

[88] This is illustrated in Cases 281, 283, 285, 287/85 *Germany v Commission* [1987] ECR 3203.

[89] For a discussion, see G Schwellnus, 'Much Ado About Nothing?' Minority Protection and the EU Charter of Fundamental Rights' ConWEB 5/2001, available at http://les1.man.ac.uk/conweb/.

acknowledgements that diversity matters within, as well as between Member States, are of EU concern.

These guarantees will take on particular significance in light of the expansion of the Community equality agenda post-Amsterdam embodied in the Framework and Race and Ethnicity Directives.[90] Particularly in light of the absence of a definition of 'race and ethnicity' in the latter Directive, and its broad definition of indirect discrimination, Article 22 EUCFR may bolster claims for accommodation of diverse cultural practices within the EU. Chalmers cites as disputes that could come within its ambit:

> restrictions on the preparation of Halal meat; allocation of housing by municipal authorities; employer bans on the playing of rap music on grounds of its misogynistic content; bans on wearing of the veil in school; the criminalisation of marijuana.[91]

Chalmers' choice of contentious issues is thus noteworthy, in that several are gender sensitive ones. This aspect of the multiculturalism agenda, that is, the tension between respect for cultural diversity and gender equality, is of concern here. Of particular concern is how Article 22 EUCFR may impact on gender equality, particularly if Article 22 is conceived of as embodying group-based cultural rights. EU law is set to become the locus for battles in the multiculturalism wars.[92]

Gender and Multiculturalism—the Political Discourse

Elsewhere in this volume, Wallace and Shaw refer to Raz's work on multiculturalism—'a heightened awareness of certain issues and certain needs people encounter in today's political reality'.[93] Thus, multiculturalism is a new sensitivity, a respect for diversity, rather than a discrete sets of rights or policies. Diversity is itself perceived as moral value. They argue that 'any strategy for promoting respect for cultural diversity must be able to negotiate these clashes [between gender equality and respect for diversity]'.[94] What remains to be seen, however, is how such clashes are to be appropriately negotiated. Various approaches have been advocated.

In a provocative essay, Moller Okin argues that multiculturalism and feminism are in 'tension' and sometimes even in opposition to each other. She argues

---

[90] Above n 18.

[91] D Chalmers, 'The Mistakes of the Good European?' Queen's Papers on Europeanisation No. 7/2000, available at http://www.qub.ac.uk/ies/onlinepapers/poe7.pdf 21. This paper has now been formally published in S Fredman (ed) *Discrimination and Human Rights: The Case of Racism* (Oxford, OUP, 2001) 193.

[92] The reference to the multiculturalism wars is taken from Kymlicka. See W Kymlicka, 'An Update from the Multiculturalism Wars: Commentary on Schachar and Spinner-Halev' in S Lukes and C Joppke (eds), *Multicultural Questions*, (Oxford, OUP, 1999) 112.

[93] See Wallace and Shaw, in this collection, at p 227.

[94] See Wallace and Shaw, in this collection, at p 228.

that defenders of 'cultural' and 'group rights' for minority cultures have failed to notice that there are considerable differences of power within those cultures, and that those differences are gendered, with men having power over women. A supporter has expressed the dilemma pithily:

> in its demand for equality for women, feminism sets itself in opposition to virtually every culture on earth. You could say multiculturalism demands respect for all cultural traditions, while feminism interrogates and challenges all cultural traditions. . . . [F]undamentally, the ethical claims of feminism run counter to the cultural relativism of 'group' rights multiculturalism.[95]

Perceived clashes between gender equality and cultural recognition arise in such diverse areas as female genital mutilation, violence against women,[96] polygamous marriages, veiling and restriction of access to the public sphere generally.

In this vein, Kymlicka, the chief liberal proponent on minority group rights,[97] acknowledges that his theory of liberal multiculturalism does not tolerate 'internal restrictions' on members of minority groups, as these violate the autonomy of individuals and create injustice within the group. Rather, it is concerned with claims to 'external protections' the group may claim against the majority. Thus, he argues that the right to gender equality is a limiting condition of minority rights. Similarly Taylor only considers that cultures should be supported where they contribute to benign forms of individual identity and are not suppressive or exclusive.[98] In this regard, much turns on what is conceived of as an 'internal restriction' in Kymlicka's sense or 'suppressive' for Taylor. It would appear that very different visions of gender equality issues may well emerge under these approaches.

In contrast, Moller Okin, in her thought-provoking, if polemical contribution to the debate, treats the recognition of gender equality as a non-negotiable condition for any policies of multiculturalism and any recognition of minority rights.[99] This, however, fails to acknowledge the importance women themselves may attach to their culture. However, if gender equality is limited in favour of group rights, this ignores the protection of sub-groups, notably women, within minority cultures. While limiting the principle of non-discrimination in certain

---

[95] K Pollitt, 'Whose Culture?' in S Moller Okin & Respondents, *Is Multiculturalism Bad for Women?* (New Jersey, Princeton University Press, 1999) 27–34.

[96] Most notoriously, in the USA some courts have accepted a 'cultural defence' in wife-murder cases. For discussion of such cases, see for example, D L Coleman, 'Individualizing Justice though Multiculturalism: The Liberal's Dilemma' (1996) 96 *Columbia Law Review* 1093; NS Kim, 'The Cultural Defense and the Problems of Cultural Preemption: A Framework for Analysis' (1997) *New Mexico Law Review* 101.

[97] W Kymlicka, *Multicultural Citizenship; A Liberal Theory of Minority Rights* (Oxford, Oxford University Press, 1995).

[99] C Taylor, 'The Politics of Recognition' in A Gutmann (ed), *Multiculturalism: Examining the Politics of Recognition* (New Jersey, Princeton University Press, 1994) 51.

[99] S Moller Okin, 'Feminism and Multiculturalism: Some Tensions' (1998) *Ethics* 108; S Moller Okin and Respondents, *Is Multiculturalism Bad for Women?* (New Jersey, Princeton University Press, 1999).

contexts may be acceptable, any automatic rule of priority is undesirable, due to its tendency to calcify cultural practices.

Other approaches focus on the need for political dialogue to diffuse these apparent tensions. In this vein Parekh argues that specific mechanisms should be established to evaluate disputed practices in an intercultural manner.[100] A more gender-sensitive process-based view is that propounded by Schachar, which advocates promoting methods of empowerment that will enable women within each cultural group to participate more forcefully in determining the principles and practices of their culture.[101] This approach is well-reasoned and has much to recommend it. However it is a long-term strategy. The legal resolution of these disputes will not be avoided. While political solutions are required, the legal arena will, in likelihood, be occupied with these disputes also.

An approach that appears appropriate in the legal context under examination is to conceptualise these issues as competing equality claims. This appears to 'fit' the structure of the Charter, which places both guarantees under the general 'equality' rubric. Its greatest advantage is to avoid the either/or dilemmas of the most strident participants in the debate[102] and to emphasise the parallels between various forms of inequality. In this respect, it avoids one of the most disturbing features of the current political discourse on ethnic minorities in Europe, namely to view gender equality as a particularly 'European' value, to be contrasted with less evolved cultures, which are characterised by unaltered patriarchal structures. Such arguments have a certain political resonance, but the reality should be borne in mind. First, the elevated position of gender equality in EU policy is a matter of happenstance. The original economic aims of Article 119 EEC, the saga of the activation by strategic litigants, and later institutionalised development into a market-orientated gender equality policy, reminds that gender equality was and remains a struggle, not a *fait accompli* in Europe.[103] Second, the notion that other cultures are inherently more sexist is clearly open to question.

In the debate on the intersection between gender and race/ethnicity equality, the value of multiculturalism must be brought to bear in order to avoid this caricature euro-centrism. Conceiving of multiculturalism as establishing competing equality claims has several advantages in this regard. First, this avoids the strictures of treating one or other as 'exceptions' to the general guarantee, which legally leads to a narrow construction of exceptions and an exacting standard of

---

[100] B Parekh, *Rethinking Multiculturalism: Cultural Diversity and Political Theory* (London, Palgrave Press, 2000). See also J Spinner-Halev, *Surviving Diversity: Religion and Democratic Citizenship* (Baltimore, Johns Hopkins University Press, 2000).

[101] A Schachar, *Multicultural Jurisdictions: Cultural Differences and Women's Rights* (Cambridge, Cambridge University Press, 2001).

[102] S Moller Okin, above n 95, cf B Barry, *Culture and Equality: An Egalitarian Critique of Multiculturalism* (Cambridge, Polity Press, 2001) and 'The Muddles of Multiculturalism' (2001) *New Left Review* 56.

[103] See for example, C Hoskyns, *Integrating Gender—Women, Law and Politics in the European Union* (London, Verso, 1996).

review. Second, it emphasises the commonality of purpose between gender equality and multiculturalism guarantees. Third, it is likely to facilitate fact-specific case-by-case outcomes, rather than pre-empting deliberation and evaluation of the various practices deemed 'cultural'. Finally, it is likely to lead to sensitivity to local policy choices.

However, the 'competing equality claims' approach is not without its detractors. Phillips notes several drawbacks,[104] principally that it sets up gender and culture as distinct systems. This may reinforce patriarchal interpretations of cultural practices and even the 'reactive culturalism' identified by Schachar.[105] It also threatens to impose a clichéd version of cultures.[106] In addition, she argues that this approach leads to a tendency to treat such issues in a judicial manner. This drawback may be unavoidable in the context of the current discussion. In particular, Phillips notes that the gender/culture debate is more often than not mobilised in the context of discourses that egalitarians may wish to avoid—anti-immigrant and anti-Muslim in particular. One need only cite the recent curtailment of the right of family reunification in Denmark, justified by the need to protect certain 'European values' in the face of the sexist practice of arranged and forced marriage, in order to appreciate this threat.[107] The gender/culture debate has negative aspects, which can only be avoided if, in reconciling these issues, we 'do not feed on and into cultural stereotypes'.[108]

The chapter now turns to examine the pertinent legal responses, in order to consider whether that challenge will be met by the provisions in the Charter, within the context of other relevant international and EU law.

---

[104] A Phillips, 'If it's all about equality, what's wrong with competing equality claims?' Paper prepared for conference on 'Minorities within Minorities: Equality, Rights and Diversity', University of Nebraska at Lincoln, 4–5 October 2002, on file with the author.

[105] Schachar defines 'reactive culturalism' as one of the ways in which group members may respond to assimilationist pressures, all of which raise challenges for the multicultural state. It is a response 'aimed at group self-preservation which takes as its goal the maintenance of a separate and distinct ethos. It may in the process, however, enforce hierarchical and rigid interpretations of group traditions which can, once multiculturalism is introduced into the equation, exacerbate the costs imposed upon traditionally less powerful group members.' A Schachar, above n 101, 11.

[106] U Narayan, *Dis/locating Cultures/Identitites, Traditions, and Third World Feminism* (London, Routledge, 1997). See also L Volpp, 'Blaming Culture for Bad Behaviour' (2000) *Yale Journal of Law and the Humanities* 89.

[107] Bertel Haarder, the Danish Immigration Minister, said that he was trying to protect young immigrant women with the new restrictive law on family reunification introduced in 2002: 'The vast majority of immigrant marriages are arranged marriages. If you are 18 years old and everyone says that you have to marry your cousin—and it usually is cousins in Pakistan—how can you resist? We are fed up with forced marriages and the systematic use of the right of family reunification to get families to Denmark at the expense of the young. For a Nordic mind this is a huge offence to freedom, human dignity and self-determination and something we Danes simply cannot accept.' Source: Migration News (August 2002), available at http://migration.ucdavis.edu/mn/Archive_MN/aug_2002-08mn.html.

[108] See Phillips, above n 104, 21.

The International and EU *Acquis* on Gender/Multiculturalism

(i) CEDAW

In contrast to the subtleties of the political discourse outlined above, the international legal framework purports to establish a clear normative hierarchy between cultural diversity and gender equality. Articles 2(f) and 5(a) CEDAW require states to take all appropriate measures to modify or abolish customs, practices and social and cultural patterns of conduct that constitute discrimination or that are based on the idea of inferiority or on stereotyped roles for women.

However, this purported hierarchy is undermined by the wide reservations permitted to states parties under CEDAW.[109] An overview of these reservations reveals that they relate principally to the maintenance of cultural practices.[110] Most notably, many states have made reservations stating that they do not consider themselves subject to Article 2 CEDAW as regards Islamic law provisions.[111] The facilitation of such sweeping reservations has been contrasted with the Convention on the Elimination of Racial Discrimination 1965 (CERD), which prohibits reservations contrary to the object and purpose of that Convention.[112] However, a process of structured dialogue on these reservations exists as part of the reporting procedures under CEDAW. Reporting requirements extend to the subject matter of the reservations. The 1999 Optional Protocol enhances this scrutiny of reservations.[113] Nonetheless, there is little incentive for states to revisit their reservations, and the process appears to anchor cultural reservations in particular.

(ii) EU Law

(a) Gender Equal Treatment Directive

Issues of cultural diversity were not raised explicitly as 'exceptions' to the gender equal treatment guarantee in the ETD. This is largely because cultural

---

[109] See generally, LA Hoq, 'The Women's Convention and Its Optional Protocol: Empowering Women to Claim Their Internationally Protected Rights' (2001) 32 *Columbia Human Rights Law Review* 677, esp 688–92.

[110] JA Minor, 'An Analysis of Structural Weaknesses in the Convention on the Elimination of All Forms of Discrimination Against Women' (1994) 24 *Georgia Journal of International and Comparative Law* 137.

[111] Iraq, Libya. In addition, Egypt has made a reservation in relation to equality of men and women in the areas of family and marriage law. *Ibid* at 145.

[112] Art 20 CERD. See LA Donner, 'Gender Bias in Drafting International Discrimination Conventions: The 1979 Women's Convention Compared with the 1965 Racial Convention' (1994) 25 *California Western International Law Journal* 241. See also, B Clark, 'The Vienna Convention Reservations Regime and the Convention on Discrimination Against Women' (1991) 85 *American Journal of International Law* 281 and RJ Cook, 'Reservations to the Convention on the Elimination of All Forms of Discrimination Against Women' (1990) 30 *Virginia Journal of International Law* 643.

[113] See generally, Hoq, above n 109.

practices in the EU are often regarded as exclusive to 'others' (immigrant and minority communities in particular). Where defences to gender discrimination are raised, these are usually cast in culturally neutral language. Thus for example, on whether it is permissible to reserve the profession of midwifery to women, no attempt is made to cast this as a 'cultural' issue. Rather, the gender segregation is justified on the grounds of the sensitivity of patients (notwithstanding the fact that the more lucrative profession of obstetrics is predominantly male). This illustrates one of the pitfalls in the gender/multiculturalism debate, that culture is attributed to the 'other', while 'our' behaviour is rational, and not culturally dictated.[114]

(b) Framework Directive

The EU has, however, sought to reconcile equality and respect for religious diversity in the Framework Directive. Article 4(2) of that Directive permits Member States to maintain in force provisions or practices allowing religious organisations[115] to differentiate between employees on the basis of their religion or belief.[116] This provision arguably encompasses measures such as Section 37(1) of the Irish Employment Equality Act 1998.[117] What remains to be seen is the extent to which such religious differentiation may have a gendered impact. In this respect it must be noted that the final caveat to Article 4(2) is that such differences in treatment should not justify discrimination on non-religious grounds.

An example cited frequently in the drafting of the Irish section, and hence relevant to the assessment of the Directive, is that of Eileen Flynn.[118] Ms Flynn was employed as a teacher in a Catholic school and was openly having a relationship with a married man. Her dismissal was held to be fair in order to prevent the undermining of the religious ethos of the school. This case predates the 1998 Act, and so the court did not canvass the possibility that this would amount to gender discrimination or discrimination on another ground. In contrast, in the

---

[114] See eg Volpp, above n 106.

[115] Namely 'churches and other public or private organisations, the ethos of which is based on religion or belief'.

[116] It provides that 'a difference of treatment based on a person's religion or belief shall not constitute discrimination where, by reason of the nature of these activities or of the context in which they are carried out, a person's religion or belief constitute a genuine, legitimate and justified occupational requirement, having regard to the organisation's ethos.' A key restriction is that the provision only permits Member States to 'maintain national legislation in force or provide for future legislation incorporating national practices existing at the date of adoption of [the Directive]'.

[117] Section 37(1) Employment Equality Act 1998 states: 'A religious, educational or medical institution which is under the direction or control of a body established for religious purposes or whose objectives include the provision of services in an environment which promotes certain religious values shall not be taken to discriminate against a person for the purposes of this Part or Part II if—(a) it gives more favourable treatment, on the religion ground, to an employee or a prospective employee over that person where it is reasonable to do so in order to maintain the religious ethos of the institution, or (b) it takes action which is reasonably necessary to prevent an employee or a prospective employee from undermining the religious ethos of the institution.'

[118] *Flynn v Power* [1985] IR 648.

recent UK case of *O'Neill*[119] where a schoolteacher in a Catholic school was dismissed when she became pregnant with a priest, the dismissal was held to be sex discrimination under the UK 1975 Sex Discrimination Act 1975. As that legislation contains no 'religious exemption' and the UK lacks legislation prohibiting religious discrimination,[120] the right of the institution to take action to maintain its religious ethos was not canvassed. The final caveat in Article 4(2) of the Framework Directive reveals that gender equality is effectively privileged over religious ethos, to the effect that the religious differentiation may not amount to discrimination on another ground. Thus gender equality (and—probably more importantly in practice—sexual orientation equality[121]) generally trump restrictions arising out of religious identity.

The Charter and Gender/Multiculturalism

How might the Charter influence these debates? The Charter does not establish a hierarchy between gender equality and religious and cultural diversity, so it will fall to the Court to determine the appropriate balance between the two. The appropriate approach would seem to be a balancing of competing equality claims on a case-by-case basis.[122] As the political discourse illustrates, this is an unenviable task, and fraught with risks. That such controversies are likely to come to resolution at EU level is now clear. The debate is no longer about competence, but substance. When we look at the way the Court has dealt with gender positive action, certain reservations must be expressed as to the capability of the Court to deal with these features. As is evidenced in the positive action discussion above, the Court's mode of reasoning does not lend itself to a rich constitutional jurisprudence. As argued above, the Charter may open the process of constitutional reasoning, and lead the Court to greater frankness as to its role.[123] This would certainly be a prerequisite for any satisfactory resolution of disputes as sensitive as those in this area.

A range of possible gender/multiculturalism issues could well arise. Examining even one, well-documented controversy, namely the prohibition on

---

[119] *O'Neill v Governors of St Thomas More Roman Catholic Voluntarily Aided Upper School* [1997] ICR 33.

[120] The Race Relations Act 1976 does protect those religious groups which can establish a distinct ethnicity, such as Sikhs (*Mandla v Dowell Lee* [1983] 2 AC 548; [1983] IRLR 209), but there is no general prohibition of religious discrimination. Religious freedom is however guaranteed at the EHCR standard under the Human Rights Act 1998. However, its provisions on freedom to manifest religion (as opposed to simply holding religious beliefs) are relatively weak. See, for discussion, G Moon, 'Substantive Rights and Equal Treatment in Respect of Religion and Belief: Towards a Better Understanding of the Rights, and Their Implications' (2000) *European Human Rights Law Review* 580.

[121] See M Bell, ch 14, in C Costello and E Barry, above n 27.

[122] For discussion of a number of possible approaches, see Wallace and Shaw, in this collection, at pp 229–31.

[123] See M Poiares Maduro, in this collection, text at p 279–81.

wearing the Muslim headscarf in state schools, provides an insight into the complex conflict of values at issue. This issue has arisen in several Member States,[124] but has been most controversial in France.[125] Community law is pertinent as the Race and Ethnicity Directive applies to the educational context.[126] As yet, of course, the Community gender equality legislation is confined to the employment/social security context,[127] but there is now competence to adopt Community legislation to extend the gender equality guarantee to non-employment areas. In any event, one could argue that as a transversal policy objective, a gender equality perspective should be read into the Race and Ethnicity Directive. The controversy therefore raises questions of Community law. It follows that the Charter is relevant as an interpretative tool and ultimately, the touchstone to determine the validity of those Community measures.

The schoolchildren may argue that the prohibition violates the obligation to respect ethnic diversity in the educational context, indirectly discriminating against them on ethnicity grounds. Indeed, this interpretation has been accepted by the UK authorities in the context of the interpretation of the Race Relations Act.[128] The prohibition of indirect discrimination in the Directive is copper-fastened by the Charter's guarantee of respect for cultural and religious diversity. This requires sensitivity to religious and cultural practices. In contrast, the national authorities may well cite gender equality concerns. How are the ostensibly competing claims to be evaluated? The language of the Charter suggests that it cannot be maintained that gender equality trumps diversity, nor that cultural diversity is normatively superior. The task requires a balancing of the equality claims. The balance requires an articulation of the underlying values of the guarantees, as well as impact assessment of the practices at issue.

In this instance this would entail an assessment of the alleged infringement of gender equality. The role of dress codes generally and, in particular, arguments of Muslim feminists in favour of veiling as an empowering practice should be acknowledged.[129] In addition, the inherent religious value of the practice deriv-

---

[124] In Germany, headscarf disputes have arisen predominantly in the employment context. It has been held that it is permissible to dismiss teachers in state schools for wearing the headscarf (Judgment of the *Bundesverwaltungsgericht*, 4 July 2002, BVerwG 2C21.01). In contrast more recently, the Federal Labour Court ruled that the wearing of the headscarf more generally was protected by religious freedom. (*Bundesarbeitsgericht*, 10 October 2002–2 AZR 472/01). In the UK, excluding pupils for complying with 'ethnic' dress codes is prohibited under the Race Relations Act. The House of Lords held that excluding a Sikh pupil for wearing a turban amounted to ethnicity discrimination in *Mandla v Dowell Lee* [1983] IRLR 209.

[125] In France, the Conseil d'Etat has ruled that 'ostentatious' wearing of headscarves violates the law prohibiting proselytising in schools; *Conseil d'Etat*, Case No 159981, Judgment 10 March 1995; *Conseil d'Etat*, Case No 130394, Judgment, 2 November 1992. For discussion see, S Poulter, 'Muslim headscarves in school: contrasting legal approaches in England and France' (1997) 17 *Oxford Journal of Legal Studies* 43.

[126] The Race and Ethnicity Directive applies to vocational training (Art 3(1)(b)) and education (Art 3(1)(g).

[127] See above n 8.

[128] Case No 247738/88 Equal Opportunities Review Discrimination Case Law Digest 2.

[129] See eg L Ahmed, *Women and Gender in Islam: Historical Roots of Modern Debate* (New Haven, Yale University Press, 1992) 223.

ing from its roots in religious doctrine must be acknowledged. On the other hand, the mechanisms that make the veil an *imposed* practice should also be placed in the balance. Crucially, the French cultural origins of the prohibition should be interrogated. It is a particular local vision of secularism that informs the prohibition in France.[130] In weighing all these factors, what is crucial in effect is that neither 'gender' nor 'culture' is viewed as monolithic. In fact, the understanding of the requirement of gender equality must be viewed in a cultural context, just as the gendered aspects of culture must be exposed. In effect, this is a plea to acknowledge the complexity and difficulty of the issue.[131]

This example is but one of many that may yet come for EU policy consideration and ultimately, legal adjudication. While the Charter is clearly not determinative of outcomes of such cases, its added value is that its diverse provisions help avoid the either/or, rule/exception dichotomies which have structured EU equality law to date. They direct decision-makers to the different equalities and values that must be placed in the balance. This could well be a healthy development, provided the balancing process is conducted in a frank and open way, which demonstrates due respect and sensitivity to the respective values at stake. If however, the legal discourse is conducted in a conclusory manner, as is currently the predominant style of the Court, deep alienation could result. Proper constitutional discourse is imperative.

CONCLUSIONS

This chapter set out to illustrate the transformative potential of the Charter. It has demonstrated that the Charter's impact in legal adjudication may well be significant. Despite its modest codificatory ambitions, the Charter's potential may well lie in its anomalous status, as embodiment of all existing protection and yet replete with all the promise of innovative development of any such open-textured instrument. The conclusion is ultimately (and admittedly somewhat surprisingly, to the author at least) that there is added-value in the existence of the legal text itself. While we may all be legal realists now, in that the determinacy of text is cursorily dismissed, the value of text in this context is manifold.

First, the very existence of the Charter may lead to a more 'honest' constitutional-type review by the Court, which openly articulates value clashes and standard of review. Second, the Charter provides space to re-examine some of the restrictive features of the *acquis* which arise out of the tendency to treat all 'exceptions' to the non-discrimination principle as violations of equality. This has been illustrated with reference to the positive action *acquis*, but in likelihood, will have broader application. Finally, the Charter rescues EU gender

---

[130] See for example, J Baubérot, *Histoire de la laïcité francaise*, (Paris, Que sais-je?, 2000); J Boussinesc, *La laïcité française, mémento juridique*, (Paris, Seuil, 1994).

[131] In this vein, see also M Nussbaum, 'A Plea for Difficulty' in S Moller Okin and Respondents, *Is Multiculturalism Bad for Women?* (New Jersey, Princeton University Press, 1999) 105.

equality law from its previous essentialism. Now, gender equality is placed in the context of other issues of liberty, equality and indeed, diversity. Its provisions point towards nuanced and varied solutions, as competing equality claims gradually come to be adjudicated, both legislatively and judicially.

7

The Unsolved Conflict: Reshaping Family Work and Market Work in the EU Legal Order

MARZIA BARBERA*

INTRODUCTION

IT HAS BEEN said that the Charter of Fundamental Rights of the European Union exerts a peculiar fascination on legal scholars, which neither its supporters nor its opponents can resist. This fascination, however, is not to be found in its novelty or in the typically ground-breaking nature of modern constitutional charters but, on the contrary, in the fact that the Charter is, at the same time, the point of arrival of an inheritance with a long history and the starting point of a new constitutional dialogue between different principles and values.[1] The future of this inheritance has been entirely entrusted to a dialogic process involving all the European Union and national institutional actors, which could be favoured by that very minimalist approach that many consider to be the Charter's main weakness.

In this chapter I will examine whether this evaluation is justified with respect to the Charter's few provisions on the reconciliation of family and professional life (Article 33 EUCFR), or whether, in this case, the Charter's reticence masks an unresolved conflict within the EU on how to reshape the relationship between family work and market work. I will consider too whether this political delay is also the result of a delay in the legal discourse in perceiving what is at stake in the debate about reconciliation policies. In discussing this issue, legal scholars have often focused their criticisms on the limits of the traditional anti-discrimination law, on the alternative between the equality approach and the substantive rights approach, and, within this latter approach, on the need to move from sex-based special rights to neutral-parenting rights. In some cases

* Professor of Labour Law, University of Brescia, Italy. I should like to thank Clare McGlynn and Tamara Hervey for their valuable comments on an earlier draft of this chapter.
[1] See R Bifulco, M Cartabia, A Celotto, 'Introduzione' in R Bifulco, M Cartabia, A Celotto (eds), *L'Europa dei diritti. Commento alla Carta dei diritti fondamentali dell'Unione Europea* (Bologna, il Mulino, 2001) 11. See also M Poiares Maduro, in this collection.

changes in Community law have vindicated these criticisms, in others they have pointed out certain conceptual weaknesses of the legal debate, in particular as regards the apparent dichotomy between the equality approach and the substantive rights approach. Another controversial point is the insistence that policies which aim to reconcile paid work and family life should be gender-neutral,[2] where instead a diverse feminist approach seeks to maintain different rules in order to reflect the different experiences of women and men, not only as regards the biological fact of birth, but also as regards the emotional relationship with, and care of children.

The focus of this legal discussion has so far been on the case law of the European Court of Justice (the Court), due to the residual or relatively new nature of the intervention of the political actors in this field. The approval of the EU Charter of Fundamental Rights, as well as the inclusion of reconciliation policies, regarded as flexibility policies, within the European Employment Strategy, offer an opportunity to extend the horizon of the legal debate, and to reconsider the relationship between social, employment and family policies. Attention will also be drawn, in this context, to the intertwining of various regulatory techniques, which fulfil overlapping functions, and to the strains that this changing frame of governance puts on the traditional role of labour law norms.

FAMILY AND PROFESSIONAL LIFE IN THE CHARTER:
THE PROVISIONS OF ARTICLE 33 EUCFR

Since the Community had no competence in the family field, for a long time family regulation was a classic spillover of policies adopted in other areas of European integration, such as those regarding protection of migrant workers, sex equality, or, more recently, judicial co-operation.[3]

With the EU Charter, the family becomes an autonomous legal entity within EU law. The first paragraph of Article 33 EUCFR reads: 'The family shall enjoy legal, economic and social protection'. The provision draws on Article 16 of the European Social Charter 1961 (ESC) and must be interpreted in connection with the other provisions of the Charter dealing with the family, ie Article 7 EUCFR, which guarantees each individual the 'respect for private and family life', and Article 9 EUCFR, which protects the 'right to marry and found a family'. Both provisions affirm rights already entrenched in the European Convention on Human Rights and Fundamental Freedoms (ECHR).[4] But while under the lat-

---

[2] See C Costello, in this collection, at pp 127–8, who considers the application of Art 24 EUCFR on the rights of the child in the context of reconciliation of paid work and family life; and especially at p 128, where Costello adopts precisely this view.

[3] See C McGlynn, 'Families and the European Union Charter of Fundamental Rights: Progressive Change or Entrenching the Status Quo?' (2001) 26 *European Law Review* 582 at 585.

[4] The rights guaranteed in Art 7 EUCFR correspond to those guaranteed by Art 8 ECHR, while Art 9 EUCFR is based on Art 12 ECHR.

ter articles the family falls inside the protection of an individual right to freedom, under Article 33 (1) EUCFR it stands out as a collective subject possessing its own rights.

Article 33 (2) EUCFR is a recognition and reaffirmation of existing rights, and links together the different phases of the Community reconciliation policies: the early anti-discrimination phase, the more controversial protective legislation phase and the more emancipatory equal parenting phase. The provision reads:

> To reconcile family and professional life, everyone shall have the right to protection from dismissal for a reason connected with maternity and the right to paid maternity leave and to parental leave following the birth or adoption of a child.

The text draws on the provisions of the Pregnancy and Maternity Directive [5] and of the Parental Leave Directive[6] and it is also based on Article 8 (protection of maternity) ESC and on Article 27 (right of workers with family responsibilities to equal opportunities and equal treatment) of the Revised European Social Charter 1996 (RevESC).

What Family is Referred to Under the Provisions of Article 33 EUCFR?

We can no longer rely, in this regard, on the narrow concept of family construed by the European Court of Justice (the Court) and the Court of First Instance (CFI) in the past, where they were asked to extend protection due to the heterosexual family founded on marriage to other alternative forms of family that have emerged in society, such as families based on de facto unions or on same-sex couples. As is well known, in all these cases the attitude of the EU courts was negative.[7] The judges then had to face up to an array of norms and practices reflecting the diversity of national legal regulations and social values (as well as to the rather restrictive rulings of the European Court of Human Rights) which, while making it difficult to identify a common normative family model, did, however, make it possible to point out 'the absence of any general assimilation of marriage and other forms of statutory union'.[8] Neither the CFI nor the Court felt capable of going, on this basis, against the decision of the Council, as legislature, to favour the traditional married family model.

Now, however, the EU courts will be able to rely on a new Community source, whose interpretative authority is widely recognised (irrespective of the controversial question as to its legal status).[9] This source does not give any

---

[5] Council Dir 92/85/EEC OJ 1992 L 348/I.

[6] Council Dir 96/34/EC OJ 1996 L 145/9.

[7] Case 59/85, *Netherlands v Reed* [1986] ECR I–1283; Case C–249/96, *Grant v South West Trains* [1998] ECR I–621; Case T–264/97, *D v Council* [1999] ECR I–A 1, II–1; Joined Cases C–122, 125/99 *D and Sweden v Council* [2001] ECR I–4319.

[8] Joined Cases C–122, 125/99 *D and Sweden v Council* [2001] ECR I–4319, para 50.

[9] See B De Witte, ' The Legal Status of the Charter: Vital Question or Non-Issue?' (2001) 8 *Maastricht Journal of European and Comparative Law* 81 at 84. The same opinion is shared by the

preference *to any specific form of family.* Though scant, the indications of Article 33 (2) EUCFR delineate a variety of family models. Alongside the bread-winner family model (exemplified by maternity leave provisions) and the dual breadwinner family model (exemplified by the more gender-neutral parental leave provisions), the provision covers families based on marriage and others based on free union, dual-parent families and single-parent families, families based on natural filiation and others based on adoptive filiation.[10] On the whole, the family envisaged by paragraph 2 focuses on the vertical dimension of parenthood, and not on the horizontal dimension of marriage, a choice whose importance should not be underestimated in the interpretation of what consti-tutes a family for the purposes of Article 33 (1) EUCFR.[11]

Considerations of the same nature could be made with regard to the other provisions of the Charter dealing with the family. As the Explanations relating to the complete text of the Charter (the Explanatory Document)[12] expressly explains under Article 9, the Charter family provisions are *wholly permissive* in character, ie they neither *prohibit* nor *guarantee* protective status, let alone specify the type or extent of protection to be granted. In other words, the provi-sions have an open texture that leaves room for both progressive interpretation and conservative interpretation.

A great deal depends on how the rights of the family will be connected to the principles of freedom and equality proclaimed by the Charter, and on how the substantive rights approach which underpins the provisions dedicated to the family will operate within the broader anti-discrimination framework laid out under Articles 20 and 21 EUCFR. Should the Court view the rights of the family as a projection of the rights to freedom of the individual, it might then construe the wording of the Charter as applying to a 'destructured' notion of the family. The family entitled to protection may take on *such different forms as those which permit the accomplishment of the personality of each of us.*[13] Should the Court, on the other hand, hold that the rights of the family are related to the Chapter devoted to Equality, then the main issue, when trying to delineate the boundaries of the family deserving of protection, will be to stake out a ground that reflects not only the values of the majority, but also those of minorities.

The Court again remained silent on the issue in *D and Sweden v Council,* but soon or later the judges must face it as a result of the adoption of the Charter,

Commission (COM (2000) 644 final, *Communication from the Commission on the Legal Nature of the Charter of Fundamental Rights of the European Union).* For the opposite view cf U De Siervo, 'L'ambigua redazione della Carta dei diritti fondamentali nel processo di costituzionalizzazione dell'Unione Europea' (2001) *Diritto Pubblico* 33.

[10] See A Giorgis, 'Art. 33. Vita familiare e professionale' in Bifulco, Cartabia, Celotto (eds), above n 2 at 237.

[11] But for a different view see McGlynn , above n 3 at 589 fn 38.

[12] See Council of the EU, *Charter of Fundamental Rights of the European Union. Explanations Relating to the Complete Text of the Charter,* (Luxembourg, Office for Official Publications of the European Communities, 2001).

[13] See R Bin, 'La famiglia: alla radice di un ossimoro' (2001) *Lavoro e diritto* 9 at 10.

which assigns a pre-eminent value to the principle of equality. I will return to this point below when discussing the role of the equality principle in the field of reconciliation policies.

The other innovative aspect of Article 33 EUCFR is that it allows reconciliation rights to be reconceptualised as individual fundamental rights. As we will see, this has important implications with regard to the enrichment of the normative function played by the contract of employment. The first and most important implication is that working arrangements must take into account the personal needs of the employees in so far as, by virtue of the principle of *Drittwirkung*, the interest satisfied by the contract is not solely the economic interest of the employer, but also the personal interest of the worker, recognised as a protected right that takes precedence over managerial prerogatives.[14]

Admittedly, these remarks are based on a text that is parsimonious. As I have already mentioned, it has been argued that the very minimalism of the Charter should favour the furtherance of that constitutional dialogue which has contributed so much to the process of European integration. The problem, however, is that in the area of reconciliation the laconic wording of the Charter comes across as more expressive of reluctance than vagueness. We are confronted here not with a normatively strong, though textually indeterminate, enunciation, but instead with fragments of a legal discourse.[15] Then again, these fragments are the very ones which helped build an *institutional* consensus (though not always a social or cultural consensus) in an area where uncertainties and unresolved conflicts prevail. The first step towards the construction of a system of effective reconciliation rights is thus to single out clearly such conflicts and to define what is at stake. In order to place this discussion in context, I will therefore first summarise the different phases of EU reconciliation policies.

THE EQUALITY APPROACH TO RECONCILIATION AND ITS CRITICS

Equality and non-discrimination have long been the main instruments through which Community law has dealt with the complex problems of the gendered division of labour and the relationship between market work and family work. This strategy did not arise by chance, but had a precise meaning and value, both at a practical and legal level. On the one hand, the Community institutions acted on the basis, so to speak, of the 'law of necessity': if they were to enter into a decision-making area that was apparently very remote from the main goal of the Community—the creation of a common market—there was no route other than to use the only binding provision which was relevant within the above mentioned sphere, namely Article 119 EEC (now Article 141 EC).[16] On the other

[14] See P Ichino, *Il tempo della prestazione nel rapporto di lavoro* (Milano, Giuffrè, 1984) at 88.
[15] See C Costello, in this collection, at p 114.
[16] See E Caracciolo di Torella and A Masselot, 'Pregnancy, Maternity and the Organisation of Family Life: An Attempt to Classify the Case Law of the Court of Justice' (2001) 26 *European Law*

hand, the Community actors implemented a conscious decision to create a legal policy model aimed at orienting women's individual decisions to the market, by acting on both the demand and the supply of labour. We can interpret in this same light not only Article 119 EEC, but all the directives on equality between men and women that stemmed from that Treaty provision during the seventies (the Equal Pay Directive, the Equal Treatment Directive and the Social Security Directive).[17] Enshrining the principle of equal pay for equal work (and later for work of equal value) meant working towards raising women's incomes in paid employment and, hence, lowering the threshold of convenience of working for the market and making it more unlikely for women to choose to devote themselves exclusively to the family. The same can be said about the opening up of male professions to women through the prohibition of discrimination established by the Equal Treatment Directive; about the abolition, prescribed by the same Directive, of protective legislation based on prohibitions of work, which presupposed the secondary nature of women's paid employment; and about the (partial) individualisation of welfare rights following the application of the principle of equal treatment in matters of social security.[18]

This policy led to a heated debate, which highlighted its weaknesses and contradictions. One of the main objections was that its guiding principle was formal equality, and not substantive equality. Formal equality seeks to correct market imperfections (that generate discrimination) on the assumption that women and men are *equal* in all relevant aspects. However, since women and men are *different* in many relevant respects, and principally in the roles they play within the family, and since these differences determine their role as workers, the idea of opening up access to the labour market to women without altering the division of family responsibilities amounted to not creating the very conditions necessary for the principle of equality to function.[19]

It was also argued that if we considered what women stood to gain from such a strategy, it was soon to be realised that equality was a gift of dubious value. The market to which women acquired access was a male oriented market: the typical worker was a full-time worker, employed on a fixed term contract, with long working hours, no career breaks, and a degree of flexibility which presupposed the absence of family commitments. Either women adapted to this model, and added to the family burden a heavy productive burden, thus aggravating their traditional double shift; or they did not adapt and left the labour market, thereby reinforcing the stereotype of their marginal productive role.

Review 239 who point out that references on this issue could only be found in soft law instruments, such as the Social Action Plan 1974.

[17] Council Dir 75/117/EEC OJ 1975 L 45/19; Council Dir 76/207/EEC; OJ 1976 L 39/40 Council Dir 79/7/EEC OJ 1979 L 6/24. Art 119 EEC did not provide a formal legal basis for these provisions, which are therefore formally based on either Art 100 (now 94) EC or Art 235 (now 308) EC or both.

[18] See J Lopez Lopez, 'Famiglia e condivisione dei ruoli in Spagna' (2001) *Lavoro e diritto* 163.

[19] See H Fenwick and T Hervey, 'Sex Equality in the Single Market: New Directions for the European Court of Justice' (1995) 32 *Common Market Law Review* 443.

The 'indifference' long shown by Community law to the interdependence of market work and family work in the social construction of gender,[20] and indeed its fundamental acceptance of the traditional division of sex roles,[21] were pointed to as confirmation of the intrinsically limited character of the Community principle of non-discrimination and of its liberal assumptions. A perfect illustration of this attitude is found in the *Hofmann* and *Stoeckel* cases,[22] where the Court made a radical distinction between formal equality in the workplace (the subject of the Equal Treatment Directive) and substantial inequality within the family, which was seen as a 'concern' outside the ambit of Community law. It has been observed that this line of reasoning runs counter to the entire history of labour law, which has consisted precisely in recognising the personal dimension of the performance of work, that is in not considering the worker as a simple actor of the labour market, but as a concrete man or woman.[23]

The development of the concept of indirect discrimination, as we know, is an attempt to enable the traditional anti-discrimination law to take account of the group structural differences which lead to inequality. It is no coincidence that, in elaborating the concept of indirect discrimination, the Court based its analysis on the conditions of workers with a part-time contract, since that form of contract has been the main means of accommodating the workplace to women's difference from men. However the legal doctrine soon pointed out that the heuristic usefulness of the distinction between direct discrimination and indirect discrimination crumbles in the case of a condition which is specific to women, namely pregnancy and maternity. This can be seen in the uncertainties and inconsistencies that have arisen in classifying discrimination based on pregnancy or maternity as direct or indirect discrimination,[24] and in the fact that in some cases the Court has abandoned the comparative exercise which is inherent to the application of the principle of equality.[25]

The uncertainties of the Court are not only of a theoretical nature, but reflect political uncertainty as to how to distribute the social costs of pregnancy and

---

[20] See Case 184/83 *Hofmann v BarmerErsatzkasse* [1984] ECR 3047; Case C–345/89 *Criminal Proceedings v Stoeckel* [1991] ECR I–4047.

[21] See Case 163/82 *Commission v Italy* [1983] ECR 3273; Case C–218/98 *Abdoulaye v Renault* [1999] ECR 911.

[22] Case 184/83 [1984] ECR 3047; Case C–345/89 [1991] ECR I–4047.

[23] See A Supiot, 'Principe d'égalité et limites du droit du travail (en marge de l'arret Stoeckel)' (1992) *Droit Social* 385. See J Hunt, in this collection, at p 65 who observes that the EU has not adopted the principle that 'labour is not a commodity'.

[24] See Case 177/88 *Dekker v Stichting Vormingscentrum voor Jong Volwassenen* [1990] ECR I–3941 and Case 179/88 *Handels-og Kontorfunktionærernes Forbund v Dansk Arbejdsgiverforening* [1990] ECR I–3979, decided on the same days. The first decision links pregnancy and maternity to direct discrimination, the second to indirect discrimination.

[25] The Court applied a substantive test as regards pregnancy in *Dekker* and a comparative test as regards the consequences of pregnancy in *Hertz*. The Court departed from this dual approach in Case C–394/96 *Brown v Rentokil* [1998] ECR I–4185, where dismissal due to pregnancy-related illness was deemed discriminatory because it occurred during the pregnancy itself, and was therefore regarded as essentially based on the fact of pregnancy.

child-bearing between individual employers, female workers and society as a whole. It has been noted that the highly questionable distinction drawn in *Hertz* and in *Brown* between pre- and post-confinement pregnancy-related illness should probably be attributed to some kind of utilitarian concern based on the classical argument that minimal risk should have less protection when costs exceed benefits[26] and that it was the spectre of indeterminate liability for post-pregnancy conditions which led the Court to impose a finite period of protection.[27] The problem is that the apparently neutral character of the anti-discrimination scrutiny conceals the judgements of a distributive nature made de facto by the Court, which can manipulate the case by simply widening or narrowing the scope of comparison.

For all these reasons the equality approach has been judged quite insufficient to deal with the problem of re-balancing the traditional division of sex roles within the family and the market. The focus has thus shifted from sex discrimination to a more general rights approach, on which *any* parent may rely.

THE SHIFT TO A SUBSTANTIVE RIGHTS APPROACH AND ITS TRAPS

It has been argued that a more effective way of tackling structural gender inequalities is to establish specific legal rights 'to equitable (rather than equal) treatment'.[28] This would not only eliminate the need for a male comparator in an area where comparison between women and men is often impossible, and would challenge the idea that the very existence of a woman's right depends on the existence of a comparable right afforded to a comparable man, but would also make more evident the fundamental choices of economic redistribution involved in the decision on how to spread the social cost of bearing children. While a legal duty formulated in a negative way (such as the prohibition of discrimination) provides no guide as to such substantive issues as the length of maternity and paternity leave, or the level of pay or the condition on return to work and so on, detailed legislative intervention, it is maintained, could explicitly establish what level of security to provide women in relation to the risks of pregnancy and maternity, and pre-empt the conflicts between the economic interests of the employer and the rights of the woman worker.

The merits of a substantive approach are illustrated in a number of essays published at a time when Community law has already taken this direction. It is difficult to state whether the renewed interest that the Community showed in the early Nineties on the subject of reconciliation was due to concerns about

---

[26] F Mancini and S O'Leary, 'The New Frontiers of Sex Equality Law in the European Union' (1999) 24 *European Law Review* 331 at 341.

[27] See on this point M Wynn, 'Pregnancy Discrimination: Equality, Protection or Reconciliation?' (1999) 62 *Modern Law Review* 435 at 446.

[28] See T Hervey, 'Sex Equality as Substantive Justice' (1999) 62 *Modern Law Review* 614 at 622.

birth rates, related to the decline in population in many European countries,[29] or whether it was the result of women's growing labour market participation which turned the combination of work and care into a major political issue.[30] The fact is that with the Community Charter of the Fundamental Social Rights of Workers 1989 (Community Social Charter) and the Council Recommendation on Childcare,[31] EU policy saw a change of direction. Thereafter the intervention took two paths: on the one hand it followed the historical path of protective legislation, granting women workers a number of specific rights through the Pregnancy and Maternity Directive,[32] on the other it followed the more innovative path of re-organising working and care time through the adoption of the Parental Leave Directive.[33] It was the first time that the Community introduced binding measures in an area previously only covered by soft law, and this indicates the new importance attributed to the problem of reconciliation. Nevertheless the compromise underlying Community intervention betrays not only a degree of commitment on the part of national political actors which was, to say the least, dubious, but also the fact that each of the directives provided national and Community institutions with the instrumental means to play out more important games on the chessboard of European integration.

The Pregnancy Directive reflects the long resistance that Member States put up during the Eighties to what was perceived as a threat to their sovereignty in an area (the regulation of the employment relationship) that was at the time their exclusive domain. This not only explains the rather low standard of protection (except for some Member States), but also the general framework of the Directive, which filters its substantive regulatory content through the only gap left open to qualified majority voting, namely health and safety measures. The Parental Leave Directive, on the other hand, was the first result of institutionalised collective bargaining at European level. As has been pointed out, the support given by the Community to supranational collective bargaining serves the institutions' interest in utilising collective bargaining as a resource to be deployed for the purposes of overcoming regulatory difficulties at Community level, and is therefore primarily instrumental.[34] Having performed the task of bridging the regulatory deficit, which has existed within the Community for a long time, European collective bargaining can only go as far as its (limited) Community competence will allow, and no further.[35]

---

[29] As suggested by C McGlynn, 'Reclaiming a Feminist Vision: the Reconciliation of Paid Work and Family Life in European Union Law and Policy' (2001) 7 *Columbia Journal of European Law* 241 at 253.

[30] See G Bruning and J Plantenga, 'Parental Leave and Equal Opportunities: Experiences in Eight European Countries' (1999) 9 *Journal of European Social Policy* 195.

[31] Council Rec 92/241/EEC OJ 1992 L 123/16.

[32] Council Dir 92/85/EEC OJ 1992 L 348/1.

[33] Council Dir 96/34/EEC OJ 1996 L 145/4.

[34] See A Lo Faro, *Funzioni e finzioni della contrattazione collettiva comunitaria* (Milano, Giuffrè,1999) p 257; B Ryan, in this collection, at pp 89–90.

[35] See B Ryan, in this collection, section on competence at pp 84–7.

As an indication of how restricted the EU's competence on the subject of reconciliation was at the time of the directive's adoption, it is sufficient to say that its legal basis lies in the Community Social Charter. Point 16(3) of the Community Social Charter, in particular, states: 'measures should be developed enabling men and women to reconcile their occupational and family obligations'. As is well known, the majority of these measures have always had a strong local character, in terms of social policy, of informal support networks, of gender cultures as reflected in social legislation.[36] Things did not change with the adoption of the Parental Leave Directive. The fundamental decisions on reconciliation policy (such as those concerning the distribution of the costs of reconciliation between workers, employers and the state) continued to remain firmly in the hands of Member States also after the intervention of the Community legislator, as can be seen in the fact that the Directive did not provide for the right to remuneration or social security benefits for the duration of the parental leave. All matters relating to pay and social security are to be determined by Member States according to national law, taking into account the importance of the continuity of the entitlements to social security cover under the different schemes, in particular healthcare.

This is one of the Directive's most criticised provisions. Several studies show a close connection between financial cover and the level of demand of parental leave, an income linked to parental leave being also a condition of it being effectively taken up.[37] In addition, the payment system is likely to affect the percentage of women and men taking leave. Given the existing gender wage differentials, men are much less inclined than women to take unpaid (or flat rate) parental leave.[38]

It is the lack of any real content given to the declared purpose of encouraging men to assume an equal share of family responsibility that casts doubt on the sincerity of the Directive. Although 'promoted as the jewel in the EU's reconciliation crown', the Parental Leave Directive appears to one author 'symbolically important, but substantially meaningless' and unlikely to affect the lives of individual women and men.[39] Some years before, the Pregnancy Directive had aroused no less disappointed reactions, not only due to the very limited protection accorded, but also due to the fact that it was seen as a re-confirmation of the more traditional assumptions about the division of employment and childcare responsibilities, proved by the absence of the father figure.[40]

---

[36] See C Saraceno, 'Un'Europa di donne e di uomini?' (1999) *il Mulino* 46; S Scarponi, 'Il lavoro delle donne fra produzione e riproduzione' (2001) *Lavoro e diritto* 97.

[37] See M Schmidt, 'Parental Leave: Contested Procedure, Creditable Results' (1997) 13 *International Journal of Comparative Labour Law and Industrial Relations* 113 at 121.

[38] See Bruning and Plantega, above n 30 at 205. The authors also underline the role that cultural factors play in the low user rates of fathers, such as the fact that, in general, men display great hesitation when contemplating full-time care and that employers in typically male sectors are usually less inclined to accommodate the wishes of employees in that respect than employers in typically female-dominated sectors.

[39] McGlynn, above n 29 at 258.

[40] For an account of the debate on the Pregnancy Directive see McGlynn, above n 28 at 256 ff.

Thus, the supporters of the substantive rights approach had to learn a hard lesson, namely that 'rights (are) only as good as their content and the remedies available to enforce them'.[41] However, this is not a new lesson: the quest for rights always conceals more than one trap.

The first trap is that of thinking that providing a ground for rights, citing reasons for justifying the existence of a right, is the most appropriate means of obtaining recognition of that right, as though the existence of rights depended either on the good reasons cited, or on the goodwill of the rulers, and not on their *conditions of possibility*, on the situations and means that make them achievable.[42]

Looking both at the *factual and cultural conditions* which were expected to favour the development of a system of reconciliation rights, we must admit that the redefinition of family and work obligations and what role such redefinition might play in the restructuring of employment relations and welfare regimes are both very controversial issues. Cross-national differences in family and in labour market behaviours make this issue even more complicated. Differences cannot be explained by referring only to differences in the welfare state regimes, or to the different orientation of women, but rather to complex interrelations of culture, institutions and social actors, which have been termed 'gender arrangements'.[43] When, for example, a UK and an Italian lawyer speak of family, maternity, paternity, and work, they speak of different things.[44] No wonder, then, that the way of looking at the reconciliation issue can be quite different in the two countries.[45]

---

[41] See Mancini and O'Leary, above n 26 at 341, quoting S Fredman, 'A Difference with Distinction: Pregnancy and Parenthood Reassessed' (1994) 110 *Law Quarterly Review* 106.

[42] N Bobbio , *L'età dei diritti* (Torino, Einaudi, 1990) at 6.

[43] See B Pfau Effinger, 'The Modernization of Family and Motherhood in Western Europe', in R Crompton (ed), *Restructuring Gender Relations and Employment. The Decline of the Male Breadwinner* (Oxford, OUP, 1999) p 78.

[44] See S Yeandle, 'Women, Men, and Non-Standard Employment: Breadwinning and Caregiving in Germany, Italy and the UK', in Crompton (ed), above n 43 at 102. While the UK system has been characterised in the past as a 'strong male breadwinner model' and is now conceptualised as a 'dual-breadwinner/dual-carer model manqué (more precisely a 'male breadwinner/female part-time care model'), with the nuclear family as the basic unit, in Italy 'familism' has prevailed over the male breadwinner model (we could talk of a 'strong male breadwinner model manqué') and the extended family continues to play a very important role even now, when a 'male breadwinner/female carer model' is emerging. Italy has one of the lowest rates of divorce, extramarital births, cohabitation, single-person households; the UK has among the highest rates on all of these indicators. Italy has the lowest rate of fertility, in spite of a relatively high level of state care provision (albeit with significant regional variations). The UK has one of the highest rates of fertility and one of the lowest levels of childcare provision. Italy has one of the lowest rates of active and employed women in Europe and one of the highest rates of full-time employment; the UK the exact opposite. In Italy the Catholic Church makes its voice heard on family morals and on the obligations of women and men; in UK it does not do so particularly effectively, but the refusal of the state to accept the burden of care since the mid-1970s has been perhaps an even more powerful exogenous force affecting women and men's attitudes towards family and labour work.

[45] On the Italian legal experience see generally D Gottardi, 'Lavoro di cura. Spunti di riflessioni (2001) *Lavoro e diritto* 121; L Calafà 'La prestazione di lavoro tra assenze e (dis)equilibri familiari' (2001) *Lavoro e diritto* 143.

Moreover, the feminist movement has been culturally split on how to config-ure reconciliation rights by the long-standing issues of whether women should seek absolute equality with men and full integration into waged work, or whether they should focus on gender differences (particularly in relation to caring and nurturing) and ask that these differences be taken into account in shaping rules and institutions. The claim by some authors that EU reconcilia-tion policy should mirror the feminist vision more accurately, by recognising sex specific rights only when considering pregnancy, which remains the realm of biology, while post-birth rights, which refer to a socially constructed realm, should be gender neutral,[46] fails to consider that this is just *one* of the feminist visions.[47] Other feminists assert a different 'truth', maintaining that the redefi-nition of the female subject starts with the revaluation of the bodily roots of subjectivity,[48] and arguing that to deny the maternal component of gender iden-tity risks pushing it into the realm of the repressed and unexpressed.[49] Others still try to avoid categorisations and the fateful effects of essentialism on the one hand, and relativism on the other, by proposing an anti-dogmatic approach which links together the challenging of stereotypical and conventional classifi-cations, and the consciousness that gender structures reflect not only stereo-types, but also women and men's different biographies, different experiences of working and caring.[50]

The limited nature of the reconciliation rights recognised by the two direc-tives also reflects these profound, unsolved conflicts, and the disappointment that they have encountered is perhaps due to a mistaken or wrongfully nurtured belief in the power of law to put right unsolved social problems and to act as a medium through which to bring about social change.[51]

The second trap lurking behind the quest for substantive rights is that of pre-suming that it is possible to do without equality. I will not consider again the objections as to the manner in which the principle of equality operates, but rather I shall ask the question whether, despite the reasons offered by its critics, we can really do without equality in seeking to achieve objectives of substantive justice. My answer is that the Community's very experience on the subject of reconciliation policies shows that we cannot (do without).

---

[46] McGlynn, above n 29 at 267 and 271; Caracciolo di Torella and Masselot, above n 16 at 258.

[47] But cf McGlynn, above n 29 at 243, fn 10.

[48] R Braidotti, 'On the Female Feminist Subject', in G Bock and S James (eds), *Beyond Equality and Difference. Citizenship, Feminist Politics and Female Subjectivity* (London, Routledge, 1992) at 182.

[49] See S Vegetti Finzi, 'Female Identity between Sexuality and Maternity', in Bock and James (eds), above n 48 at 141.

[50] See K Barlett, 'Feminist Legal Method' (1990) 103 *Harvard Law Review* 829 at 880 ff.

[51] Jurists generally emphasise that they do not believe that law and legal institutions are capable on their own of modifying social systems. The problem is that reliance on the force of the law often acts at a pre-comprehension level of a problem. But for a sensitive view of the problem see K Armstrong, 'Legal Integration: Theorizing the Legal Dimension of European Integration' (1998) 36 *Journal of Common Market Studies* 154.

In an article written together with Siofra O'Leary, Advocate General Federico Mancini noted that the decision by the Community legislator in the Pregnancy Directive to opt for a special protection regime had relieved the Court of the need to wrestle with the equal treatment/non-discrimination instruments, which had proved to be insufficient as a means of distributing the burden of pregnancy and maternity.[52] This is in fact what has happened, but its effect has been to remove the above-mentioned distributive question from legal analysis.

Despite the warning in the Pregnancy Directive that protection of women shall not be at the expense of the principle of equality, since *Gillespie*[53] the Court has abandoned the comparative approach, assigning women on maternity leave to a 'special position' which is not to be compared to any other worker's position, be it a woman's or a man's, a position in which the rights that are protected are only *self-referential rights*, in other words rights established by the Directive itself. As to how these 'special rights' should be quantified, it is for the national legislature, the Court says, to set the minimum amount of benefit to be paid during maternity leave, having regard to the duration of such leave and the existence of any other social advantages.

It is not the first time that the principle of subsidiarity has turned out to clash with the Community principle of equality. Nevertheless in this case the Court ends up contradicting itself. In *Gillespie*, the Court held that maternity pay must not be so low as to undermine the purpose of maternity leave and that it must be 'adequate'. But how to check the instrumental fit of a given public choice (in this case a welfare choice), and how to measure the adequacy of a social benefit? The missing piece of the Court's reasoning is equality and the two distinct functions (of several attributed to it) played by this principle in European constitutional traditions.

As for the first function, the principle of equality constitutes the obligatory test of the rationality and reasonableness of the political process. This function derives from a core idea of means-end rationality, according to which the principle of equality requires, as a limit to arbitrariness, that a rule bear a rational relationship to a given purpose (with a request of a tighter fit when a suspect classification is used).

The second function of the principle of equality refers to the problems of distributive justice faced by all political and social institutions, problems that equality can help to solve because it looks not only at the commutative justice of the individual exchanges, but also *at the global properties of the distribution*. Going back to the example discussed above, the 'adequacy' of a minimum income can hardly be estimated without looking at other benefits paid in similar cases (it is no coincidence that the Pregnancy Directive uses sickness benefit

---

[52] See Mancini and O'Leary, above n 26 at 341.

[53] Case C–342/93 [1996] ECR I–475. The Court interpreted the equality legislation in the light of the Pregnancy Directive, even though it had not yet come into force. The logic of *Gillespie* has been further developed in Case C–411/96 *Boyle v EOC* [1998] ECR I–6401 and Case C–333/97 *Lewen v Denda* [2000] ECR I–7243.

as a term of reference on this matter, leaving aside the appropriateness of this comparison).

It is only by putting women on maternity leave into a category of 'non-workers', separated from all others, that the Court has been able to 'neutralise' the principal of equality. But in doing so it has deprived itself of the normative instrument which it has always used in drawing up the boundaries of the legitimate use of power and has entrusted the *content* of substantive rights of women to the pure discretion of the political decision-maker.

Through its express proclamation of the principle of equality, Article 20 EUCFR now allows the EU courts to scrutinise the distribution by Community and national legislators of public goods that have a quasi-constitutional nature, such as those referred to by Article 33 EUCFR. According to a cautious reading of the Charter, given the constraints imposed by Article 51 EUCFR, only if the individual is subjected to less favourable treatment in an area regulated by Community law would the equality clause be a relevant cause of action.[54] But the consequences of the recognition and application of the principle of equality may be indeed more wide-ranging. While Article 51 EUCFR does set constraints to the expansion of Community competence, the principle of equality and the prohibitions of discrimination enshrined in Article 21 EUCFR (especially if the Charter is incorporated into the Treaties) could nevertheless become the 'jemmy' with which to prise open those constraints, eroding the rule of enumerated powers to the benefit of the supranational institutions, as has happened in federal systems, and expanding the jurisdiction of the EU courts beyond any limits imposed by contingent political decisions.[55]

In the Charter the principle of equality operates, as we have seen, as a mainstreaming principle,[56] and as for the prohibitions on discrimination set forth by Article 21 EUCFR, unlike those enshrined by Article 14 ECHR, they are not instrumental, ie they do not serve to grant protection to rights already recognised by substantive provisions, but have an autonomous scope, also covering fields of exercise of discretionary powers that are 'empty' of rights. In other words, both the principle of equality and the prohibitions on discrimination help to determine that 'context of Community law' within which Member States are obliged to respect the 'requirements flowing from the protection of fundamental rights at the Community level'.[57]

In this vein, reading Article 33 EUCFR through the lens of the principles of equality and non-discrimination could, for example, enable the Court to scrutinise not only any restrictions by EU institutions and by Member States of the

---

[54] See J Kenner, in this collection, at p 19.

[55] The differences between the EU system of scrutiny of Member States' acts affecting fundamental rights, and a federal system such as that of the USA have been explored by K Lenaerts, *Le juge et la constitution aux Etas-Unis d'Amerique and dans l'ordre juridique européen* (Brussels, Bruylant, 1998).

[56] See C Costello, in this collection, at p 116; and M Bell, in this collection, after pp 103–4.

[57] In the words of the Explanatory Document under Art 51 EUCFR, which in turn refer to the Court's case law.

right to protection from dismissal for a reason connected with maternity set forth by Community law, but also the unequal distribution of discretionally attributed benefits, such as parental leave paid only to women workers and not to men workers as well.

This use of the principle of equality is not unknown to the Court. When the Court first ruled on atypical work there was no specific Community legislation on this subject. However, the Court did rule on the matter through the medium of the principle of equality, which enabled it to evaluate the adverse consequences on these categories of workers of the discretionary decisions taken by national legislators.[58] As a result, by applying the principle of equality (as prohibition of sex discrimination), the Court exceeded the limits of its jurisdiction.

The 'jemmy' may not be used. As I have argued elsewhere, the importance of the Court has grown in the new Community anti-discrimination context, but so has its difficulty in playing its role and perpetuating that consensus-building exercise which is so crucial for its legitimacy.[59] With regard to reconciliation issues, this difficulty is compounded by the profound contradictions that exist in this field. The decision in the recent *Lommers* case,[60] which ruled that the principle of equal treatment does not preclude a scheme set up by the Dutch Minister of Agriculture under which a limited number of subsidised nursery places was reserved for female officials, because its aim was 'to tackle extensive under-representation of women' in the workplace, confirms the ambiguity of the doctrine of the Court on the issue of the legality of positive action.[61] It also reflects a dilemma that is hard to solve, namely how reconciliation policies that facilitate women's access to employment serve to increase equality and how they leave the division of labour and care within the household unaltered. However, there remains the fact that the Charter's principles of equality and non-discrimination have a potential capacity to expand the Community's competences.

RECONCILIATION AS A POLICY AND RECONCILIATION AS A RIGHT

The most recent phase of the EU strategy on reconciliation is taking place in the context of a conceptual framework that is quite different from the one described so far. Here, too, there is a dichotomy—that of reconciliation as a policy and reconciliation as a right—but the contours of the two alternatives are much more vague, as befits the current phase of EU social policy, where the

---

[58] See M Roccella and T Treu, *Diritto del lavoro della Comunità europea* (Padova, CEDAM, 2002) 177; G De Simone, 'La giurisprudenza comunitaria sui lavori flessibili', paper presented at the AIDLASS Conference *Interessi e tecniche nella disciplina del lavoro flessibile* (Urbino, 2002).

[59] See M Barbera, 'Not the Same? The Judicial Role in the New Community Anti-discrimination Law Context' (2002) 31 *Industrial Law Journal* 82.

[60] Case C–476/99 [2002] ECR I–2891.

[61] See C Costello, in this collection, at pp 119–22.

boundaries between employment policies and labour law and between soft law and hard law become indistinct.[62]

Following the Amsterdam Treaty and the transformation of employment into a matter of common concern, reconciliation has become part of the European Employment Strategy (EES). The new approach is a holistic one: reconciliation is seen as a means of promoting equal opportunity, as a condition facilitating women's employment, and as a means of creating jobs.[63] Both the Employment Guidelines devoted to these issues and the Part-time Work Directive[64] fit into this pattern since their guiding principles are, if not formally, substantially the same, not only because the Directive's objectives fit with those of the EES, but also because the language and the content of soft law and of hard law in this case are very similar.[65]

The general impression is that, in the area of reconciliation as in other areas, the centre of gravity of public policies has shifted from traditional labour policies to employment policies. The detachment with which some legal scholars have followed the events leading to the approval of the Employment Title of the Amsterdam Treaty and its initial implementation phase is perhaps due to this circumstance, which has made them reluctant to wander into territory that is seen as being dominated by a prevalently procedural rationale, which is difficult to translate into the language of rights. Having to deal with what has been defined as a new, vague category of 'non rights'[66] has created a sense of displacement, if not one of estrangement, from this new field of Community intervention.

In reality even the latest products of Community labour law—the aforementioned Part-time Work Directives and the Fixed Term Work Directive[67]—favour a procedural and programmatic method of regulation, which creates a framework of general principles whose binding nature is dampened by the use of vague terms, and establishes a set of social objectives to be pursued, the main one being to increase employment.[68] Nevertheless the minimalism of the two Directives is counterbalanced by the prohibition of discrimination, whose central importance opens the doors to new developments in anti-discrimination protection.

---

[62] See M Barbera, *Dopo Amsterdam. I nuovi confini del diritto sociale comunitario* (Brescia, Promodis, 2000).

[63] The Commission welcomed this broader approach to reconciliation in the proposal of the 5th Action Programme on gender equality for the period 2001–2005 (Communication *Towards a Community Framework Strategy on Gender Equality (2001–05)* COM (2000) 335 final).

[64] Council Dir 97/81/EC OJ 1998 L 14/9.

[65] See De Simone, above n 59.

[66] See S Sciarra, 'The Employment Title in the Amsterdam Treaty. A Multi-language Legal Discourse', in D O'Keeffe and P Twomey (eds), *Legal Issues of the Amsterdam Treaty* (Oxford, Hart, 1999) p 170.

[67] Council Dir 99/70/EC OJ 1999 L 175/43.

[68] See S Scarponi, 'Luci ed ombre dell'accordo europeo in materia di lavoro a tempo parziale' (1999) *Rivista Giuridica del Lavoro* 399.

All this seems to indicate a tendency for the two areas of Community intervention to converge. In the EU context, labour law is seeking to legitimise itself not only as an instrument of social protection, but also as a means of optimising the economic efficiency and rationalisation of productive relationships. Conversely, EU employment policies are seeking accreditation not only as macro-economic policies, but also as policies intended to construct a 'social citizenship', in the form of equal work opportunities.[69]

I do not wish to suggest that labour law and employment policies are being confused with each other: that, for example, the measures promoting reconciliation of family and professional life under the Fourth Pillar on Equal Opportunities of the European Guidelines must necessarily be translated into individual rights and public obligations, or that, to provide an example to the contrary, the right to protection from dismissal for a reason connected with maternity can lose its status as a fundamental right in the presence of possible employment goals. What I do wish to underline is that the two areas now tend to overlap in a complex, changing relationship that is not without its tensions.

The tensions I am talking about will become clear if we examine the way in which the EES presents the problem of reconciliation, that is, mainly as a problem affecting the functioning of the labour market and the welfare system. As a result, there is a tendency to shift attention from the mechanisms whereby the contract of employment has realised its historical function of redistributing risk, and to forget the role that fundamental rights can play *within* the individual contract. If reconciliation rights become generic welfare rights, they run the risk of being watered down and losing all contact with productive work.

The manner in which the Court treats the question of the relationship between pregnancy, maternity and pay perfectly illustrates the risks involved with this approach. As I have said, in *Gillespie* the Court ruled that:

> women on maternity leave. . . . are in a special position which requires them to be afforded special protection, but which is not comparable either with that of a man or with that of a woman actually at work.[70]

Having stated this, in *Boyle*[71] and in *Lewen*[72] the Court, relying on the distinction made between 'pay' and 'allowance' under Article 11(2)(b) of the Pregnancy Directive, differentiates between the 'remuneration' derived from the employment relationship, and an 'adequate income' whose amount is to be

---

[69] M Freedland, 'Employment Policy', in P Davies, A Lyon-Caen, S Sciarra and S Simitis (eds), *European Community Labour Law: Principles and Perspectiva, Liber Amicorum Lord Wedderburn* (Oxford, OUP, 1996) p 287. More recently, in an essay written with Kilpatrick, the same author has noted that the overlapping of various regulatory instruments with multiple and inter-linked roles seems to typify 'a "third way" labour law governance'; see M Freedland and C Kilpatrick, 'How is EU Governance Transformative? Part-time Work in the UK', forthcoming. See also J Hunt, in this collection, at pp 57–9.

[70] Case C–342/93 [1996] ECR I–475 para 17.

[71] Case C–411/96 [1998] ECR I–6401.

[72] Case C–333/97 [2000] ECR I–7243.

set by the national legislature, having regard to the duration of such leave and the existence of any other social advantages.

The Court, therefore, abandons the male norm as a term of reference, but at the cost of transforming the woman on maternity into a 'non-worker', who cannot compare her condition to anyone else, be it a woman or a man, and at the cost of allocating her to the realm of social protection, where economic justification is more likely to gain recognition thanks to the principle of subsidiarity.[73]

The Court in *Lewen* held that:

> a worker who exercises a statutory right to take up parenting leave, which carries with it a parenting allowance paid by the State is in a special situation, which cannot be assimilated to that of a man or a woman at work since such leave involves the suspension of the contract of employment and, therefore, of the respective obligations of the employer and the worker.

It seems, thus, that the legal basis for placing a woman on maternity leave in a separate category, deprived of all comparison with other workers, is the *suspension of the contract of employment*, but the statement is at odds with the refusal in *Boyle* to compare the situation of a woman on maternity leave with that of a woman or a man on sick leave (that is to say with another case of suspension of the contract of employment).

It has been argued that the unique status accorded to a woman on maternity leave probably relies on the assumption that while a worker on sick leave remains a (potentially productive) worker, a woman on maternity leave becomes an (unproductive) mother.[74] It seems to me instead that the Court's reasoning gives more weight to the implicit use of traditional legal categories which link the cases of suspension of the contract of employment to a list of incapacities for work which: a) make the performance of contract impossible, and b) are independent of the mere will of the worker.

The Court appears to think that these are the very conditions in which the contract of employment continues to function as a re-distributing risk mechanism, and that the worker's security expectations (security of income, security of employment) continue to be fully protected. While a pregnant woman still fits into this conceptual framework, according to the Court, this is not the case of a woman on maternity leave. In this case there is no unfitness for work (which could allow a comparison with a sick male), and the suspension of the contract is the result of the woman's *choice* not to work. This seems to require, in the Court's view, a different sharing of loss between the employer, the woman and the state. It is for this reason that pregnancy rights are termed *employment rights* and maternity rights *welfare rights*.

The Court has not always followed this demarcation line: for example in *Gillespie* it held that during maternity leave a woman must, like any other

---

[73] See Wynn, above n 27 at 443.
[74] See Caracciolo di Torella and Masselot, above n 16 at 252.

worker, benefit from any pay rise, and in *Thibault*[75] it ruled that denying an annual performance assessment to a woman on maternity leave breached the Equal Treatment Directive. It may also be the case that the particularly long period of maternity leave (three years) brought to the Court's attention in *Lewen* led it to rule that the employer should not be over-burdened by what continue to be perceived as women's reproductive problems.

There remains the fact that the Court's doctrine, in insisting on the 'special situation' of the woman on maternity leave, appears to ignore some important developments that have occurred in national legal systems regarding the very concept of suspension. Focusing on the case of Italy, over time both the law and collective bargaining have granted the suspension of the employment relationship a number of different functions, so much so that legal scholars have proposed a sort of 'cumulative de-structuring' of the concepts of employment relationship and its suspension.[76] Suspension has shifted from the function of guaranteeing income security and job security in the event of incapacity for work due to circumstances beyond the worker's control, to the function of making the full development of the worker's personality possible through the exercise of a number of rights related to his or her personal and social life. The term used by some authors is 'discretionary suspension' and this refers to cases such as leave for trade union activities, leave for education and training, leave for public duties or voluntary work. The term indicates the fact that the suspension of the employment relationship is no longer due to an *objective* incapacity for work, but to the worker's *subjective* decision to use his or her energy to achieve personal or social interests,[77] a decision which is given recognition by the law. This development also affected parental leave, which, extended first to adopting mothers and then to fathers, has also departed from the perspective of the incapacity for work to enter fully into this new theory.[78]

A NEW FUNDAMENTAL RIGHT DIMENSION

The process so far described has not taken place outside, but *within* the contract of employment, through a law-made integration of its content. This means that even during non-working time, the *contract continues to be performed*, but in order to satisfy the employee's *personal* interests, which are different from the employer's *economic* interests. The process is counter-balanced by a strengthening of state intervention in supporting the worker's income, to avoid burdening employers with the direct economic costs of the new rights.

[75] Case C–136/95 [1998] ECR I–2011.
[76] See M Dell'Olio, 'Sospensione del rapporto di lavoro' (1999) *Digesto Italiano IV*, vol XV, 22 at 23.
[77] Italian labour lawyers therefore distinguish between 'impossibilità' and 'inesigibilità'. See R Del Punta, *Commentario al Codice civile, sub artt. 2110, 2111* (Milano, Giuffrè,1992) at 592.
[78] *Ibid.*

Supiot has described these changes as a process of 'concordance des temps', which re-writes the contractual organisation of working time so as to include non-productive work (care work, community work, education).[79] Italian law on parental leave even includes in this *concordance of time* the rhythm of collective life, a prospect which is not as utopian as it first sounds, given its recent experimentation in some Northern Italian cities.

These developments until recently may have seemed difficult to understand for a common lawyer. In the UK, it is contract that establishes the main duties of the parties and, with a few exceptions, statutory obligations do not enter the contract of employment, not even in the form of implied terms of the contract. There is therefore a historical difficulty in conceiving of a contract that is modified by *ius cogens*. The lack of familiarity with the concept of 'inderogability'[80] has often led common lawyers to consider that everything that is imperative is due to status and not to contract.[81] Nevertheless, for some time, even in the common law system the question of how to enlarge the so called 'relational dimension' of the contract has been widely discussed, as has the question of the relationship between common law principles and fundamental rights principles, such as those recognised by the EU's legal order or by international law.[82]

Article 33 EUCFR introduces a new fundamental rights dimension into the EU discourse on reconciliation, a dimension which can no longer be ignored when discussing how to distribute the social costs of reconciliation, and which projects into the EU legal system the issue of discontinuous work in the contract of employment. What is not clear is the extent to which this new dimension will bring about significant changes to existing reconciliation policies and rules.

The Charter clearly speaks the language of individual rights: 'everyone shall have the right . . .'. But, as I noted at the beginning, its language is fragmentary and full of gaps, and does not go so far as to state a general 'right to reconciliation' (unlike an earlier version of the Charter). It has been observed that, as a result, the provisions of the Charter on reconciliation 'merely replicate(s) the existing inadequacies of the law', while instead, as there are many examples of rights listed in the Charter that had no previous basis in Community law, it would accordingly be possible 'to draft reconciliation provisions in greater breath'.[83]

Perhaps these observations do not take into full consideration one aspect, namely that Article 33 EUCFR contains one of the few provisions in the Charter

---

[79] See A Supiot, 'Temps de travail: pour une concordance des temps' (1995) *Droit Social* 947.

[80] See Lord Wedderburn, 'Inderogability, Collective Agreements and Community Law' (1992) 21 *Industrial Law Journal* 245.

[81] See P Loi, *La sicurezza. Diritto e fondamento dei diritti nel rapporto di lavoro* (Torino, Giappichelli, 2000) 160.

[82] On the implications for British labour law of the human rights guarantees after the Human Rights Act of 1998 see K Ewing ' The Human Rights Act and Labour Law' (1998) 27 *Industrial Law Journal* 275; C Barnard and S Deakin, 'Costituzionalizzare il diritto del lavoro. L'esperienza britannica' (2000) *Lavoro e diritto* 575.

[83] See McGlynn, above n 29 at 262.

which establishes rights explicitly encapsulating entitlements to benefits which have cost implications, and runs counter to a style of drafting that rarely succumbs to the temptation to explicitly configure social rights as 'diritti di prestazione', that is as claims on public authorities or on private parties imposing economic burdens. This is clearly a compromise linked to the concern expressed by some in the debate preceding the adoption of the Charter not to entrust courts with the task of defining issues of allocation of resources which are inherently political, and should therefore be left to the political process.[84] I do not wish to discuss here the rights and wrongs of this debate. I merely wish to point out that the real issue is precisely to what extent reconciliation is a central issue in the political decision-making process.

DISCLOSING HIDDEN CONFLICTS AND SILENT POLICIES

Labour lawyers may not fully realise the extent to which reconciliation of family and professional life stands out today as both the test to the more critical issues faced by labour law and the crucible for new equilibriums. The feeling shared by many is that reconciliation remains a women's issue and, as such, an issue of specific and limited relevance (hence the overwhelming presence of female authors in this field, at least in Italy). Yet, every employment system implies a specific gender contract, or, more to the point, a specific gendered division of labour. One cannot fully understand either current labour market regulations, or changes now under way unless one looks over and beyond the narrow sphere of production into the area of reproduction.

As the historic gender contract which had been the cornerstone of traditional welfare and employment regimes is now in crisis, the sharp lines drawn between work and non-work, paid and unpaid work, professional and non professional activity seem to be disappearing.[85] The boundary between work and non-work is becoming blurred and the same phenomenon affects traditional relations between social, employment and family policies.

All this calls for the construction of a new set of social and legal regulations and requires a more egalitarian redefinition of the obligations of women and men inside the family and at work. It is for women, that is, for the members of the very social group more directly concerned by this process, to set the new agenda.[86] Should they be sidelined, as has often been the case, change might once again take on the shape of 'silent policy changes'. One example of this is that while debate on the reform of the pension systems is raging in all countries and clashing interests jostle in broad daylight, the issue of the retrenchment of

---

[84] See N Bernard, in this collection, section at pp 254–62.

[85] See Bruning and Plantega, above n 30 at 207.

[86] For a similar suggestion with respect to other 'excluded' social groups, see M Bell, in this collection, sections on older people and cultural, religious and linguistic diversity (pp 106–8).

public expenditure on social services and economic support to families is less frequently the object of public debate and politically easier to control.[87]

The other hidden conflict refers to the policy choices involved in the transition from the traditional breadwinner model to new models of division of family work and market work. Here again options are open. Should we opt for the alternative of allowing more women to participate in the labour market on the same terms as men, pressing in the direction of a two-earner economy, with some form of collectivisation of care, or, instead, should we opt for the alternative of the one and half-earner model, with men participating in the labour market in a 'female way', and thus sharing care tasks?[88] A number of other lesser or more egalitarian options exist between these two ends of the spectrum. Here again governments and social actors tend to make silent choices, while the choices of women are hard to decipher, in so far as in the attitudes of women towards family and work, both choice and constraint come into play, and it is difficult to discern to what extent women (but also men) actively interpret their identities and steer the course of their life and to what extent, instead, they merely go along pre-set paths.[89]

It is hard to believe that the Court, even though it has until now played a major role in the development of EU reconciliation policies and still stands out as the key interlocutor of the legal doctrine, should take it entirely upon itself to decide conflicts left unresolved by the political actors who wrote the provisions of the Charter. But one of the roles that it will undoubtedly be able to play will be to strengthen anti-discrimination protection, and safeguard the values and interests of minorities, which is one of the fundamental roles that courts play in the interpretation of constitutional charters. As mentioned above, a testing ground of this role could be the elaboration of a wider concept of family that respects these values and interests.

As for the rest, the construction of a system of effective reconciliation rights at the EU level will depend primarily on the capacity to push to the centre stage of public debate the hidden conflicts and the silent policies which lurk behind the words of the Charter. This is why the issue of reconciliation is at present fundamentally linked to the issue of the empowerment of women within the political process. The Charter can further this process by expressing through the strong language of constitutional texts their claim to renegotiate the gender contract in new terms.

---

[87] See C Saraceno, 'Politiche del lavoro e politiche della famiglia: una alleanza lunga e problematica' (2001) *Lavoro e diritto* 37; J Millar 'Obligations and Autonomy in Social Welfare', in Crompton (ed), above n 43, at 26.

[88] See J Visser, 'The first part-time economy in the world: a model to be followed?' (2002) 12 *Journal of European Social Policy* 24 at 37.

[89] See R Crompton and F Harris, 'Employment, Careers, and Families: The Significance of Choice and Constraints in Women's Life', in Crompton (ed), above n 43 at 133.

8

Social Security and Social Assistance

JENNIFER TOOZE*

INTRODUCTION

ARTICLE 34 IS the primary guarantee in the Charter of Fundamental Rights of the European Union, 2000 (the Charter) for social security and social assistance. It requires the EU to recognise and respect entitlement to social security and the right to social and housing assistance and it entitles everyone residing and moving legally within the EU to social security and social advantages in accordance with Community law and national laws and practices. The precise implications of Article 34 EUCFR for Member States and for EU law and policy more generally remain unclear. Further, any attempt to predict the impact of this provision is complicated by the undeveloped and technical nature of standards encapsulated in existing international law pertaining to social security and social assistance.

This chapter considers the potential scope of Article 34 EUCFR and the implications that this provision may have for EU law and policy. Relying on the Explanations relating to the complete text of the Charter (Explanatory Document),[1] it is argued that interpretation of Article 34 EUCFR should be based largely on the right to social security contained in Article 12 of the European Social Charter, 1961 (ESC) and Articles 30 and 31 of the Revised European Social Charter, 1996 (RevESC). The well-developed standards under the relevant provisions of the ESC and RevESC (collectively referred to as (Rev)ESC) are analysed with a view to identifying issues that will be of relevance for EU law. The conclusion is that Article 34 EUCFR is unlikely to prompt great change in EU law pertaining to sex discrimination and discrimination against non-nationals in social security. But work undertaken by the European Committee of Social Rights in respect of the rights to social security and social

* Home Office sponsored legal trainee. The views expressed in my chapter are my own and do not represent the views of the Home Office or the UK Government generally. Previously, a PhD student at the University of Nottingham researching international human rights law under the supervision of Professor David Harris. I should like to thank all participants of the Workshop held in Nottingham in June 2002, in particular Tamara Hervey and Steve Peers, for the many very useful comments made on a previous draft of this paper. Any mistakes are my own.

[1] European Communities, *Explanations Relating to the Complete Text of the Charter* (Luxembourg, Office for Official Publications of the European Communities, 2001), accessible from http://www.europa.eu.int.

assistance in the (Rev)ESC demonstrates the scope for diversity between national policies under these provisions, which in turn emphasises the suitability of social security and social assistance for regulation by the Open Method of Co-ordination (OMC). Furthermore, several indicators and benchmarks used by the European Committee of Social Rights are identified as being potentially applicable under the EU Social Policy Agenda.

BACKGROUND

There is no doubt that the EU was established for purposes of economic integration rather than for the protection of human rights. States entrusted the latter task to the Council of Europe which oversees the implementation of the much-celebrated European Convention on Human Rights (ECHR). But, as the role of the EU has developed, the question of human rights protection has increasingly arisen. Are the institutions of the EU bound to protect human rights and, if so, which human rights? What human rights obligations arise for Member States when implementing EU law? In recognition of the growing relevance of human rights in EU law and policy, a preambular paragraph pertaining to human rights was included in the Single European Act 1986. In 1992 an express obligation on EU institutions to respect those fundamental rights contained in the ECHR and those derived from the constitutional traditions of the Member States was included in Article 6(2) TEU. This express obligation is accompanied by a power in Articles 6(1) and 7 TEU to impose sanctions on Member States for persistent failure to respect these fundamental rights.[2] Furthermore, the European Court of Justice (the Court) has considered the question of the protection of fundamental rights and in doing so has placed a special emphasis on the ECHR.[3] But the debate has continued and one of the primary objectives behind drafting the Charter was to clarify which rights were of relevance to the EU.[4]

The Charter encapsulates a large number of civil, cultural, economic, political and social rights. But the decision to include economic, social and cultural rights was controversial. Some states distinguished these rights on the basis that they were not justiciable or enforceable by individuals in the same way as civil and political rights.[5] A compromise was struck, whereby traditional economic,

---

[2] See generally Lord Goldsmith 'A Charter of Rights, Freedoms and Principles' (2001) 38 *Common Market Law Review* 1201 at 1203.

[3] C–84/95 *Bosphorus v Minister for Transport* [1996] ECR I–3953. In this case Advocate-General Jacobs noted that '. . . for practical purposes the Convention can be regarded as Community law and can be invoked as such both in this court and in national courts where community laws are in issue', as quoted in Goldsmith, above n 2 at 1203.

[4] Goldsmith, above n 2 at 1204.

[5] The debate in respect of the justiciability of economic, social and cultural rights is complex and there is considerable literature on it. See, for example, C Sunstein, 'Social and Economic Rights? Lessons from South Africa' (2001) Public Law and Legal Theory Working Paper No. 12, The

social and cultural rights were included as principles.[6] The Charter clarifies that rights are to be 'respected' whilst principles are to be 'observed'.[7] But the subtleties of the distinction are unclear. The term 'respect' is usually employed in international human rights law to reflect abstention from action that will interfere with the enjoyment of liberties or guarantees.[8] Yet the term 'observe' is difficult to distinguish in this regard. Could the essential distinction between rights and principles rest with the individual enforceability that is associated with rights status? If so, individuals will not be able to enforce entitlements arising under Charter principles whereas they will be able to enforce entitlements arising from rights. If this is the case, there may be a conflict between certain economic and social principles in the Charter and certain economic and social rights as guaranteed in international human rights law.

Article 34 EUCFR is found alongside a number of well-recognised economic, social and cultural rights in the Chapter of the Charter entitled 'Solidarity' and provides the primary Charter guarantee for social security and social assistance. Social security and social assistance are currently protected in international human rights law. Article 22 of the Universal Declaration on Human Rights 1948 provides for a right of everyone to social security[9] and States Parties to the International Covenant on Economic, Social and Cultural Rights 1966 'recognise the right of everyone to social security, including social insurance'.[10] However, the content of the right to social security under these instruments is

University of Chicago; A Sachs, 'Social and Economic Rights: Can they be made Justiciable?' (2000) 53 *SMU Law Review* 1381; M Craven, 'The Justiciability of Economic, Social and Cultural Rights' in R Burchill, DJ Harris and A Owers (eds), *Economic, Social and Cultural Rights: Their Implementation in United Kingdom Law* (Nottingham, University of Nottingham Human Rights Law Centre, 1999) 1; SBO Gutto, 'Beyond Justiciability: Challenges of Implementing/Enforcing Socio-Economic Rights in South Africa' (1998) 4 *Buffalo Human Rights Law Review* 79; HJ Steiner, 'Social Rights and Economic Development: Converging Discourses?' (1998) 4 *Buffalo Human Rights Law Review* 25; V Leary, 'Justiciability and Beyond, Complaint Procedures and the Right to Health' (1995) 55 *International Commission of Jurists: The Review* 105; S Leckie, 'The Justiciability of Housing Rights' in F Coomans and G Van Hoof (eds), *The Right to Complain and Economic, Social and Cultural Rights* (Netherlands, Studie-en Informatiecentrum Mensenrechten, SIM, 1995) 35.

[6] Goldsmith, above n 2 at 1212. See J Kenner, in this collection, at p 16.

[7] Art 51(1) EUCFR.

[8] The obligation to respect is typically contrasted with the obligation to 'protect', which entails preventing actions of third parties from violating rights, and with the obligation to 'ensure' or 'fulfil', which requires measures to be taken to ensure rights to those who cannot secure rights through their personal efforts. See A Eide, 'Realisation of Social-Economic Rights and the Minimum Threshold Approach' (1989) 10 *Human Rights Law Journal* 35 at 37. See also G Van Hoof, 'The Legal Nature of Economic, Social and Cultural Rights: A Rebuttal of Some Traditional Views' in P Alston and K Tomasevski (eds), *The Right to Food* (Utrecht, Stichting Studie-en Informatiecentrum Mensenrechten, 1984) 97 at 106–8; K Arambulo, *Strengthening the Supervision of the International Covenant on Economic, Social and Cultural Rights. Theoretical and Procedural Aspects* (Oxford, Intersentia-Hart, 1999) 117–26.

[9] Art 22 of the Universal Declaration of Human Rights 1948, UNGA RES 217A (III). See B Andreassen, 'Article 22' in G Alfredsson and A Eide (eds), *The Universal Declaration of Human Rights. A Common Standard of Achievement* (London, Martinus Nijhoff Publishers, 1999) 453.

[10] Art 9 of the International Covenant on Economic, Social and Cultural Rights 1966, 993 UNTS 3, reprinted in (1967) 6 *International Legal Materials* 360.

yet to be clarified in detail.[11] The ESC and the RevESC both contain a right to social security and a right to social assistance.[12] These provisions have been interpreted in considerable detail and provide the most elaborate standards in respect of *rights* to social security and social assistance. Both of these provisions are of relevance to Article 34 EUCFR since they are referred to in the Explanatory Document which provides a commentary to Article 34 EUCFR. This commentary is critical to understanding the intentions of the drafters.[13] Should the Charter ever become legally binding in its current form, the intentions of the drafters will be of relevance to interpreting legal obligations where the textual or ordinary interpretation gives rise to an ambiguous or unreasonable meaning.[14] The provisions referred to in the Explanatory Document will therefore be considered in greater detail when examining the scope of Article 34 EUCFR below.

Article 34 EUCFR must be read in conjunction with the horizontal provisions contained in Articles 51–54 EUCFR. Goldsmith has argued that Article 51 (1) EUCFR means that the EU institutions are the primary addressees of the Charter and that Member States are addressees only when they are acting as agents of the EU by implementing EU law.[15] Article 51(2) EUCFR confirms that the Charter 'does not establish any new power or task for the Community or the Union, or modify powers and tasks defined by the Treaties'. Consequently, Article 34 EUCFR will not itself provide the basis for an *extension* of Community competence in the area of social security. Rather, it will impact upon standard-setting and policy-making in the field of social security where the EU institutions undertake such standard-setting and policy-making under existing competences.

To date, the Community has enjoyed only limited competence in the field of social security and social assistance.[16] Broadly speaking, social security has largely been considered in the context of equal treatment between men and women[17] and

---

[11] See J Tooze, *Identification and Enforcement of Social Security and Social Assistance Guarantees under the International Covenant on Economic, Social and Cultural Rights* (PhD thesis, University of Nottingham, 2002).

[12] Arts 12 and 13 of the ESC ETS No 035 and the RevESC ETS No 163.

[13] Goldsmith, above n 2 at 1213.

[14] Arts 31 and 32 of the Vienna Convention on the Law of Treaties 1969, reprinted in 8 *International Legal Materials* 679 (1969).

[15] Goldsmith, above n 2 at 1205.

[16] See Art 137 EC, as amended by the Treaty of Nice, which provides that 'the Community shall *support and complement* the activities of the Member States in [the field of] . . . (c) social security and social protection of workers . . . (j) the combating of social exclusion; [and] (k) the modernisation of social protection systems without prejudice to point (c) (emphasis added).' To this end, the Council may adopt so-called 'incentive measures', 'excluding any harmonisation', and in the case of social security and social protection of workers, directives, setting minimum requirements for gradual implementation.

[17] See, in particular, Dir 79/7/EEC and Dir 86/378/EEC which provide for equal treatment in statutory and occupational social security schemes respectively (OJ 1979 L 6/24 and OJ 1986 L 283/27). These are discussed further below at pp 175–8.

free movement of Community nationals.[18] In the latter context, a proposal was recently made for the adoption of a regulation on the coordination of social security systems.[19] Furthermore, both social security and social assistance fall within the scope of the EU's Social Policy Agenda. The Social Policy Agenda provides a coherent framework for new initiatives aimed at economic and social renewal.[20] It has given rise to initiatives in the field of social security and the combating of social exclusion. Thus, the Commission adopted a communication on pensions[21] and the European Parliament and Council recently adopted a decision establishing a programme of Community action to encourage cooperation between Member States to combat social exclusion.[22] It is in this context that the three paragraphs of Article 34 EUCFR will be analysed with a view to determining the potential scope of the paragraphs and the impact they may have on EU law and policy.

ARTICLE 34(1) ENTITLEMENT TO SOCIAL SECURITY BENEFITS AND SOCIAL SERVICES

Article 34(1) EUCFR reads:

> The Union recognises and respects the entitlement to social security benefits and social services providing protection in cases such as maternity, illness, industrial accidents, dependency or old age, and in the case of loss of employment, in accordance with the rules laid down by Community law and national laws and practices.

The text of the provision itself raises several important points. First, there is no reference in Article 34(1) to a *right* to social security; Article 34(1) refers to 'entitlement to social security benefits'. This tends to confirm the status of Article 34—traditionally a social right[23]—as being that of a 'principle'. Second, employment of the phrase the EU 'recognises and respects' can be seen to emphasise the fact that there is no obligation on the EU or on Member States to

---

[18] Council Reg 1408/71/EEC (OJ 1971 L 149/2) and Council Reg 1612/68/EEC (OJ 1968 L 257/2) discussed further below at pp 178–9.

[19] COM (98) 779 of 21 December 1998, OJ C 38 of 12 February 1999. See http://europa. eu.int/prelex/detail_dossier_real.cfm?CL=en&DosId=141180. This is discussed further below at p 180.

[20] For a brief background to, and details of initiatives taken pursuant to, the Social Policy Agenda see http://europa.eu.int/eur-lex/en/com/cnc/2001/com2001_0104en01.pdf.

[21] COM(2000)622, 'The Future Evolution of Social Protection from a long-term point of view: safe and sustainable pensions'. See http://europa.eu.int/eur-lex/en/com/cnc/2001/com2001_0104en 01.pdf.

[22] See Decision 50/2002/EC of 07/12/2001 (original proposal COM (2000) 368 of 16 June 2000, OJ C 337 of 28 November 2000) discussed at http://wwwdb.europarl.eu.int/oeil/oeil_ViewDNL. ProcedureView?lang=2&procid=4259. This is discussed further below at p 186.

[23] E Dankwa, 'Working Paper on Article 2(3) of the International Covenant on Economic, Social and Cultural Rights' (1987) 9 *Human Rights Quarterly* 230 at 239–40; B Simma, 'The Implementation of the International Covenant on Economic, Social and Cultural Rights' in F Matscher (ed), *The Implementation of Economic and Social Rights. National, International and Comparative Aspects* (NP Engel Verlag, Strasbourg, 1991) 75 at 81; J Tooze, above n 11 at 78–80.

legislate in this field.[24] It confirms that there is an obligation on the EU not to violate entitlement to social security benefits when it legislates in another field in which it has competence. Third, Article 34(1) is expressly addressed to the EU; 'the Union recognises and respects'. This is not the case for all provisions of the Charter and it could be argued that this term overrides Article 51(1) EUCFR, which clarifies that 'the provisions of this Charter are also addressed to . . . the Member States . . . when they are implementing Union law'. However, since Article 51(1) EUCFR is a horizontal article of general application and contains no exceptions, it is submitted that precedence should be given to it. Consequently Article 34(1) EUCFR can be seen to be directed towards both the EU and Member States implementing EU law.

Finally, the reference to 'national laws and practices' emphasises the limited competence enjoyed by the Community in the field of social security and highlights the need to respect national differences in this field.[25] Whilst the need for respecting national differences is strongly accepted, this chapter argues that Article 34 EUCFR should not be relied upon to grant Member States *carte blanche* in the field of national social security policy generally. In particular, where the Community enjoys competence that impacts upon social security provision, Member States must operate in the spirit of the guarantee provided by Article 34 EUCFR and will not be able to completely evade this obligation by reference to respect for national differences. Rather, Member States are likely to enjoy a considerable discretion as to how they guarantee social security in this context. As will be discussed below, this emphasis on respect for national differences suggests that social security matters may be particularly amenable to regulation by the OMC rather than by legislation.

The Explanatory Document sheds further light on the meaning of Article 34(1) EUCFR. It states that Article 34(1) EUCFR is based on Articles 137 and 140 EC, point 10 of the Community Charter of the Fundamental Social Rights of Workers 1989 (the Community Social Charter)[26] and Article 12 ESC. Both Article 137 and Article 140 EC confirm that social security falls primarily within the competence of Member States. As discussed above, Article 137 EC confirms that Member States continue to play the leading role in social security and social assistance matters and that the role of Community is to 'support and complement' the activities of Member States.[27] Article 140 EC provides that the Commission, 'shall encourage cooperation between the Member States and facilitate the coordination of their action in all social policy fields . . . particularly

---

[24] Goldsmith, above n 2 at 1213.

[25] See generally, Goldsmith, above n 2 at 1213.

[26] For background to the Community Charter of Fundamental Social Rights of Workers see http://www.europa.eu.int/scadplus/leg/en/cha/c10107.htm.

[27] To this end, the Council can adopt measures to encourage cooperation between Member States and may, in respect of social security and the social protection of workers, adopt, by means of directives, 'minimum requirements for gradual implementation having regard to the conditions and technical rules obtaining in each of the Member States', Article 137 EC, as amended by the Nice Treaty.

in matters relating to . . . social security'.[28] Point 10 of the Community Social Charter pertains to the potential substance of Article 34(1) of the Charter. It provides that every worker of the European Community has a right to adequate social protection and shall enjoy an adequate level of social security benefits.[29] The greatest indication as to the substantive content of Article 34(1) EUCFR is provided by the reference to Article 12 ESC. This is because the European Committee of Social Rights, which oversees implementation of the ESC, has developed elaborative jurisprudence under Article 12 ESC.

Article 12 ESC as an Aid to Interpretation

Article 12 ESC provides for a *right* to social security. Contracting Parties to the ESC undertake, 'to establish or maintain a system of social security'; 'to maintain the social security system at a satisfactory level'; 'to endeavour to raise progressively the system of social security to a higher level'; and to take steps in order to ensure equal treatment for persons moving between the Contracting Parties and 'the accumulation of insurance or employment periods completed under the legislation of each of the Contracting Parties'.

All Member States are parties to the ESC.[30] Six Member States[31] have also ratified the RevESC, which provides for a slightly higher standard.[32] However, not all Member States have undertaken to implement the four paragraphs of Article 12 ESC pertaining to social security.[33] Sweden has not accepted Article 12(4) ESC and the UK has only accepted Article 12(1) ESC.[34]

---

[28] 'To this end, the Commission shall act in close contact with Member States by making studies, delivering opinions and arranging consultations both on problems arising at national level and on those of concern to international organisations', Article 140 EC.

[29] Point 10 of the Community Charter of Fundamental Social Rights of Workers 1989 provides: 'Every worker of the European Community shall have a right to adequate social protection and shall, whatever his status and whatever the size of the undertaking in which he is employed, enjoy an adequate level of social security benefits. Persons who have been unable either to enter or re-enter the labour market and have no means of subsistence must be able to receive sufficient resources and social assistance in keeping with their particular situation'.

[30] As of 21 April 2003 there were 26 parties to the ESC, http://conventions.coe.int/Treaty/EN/cadreprincipal.htm.

[31] Sweden, Finland, France, Ireland, Italy and Portugal as of 21 April 2003, http://conventions.coe.int/Treaty/EN/cadreprincipal.htm.

[32] The reference to Convention 102 in Art 12(2) is replaced by one to the European Code of Social Security, (1964), ETS 048.

[33] States Parties to the (Rev)ESC are, subject to certain limitations, free to select the paragraphs of Articles which they accept. Under Art 20 ESC states must accept at least five of the following Articles: 1, 5, 6, 12, 13, 16 and 19. In addition, states can select Articles or numbered paras of remaining Articles. In total, States Parties must accept a minimum of 10 Articles or 45 paras. The requirements in respect of undertakings are slightly higher under the RevESC, see Part III, Article A RevESC.

[34] Although Ireland did not accept Art 12(2) ESC it did accept Art 12(2) RevESC. See declarations of states available at http://conventions.coe.int/Treaty/EN/cadreprincipal.htm.

(i) A Right to a System of Social Security

Despite the rights terminology employed in Article 12 ESC, it is clear that acceptance by States Parties of obligations in respect of this right to social security does not require States Parties to immediately provide a specific level of social security to all persons within their jurisdiction. Rather, the obligation incumbent on States Parties is the adoption, maintenance and progressive improvement of a *system* of social security.[35] Under Article 12(1) ESC, states are required to establish a social security system that 'covers a significant percentage of the population and at least offers effective benefits in several areas'.[36] When monitoring compliance, the European Committee of Social Rights enquires into the contingencies[37] and numbers[38] covered by each branch and requests that figures be broken down into wage earners, self-employed,[39] men and women,[40] professional category[41] and dependants.[42]

Article 12(2) ESC requires maintenance of the system of social security at a satisfactory level, defined as at least the level required for ratification of International Labour Organisation (ILO) Convention 102.[43] ILO Convention 102 provides for the progressive introduction of nine recognised branches of social security: medical care; sickness benefit; invalidity benefit; unemployment benefit; employment injury benefit; old-age benefit; survivors' benefit; maternity benefit; and family benefit. By way of broad summary, States Parties to ILO Convention 102 are required to accept obligations in respect of a minimum of three branches of social security.[44] States Parties are required to provide those branches to a minimum number of persons. Generally,[45] states can provide for one of four alternative groups: 50 per cent of all employees (Group 1); classes of the economically active population that constitute at least 20 per cent of all res-

---

[35] This is inevitably of relevance to the question of the justiciability of the right to social security as enshrined in the (Rev)ESC.

[36] ECSR, General Introduction, *Conclusions XIII–4*, at 37. For eg see *Conclusions XV–1*, Addendum, at 158 (Poland).

[37] ECSR, *Conclusions XV–1* at 47 (Austria).

[38] ECSR, *Conclusions XV–1* at 84 (Belgium).

[39] States have been held to be in compliance where the self-employed are covered by maternity, old-age and survivors' benefits, ECSR, *Conclusions XV–1*, Addendum, at 28 (Ireland).

[40] States have been held to be in compliance where it is not clear how many (female) part-time workers are excluded from sickness, invalidity, unemployment and retirement benefits, ECSR, *Conclusions XIV–1*, at 702 (Spain).

[41] ECSR, *Conclusions XV–1*, at 124 (Cyprus).

[42] ECSR, *Conclusions XV–1*, at 339 (Iceland).

[43] The ILO is the main UN specialised agency operating in the field of labour standards and social security and Convention 102, the *Social Security (Minimum Standards) Convention*, was adopted in 1952. For text see http://www.ilo.org.

[44] Art 2(a)(ii) Convention 102. One of these branches must be unemployment benefit, old-age benefit, employment injury benefit, invalidity benefit or survivors' benefit.

[45] A separate standard exists for those states 'whose economy and medical facilities are insufficiently developed', whereby coverage must be extended to 50% of all employees in industrial workplaces employing at least 20 persons (Group 5). See Arts 3, 9(d), 15(d), 21(c), 27(d), 33(b), 41(d), 48(d), 55(d), 61(d) Convention 102.

idents (Group 2); all residents who lack the means to live in health and decency (Group 3); and a percentage of residents (Group 4). However, all four alternatives are not available for each benefit.[46] Benefits provided under these branches must satisfy a certain minimum level. The minimum levels of income-replacement benefits[47] range between 40–50 per cent of previous or average earnings.[48] These levels are understood to be sufficient to 'maintain the family of the beneficiary in health and decency'.[49]

The European Committee of Social Rights often determines compliance with Article 12(2) ESC by reference to the assessment made by the ILO Committee of Experts on the Application of Conventions and Recommendations in respect of compliance with ILO Convention 102.[50] Where benefit levels have dropped below the required standards, the European Committee of Social Rights has declared compliance on a provisional basis only[51] or deferred reaching a conclusion.[52] Where states have not ratified either instrument, the European Committee on Social Rights has made the assessment on the basis of other instruments ratified by the State party[53] or has deferred conclusion pending receipt of further information.[54]

Having ILO Convention 102 at the heart of Article 12 ESC confirms a number of important issues which can be seen to apply equally to Article 34 EUCFR due to the reference to Article 12 ESC in the Explanatory Document. First, it confirms that social security is defined under the ESC in accordance with the ILO definition. Consequently, social security does not include social assistance.[55] Rather, there are nine branches of social security that respond to an interruption of earning power occurring in nine situations. The non-exhaustive list contained in Article 34(1) EUCFR includes a number of these branches. Second, with the exception of family benefit, social security benefits aim to provide a replacement income (often measured in terms of percentage of previous or average wage) that is generally sufficient to provide for at least a minimum standard of living. Third, although social security may be provided privately,

---

[46] Under Convention 102 groups 1–3 are available for sickness, old-age, invalidity, survivors and family benefits (Arts 15, 27, 55, 61 & 41 respectively); 1 & 3 for unemployment benefit (Art 21); 1, 2 & 4 for medical care (Art 9); 1–2 for maternity (Art 48); 1 for employment injury (Art 33). With regard to maternity and survivors' benefit these specified groups may pertain to husbands and fathers respectively and medical care includes families.

[47] Family benefit is not an income-replacement benefit as it only aims to support the costs of raising a child/family.

[48] See Arts 65 and 66 and Schedule to Part XI Convention 102.

[49] This conclusion is drawn from Art 67(c) of Convention 102, which confirms that benefits provided to certain groups must be of such a level to 'maintain the family of the beneficiary in health and decency' and in any case as high as' benefits falling between the 40–50% of previous or average wage.

[50] ECSR, General Introduction, *Conclusions XIII–4*, at 38.

[51] ECSR, Conclusions *XIII–4*, at 395 (Germany).

[52] ECSR, *Conclusions XIV–1*, at 461–62 (Italy), regarding the total level of family benefits.

[53] ECSR, *Conclusions XIII–3*, at 354 (Finland), with reference to other ILO Conventions ratified.

[54] ECSR, *Conclusions XV–1*, Addendum, at 159–60 (Poland).

[55] For discussion of social assistance, see below at n 158 and accompanying text.

states remain ultimately responsible for their obligations under ILO Convention 102.[56] Fourth, individuals should have a right of appeal in respect of 'refusal of the benefit or complaint as to its quality or quantity'[57] unless the claim 'is settled by a special tribunal established to deal with social security questions . . . on which the persons protected are represented'.[58]

Fifth, reference to ILO Convention 102 confirms that Article 12 ESC permits conditions to be attached to social security benefits. Qualifying periods, expressed in terms of contributions, employment or residence, are stipulated in ILO Convention 102 for eight of the nine branches (not for employment injury benefit). ILO Convention 102 also permits the suspension of benefits for absence from the territory, a fraudulent claim, a related criminal offence, related wilful misconduct, failure to make use of rehabilitation services available or to confirm continuing eligibility, where the claimant is being maintained at public expense or where s/he is receiving another social security benefit.[59] Finally, reference to ILO Convention 102 in Article 12(2) ESC confirms that States Parties to this provision may adopt waiting periods (the time between day one of the contingency and day one of benefit payment) in respect of some branches.[60] These obligations apply equally under Article 34(1) EUCFR. The conditions and waiting periods may be seen to constitute limitations on social security provision thus attracting the application of Article 52(1) EUCFR.[61] However, it is submitted that Article 52(1) EUCFR is unlikely to apply, because Article 34(1) EUCFR is unlikely to be considered as encapsulating either a 'right' or a 'freedom'.

Thus, it is clear that under this system, the levels, branches and beneficiaries of social security can vary between States Parties. This sits comfortably with the reference in the text of Article 34(1) EUCFR to operating in accordance with national laws and practices. Furthermore, it suggests that social security provision may be especially amenable to regulation through the OMC. Broadly speaking, the OMC is a form of governance that operates on the basis of diversity and the spreading of best practice and which is said to 'improve transparency and deepen democratic participation'.[62] It aims to enable Member States to develop at their own pace in areas of policy that have traditionally not

---

[56] Art 71(3) Convention 102. Convention 102 emphasises the need for state regulation of actuarial studies and calculations of privately administered social security. See Art 71(3) read in conjunction with Art 72(2) Convention 102.

[57] Art 70(1) Convention 102.

[58] Art 70(3) Convention 102.

[59] See Art 69 (a)(d)(e)(f)(g)(b)(c) Convention 102 respectively.

[60] Under Convention 102 waiting periods exist in respect of certain employment injury benefits, sickness benefits and unemployment benefits and range from three to seven days. See Arts 38, 18(1)(2)(b), 24(3) Convention 102 respectively.

[61] Art 52(1) EUCFR reads: 'Any limitation on the exercise of the *rights* and *freedoms* recognised by this Charter must be provided for by law and respect the essence of those rights and freedoms. Subject to the principle of proportionality, limitations may be made only if they are necessary and genuinely meet the objective of general interest recognised by the Union or the need to protect the rights and freedoms of others' (emphasis added).

[62] C de la Porte, 'Is the Open Method of Coordination Appropriate for Organising Activities at European Level in Sensitive Policy Areas?' (2002) 8 *European Law Journal* 38 at 39.

been subject to regulatory pressure from the EU level. Common indicators and benchmarks, against which state practice is measured, are set. The European Commission and Council assess compliance and make country-specific recommendations in their periodic reports. The five-year plan of action for the EU Social Policy Agenda envisages use of the OMC alongside legislation to ensure, inter alia, respect of fundamental social rights.[63] The variations that are permitted under an ILO-based right to social security clearly lend themselves to the flexibility and discretion afforded by this form of coordination. Thus, whilst Article 34(1) EUCFR will not itself provide a basis for legislating where the EU does not already enjoy competence, it may impact upon the OMC. In particular, the number of branches and beneficiaries of social security and the level of benefits provided could represent useful indicators and benchmarks to be applied under the Social Policy Agenda.

Although it does not go directly to the impact of Article 34(1) EUCFR, there is merit in commenting briefly on the justiciability of the right to social security as espoused in the ESC. As noted, Article 12 ESC does not entitle every individual to a specific level of social security provision. In this sense the justiciability of the right to social security clearly varies from that of typical civil and political rights. But the right to social security could theoretically give rise to an individual claim where states fail to take the steps necessary to establish and maintain an adequate system of social security.[64] In this sense the right can be said to be justiciable. Although it may be argued that judges are not best placed to consider macroeconomic policies of this nature, Article 12 ESC reveals how the establishment of clear benchmarks, in the form of accepted ILO standards, greatly reduces the scope for judicial activism in this traditionally political arena.[65]

(ii) *Right to Progressive Improvement of the System of Social Security*

Under Article 12(3) ESC, states are expected to strengthen protection and to extend social security to the whole population.[66] Increases in benefit levels (vis à vis inflation,[67] cost of living,[68] prices,[69] consumer price index,[70] the minimum wage,[71] salary scales,[72] average wage rates[73]) and in duration[74] are taken as

---

[63] See P Syrpis, 'Smoke without Fire: The Social Policy Agenda and the Internal Market' (2001) 30 *Industrial Law Journal* 271 at 277 ff.

[64] J Tooze, above n 11.

[65] For discussion on the role of the judiciary in respect of economic, social and cultural rights see J Tooze, above n 11 at ch 1.

[66] ECSR, General Observation, *Conclusions XIII–4*, at 143–44.

[67] ECSR, *Conclusions XV–1*, at 484 (Portugal).

[68] ECSR, *Conclusions XV–1*, at 409 (Malta).

[69] ECSR, *Conclusions XII–1*, at 184 (Netherlands).

[70] ECSR, *Conclusions XIV–1*, at 703 (Spain).

[71] ECSR, *Conclusions XII–1*, at 184 (Netherlands).

[72] ECSR, *Conclusions XIII–2*, at 110 (Denmark).

[73] ECSR, *Conclusions XIV–1*, at 498 (Luxembourg).

[74] ECSR, *Conclusions XV–1*, at 571 (Sweden).

evidence of progress. The European Committee of Social Rights highlights increases that fail to match inflation,[75] seeks information where benefits are well below the minimum wage[76] and has on occasion requested benefit levels to be presented as a percentage of the average wage rate.[77] Not surprisingly, reduction[78] or freezing[79] of benefit levels gives rise to concern, but will not necessarily lead to non-compliance.

Notwithstanding this obligation to progress, in the last 10 years or so many States Parties to the (Rev)ESC have adopted 'regressive' measures in this field with a view to addressing demographic changes and the changing structures of employment, to reducing budget deficits[80] and to satisfying the EU economic criteria.[81] These developments have led the European Committee of Social Rights to recognise that, 'in view of the close relationship between the economy and social rights, the pursuit of economic goals is not necessarily incompatible' with the progressive obligation.[82] It therefore accepts alterations to social security systems,

> to the extent that these are necessary in order to ensure the maintenance of the system in question . . . [and on the condition that] any restrictions do not interfere with the effective protection of all members of society . . . and do not tend to gradually reduce the social security system to a system of minimum assistance.[83]

The European Committee of Social Rights insists on assessing the appropriateness of any measures adopted in pursuit of such goals.[84] To this end it requests information on the nature, extent and results of changes, the reasons underlying changes, the necessity of the reform, the adequacy of the reform in the particular situation and the existence of social assistance measures for those consequently in need.[85]

This General Observation has permitted the acceptance under Article 12(3) (Rev)ESC of many regressive measures, for example, a reduction in early retire-

---

[75] ECSR, *Conclusions XIV–1*, at 353 (Greece).

[76] ECSR, *Conclusions XIV–1*, at 704 (Spain).

[77] ECSR, *Conclusions XIII–4*, at 150 (Greece).

[78] ECSR, *Conclusions XV–1*, Addendum at 60–61 (Luxembourg), where a 13% reduction in pensions led to a deferred conclusion. Information is likely to be requested even where only a small number of benefits have been reduced in level or in duration and a positive conclusion is reached overall, *Conclusions XII–1*, at 181–82 (Denmark), where increases in 3 benefits and a decrease in 1 benefit were identified.

[79] ECSR, *Conclusions XIV–1*, at 464–66 (Italy), conclusion deferred.

[80] ECSR, General Introduction, *Conclusions XIII–4*, at 35–36.

[81] ECSR, General Introduction, *Conclusions XIV–1*, at 46; *Conclusions XIV–1*, at 80 (Austria).

[82] The ECSR accepted that 'Contracting Parties may consider that consolidating public finances, in order to prevent deficits and debt interest from increasing, is one way of safeguarding the social security system', ECSR, General Introduction, *Conclusions XIV–1*, at 39.

[83] ECSR, General Observation on Art 12(3), *Conclusions XIII–4*, at 143; General Introduction, *Conclusions XIV–1*, at 39 & 46. Concern has been expressed where states are suspected of drifting towards a system of minimum assistance, *Conclusions XIV–1*, at 185–88 (Denmark); *Conclusions XV–1*, Addendum, at 160–61 (Poland).

[84] ECSR, General Introduction, *Conclusions XIV–1*, at 39.

[85] ECSR, General Observation, *Conclusions XIII–4*, at 143–44.

ment together with restrictions in medical care[86] and removal of the state pension where adequate alternative pensions were available.[87] However, the European Committee of Social Rights did defer its conclusion where a 'capitalising scheme for pensions' had been introduced, pending information on the results arising,[88] and where public service pensions were substantially reduced until reasons were given and information regarding compensatory measures was provided.[89]

Adoption of workfare measures, whereby unemployment benefit is made conditional on certain actions being taken by the beneficiary, is a common regressive measure considered under Article 12(3) (Rev)ESC. The European Committee of Social Rights has accepted an obligation to take up reasonable job offers outside the claimant's normal occupational area after six months of unemployment[90] and suspension of unemployment benefit for between three weeks and three months on refusal to accept a job offer or to take up training or on ceasing work without a valid reason.[91] However, it has sought further information as to the interpretation given to 'suitable job'[92] and found one State party to be in violation of Article 12(3) (Rev)ESC due to the disproportionate nature of workfare measures. In the latter case, the workfare programme, which was adopted in a state enjoying close to full employment and economic growth, had entailed forfeiture of unemployment benefit to over 8000 claimants for a period of between eight weeks and six months for (repeated) refusal to accept a job anywhere in the country and regardless of skills, qualifications, family and personal circumstances.[93]

The approach taken by the European Committee of Social Rights to regressive measures demonstrates how the right to social security can be interpreted so as to respond to economic demands incumbent upon individual states.[94] Yet it also establishes the limits to which states may regress by establishing a bottom line below which social security provision must not fall. This may well be a distinguishing factor of social security provision within the Council of Europe, particularly when compared with more liberal systems of welfare provision, such as the system in the USA. By virtue of Article 34 EUCFR, this distinguishing factor may well be determinative in any EU law and policy pertaining to social security. Whilst social security standards may vary between Member States and whilst regression may be permitted in accordance with financial needs, Member

[86] ECSR, *Conclusions XV–1*, at 47–48 (Austria).
[87] ECSR, *Conclusions XV–1*, at 208–10 (Finland).
[88] ECSR, *Conclusions XV–1*, at 372 (Italy).
[89] ECSR, *Conclusions XV–1*, Addendum, at 60–61 (Luxembourg).
[90] ECSR, *Conclusions XV–1*, at 159 (Denmark).
[91] ECSR, *Conclusions XV–1*, at 209–10 (Finland).
[92] ECSR, *Conclusion XV–1*, Addendum, at 160–61 (Poland).
[93] ECSR, *Conclusions XV–1*, at 440–42 (Norway).
[94] This approach may be transferable to other economic and social rights and to other instruments. This author has argued elsewhere that a similar approach should be taken under Art 9 of the UN International Covenant on Economic, Social and Cultural Rights 1966 (ICESCR), J Tooze, above n 11.

States should refrain from reducing social security provision to a system of minimum assistance. Further, the EU should avoid any policy that encourages a reduction below this level.

How might this influence existing policy on social security? The bulk of EU legislation pertaining to social security pertains to sex discrimination and to discrimination against Community and third country nationals which prevents the free movement of these groups. These forms of discrimination in social security provision are considered below and, in any case, are unlikely to be directly affected by this orientation of social security policy away from minimum assistance. But, as discussed above, social security can also be seen to fall within the scope of the EU Social Policy Agenda which is being implemented by the OMC as well as by legislation. Article 34(1) EUCFR may provide a basis on which to insist that indicators and benchmarks set under the OMC for poverty and social inclusion should prevent social security from being reduced to a system of minimum assistance.

(iii) Equal Treatment in Social Security

Although Article 12 (Rev)ESC does not necessarily guarantee every person a particular level of social security, it does guarantee equal treatment between men and women and it prohibits discrimination on a number of commonly recognised grounds.[95] Thus, regardless of the numbers of persons covered by the social security system in operation, those covered must be treated equally. This non-discrimination requirement is not unusual; international human rights law provides for the immediate eradication of de jure discrimination in economic, social and cultural rights as well as in civil and political rights.[96] Although this extends to the equal treatment of non-nationals, states frequently flout this obligation in the field of economic, social and cultural rights.[97] It is

---

[95] Preambular para 4 ESC provides a parasitic non-discrimination provision: 'Considering that the enjoyment of social rights should be secured without discrimination on grounds of race, colour, sex, religion, political opinion, national extraction or social origin'. Part V, Article E, RevESC provides a similar provision: 'The enjoyment of the rights set forth in this Charter shall be secured without discrimination on any ground such as race, colour, sex, language, religion, political or other opinion, national extraction or social origin, health, association with a national minority, birth or other status'.

[96] See, for example, the parasitic non-discrimination provision contained in Art 2(2) ICESCR, 993 UNTS 3, reprinted in (1967) 6 *International Legal Materials* 360; Limburg Principles on the Implementation of the International Covenant on Economic, Social and Cultural Rights (1986) 9 *Human Rights Quarterly* 122, Principles 37 and 38; Y Klerk, 'Working Paper on Article 2(2) and Article 3 of the International Covenant on Economic, Social and Cultural Rights' (1987) 9 *Human Rights Quarterly* 250. There has also been a considerable amount of jurisprudence on equal treatment in social security under the free standing equality before the law guarantee contained in Art 26 of the International Covenant on Civil and Political Rights 1966 (ICCPR), 999 UNTS 171, reprinted in (1967) 6 *International Legal Materials* 368. See, for example, *Broeks v Netherlands* [1987], A/42/40, 139; *Vos v Netherlands* [1999], A/54/40, 271; J Tooze, above n 11 at chs 7 and 8.

[97] See E Dankwa, 'Working Paper on Article 2(3) of the International Covenant on Economic, Social and Cultural Rights' (1987) 9 *Human Rights Quarterly* 230 at 246–48.

perhaps not surprising therefore that Article 12(4) (Rev)ESC permits certain exceptions to the principle of equal treatment of non-nationals in the field of social security. This will be discussed below when considering the transferability of social security between Member States.

In practice the obligation to remove de jure discrimination in social security immediately may well be onerous. This is particularly· the case for sex discrimination because social security legislation must take into account and respond to factual differences between the roles traditionally played by men and women in the labour market. Failure to take such differences into account may give rise to indirect discrimination. For example, the European Committee on Social Rights does not consider it acceptable to exclude part-time workers from the social security system under Article 12(1) ESC;[98] the majority of part-time workers are usually women. Yet, since the factual situation of men and women in the labour market is evolving, social security legislation that once legitimately distinguished between men and women may become discriminatory over time.[99] Thus, the non-discrimination requirement in practice requires the continuous review of existing social security legislation. This has led some to argue that social security necessarily lags behind social developments and that the appropriate legal obligation is that of the periodic review of legislation rather than the eradication of any discrimination.[100] However, human rights bodies have generally insisted on the immediate nature of the obligation to eradicate de jure discrimination. For example, when confronted with social security legislation that discriminated against women, the European Court of Human Rights (ECtHR) did not hesitate to find a violation of Article 14 in conjunction with Article 1, Protocol 1 of the ECHR (right to property).[101]

Could Article 34(1) EUCFR give rise to any new standards in EU Law in the field of sex discrimination? Directives 79/7/EEC[102] and 86/378/EEC[103] (as amended by Directive 96/97[104]) provide for the implementation of the principle of equal treatment for men and women in matters of social security equal

---

[98] ECSR, *Conclusions XV–1, vol 1*, between 80 and 90 (Belgium), available at http://www.coe.int/T/E/Human_Rights/Esc/5_Recent_Conclusions/2_By_Control_Cycles/Social_Charter/Conclusions_XV-1Vol_1Eng.asp#TopOfPage.

[99] See, for eg four cases considered under Art 26 ICCPR: *Broeks v Netherlands* [1987], A/42/40, 139; *Zwaan-de Vries v Netherlands* [1987], A/42/40, 160; *Vos v Netherlands* [1989], A/44/40, 232; *Pauger v Austria* [1992], A/47/40, 325.

[100] Three members of the UN Human Rights Committee argued this in an individual opinion, Ando, Herndl and Ndiaye, HRC Individual Opinion in *Sprenger v Netherlands* [1992], A/47/40, 311, at 315–16.

[101] See *Van Raalte v Netherlands* [1997] 24 EHRR 503, at 514, para 44 and at 518–20, paras 39–44.

[102] Dir 79/7/EEC of 19 December 1978 on the progressive implementation of the principle of equal treatment for men and women in matters of social security (OJ 1979 L 6/24).

[103] Dir 86/378/EEC of 24 July 1986 on the implementation of the principle of equal treatment for men and women in occupational social security schemes (OJ 1986 L 283/27).

[104] Dir 96/97/EC of 20 December 1996 amending Dir 86/378/EEC on the implementation of the principle of equal treatment for men and women in occupational social security schemes (OJ 1996 L 46/20).

treatment in statutory and occupational social security schemes respectively. However, there are a number of exceptions to this principle of equal treatment.

Pensionable ages are currently excluded from the principle of equal treatment in both statutory[105] and occupational[106] social security schemes. The Court has clarified that this exception to the principle aims to 'enable [States] . . . progressively to adapt their pensions systems . . . without disrupting the complex financial equilibrium of those systems'.[107] States must demonstrate that any difference in treatment is necessary to prevent upsetting this financial equilibrium. By way of example, the Court has held that it is not necessary to gear non-contributory benefits to pensionable ages in order to avoid upsetting the financial equilibrium,[108] that different contributory requirements can no longer be justified where differences in pensionable ages have been abolished,[109] that prescriptions awarded at the statutory pensionable age (not necessarily on retirement) are not 'necessarily and objectively' tied to the pensionable age[110] and that a difference in the minimum eligibility age for invalidity benefits can not be justified simply because that benefit will be replaced by old-age benefits at different retirement ages.[111]

In practice the scope of the EU derogation varies between statutory and occupational schemes. With regard to statutory schemes, Directive 79/7/EEC requires states to periodically examine differences 'in order to ascertain, in the light of social developments . . . whether there is justification for maintaining the exclusions concerned'.[112] Notwithstanding the absence of such an obligation in Directive 86/378/EEC, the obligation regarding occupational systems appears to be more onerous. In a series of judgments the Court has in effect eroded the derogation in Directive 86/378/EEC by insisting that access to and benefits derived from occupational pension schemes constitute 'pay' and are consequently subject to equal treatment under Article 141 (ex 119) EC.[113] This line of cases suggests that differentiating between conditions of access in statutory

---

[105] Art 7(1)(a) Dir 79/7/EEC (OJ 1979 L 6/24).

[106] Art 9(a) Dir 86/378/EEC (OJ L 283/27).

[107] Case C–9/91 *R v Secretary of State for Social Security*, ex parte *Equal Opportunities Commission* [1992] ECR I–4297, para 15 (statutory scheme); Case C–92/94 *Secretary of State for Social Security v Rose Graham and others* [1995] ECR I–2521, para 12 (statutory scheme).

[108] Case C–328/91 *Secretary of State for Social Security v Evelyn Thomas and Others* [1993] ECR I–1247, paras 14–21.

[109] Case C–154/92 *Remi van Cant v Rijksdienst voor Pensionen* [1993] ECR I–3811, paras 9–14.

[110] Case C–137/94 *R v Secretary of State for Health*, ex parte *Richardson* [1995] ECR I–3407, paras 15–29.

[111] Case C–104/98 *Buchner v Sozialversicherungsanstalt der Bauern* 23 May 2000, reported in (2000) 57 *EU FOCUS* 8–9.

[112] Art 7(2) Dir 79/7/EEC (OJ 1979 L 6/24).

[113] The first case was Case 170/84 *Bilka-Kaufhaus GmbH v Karn Weber von Hartz* [1986] ECR 1607. This was followed in 1990 by Case C–262/88 *Barber v Guardian Royal Exchange Assurance Group* [1990] ECR I–1889 in which the Court held that the setting of different age conditions for the termination of employment was in violation of Art 119 (now 141) EC. The decisive criterion is whether the benefits are paid due to the employment relationship. See Case C–7/93 *Bestuur van het Algemeen Burgerlijk Pensioenfonds v Beune* [1994] ECR I–4471; *Podesta (CRICA)* [2002] ECR I–4039.

systems cannot be replicated in occupational systems[114] and differences in benefit levels may only be replicated where they aim to achieve substantive equality[115] and not to perpetuate the statutory discrimination.[116] Article 141 includes employer[117] and worker[118] contributions. The willingness of the Court to justify differences in occupational systems that promote *substantive* equality on the basis of differences in statutory entitlement permits statutory inequality to be rectified by occupational inequality.[119]

EU Directive 79/7EC also permits the granting of benefits for dependent wives but again calls on Member States to, 'periodically examine [this] matter . . . in order to ascertain, in the light of social developments in the matter concerned, whether there is justification for maintaining the exclusions concerned'.[120]

Will Article 34(1) EUCFR place pressure on Member States to remove any remaining sex discrimination immediately or will states continue to periodically review these excluded areas with a view to determining whether the difference in treatment is justified? On the one hand, it could be argued that the guarantee in Article 34(1) EUCFR, particularly when read in conjunction with the reference to Article 12 ESC in the Explanatory Document, requires the immediate eradication of de jure sex discrimination in social security. However, a number of factors support the retention of these exceptions to the principle of equal treatment between men and women in social security. First and foremost, Member States have not been found to be in violation of Article 12 (Rev)ESC on the basis of these exceptions.[121] Moreover, it is not evident that there is sufficient support within the EU for the removal of these exceptions. The importance of maintaining the financial equilibrium of social security systems was recognised when Article 137 EC was amended by the Nice Treaty. Thus, Article 137 EC as amended insists that provisions adopted under that article 'must not significantly affect the financial equilibrium' of the social security systems of

---

[114] See Case C–110/91 *Michael Moroni v Collo GmbH* [1993] ECR I–6591, paras 9–20.

[115] This was the case in Case C–132/92 *Birds Eye Walls Ltd v Friedel M Roberts* [1993] ECR I–5579, paras 12–24.

[116] See Case C–7/93 *Bestuur van het Algemeen Burgerlijk Pensioenfonds v Beune* [1994] ECR I–4471. See in this regard E Whiteford, 'Occupational Pensions and European Law: Clarity at Last?' in TK Hervey and D O'Keeffe (eds), *Sex Equality Law in the European Union* (Chichester, Wiley, 1996) 21.

[117] Case 192/85 *George Noel Newstead v Department of Transport and HM Treasury* [1987] ECR 4753. Except where actuarial tables are used since these do not fall within Art 141 EC, Case C–152/91 *David Neath v Hugh Sleepner Ltd* [1993] ECR I–6935, paras 19–34.

[118] Case C–200/91 *Coloroll Pension Trustees Ltd v Russell and others* [1994] ECR I–4389, paras 86–93.

[119] In Case C–132/92 *Birds Eye Walls Ltd v Friedel M Roberts* [1993] ECR I–5579 the Court permitted different levels of bridging pensions for men and women on the basis that it gave rise to substantive equality, taking into consideration the different statutory pension system. See E Whiteford, above n 116 at 29–34.

[120] Art 7(1)(c) & (d) (2) Dir 79/7/EEC (1979) (OJ 1979 L 6/24).

[121] In a similar vein, states can exclude social security from the protection of Art 1(1) of the 1988 Additional Protocol to the ESC which provides for equal treatment in, inter alia, remuneration. See Council of Europe, *Equality between women and men in the European Social Charter*, Social Charter Monograph No 2 (Council of Europe, Strasbourg, 1999) at 25–26.

Member States.[122] Furthermore, a Commission proposal in 1987 for a Council Directive completing the implementation of the principle of equal treatment for men and women in statutory and occupational social security schemes[123] has not yet obtained the acceptance of the EU Parliament or Council.[124] It is also worth emphasising that the judicial scrutiny exercised by the Court over the necessity of any exceptions made by Member States provides a solid safeguard and reduces scope for abuse. For these reasons, it is submitted that Article 34 EUCFR is unlikely by itself to place pressure on Member States to withdraw their exceptions to the principle of equal treatment between men and women in the field of social security. To this limited extent, therefore, the eradication of discrimination on the grounds of sex can be seen to be progressive in the field of social security.

ARTICLE 34(2): TRANSFERABILITY OF SOCIAL SECURITY BETWEEN MEMBER STATES

Article 34(2) EUCFR reads, 'Everyone residing and moving legally within the European Union is entitled to social security benefits and social advantages in accordance with Community law and national laws and practices'. It is clear from the text of Article 34(2) that both social assistance and social security fall within the scope of this provision. This is because the term 'social advantages', has been interpreted as including social assistance under Regulation 1612/68/EEC.[125] The inclusion of social assistance under Article 34(2) EUCFR is further confirmed by the reference in the Explanatory Document to Article 13(4) ESC. It is less clear from the text of Article 34(2) EUCFR which groups are going to enjoy protection and whether those groups are to enjoy equal treatment. A literal interpretation of Article 34(2) suggests that this provision includes 'everyone residing and moving legally within the European Union', regardless of whether they are Community nationals. Yet the provisions referred to in the Explanatory Document generally extend protection to Community nationals only.[126] Furthermore, although there is no express reference in Article 34(2) to equal treatment, some of the references in the Explanatory Document suggest that equal treatment may be envisaged.

The Explanatory Document states that Article 34(2) EUCFR is based on Article 13(4) ESC, point 2 of the Community Social Charter and reflects the rules

---

[122] Art 137(4) EC, as amended by the Nice Treaty.

[123] COM(87)494 final, 23 October 1987, discussed at http://www.europa.eu.int/scadplus/leg/en/cha/c10907.htm. OJ C 309 19 November 1987 at 10.

[124] On 16 September 1999, the EU Parliament decided not to accept the Commission's proposal at first reading and invited the Commission to present a revised proposal taking account of the Commission's political commitments and developments in the areas concerned, see http://europa.eu.int/smartapi/cgi/sga_doc?smartapi!celexapi!prod!CELEXnumdoc&lg=en&model=guicheti&numdoc=587PC0494.

[125] See T Hervey, *European Social Law and Policy* (London, Longman, 1998) at 92.

[126] See further below.

arising from Regulation 1408/71/EEC[127] and Regulation 1612/68/EEC.[128] Point 2 of the Community Social Charter provides:

> The right to freedom of movement shall enable any worker to engage in any occupation or profession in the Community in accordance with the principle of equal treatment as regards access to employment, working conditions and social protection in the host country.

Article 13(4) ESC provides for treatment of non-nationals in respect of social assistance and Regulations 1408/71/EEC and 1612/68/EEC concern treatment of non-nationals in respect of social security. Since Regulations 1408/71/EEC and 1612/68/EEC go to the very heart of the obligations contained in Article 12(4) (Rev)ESC, it is submitted that Article 12(4) ESC is also applicable to Article 34(2) EUCFR. Thus, Article 12(4) (Rev)ESC provides interpretative guidelines in respect of social security whilst Article 13(4) ESC does so in respect of social assistance.

Transferability of Social Security

Regulations 1612/68/EEC and 1408/71/EEC pertain to the question of the free movement of persons, in particular Community nationals, within the EU.[129] Regulation 1612/68/EEC provides for the equal treatment of migrant workers who are Community nationals under the national social security scheme of the Member State in which they work.[130] Regulation 1408/71/EEC prohibits discrimination on the grounds of nationality, supports aggregation and apportionment of benefit rights and supports the exportability of benefits from one Member State to another.[131] Broadly speaking, Regulation 1408/71/EEC extends to workers who are, or have been, subject to the legislation of one or more Member States and who are nationals of one of the Member States and to their families and survivors.[132] The need to simplify and improve the coordination rules contained in Regulation 1408/71/EEC was recognised as early as 1992[133] and in 1998 the Commission proposed to replace Regulation

---

[127] Reg 1408/71/EEC of the Council of 14 June 1971 on the application of social security schemes to employed persons and their families moving within the Community (OJ 1971 L 149/2).

[128] Reg 1612/68/EEC of the Council of 15 October 1968 on freedom of movement for workers within the Community (OJ 1968 L 257/2).

[129] Although not referred to in the Explanatory Document, the EU Council adopted another directive in this field; Dir 98/49/EC of 29 June 1998 on safeguarding the supplementary pension rights of employed and self-employed persons moving within the Community (OJ 1998 L 209/46).

[130] See T Hervey, above n 125 at 84 ff.

[131] *Ibid.*

[132] Art 2(1) Reg 1408/71/EEC (OJ 1971 L 149/2). Amongst other groups covered by this regulation are stateless persons and refugees residing within the territory of a Member State (Article 2(1)) and survivors of workers who have been subject to the legislation of a Member State but who are not nationals of a Member State so long as those survivors are a national of a Member State (Article 2(2)).

[133] Edinburgh European Council, 11–12 December 1992, Presidency Conclusions (SN 456/92).

1408/71/EEC.[134] The new regulation would extend protection to third country nationals who are or have been subject to the social security legislation of one or more Member States and to their families and survivors.[135] Discussions were held by the Council in June 2002 at which a compromise that allows certain limited derogations concerning the inclusion of family benefits in the material scope of the Regulation was struck. This compromise responded to the desire of two delegations to maintain their current practice, whereby the status of third country nationals is not fully equivalent to that of EU citizens.[136]

The practice under Article 12(4) (Rev)ESC demonstrates the difficulties arising from the extension of equal treatment to third country nationals. As noted above, Article 12(4) (Rev)ESC deals with the issue of the transferability of social security benefits. As such it has been described as the 'cornerstone . . . of the whole European social security coordination edifice'.[137] Under Article 12(4)(a) (Rev)ESC States Parties undertake to:

> take steps, by the conclusion of appropriate bilateral and multilateral agreements or by other means, and subject to the conditions laid down in such agreement, in order to ensure . . . equal treatment of non-nationals of other Parties in respect of social security rights, including the retention of benefits arising out of social security legislation, whatever movements the persons protected may undertake between the territories of the Parties.

This provides for the equal treatment in social security of nationals of other States Parties, regardless of whether those States Parties have undertaken to reciprocate this treatment by accepting Article 12(4)(a) (Rev)ESC. It applies to non-nationals regardless of whether they are lawfully resident or working regularly within the territory.[138] The European Committee of Social Rights has confirmed that this provision of equal treatment generally applies to all general and special contributory, non-contributory and combined social security schemes.[139]

---

[134] Proposal for a Council Regulation on coordination of social security systems, COM(98) 779 final—AVC 98/0360, OJ C038, 12 February 1999, at 10. For background see http://www.europa.eu.int/scadplus/leg/en/cha/c10521.htm.

[135] See Art 1 of the proposal, COM(98) 779 final. For discussion see H Verschueren, 'EC Social Security Coordination Excluding Third Country Nationals: Still in Line with Fundamental Rights after the *Gaygusuz* Judgment?' (1997) 34 *Common Market Law Review* 991.

[136] See http://europa.eu.int/smartapi/cgi/sga_doc?smartapi!celexapi!prod!CELEXnumdoc&lg=en&numdoc=51998PC0779&model=guicheti. The European Economic and Social Committee also expressed support for the inclusion of third country nationals who are affiliated to the social security regime of a Member State, Opinion of the Economic and Social Committee on the 'Proposal for a Council Regulation on coordination of social security systems' (2000/C 75/11) 27 January 2000. See http://europa.eu.int/smartapi/cgi/sga_doc?smartapi!celexapi!prod!CELEXnumdoc&lg=en&numdoc=52000AC0090&model=guichett.

[137] Council of Europe, *Social Protection in the European Social Charter*, (Strasbourg, Council of Europe, 1999), at 40.

[138] See Appendix, para 1, (Revised) ESC; DJ Harris, *The European Social Charter*, 2nd edn (New York, Transnational Publishers Inc, 2001) at 162.

[139] ECSR, General Introduction, *Conclusions XIII–4*, at 43.

The equal treatment required under Article 12(4)(a) (Rev)ESC proscribes states from granting social security benefits to nationals only[140] and from varying the duration of benefits between nationals and non-nationals.[141] As a general rule, Article 12(4)(a) (Rev)ESC proscribes states from attaching additional conditions to non-nationals from other States Parties to the (Rev)ESC.[142] However, residency requirements are permitted in respect of all non-contributory social security benefits[143] so long as they are proportionate.[144] (This reflects that these benefits are funded from taxation.[145]) During its 15th cycle the European Committee of Social Rights found 12 of the 17 states considered under Article 12(4) (Rev)ESC to be in violation of that provision where contributory or non-contributory[146] family or child benefits were conditioned to the residence of the child in the awarding state.[147]

Article 12(4)(a) (Rev)ESC provides for 'the retention of benefits arising out of social security legislation, whatever movements the persons protected may undertake between the territories of the Contracting Parties'.[148] This essentially permits non-nationals who are nationals of any State party to the (Rev)ESC to export their accrued entitlement from one to any other State party to the (Rev)ESC. During the 13th cycle the European Committee of Social Rights recognised that this aspect of Article 12 (Rev)ESC was undeveloped and called on states to indicate how the principle was implemented.[149] The European Committee of Social Rights has since found violations where retention is not available to nationals of all States Parties to the (Rev)ESC.[150]

Article 12(4)(b) (Rev)ESC provides for the 'granting, maintenance and resumption of social security rights by such means as the accumulation of insurance or employment periods completed under the legislation of each of the

---

[140] ECSR, General Introduction, *Conclusions XIII–4*, at 43; *Conclusions XIV–1*, at 708–9 (Turkey).

[141] ECSR, *Conclusions XV–1*, at 261–62 (France).

[142] ECSR, General Introduction, *Conclusions XIII–4*, at 43–44; *Conclusions XIV–1*, at 82 (Austria).

[143] Appendix, Art 12(4) (Rev)ESC. The fact that residency requirements are not permitted for all benefits confirms that 'lawfully resident' does not imply satisfaction of any residence requirement.

[144] ECSR, *Conclusions XIII–3*, at 357–58 (Finland).

[145] ECSR, *Conclusions XV–1*, at 162 (Denmark).

[146] The residence requirement that may be imposed under the Appendix to the (Rev)ESC pertains only to the beneficiary (the parent in the case of family benefit) and not to the child thereof in respect of which the benefit is granted, ECSR, *Conclusions XIII–4*, at 404 (Germany).

[147] ECSR, *Conclusions XV–1*, at 88 (Belgium).

[148] See DJ Harris, above n 138 at 164.

[149] ECSR, General Introduction, *Conclusions XIII–4*, at 45. The ECSR confirmed that 'without taking a determinative position on this point . . . this principle is obviously applicable to benefits such as invalidity, old-age, survivors' benefits, employment, injury, pensions, death grants accruing under the legislation' (that is, long-term benefits) General Introduction, *Conclusions XIII–4*, at 45. It also noted that 'a variety of arrangements, whose scope the Committee reserves the right to assess, can be made for other benefits (particularly unemployment and sickness benefits)', *ibid*, and confirmed that it does not require retention of short-term benefits that are linked to the labour-market, *Conclusions XIV–1*, at 630 (Norway), in relation to unemployment benefit.

[150] ECSR, *Conclusions XV–1*, Addendum at 31 (Ireland).

Contracting Parties'. This provision ensures that nationals of States Parties to the (Rev)ESC can move between States Parties without losing the periods of employment, insurance and residence they have accumulated.[151] Again, this is a relatively undeveloped provision and during the 13th cycle the European Committee of Social Rights requested states to report on how this is achieved.[152] It was not until the 15th cycle that the European Committee of Social Rights found violations on the basis that states failed to take periods spent by non-EU and non-EEA nationals in other States Parties into account.[153]

All 15 Member States of the EU and the States Parties to the Agreement on the European Economic Area that have accepted Article 12(4) (Rev)ESC satisfy the requirements of this provision in respect of *each other*.[154] But EU states do not necessarily satisfy the requirements in respect of non-EU and non-EEA states. In practice, it seems that they are not required to under Article 12(4)(b) (Rev)ESC. This is because the European Committee of Social Rights has generally accepted that ratification by states of the European Convention on Social Security 1972 is sufficient for the purposes of Article 12(4)(b) (Rev)ESC.[155] States Parties to the 1972 Convention need only adopt measures in respect of each other's nationals (as well as refugees and stateless persons).[156] Since there are only eight States Parties to the 1972 Convention, seven of which are members of the EU,[157] this approach only requires EEA states, including Member States, to extend equal treatment to nationals of one non-EEA state. In this way, Article 12(4)(b) (Rev)ESC can be seen to be subject to progressive implementation.

The progressive nature of the obligation imposed in practice under Article 12(4)(b) (Rev)ESC demonstrates how difficult it has proven to extend equal treatment to non-nationals who are nationals of the States Parties to the (Rev)ESC. This is of relevance to the debate in EU law regarding extension of equal treatment in social security to third country nationals and casts doubt on whether Article 34 EUCFR is itself going to provide a strong basis for requiring the immediate equal treatment of all third country nationals in matters of accrual and maintenance of social security benefits.

Transferability of Social Assistance

Social assistance can be distinguished from social security on the basis of the contingency to which it responds. Rather than responding to any of the nine

---

[151] ECSR, General Introduction, *Conclusions XIII–4*, at 45–46.

[152] ECSR, General Introduction, *Conclusions XIII–4*, at 46.

[153] ECSR, *Conclusions XV–1*, at 162 (Denmark).

[154] This was the case during the 14th & 15th supervision cycles by virtue of European legislation.

[155] ECSR, *Conclusions XV–1*, 51 (Austria).

[156] Art 4 of the 1972 Convention ETS No. 078.

[157] As of 21 April 2003 Austria, Belgium, Italy, Luxembourg, Netherlands, Portugal, Spain and Turkey are parties to the 1972 Convention, http://conventions.coe.int/Treaty/EN/cadreprincipal.htm.

contingencies falling within social security, social assistance provides a safety net of last resort to all those in need.[158] It is not contributory, is almost always means-tested and is provided in cash or in kind. It is almost always funded through general taxation. Inevitably, there is some overlap between social security and social assistance. For example, a non-contributory old-age pension may provide an income of last resort to the elderly. Nevertheless, according to this distinction, this benefit would fall within social security because it responds to one of the nine contingencies; old-age.

Regulation 1612/68/EEC provides that a worker who is a national of a Member State shall, when in the territory of another Member State, enjoy the same social advantages as national workers.[159] A broad interpretation is given to the meaning of worker, where a worker is one who carries out 'general and effective' economic activity that is not 'marginal and ancillary'.[160] The crucial factor is whether the non-nationals are lawfully resident.[161] Article 13(4) (Rev)ESC covers a different group of non-nationals. It provides social assistance protection to nationals of other States Parties to the (Rev)ESC that are neither lawfully resident nor working regularly within the territory but that are simply lawfully within the territory. This group includes tourists and students.[162]

On the face of it, Article 13(4) (Rev)ESC appears to require equal treatment of these non-nationals to the extent required under Article 13(1) (Rev)ESC.[163] Article 13(1) (Rev)ESC requires equal treatment of non-nationals of other States Parties that are working regularly or are legally resident in the State party in question.[164] States Parties will not comply with Article 13(1) (Rev)ESC where some assistance benefits are provided to nationals only[165] or to nationals of only some States Parties to the (Rev)ESC,[166] where benefits are of more limited duration for non-nationals[167] or where residence requirements are attached to social and medical assistance.[168] However, it is clear that the social and medical assistance provided under Article 13(4) (Rev)ESC need not be identical to that provided under Article 13(1) (Rev)ESC. Indeed, the European Committee of Social Rights has specifically recognised that the most appropriate form of social assistance in light of the essentially temporary nature of stay involved is emergency

---

[158] See ECSR, General Introduction, *Conclusions XIII–4*, at 36–37.

[159] Art 7(1) & (2) Reg 1612/68/EEC.

[160] Case 53/81 *Levin* [1982] ECR 1035, as discussed in T Hervey, above n 125 at 91.

[161] See T Hervey, above n 125 at 92.

[162] ECSR, General Introduction, *Conclusions XIII–4*, at 62.

[163] Under Art 13(4) (Rev)ESC States Parties undertake to apply Art 13(1) (Rev)ESC to those lawfully within their territory 'on an equal footing with their nationals'.

[164] Art 13(1) & Appendix, para 1 (Rev)ESC. See ECSR, General Introduction, *Conclusions XIII–4*, at 61. Before this cycle the ECSR considered non-nationals under Article 13(4) only. For analysis see DJ Harris, above n 138 at 174–76.

[165] ECSR, *Conclusions XIII–4*, at 187 (Malta).

[166] ECSR, *Conclusions XIV–1*, at 322–33 (Germany).

[167] ECSR, *Conclusions XIV–1*, at 193 (Denmark).

[168] ECSR, General Introduction, *Conclusions XIII–4*, at 61; *Conclusions XV–1*, at 644–46 (UK). The ECtHR has also found differential treatment of non-nationals in respect of contributory related emergency assistance to be discriminatory, *Gaygusuz v Austria* [1996] 23 EHRR 364 at paras 40–52.

aid to respond to immediate need, including food, accommodation, emergency care and clothing.[169] Thus, a guaranteed minimum income to this group is not foreseen under Article 13(4) (Rev)ESC. However, the European Committee of Social Rights has found the provision of assistance for 'very urgent reasons' (where life is threatened or where permanent serious injury may result) to be too restrictive.[170] Residence conditions cannot be applied under this provision[171] and states have been found non-compliant where benefits are only afforded to nationals.[172]

Does the reference in the Explanatory Document to Article 13(4) (Rev)ESC mean that Article 34(2) EUCFR only pertains to emergency assistance in respect of non-nationals who are 'residing and moving legally within the European Union'? Since Regulation 1612/68/EEC requires equal treatment of workers who are nationals of a Member State living in another Member State, it is clear that the drafters did not intend to limit the scope of Article 34(2) EUCFR to the provision of urgent assistance to working Community nationals. Rather, it is more likely that the reference to Article 13(4) of the (Rev)ESC was included in the Explanatory Document to confirm that the obligation under Article 34(2) EUCFR extends beyond those non-nationals who are *lawfully resident in* the territory (protected by Regulation 1612/68/EEC) to those who are simply *lawfully within* the territory. Thus, persons need only reside within the EU and not the Member States in question. Furthermore, the reference to Article 13(4) (Rev)ESC may be read as implying that equal treatment is not envisaged in respect of those who are not Community nationals working in another Member State. Rather, emergency assistance to this latter group may be sufficient.

Because the provision of social assistance to non-nationals would promote the free movement of Community nationals and third country nationals, the Community would seem to have an existing competence in this field. The Community could therefore legislate regardless of the text of Article 34 EUCFR. The existence of Article 34(2) EUCFR, together with the reference in the Explanatory Document to Article 13(4) ESC, may be seen to lend support to extending social provision protection to Community nationals who are not workers and to third country nationals, albeit without requiring equal treatment of these groups. Such an extension would represent a development in Community law.

---

[169] ECSR, General Introduction, *Conclusions XIII–4*, at 62; General Introduction, *Conclusions XIV–1*, at 55.
[170] ECSR, *Conclusions XIV–1*, at 572–73 (Netherlands).
[171] ECSR, *Conclusions XIII–2*, at 138 (Greece).
[172] ECSR, *Conclusions XIII–3*, at 368–69 (Turkey).

ARTICLE 34(3): THE RIGHT TO SOCIAL ASSISTANCE

Article 34(3) EUCFR reads:

> In order to combat social exclusion and poverty, the Union recognises and respects the right to social and housing assistance so as to ensure a decent existence for all those who lack sufficient resources, in accordance with the rules laid down by Community law and national laws and practices.

The text of Article 34(3) EUCFR confirms several issues. First, in contrast to Article 34(1), Article 34(3) EUCFR contains a *right* to social and housing assistance. This is important since it implies an enforceable individual right where there is none in respect of social security entitlement generally under Article 34(1) EUCFR. Second, the text replicates Article 34(1) to the extent to which it employs the phrase 'the Union recognises and respects' the right. The Explanatory Document notes that the EU must respect the right 'in the context of policies based on Article 137(2) of the Treaty establishing the European Community, particularly in the last sub-paragraph'. This seems to pertain to Article 137(2) EC before it was amended by the Nice Treaty and thus relates to the measures the Council may adopt to encourage cooperation between Member States. Again, the text emphasises that the EU is to abstain from interfering with the right when it is operating within its sphere of competence but that it is not to adopt legislation on the basis of Article 34(3) EUCFR. By virtue of Article 51(1) EUCFR, Member States will also be bound by Article 34(3) EUCFR. Third, the reference to operating in accordance with 'national laws and practices' again emphasises the limited competence enjoyed by the Community in the field of social assistance and the need to respect national differences in this field.

The Explanatory Document notes that Article 34(3) EUCFR is drawn from point 10 of the Community Social Charter[173] and Articles 30 and 31 RevESC. Articles 30 and 31 RevESC pertain to the eradication of poverty and of social exclusion. Article 30 RevESC—the right to protection against poverty and social exclusion—expressly refers to housing and social assistance. Article 30 RevESC reads:

> With a view to ensuring the effective exercise of the right to protection against poverty and social exclusion, the Parties undertake:
> (a) to take measures within the framework of an overall and co-ordinated approach to promote the effective access of persons who live or risk living in a situation of social exclusion or poverty, as well as their families, to, in particular, employment, housing, training, education, culture and social and medical assistance;
> (b) to review these measures with a view to their adaptation if necessary.

---

[173] For the text, see n 29 above.

Social assistance is just one element of Article 30, which envisages a coordinated approach to poverty reduction and social exclusion. Under Article 30 RevESC States Parties must adopt a 'series of measures, which may or may not imply financial benefits, and which concern both persons in a situation of exclusion and those who risk finding themselves in such a situation'.[174] Thus, measures adopted under Article 30 RevESC must be pre-emptive as well as reactive. Poverty eradication and the combating of social exclusion are amongst the objectives of the EU's Social Policy Agenda and of Decision 50/2002/EC establishing a programme of Community action to encourage cooperation between Member States to combat social exclusion.[175] The programme is part of an OMC between Member States entailing the setting of appropriate objectives at EU level and the implementation of national action plans.[176] The OMC is designed to support cooperation that enables the effectiveness of policies to combat social exclusion by improving understanding of social exclusion with the help of comparable indicators, by organising exchanges on the impact of policies and promoting learning in the context of national action plans and by developing the capacity of actors to address social exclusion and poverty.[177]

Article 31 RevESC enshrines a right to housing. Under it, States Parties undertake to take measures designed to 'promote access to housing of an adequate standard'. Article 31(2) and (3) RevESC refer to measures designed 'to prevent and reduce homelessness with a view to its gradual elimination' and 'to make the price of housing accessible to those without adequate resources'. These provisions contain what might usually be associated with housing assistance. Indeed, housing assistance can be regarded as forming one 'branch' of social assistance. The reference to Article 31 RevESC in its entirety may suggest positive obligations for states to ensure that housing generally is of an adequate standard.

The principal guarantee of social assistance in the (Rev)ESC is contained in Article 13(1) (Rev)ESC, which provides for a right to social and medical assistance. It is submitted that the detailed standards developed under Article 13(1) (Rev)ESC are of relevance to Article 34(3) EUCFR. Almost undoubtedly, an identical meaning will be given to the term 'social and medical assistance' under Article 13 of (RevESC) and Article 30 RevESC. Indeed, the explanatory report to the RevESC confirms that, although the purpose of Article 30,

> is not to repeat the juridical aspects of the protection covered by other Articles of the revised Charter . . . Parties may naturally refer to information given in respect of other provisions when reporting under this provision.[178]

Furthermore, the Explanatory Document notes that Article 30 RevESC does not expressly mention the guarantee of minimum resources because such

---

[174] Council of Europe, Explanatory Report to the RevESC, para 116.
[175] See above n 22.
[176] See http://wwwdb.europarl.eu.int/oeil/oeil_ViewDNL.ProcedureView?lang=2&procid=4259.
[177] See http://wwwdb.europarl.eu.int/oeil/oeil_ViewDNL.ProcedureView?lang=2&procid=4259.
[178] Council of Europe, Explanatory Report to the RevESC, para 113.

protection is provided for by Article 13 (Rev)ESC and is 'covered by . . . Article [30] where reference is made in paragraph a to "effective access to [. . .] social assistance" '.[179]

For this reason, the content of Article 13(1) (Rev)ESC is very likely to be of relevance to Article 34(3) EUCFR. Article 13(1) (Rev)ESC reads:

> With a view to ensuring the effective exercise of the right to social and medical assistance, the . . . Parties undertake:
> 1. to ensure that any person who is without adequate resources and who is unable to secure such resources either by his own efforts or from other sources, in particular by benefits under a social security scheme, be granted adequate assistance, and, in case of sickness, the care necessitated by his condition.

Under Article 13(1) (Rev)ESC social assistance must be guaranteed by the state[180] and can be awarded in cash or in kind. It must be made available as of right to all people in need and must be sufficient to permit a decent life.[181] Medical assistance entails the provision of free health care or of the financial assistance necessary to meet the costs of necessary medical treatment to those in need.[182] The European Committee of Social Rights does not 'define the nature of the care required, or the place where it is given'.[183] Thus, states are given considerable discretion and will respond differently with a view to complying with Article 13(1) (Rev)ESC.

States Parties to the (Rev)ESC are under an obligation to gradually remove the need for assistance.[184] Notwithstanding the obligation to remove the need for social assistance, the European Committee of Social Rights has not based a finding of non-compliance on an increase in the number of claimants.[185] To the contrary, progress is often illustrated by the extension in the number of benefits[186] and claimants.[187] Only substantial variations in coverage over time need to be justified. Not surprisingly, concern is expressed where *lacunae* remain in coverage[188] and exclusion of particular groups has given rise to findings of non-compliance under Article 13(1) (Rev)ESC.[189] The European Committee of

---

[179] Council of Europe, Explanatory Report to the RevESC, para 115.

[180] ECSR, *Conclusions XII–1*, at 188 (Greece). Social assistance must be seen within a programme of poverty alleviation and in conjunction with the provision of advisory services. See General Introduction, *Conclusions XIV–1*, at 52; Art 13(3) (Rev)ESC.

[181] ECSR, General Introduction, *Conclusions XIII–4*, at 54–56.

[182] ECSR, General Introduction, *Conclusions XIII–4*, at 57.

[183] ECSR, General Introduction, *Conclusions XIII–4*, at 57.

[184] ECSR, General Introduction, *Conclusions XIII–4*, at 55–57. Nonetheless, the ECSR is keen to establish reasons behind substantial decreases in claimants, *Conclusions XIV–1*, at 318–19 (Germany).

[185] See ECSR, *Conclusions XIII–4*, at 183 (Ireland). It has enquired into problems caused by a 20% increase in claimants, *Conclusions XIV–1*, at 271 (France).

[186] ECSR, *Conclusions XIII–2*, at 344 (Malta).

[187] ECSR, *Conclusions XII–2*, at 183 (Spain).

[188] ECSR, *Conclusions XIII–5*, at 223–25 (Portugal). Non-compliance has resulted from a lack of assistance in certain regions, *Conclusions XIII–4*, at 185–87 (Italy).

[189] ECSR, *Conclusions XV–1*, at 269–71 (France), regarding under 25s; Addendum, at 64 (Luxembourg), regarding under 30s.

Social Rights also requests information on the types of benefits available[190] and the frequency of payment.[191]

The European Committee of Social Rights has developed a number of indicators and benchmarks by which it assesses the adequacy of social assistance provided under Article 13(1) (Rev)ESC. First, it uses an increase[192] or decrease[193] in expenditure as an indicator of adequate provision under Article 13(1).[194] However, it is very difficult to discern specific standards from the European Committee of Social Rights' jurisprudence.[195] Occasionally, the European Committee of Social Rights has sought information where the increase in expenditure is lower than the increase in beneficiaries.[196]

Second, the European Committee of Social Rights identifies the cost of living, together with minimum subsistence, as being the test for determining the adequacy of social assistance.[197] Moreover, the European Committee of Social Rights often measures the cost of living in terms of inflation[198] and indicators are sought by reference to minimum and average wages.[199] Alternative bases of comparison referred to on occasion include the level of unemployment insurance,[200] the consumer price index,[201] and household consumption data.[202] A failure to match inflation will not necessarily lead to a finding of non-compliance under the (Rev)ESC.[203] However, a rise of 0.5 per cent in assistance levels[204] or a failure to increase them at all[205] in the wake of 2 per cent average inflation led the European Committee of Social Rights to request an explanation.

---

[190] ECSR, General Introduction, *Conclusions XIII–4*, at 57; *Conclusions XIII–4*, at 172 (Denmark).

[191] See generally, ECSR, *Conclusions XIV–1*, at 470 (Italy).

[192] For example, a 25% increase in expenditure together with a 10.5% increase in beneficiaries met with approval, ECSR, *Conclusions XII–1*, at 188 (Denmark).

[193] ECSR, *Conclusions XIV–1*, at 359 (Greece), 67% reduction; *Conclusions XV–1*, at 215 (Finland), 15% reduction.

[194] ECSR, *Conclusions XIII–2*, at 126–27 (France). The ECSR has also held that the conditioning of benefit levels to the availability of (governmental) funds fails to comply with Art 13 (Rev)ESC, *Conclusions XV–1*, at 532–35 (Spain).

[195] 27% of the entire public spending, 6.6% GDP, 3.5% of the social protection budget and 8.4% of social security spending have not given rise to comment. Whereas 6% of the social services budget permitted a positive conclusion, 1% of the social expenditure budget led the ECSR to enquire as to the levels of benefits and numbers covered. See ECSR, *Conclusions XIV–1*, at 537 (Malta); *Conclusions XV–1*: at 602 (Turkey); at 268 (France); Addendum, at 104–5 (Netherlands); *Conclusions XIV–1*: at 741 (Sweden); at 396 (Iceland) respectively. 4% on medical assistance did not prompt any comment, *Conclusions XIV–1*, at 321–22 (Germany).

[196] ECSR, *Conclusions XII–2*, at 181 (Germany), where a 6.5% increase in expenditure in relation to a 8% increase in beneficiaries did not prevent a positive conclusion from being drawn.

[197] ECSR, General Introduction, *Conclusions XIII–4*, at 56.

[198] ECSR, *Conclusions XIV–1*, at 359–60 (Greece). Information has been sought on the indexing of benefits, *Conclusions XV–1*, at 344 (Iceland).

[199] ECSR, *Conclusions XIV–1*, at 85 (Austria).

[200] ECSR, *Conclusions XIV–1*, at 632 (Norway).

[201] ECSR, *Conclusions XIV–1*, at 429 (Ireland).

[202] ECSR, *Conclusions XV–1*, at 489 (Portugal).

[203] ECSR, *Conclusions XIII–4*, at 171 (Austria); *Conclusions XV–1*, at 643 (UK).

[204] ECSR, *Conclusions XV–1*, at 164–65 (Denmark).

[205] ECSR, *Conclusions XIV–1*, at 85 (Austria).

Third, the European Committee of Social Rights has also focused on the relationship between social assistance and the minimum wage. Where assistance corresponds to 50 per cent of the minimum wage the European Committee of Social Rights has sought assurance that individual basic needs can be met.[206] Where levels drop below 50 per cent of[207] or 'well below'[208] the national minimum wage, further information has been requested and conclusions have been deferred. Benefits below 10 per cent[209] and 14 per cent[210] of the minimum wage are not acceptable.

These indicators and benchmarks could be used under the OMC pursuant to Decision 50/2002/EC establishing a programme of Community action to encourage cooperation between Member States to combat social exclusion. For example, an increase in expenditure, the increase in assistance levels vis à vis any increase in inflation and the relationship between assistance benefits and the minimum wage could all provide useful indicators for improving understanding of social exclusion.[211]

A further possible indicator of the enjoyment of social assistance is the existence of a right to an independent appeal. Under Article 13(1) (Rev)ESC states must provide an independent appeal that includes examination of the merits of the case.[212] The European Committee of Social Rights has sought to clarify the independence of,[213] and sought examples arising under,[214] such a procedure and has based non-compliance with Article 13(1) of the (Rev)ESC on the absence of such an independent appeal procedure.[215] The European Committee of Social Rights also enquires as to the availability of assistance[216] and legal aid[217] during such an appeal process. This right of appeal represents a vital element of a right to social assistance since it enables individuals to enforce their individual entitlements. Arguably, the recognition of a *right* to social assistance in Article 34(3) EUCFR may provide support for the availability of such a right of appeal in national laws to be used as an indicator of enjoyment of social assistance under the OMC pursuant to Decision 50/2002/EC establishing a programme of

---

[206] ECSR, *Conclusions XIV–1*, at 569–70 (Netherlands).

[207] ECSR, *Conclusions XIV–1*, at 671–72 (Portugal).

[208] ECSR, *Conclusions XII–2*, at 182–83 (Malta).

[209] ECSR, *Conclusions XIV–1*, at 771–73 (Turkey).

[210] ECSR, *Conclusions XV–1*, at 601–2 (Turkey), notwithstanding a 280% increase in expenditure.

[211] See above p 186.

[212] ECSR, General Introduction, *Conclusions XIII–4*, at 55–57. See also *Conclusions XII–1*, at 192 (UK).

[213] For example, the ECSR has enquired as to the appointment process and length of office of members and for the body's statute, *Conclusions XIII–4*, at 175 (Denmark).

[214] ECSR, *Conclusions XIII–5*, at 97 (Finland).

[215] ECSR, *Conclusions XIII–2*, at 129 (Italy).

[216] ECSR, *Conclusions XIII–2*, at 125 (Denmark).

[217] The ECSR has recognised that individuals should benefit from legal assistance when appealing and has sought reasons for the lack of legal aid, General Introduction, *Conclusions XIII–4*, at 56; *Conclusions XV–1*, at 166 (Denmark).

Community action to encourage cooperation between Member States to combat social exclusion.

It is also worth mentioning that regressive measures have been accepted under Article 13(1) (Rev)ESC. Thus, the European Committee of Social Rights has specified that workfare measures are compatible with the (Rev)ESC 'in so far as such conditions are reasonable[218] and fully consistent with the objective of providing a long-lasting solution to the problems of deprivation experienced by the individual'.[219] The European Committee of Social Rights enquires as to the numbers adversely affected by workfare measures, the existence of any reasons for which claimants may refuse work,[220] the extent of any reduction of benefit[221] and the availability of an appeal process.[222] It also enquires as to the purpose of such conditions, how the overall social policy avoids dependency and whether services are given sufficient means to monitor case studies.[223] Workfare measures for social assistance have not yet given rise to a finding of non-compliance under Article 13(1) (Rev)ESC, even where questions remain unanswered.[224] Again, this demonstrates the wide discretion granted to states in realising the right to social assistance and demonstrates how the right can be interpreted so as to respond to the economic demands incumbent on individual states.

Although these developed standards in the field of social assistance are likely to be of relevance to the EU Social Policy Agenda, the reference to Articles 30 and 31 RevESC emphasises the need for a coordinated and integrated approach to poverty reduction. States should identify and target vulnerable groups and should act pre-emptively rather than simply reacting to existing poverty. Pre-emptive action under Article 30 RevESC may well focus in particular on education and training of vulnerable groups. Evidence of such an integrated approach could be sought in the national action plans that are drawn up by states pursuant to Decision 50/2002/EC establishing a programme of Community action to encourage cooperation between Member States to combat social exclusion under the EU Social Policy Agenda.[225]

---

[218] Regarding reasonableness see ECSR, *Conclusions XV–1*, at 446 (Norway).

[219] ECSR, General Introduction, *Conclusions XIV–1*, at 52.

[220] ECSR, *Conclusions XIII–4*, at 190 (Spain).

[221] ECSR, *Conclusions XIII–4*, at 188 (Norway). Reductions of 20% and 25% prompted enquiries and a reduction of 50% led the ECSR to enquire as to the steps taken to find an alternative solution, *Conclusions XIV–1*, at 231 (Finland); at 320 (Germany); at 396 (Iceland) respectively.

[222] ECSR, *Conclusions XIV–1*, at 632 (Norway).

[223] ECSR, General Introduction, *Conclusions XIV–1*, at 52.

[224] See, for example, ECSR, *Conclusions XV–1*, at 92 (Belgium).

[225] Assistance on the inclusion of social guarantees in national action plans may be sought from the guidelines that are currently being drawn up by the UN Office of the High Commissioner for Human Rights on the inclusion of economic, social and cultural rights in Poverty Reduction Strategy Programs (PRSPs). These PRSPs are drawn up by developing and transition States in conjunction with the International Monetary Fund and World Bank as a condition for debt alleviation and future concessional lending. For information on the UN guidelines see http://www.unhchr.ch/development/poverty-03.html. And for information on the PRSP process and economic, social and cultural rights see J Tooze, 'Aligning States' Economic Policies with Human Rights Obligations: The CESCR's Quest for Consistency' (2002) 2(2) *Human Rights Law Review* 229.

CONCLUSIONS

At first glance, the guarantee of social security and social assistance in Article 34 EUCFR may seem to offer little in the way of clear obligations to the institutions of the EU and to Member States when they are implementing EU law. Little is known of the detailed standards developed under Articles 12 and 13 (Rev)ESC and it is less clear still as to how these standards can be of relevance to the EU in light of its areas of competence.

To date, the EU has primarily developed standards on sex discrimination and discrimination against non-nationals in the field of social security. This is due to its competence in matters of equal treatment and pay and free movement of workers and Community nationals more generally. The conclusion of this chapter is that Article 34 EUCFR is unlikely to impact greatly on these well-developed EU standards. EU laws in respect of sex discrimination in social security have narrowly crafted exceptions to equal treatment of men and women that are deemed to be justified by the need to maintain the financial equilibrium of contributory social security schemes and the necessity of which is carefully monitored by the Court. Arguably, Article 34 EUCFR may place pressure on the EU and on Member States to abandon these exceptions since sex discrimination in social security is strongly protected against in international human rights law. But in practice, states have not been found to be in violation of the (Rev)ESC in respect of these exceptions and the Nice Treaty confirmed that action in this area should not significantly affect the financial equilibrium of social security systems. For this reason, it has been argued that Article 34 EUCFR is unlikely to prompt change in the field of sex discrimination in social security. The EU standards in respect of the entitlement of non-nationals to social security are also very well developed. The current proposal to extend equal treatment to third country nationals preceded the adoption of Article 34 EUCFR. Although Article 34(2) may be seen to provide support for a higher level of protection for third country nationals, jurisprudence under Article 12(4) (Rev)ESC emphasises the difficulties that states have in practice when extending equal treatment to third country nationals.

Rather, the main impact of Article 34 EUCFR is likely to be in the field of EU Social Policy Agenda. There is scope for certain limited 'regulation'—in terms of the EU's 'new' methods of governance'[226]—of social security and social assistance under this Agenda. It has been demonstrated that the rights to social security and social assistance, as guaranteed under the (Rev)ESC, grant states considerable discretion as to how these rights are to be realised. Different states will adopt different branches of social security and will provide them to different groups at different levels. Yet they may all comply with their obligations in respect of the right to social security. States also enjoy discretion as to the form

[226] See further N Bernard, in this collection.

and delivery of social assistance benefits. Thus the standard-setting undertaken on the *rights* to social security and social assistance confirms the need for such discretion and emphasises the suitability of social security and social assistance for regulation by the OMC. More specifically, the indicators and benchmarks adopted by the European Committee of Social Rights under Articles 12 and 13 (Rev)ESC may well be applicable under the Social Policy Agenda OMC. Reference to Articles 30 and 31 RevESC emphasise the need for a coordinated approach to poverty reduction with pre-emptive as well as reactive measures. Such an integrated approach could be reflected in the national action plans drawn up by Member States under the EU Social Policy Agenda. Finally, the minimum baseline below which states must not regress when providing social security and social assistance under Articles 12 and 13 (Rev)ESC can provide a benchmark for the Social Policy Agenda. In this regard, the maintenance of a social security system distinct from a system of minimum assistance could provide the hallmark of any evolving European welfare policy.

9

The 'Right to Health' in European Union Law

TAMARA K HERVEY*

INTRODUCTION

T HE CHARTER OF Fundamental Rights of the European Union, 2000 (the
Charter) contains a number of provisions relevant to a 'right to health'. The
language of rights carries significant normative power, in particular with respect
to relationships between individuals and repositories of collective power, typically states, but also non-state polities such as the EU. However, the notion of a
'right' to health is contentious for a number of reasons. Therefore its utility or
appropriateness may be called into question. This chapter explores the differences that a rights-based approach to health might make within elements of EU
law and policy with respect to the protection of human health. For instance,
would conceptualising along the lines of a 'right to health' make a difference in
terms of resolution of conflicts, such as those concerning the relationships
between majorities and minorities, 'insiders' and 'outsiders'; resource allocation; spheres of competence or others? Would it make a difference in terms of
relationships between relevant actors, such as the EU and governments of third
states; private individuals; non-governmental organisations?

WHAT IS THE 'RIGHT TO HEALTH'?

The Relevance of Rights Discourse

The debates concerning the inclusion of social rights, such as the right to health,
in the Charter have many historical antecedents. Arguments over the nature,
content, form and structure of social rights are not new.[1] As is the case with

* School of Law, University of Nottingham, UK. I am indebted to the participants at the workshop in June 2002, and especially Jeff Kenner, Jean McHale, Therese Murphy, Patrick Twomey and
Lisa Waddington. The usual disclaimer applies.

[1] M Craven, 'A View from Elsewhere: Social Rights, International Covenant and the EU Charter
of Fundamental Rights', in C Costello, ed, *Fundamental Social Rights: Current European Legal
Protection and the Challenge of the EU Charter on Fundamental Rights* (Dublin, Irish Centre for
European Law, 2001) p 77.

other rights, the phrase 'right to health' is shorthand, encapsulating entitlements with respect to health care and health protection.[2] Just as the 'right to life' does not mean the 'right to eternal life', so the right to health does not mean a right to be healthy, or a claim to maintain or attain perfect health.[3] Further, it is often argued that social rights, such as the right to health, do not merit the term 'rights', being merely a luxury affordable only by developed states.[4] Indeed the cost of health care is a problem also for wealthy states.[5] The main emphasis of such social rights consists in a *claim on* the public authorities for protection and assistance, rather than the *freedom from* state interference that is said to characterise civil and political rights.[6] It is argued that treating such matters as 'rights' devalues the currency of (civil and political) rights, and justifies inappropriate state intervention in the functioning of free market economies.[7] Worse, a strong claim of right may serve as proxy for appropriate political debate leading to the proper allocation of socio-economic resources, and may in fact bring about a substantively unjust result in terms of their allocation.[8] Alternatively, in spite of the official position that human rights are indivisible and inter-related,[9] social rights are often seen as 'second class' rights,[10] aspirational only and programmatic in nature. As they constitute a 'positive' claim on the state, rather than a 'negative' freedom from state interference, such rights are not seen as enforceable by individuals before judicial bodies. However, as will be seen, the right to health encapsulates a cluster of rights, not all of which

[2] V Leary, 'The Right to Health in International Human Rights Law' 1 *Health and Human Rights* (1994) 3–5; B Toebes, *The Right to Health as a Human Right in International Law* (Antwerp, Intersentia/Hart, 1999), pp 16–18; 24.

[3] B Toebes, 'The Right to Health', in A Eide, C Krause and A Rosas (eds), *Economic, Cultural and Social Rights* (The Hague, Kluwer, 2001), p 170.

[4] H Steiner and P Alston, *International Human Rights in Context: Law, Politics, Morals* (Oxford, OUP, 2000), pp 300–5.

[5] Leary, above n 2, 13. Recent reforms of national health care systems have been, at least in part, driven by a desire to contain spiralling costs, see, eg RB Saltman, J Figueras and C Sakellarides (eds), *Critical Challenges for Health Care Reform in Europe* (Open University Press, Buckingham, 1998); RB Saltman, 'A Conceptual Overview of Recent Health Care Reforms' (1994) 4 *European Journal of Public Health* 287–93; Dunning Report *Choices in Health Care: A Report by the Government Committee on Choices in Health Care, the Netherlands* (Rijswijk, Minister of Welfare, Health and Cultural Affairs, 1992); C Barker, *The Health Care Policy Process* (London, Sage, 1992), pp 151–57; R Freeman, *The Politics of Health in Europe* (Manchester, MUP, 2000), pp 66–85.

[6] See further A Rosas and A Eide, 'Economic, Social and Cultural Rights: A Universal Challenge' and A Eide, 'Economic, Social and Cultural Rights as Human Rights' in A Eide, C Krause and A Rosas, above n 3.

[7] See Steiner and Alston, above n 4, p 237.

[8] See contributions of M Minow, K Anderson and M Mandler, Human Rights Program, Harvard Law School and François-Xavier Bagnoud Center for Health and Human Rights Workshop, *Economic and Social Rights and the Right to Health*, September 1993, www.law.harvard.edu/programs/HRP/Publications/economic1.html, p 4.

[9] See Universal Declaration of Human Rights, Vienna World Conference on Human Rights Declaration, para 5.

[10] Vienna World Conference 1993, UN Committee on Economic, Social and Cultural Rights UN Doc. E/1993/22, Annex III, paras 5 and 7, cited Steiner and Alston, above n 4, p 238, 'The reality is that violations of civil and political rights continue to be treated as though far more serious and more patently intolerable, than massive and direct denials of economic, social and cultural rights'.

fall within the category of 'positive rights', and even if they do, may have value in terms other than individual judicial enforcement.[11]

While I agree that we should reject the rhetoric of 'rights' if it is inappropriate in terms of the aims to be achieved by espousing and promoting such rights,[12] I tend towards the view that, as others have argued, if the value of civil and political rights is appreciated, it is certainly worth exploring what may be gained by applying the notion of rights to social entitlements such as the 'right to health'.[13] Further, the realisation that, in practice, civil and political rights may be rendered meaningless without the means to enjoy them has led some to argue that social rights are *higher* in value than civil and political rights.[14] Civil and political rights also have economic costs and impose economic burdens; this has not been an insurmountable impediment to their utility and widespread support. Civil and political rights may also be (or have been) under-determined in terms of substantive content. It follows that, like civil and political rights, social rights may become more determined through the historical contexts provided in human rights practice. If human rights most urgently need defending where they are most denied, a rights agenda is by definition aspirational; but this does not necessarily reduce it to mere rhetoric.[15] The various roles of soft law and the existence of alternative enforcement mechanisms extend the value of rights beyond their formal judicial enforceability. Not least, in human rights practice and the work of non-governmental organisations, the rhetoric of rights buys time and attention from those in power: 'Rights talk buys ten minutes of their attention. I use it like a magic wand'.[16]

It has been observed that 'health and human rights are complementary approaches to the central problem of defining and advancing human well-being'.[17] Indeed, current public health practice, in particular in HIV/AIDS, is drawing clear links between health and human rights protection. The vulnerability of certain individuals or groups to disease, disability and premature death may be clearly linked to the extent to which the human rights and dignity

---

[11] Cf A Von Bogdandy, , 'The European Union as a Human Rights Organization? Human Rights and the Core of the European Union' 37 *Common Market Law Review* (2000) 1307–38 at 1316 'the very essence of a right is that it is accorded immediate protection by the courts'.

[12] 'If our commitment to rights arises out of our humane concerns about the object of those rights—such as good health or health care—then we should feel free to eschew rights rhetoric for other serviceable forms of argument: theories of political community, of distributive fairness and social justice, or of maximising utility'. (H Steiner, Harvard Law School Workshop, above n 8, p 2).

[13] Gostin, Harvard Law School Workshop, above n 8, p 7.

[14] 'What permanent achievement is there in saving people from torture, only to find that they are killed by . . . disease that could have been prevented?' Eide and Rosas, in Eide, Rosas and Krause (eds), above n 3, p 7; 'Of what use is the right to free speech to those who are starving and illiterate?' Steiner and Alston, above n 4, p 237.

[15] D Beetham, 'What Future for Economic and Social Rights' 43 *Political Studies* (1995) 41, cited in Steiner and Alston, above n 4, p 255.

[16] J Osborn, Harvard Law School Workshop, above n 8, p 7.

[17] J Mann, L Gostin et al, 'Health and Human Rights' 1 *Journal of Health and Human Rights* (1994) 7.

of those individuals are protected.[18] This realisation may be linked to the notion of the interdependence and indivisibility of human rights—the right to health cannot be effectively protected without respect for other recognised rights and vice versa. Rights discourse as applied to health may therefore be useful or appropriate for this and a number of further, related reasons.[19]

First is the notion of rights as a legal or quasi-legal expression of the values fundamental to a particular socio-political order. In the context of a right to health, the claim here is not that health rights should always take precedence over other rights, but rather that the terminology of rights helps to emphasise the importance of health status in terms of the survival and quality of life of individuals. Further, a notion of a 'right' to health helps move away from the conceptualisation of health as simply a medical, technical problem, by emphasising health as a social good.[20]

Second, using the terminology of the right to health emphasises the notion of individualisation of health as a social right. This is illustrated, for instance, by the practice of the UN Committee on Economic, Social and Cultural Rights in its role as supervisory organ of the International Covenant of Economic, Social and Cultural Rights, 1966 (ICESCR). The Committee has developed an understanding of social rights as not simply generalised policy goals, but also, in some circumstances, as individual entitlements.[21] There are two possible routes to this conclusion, which can be used individually or in combination. One is to stress the conservative, negative or freedom-related dimension of social rights. So the right to health care does not simply mean a positive claim on the state, but also a negative freedom from state intervention in health. This would suggest for instance that crude public health schemes (such as forced sterilisation, or compulsory immunisation) are not consistent with an individual's right to health, irrespective of their utilitarian results in terms of the health of the collectivity. The other approach ('social rights plus') is to combine social rights with other 'foundational' rights, in particular rights to dignity, due process and non-discrimination.[22] A right to health implies protection for the dignity of the most vulnerable in society[23] and their equal treatment in terms of access to health provision, at whatever levels this is made available in a particular state or

---

[18] Mann, Gostin et al, above n 17, cite the example of women in East Africa who are vulnerable to HIV infection: 'women's vulnerability to HIV is now recognised to be integrally connected with discrimination and unequal rights, involving property, marriage, divorce and inheritance'.

[19] Leary, above n 2.

[20] Leary, above n 2, p 8.

[21] Craven, above n 1, pp 82–86.

[22] See UN Committee on Economic, Social and Cultural Rights, General Comment No 3 (1990) UN Doc E/1991/23, Annex III '[W]hile the Covenant provides for progressive realisation and acknowledges the constraints due to the limits of available resources, it also imposes various obligations which are of immediate effect. Of these, two are of particular importance . . . One of these . . . is the "undertaking to guarantee" that relevant rights "will be exercised without discrimination"', cited in Steiner and Alston, above n 4, p 265.

[23] In particular those socially excluded by poverty, race or ethnicity, nationality, gender, age, mental or physical disabilities.

society. The emphasis on dignity and non-discrimination implicit in a right to health also implies 'the rejection of a solely market-based approach to the social good of health care and health status'[24] and that cost containment cannot be a sole determinative goal in health care management and financing. Of course, non-discrimination in the context of the right to health does not mean the same treatment for all, as health care needs will vary widely among individuals.[25] However, it does mean that irrelevant grounds for different treatment must be eradicated. It means that the rights of people to health care must be determined on the basis of their humanity, not status. It also probably means that different clinical needs[26] should be treated with equal concern, within the context of an overall health budget.[27]

Third is the notion of entitlement, or as the Helsinki Accords put it: individuals are entitled to 'know and act on their rights'. Entitlement can mean justiciability, in the 'restraint on states' or 'social rights plus' senses. But it does not necessarily mean justiciability, but rather the normative cachet of rights.[28] The notion of the 'visibility' of rights was particularly stressed by some, notably the UK government, during the Charter negotiations. In the context of health, the notion of a right to health may help to raise the profile of health entitlements.

Finally, although international human rights law primarily addresses the individual as the holder of human rights, the full enjoyment of individual human rights may, in some circumstances, require the protection of *groups* of persons. This perspective has prompted the notion of a 'third generation' of human rights, as a response to the phenomenon of global interdependence.[29] The right

---

[24] Leary, above n 2, p 9.

[25] See M Brazier, 'Rights and Health Care' in R Blackburn (ed), *Rights of Citizenship* (London, Mansell, 1993), p 58 'Basic human needs for food and clothing and other material resources are susceptible to some sort of objective assessment and differ relatively little from person to person. . . . Needs for medical care vary widely. A baby born with severe disabilities at 25 weeks' gestation will probably consume health care resources sufficient for the basic care required for 20–30 normal infants delivered at full term. The cost of a single heart transplant will cover the cost of chiropody services for elderly patients in a health district for a year or more. The older the patient the more, and more expensive, medical care she needs. Where resources for health care are limited the question becomes not one of an absolute right to care, but one of defining to what share of available resources the citizen has a right. Emphasis on individual rights to health care, high-flown rhetoric that each and every citizen has a right to health care, obscures the issue, which is who has or should have the ultimate responsibility for allocating available resources and determining my proper share of, and claim to, those resources.' On models of equality and non-discrimination, see M Bell, in this collection.

[26] And here there is scope for argument as to what constitutes a clinical need: should infertility treatment be included? Cosmetic surgery? What if the sufferer has clinical depression arising from their infertility or the shape of their nose? See Brazier, above n 23.

[27] Brazier, above n 23, p 67.

[28] 'A rights approach offers a normative vocabulary that facilitates both the framing of claims and the identification of the right holder. This means that the addressee of the rights or duty bearers . . . have the duty to provide the entitlement, not to society in general, but to each member. This standing has very important implications for efforts to seek redress in cases where the entitlement is not provided or the right violated.' A Chapman, *Exploring a Human Rights Approach to Health Care Reform* (Washington DC, American Association for the Advancement of Science, 1993).

[29] See K Vasak, 'A Thirty Year Struggle' *UNESCO Courier* (No 1977), 29, cited R Rich, 'Right to Development: A Right of Peoples' in J Crawford (ed) *The Rights of Peoples* (Oxford, Clarendon, 1988).

to health is not generally regarded as such a 'third generation' human right in itself, but may be closely related to the rights to peace, to a protected environment, and to development. If the benefits of a rights discourse as applied to collectively held rights[30] are accepted, a collective notion of a right to health may be useful in this respect.[31]

The Content of the Right to Health

The Preamble to the Constitution of the World Health Organisation, 1946, was the first international instrument to explicitly formulate a 'right to health'.[32] The right to health is now found in several international human rights conventions,[33] including the European Social Charter, 1961 (ESC) and Revised European Social Charter, 1996 (RevESC), and also in a number of national constitutions,[34] including, in the EU, Belgium,[35] Finland,[36] Italy,[37] Luxembourg,[38] the Netherlands,[39] Portugal[40] and Spain.[41] The presence of such a right in national constitutions and regional international legal instruments may be particularly important in terms of the notion of the Charter as expressing (pre-existing) 'general principles' of Community law.

[30] For discussion and elaboration, see Rich, above n 29, pp 53–54.

[31] For further discussion, see below.

[32] B Toebes, *The Right to Health as a Human Right in International Law* (Antwerp, Intersentia/Hart, 1999), p 15; Toebes, in Eide, Krause and Rosas, above n 3, p 171.

[33] See Universal Declaration of Human Rights, 1948, Art 25; International Covenant on Economic Social and Cultural Rights, Art 12; Convention on the Elimination of all forms of Discrimination Against Women, 1979, Art 12; Convention on the Rights of the Child, Article 24; European Social Charter, 1961, Art 11 and 13; Revised European Social Charter, 1996, Arts 11 and 13; Convention on Human Rights and Biomedicine, Art 3; Protocol of San Salvador, Art 10. See Toebes, in Eide, Krause and Rosas, above n 3, p 173.

[34] See, for instance, Art 70 D of the Hungarian Constitution; Art 27 of the South African Constitution; Art 39(e) and (f), 46 and 47 of the Indian Constitution; S 15 of Article II of the Philippines Constitution. See Toebes, in Eide, Krause and Rosas, above n 3, p 174.

[35] Art 23 '(1) Everyone has the right to lead a life in conformity with human dignity. (2) To this end, the laws, decrees and rulings alluded to in Article 134 guarantee, taking into account corresponding obligations, economic, social and cultural rights, and determine the conditions for exercising them. (3) These rights include, notably: . . . (2) The right to social security, to health care and to social, medical and legal aid'.

[36] Ch 2, s 19(3) 'The public authorities shall guarantee for everyone . . . adequate social, health and medical services and promote the health of the population'.

[37] Art 32 'The Republic protects health as a fundamental right of the individual and as a concern of the collectivity and guarantees free care to the indigent'.

[38] Art 11(5) 'The law organises social security, health protection'.

[39] Art 22(1) 'The authorities shall take steps to promote the health of the population'.

[40] Art 64(1) 'Health: All have the right to health protection and the duty to defend it and to promote it'.

[41] Art 43 '(1) Se reconoce el derecho a la protección de la salud. (2) Compete a los poderes públicos organizar y tutelar la salud pública a través de medidas preventivas y de las prestaciones y servicios necasarios. La ley establecerá los derechos y deberes de todos al respecto. (3) Los poderes públicos fomentarán le educación sanitaria, la educación fisica y el deporte. Asimismo facilitarán la adecuada utilización del ocio'.

The right to health, as found in international and national law, has multiple and contested meanings,[42] with respect both to the types of obligations it imposes and the substantive content of those obligations. The notion of a right to health tells us little unless we know what kinds of duties states and other holders of public power such as the EU have to enable people to realise it.[43] Human rights are said to impose three types of obligations on the holders of public power: obligations to respect, to protect and to fulfil.[44] Thus the right to health may be used to mean a negative obligation to *respect* people's health, to restrain the holders of public power from infringing the health of individuals. For instance, it may provide a curb on state acts which encroach upon people's health, such as environmental pollution. It may require states not to impede individuals or groups of people from access to available health services.[45] Or the right to health may involve a positive obligation on the part of the state or other polity, to *protect* health. This would require taking legislative action for instance to ensure (equal) access to health services if they are provided by third parties, or to provide health care to the impoverished; or to protect people from health infringements by third parties.[46] Or the right to health may involve more extensive action on the part of the state or other polity, to *fulfil* the right to health, by facilitating its enjoyment or by providing the means for so doing. In the context of obligations imposed on states, this may require states to adopt a national health policy, and moreover, to devote a sufficient proportion of national revenues to health. It may require states to create the conditions where all people within the state have access to health services, and to the necessary preconditions for good health, such as clean water and adequate sanitation.[47]

The specific meaning of rights becomes clear through their application in international and national judicial and quasi-judicial fora.[48] Basing her analysis on texts of international treaties, existing case law and other elements of human rights discourse, in particular the reporting procedures of the UN Committee on Economic, Social and Cultural Rights and of the Committee of Independent Experts under the European Social Charter,[49] Toebes has developed a sophisticated typology of the core substantive content of the right to health in

[42] See Minow, Harvard Law School Workshop, above n 8, p 4.

[43] See Steiner and Alston, above n 4, p 267; Nussbaum, Harvard Law School Workshop, above n 8, p 7.

[44] See H Shue, 'The Interdependence of Duties' in P Alston and K Tomasevski, *The Right to Food* (Utrecht, Stichting Studie en Infomatiecentrum Mensenrechten, 1984); see also eg Committee on Economic Social and Cultural Rights, General Document No 12, (1999) UN Doc E/C.12/1999/5, cited in Steiner and Alston, above n 4, p 267; A Eide, 'Economic, Social and Cultural Rights as Human Rights' in Eide, Krause and Rosas, above n 3, p 23.

[45] Toebes, in Eide, Krause and Rosas, above n 3, pp 179–80.

[46] Toebes, in Eide, Krause and Rosas, above n 3, p 180.

[47] Toebes, in Eide, Krause and Rosas, above n 3, p 180.

[48] As Leary, above n 2, points out, 'it is not unusual for the full implications of a right enshrined in a bill of rights or a human rights treaty to be perceived only gradually: rights proclaimed in national constitutions and in international legal instruments are expressed in succinct language whose meaning is rarely self-evident.'

[49] Now the European Committee of Social Rights.

international law. Toebes concludes that the *core content* (the bare minimum) of the right to health in international law includes elements with respect to both health care and the underlying pre-conditions for health. The former comprises 'maternal and child care, including family planning; immunisation against the major infectious diseases; appropriate treatment of common diseases and injuries; and provision of essential drugs'. The latter comprises an 'adequate supply of safe water and basic sanitation; and freedom from serious environmental health threats'. The scope of the right to health is drawn so that interaction with other rights, in particular the right to life, to physical integrity and privacy, to education and information and to housing, food and work, are clarified.[50]

Toebes' definition of the right to health has the advantage of being 'international', in the sense of drawn from international human rights documents and practice. However, this entails certain drawbacks. In defining the scope of the right to health, Toebes has reduced the right to health to its bare minimum. This is consistent with an approach starting from economic development,[51] in that the entitlements under the right to health are such that every state, no matter at what stage of development, may reasonably be expected to comply. However, in the context of the EU, or at least its internal policies, it might be objected that such a 'lowest common denominator' definition finds no real meaning. It would seem unquestionable that the Member States of the EU allocate sufficient resources to respect, protect and even fulfil the right to health in that minimal sense.[52] However, if that is all that the right to health means in the EU context, then it may be a concept devoid of the usual utility of rights language.

Other approaches to defining the right to health may derive from national (constitutional) provisions.[53] For instance, Brazier, essentially determining 'rights to health care' in terms of their justiciability at the suit of an individual, sees the core content of such rights in English law as including simply a 'right to equal access to health care' and patients' rights against their carers, in terms of determination of the form of treatment, ensuring proper treatment, and

---

[50] See Toebes, above n 32, pp 243–89 and table on p 289.

[51] Beetham, in Steiner and Alston, above n 4, p 256 'Both the defenders of a "basic needs" approach within development economics and human rights theorists would converge on a minimum core of rights such as . . . the right to . . . basic (or primary) health care, clean water and sanitation.' This list provides the 'foundation, together with the crucial principle of non-discriminatory access'. In terms of specificity, Beetham argues that, although 'there will inevitably be a certain arbitrariness about defining the required standard for a human right as that of primary health care, such a core content can be defined.'

[52] But see below, in terms of guaranteeing the right to health for 'outsiders', for instance asylum seekers.

[53] For reasons of space, discussion has been limited to literature on English health law. For further information on the right to health in other national constitutions, see the contributions to A den Exter and H Hermans (eds), *The Right to Health Care in Several European Countries*, proceedings of a conference held in Rotterdam, the Netherlands, 1998, (1999) *Studies in Social Policy* No 5.

control of information relating to the patient and the state of his health.[54] Montgomery,[55] exploring the implications of realising a 'right to health' in the context of the English legal system, identifies a four-fold typology of obligations: protection from disease and accidents; protection from adverse environmental factors; promotion of a healthy environment; and provision of health care services. The obligation to protect from disease and accidents means, for instance, that the state has a responsibility to immunise children, and to take measures necessary to confine contagious diseases. The obligation to protect from adverse environmental factors means that the state has a duty to minimise known risks, for instance, to ensure employers provide safe working systems, to eradicate poor housing, or to provide that public places be free from tobacco smoke. Promotion of a healthy environment will require action taken to increase standards of health, such as the provision of free milk for school children, and action to prevent ill-health, such as control of food additives, screening for cancer and provision of leisure services. Finally, the 'right to health' includes a 'right to health care'. The right to health care is held by all citizens equally, and thus access to health care should be comprehensive. Such a maximalist interpretation clearly extends the scope of the 'right to health' beyond both Toebes' minimalist international core content, and rights justiciable at the suit of individuals.[56]

Both the international (represented by Toebes) and the national constitutional (represented by Montgomery) core content of the right to health include elements of the pre-conditions for good health. The benefit of this is that it allows the notion of the right to health to encompass the practice of public health promotion. This is defined as what a society can do collectively to ensure the conditions in which people can be healthy. These are more than simply the provision of health care for the unhealthy, but include clean water and air, (health) education, and a social environment that respects and supports human dignity.[57] A public health approach focuses on the preconditions for health, rather than the notion of fixing the defective human machine.[58] As its emphasis is on prevention rather than cure, it reflects best practice in the health world, and in particular most efficient use of limited resources. However, this approach can

---

[54] Brazier, above n 23, pp 67 and 69–70. This approach may also be found in McHale, 'Enforcing Health Care Rights in the English Courts' in R Burchill, D Harris and A Owers (eds), *Economic, Social and Cultural Rights: Their Implementation in United Kingdom Law* (Nottingham, University of Nottingham Human Rights Law Centre, 1999); the contributions to L Westerhäll and C Phillips (eds), *Patients' Rights: Informed Consent, Access and Equality* (Stockholm, Nerenius & Santérus, 1994); and R Plant, *Can There be a Right to Health Care?* (Southampton, Institute for Health Policy Studies, 1989), cited in J Montgomery, *Health Care Law* (Oxford, OUP, 1997), p 54.

[55] 'Recognising a Right to Health' in R Beddard and D M Hill (eds), *Economic, Social and Cultural Rights: Progress and Achievement* (Basingstoke, Macmillan, 1992), pp 188–92. See also Montgomery, above n 3.

[56] See also, for a similar approach, J McHale and M Fox, *Health Care Law: Text, Cases and Materials* (London, Sweet and Maxwell, 1997), ch 1.

[57] J Mann, L Gostin, et al, 'Health and Human Rights' above n 17.

[58] Montgomery, above n 54, pp 2–4.

only be accommodated within rights discourse if a notion of collectively held rights is accepted.

Having considered the 'right to health' in international and national (constitutional) law, we now turn to the right to health in the Charter. The first thing to note is that the Charter does not include a 'right to health' as such. Article 35 EUCFR concerns the 'right to health *care*', and provides that,

> Everyone has the right of access to preventive health care and the right to benefit from medical treatment under the conditions established by national laws and practices. A high level of human health protection shall be ensured in the definition and implementation of all Union policies and activities.

This provision has two elements: an expression of individual entitlement and a mainstreaming obligation. The individual entitlements ('everyone has the right . . .'), taken from the ESC,[59] are both to medical treatment in the case of ill-health, and to preventive health care. This latter could potentially encompass the notion of the pre-conditions for good health, as elaborated in the international and national literature on the (collective) right to health. The fact that the title of this provision is the 'right to health *care*' may therefore be of less relevance than it appears. The second sentence repeats the 'mainstreaming' provision in Article 152 (1) EC,[60] and extends the obligation placed on the EU institutions in the context of *Community* policies and activities to *Union* policies and activities. This element of the Charter may be seen as a kind of 'super-mainstreaming'[61] expression of the values that should underpin EU law and policy.

In addition to Article 35 EUCFR, the Charter contains a number of other provisions relevant for the right to health. Article 1 EUCFR on human dignity may be said to be the basis of all elements of the right to health. Its close relative is Article 3 EUCFR on the integrity of the person, which draws from and is stated to be consistent with[62] the Council of Europe's Convention on Human Rights and Biomedicine, 1997. Article 8 EUCFR[63] on the protection of personal data may be relevant in terms of data that medical professionals may hold on their patients, data with respect to medical research, and patients' entitlements to

---

[59] Art 11 ESC.

[60] See Council, Explanations Relating to the complete text of the Charter (Luxembourg, Office for Official Publications of the European Communities, 2001), accessible from http://www.europa.eu.int/(Explanatory Document); CHARTE 4473/00 CONVENT 49.

[61] Kenner, *EU Employment Law: From Rome to Amsterdam and beyond* (Oxford, Hart, 2002) p 544.

[62] See Explanatory Document; CHARTE 4473/00 CONVENT 49.

[63] Based on Art 286 EC, Dir 95/46/EC and also Art 8 ECHR and the Council of Europe Convention of 28 January 1981 for the Protection of Individuals with regard to Automatic Processing of Personal Data, which has been ratified by all Member States.

view their medical records. Article 13 EUCFR on the freedom of the arts and sciences may be relevant to medical research. Finally, Article 21 EUCFR on the non-discrimination principle is extremely important:

> Any discrimination based on any ground such as sex, race, colour, ethnic or social origin, genetic features, language, religion or belief, political or other opinion, membership of a national minority, property, birth, disability, age or sexual orientation shall be prohibited.

The phrase 'any ground such as' is crucial here, as it implies that other suspect grounds, for instance citizenship or nationality,[64] might also found a complaint of discrimination. The provision draws on Article 13 EC, Article 14 ECHR and Article 11 of the Convention on Human Rights and Biomedicine, with respect to genetic heritage. According to the Explanations relating to the complete text . of the Charter (Explanatory Document), 'insofar as this provision corresponds to Article 14 of the ECHR, it applies in compliance with it'.[65]

The legal status of the Charter is, infamously, to be determined at a later date.[66] It may be that the social rights in the Charter would never be justiciable at the suit of an individual, even if the Charter were to be 'hardened up' as a legal instrument.[67] The Cologne Conclusions state that:

> in drawing up such a Charter account should furthermore be taken of economic and social rights as contained in the European Social Charter and in the Community Charter of Fundamental Social Rights for Workers *insofar as they do not merely establish objectives for action by the Union.*

The Charter does not, however, elaborate on the distinction implicit here between 'economic and social rights' and mere 'objectives for action'.[68] Drawing on the wording of the Charter, Hepple suggests that the provisions on economic and social rights within it fall into three categories: clear individual rights; rights that 'the Union recognises and respects'; and pure objectives. Article 35 EUCFR falls into the third category. This is also reflected in the constitutional traditions of some Member States, which draw a distinction between

---

[64] But see Art 21(2) EUCFR.

[65] See Explanatory Document; CHARTE 4473/00 CONVENT 49.

[66] See Cologne European Council Conclusions, June 1999. Apparently at least 6 Member States are, or at least were, against the Charter being incorporated into the Treaties, see L Betten, 'The EU Charter on Fundamental Rights: A Trojan Horse or a Mouse?' (2001) 17 *International Journal of Comparative Labour Law and Industrial Relations* 151–64, p 152, citing *Times, Guardian* 20 June 2000; see also B de Witte, 'The Legal Status of the Charter: Vital Question or Non-Issue?' (2001) 8 *Maastricht Journal of European and Comparative Law* 81–89, p 82.

[67] See Goldsmith's argument in terms of 'principles' as opposed to 'rights and freedoms', in Lord Goldsmith, 'A Charter of Rights, Freedoms and Principles' (2001) 38 *Common Market Law Review* 1201–16. Cf M Gijzen, 'The Charter: a milestone for social protection in Europe?' (2001) 8 *Maastricht Journal of European and Comparative Law* 33–48, p 42 'the Charter has the potential to become the first legally binding document which guarantees both fundamental socio-economic rights and which provides, at the same time, for a system of individual petition'.

[68] B Hepple, 'The EU Charter of Fundamental Rights' (2001) 30 *Industrial Law Journal* 225–31, p 228.

justiciable rights and 'directive principles of social policy'.[69] This might pose obstacles to the development of the right to health care in the Charter as an individually justiciable right,[70] even if the Charter gains a formal legal status in Community law.

However, even without incorporation or other formal legal status, and even if some provisions remain non-justiciable at the suit of individuals, the provisions in the Charter may be relevant for a number of reasons. For instance, the Charter clearly imposes obligations on the institutions of the EU. Article 51 (1) EUCFR, understood in the context of Article 6 (2) TEU, suggests a positive obligation on the institutions to take full account of the Charter when performing their legislative tasks.[71] If the provisions of the Charter are construed by the European Court of Justice (the Court) or the Court of First Instance as merely expressing *existing* 'general principles of Community law',[72] the Charter's provisions may in effect become the basis for judicial review[73] of action of the EU institutions, both administrative and legislative. Review of acts of the Member States *implementing* Community law,[74] or derogating from Community law when exercising one of the 'four freedoms',[75] may also be possible on this basis. Further the inclusion of social rights in the Charter, the explicit references to the ESC and RevESC in the Preamble, and the notion of 'indivisibility' of rights in the Charter, may encourage courts applying Community law to draw on the ESC and RevESC. The EU Charter brings the jurisprudence of the European Court of Human Rights even more firmly within Community law.[76] Although there is no express mention of the European Committee of Fundamental Social Rights, some have argued that the European Court of Justice is now required, in cases concerning the interpretation of provisions derived from the ESC (which of course includes Article 35 EUCFR) to consider the (quasi) jurisprudence of the European Committee of Social Rights.[77] Moreover, as discussed above, the right to health *plus* other general principles of Community law, either in the Charter or not, may form a basis for the development of individually enforceable rights to health. For instance, the right to health may be combined with the right to dignity in Article 1 EUCFR, the right to non-discrimination in

---

[69] B Hepple, *ibid*; see, for instance, the Spanish constitution and the Irish constitution, Art 45.

[70] K Lenaerts and P Foubert, 'Social Rights in the Case-Law of the European Court of Justice' (2001) 28 *Legal Issues of European Integration*, 267–96, p 271 'It seems, however, obvious, that the social rights contained in the Charter cannot as such serve as a basis for claims by EU citizens against the Community or a Member State. They should rather be seen as a "touchstone" against which Community and Member State action can be tested.'

[71] Kenner, above n 61, p 531.

[72] Or, as the British delegation insisted, 'a showcase of existing rights'.

[73] Under Arts 230 EC and 234 EC; also potentially under Art 68 EC.

[74] Case 5/88 *Wachauf* [1989] ECR 2609.

[75] Case 260/89 *ERT* [1991] ECR I–2925.

[76] Art 52(3) EUCFR.

[77] Kenner, above n 61, p 537; N Casey, 'The European Social Charter and Revised European Social Charter'; and B Fitzpatrick, 'European Union Law and the Council of Europe Conventions' in Costello (ed), above n 1. But see J Kenner, in this collection, at pp 23–24.

Article 21 EUCFR, or the right to good administration in Article 41 EUCFR.[78] Alternatively, even if the provision on the right to health care is simply an expression of an objective, merely setting tasks to be translated into enforceable rights by secondary Community or (largely) national law, the status of these secondary provisions may be affected by their relationship with a fundamental right set out in the Charter. Such provisions may take on a 'constitutionalised' status, as has been the case, for instance with the Court's development of the secondary legislation on sex equality.[79]

Further, as soft law, the Charter may be used to interpret existing Community law,[80] and as a platform for the development of measures of hard Community law.[81] Although the Charter explicitly does not give any new powers or tasks to the EU institutions, it may provide a source of inspiration for the Community legislature, may constrain or direct the substantive contents or focus of Community law and policy (through the 'super-mainstreaming' element of some of its provisions) and may consequently give added support to certain actors in the legislative process.[82] In terms of social rights, the Charter may increase the influence of the ESC and RevESC in the EU's legal order, or those of its Member States.[83] Less tangibly still, the Charter may be seen as an important expression of the *values* underpinning the EU as a polity,[84] and thus may influence legislative, administrative and judicial activity in perhaps more subtle ways.

This overview suggests a number of possible roles for social rights, such as the right to health, in the Charter, including the protection of the vulnerable from the interests of the collectivity; the curbing of the power of the EU as a non-state polity; providing a focus for pressure on 'third party' state governments; and resolving matters concerning resource allocation and the interactions of public

---

[78] For discussion of this right, see Case T–54/99 *Max Mobil* [2002] ECR II–313.

[79] Directive 76/207/EC OJ 1976 L 39/40 as encapsulating a fundamental right, see Cases 75 & 117/82 *Razzouk and Beydoun* [1984] ECR 1509, para 16; see Von Bogdandy, above n 11.

[80] See eg Case C–322/88 *Grimaldi* [1989] ECR 4407; Opinion of the Advocate-General in Case C–173/99 *BECTU* [2001] ECR I–4881.

[81] On the roles of soft law, see, eg, L Cram, *Policy-making in the EU: Conceptual Lenses and the Integration Process* (London, Routledge, 1997), pp 107–11; K Wellens and R Borchardt, 'Soft Law in European Community Law' (1989) 14 *European Law Review* 267; J Kenner, 'The EU Employment Title and the "Third Way": Making Soft Law Work?' (1999) 15 *International Journal of Comparative Labour Law and Industrial Relations* 33; see also specifically in the context of social policy, Betten, above n 66, p 152. For examples in the areas of sex equality and racism/xenophobia see, respectively, C Hoskyns, *Integrating Gender* (London, Verso, 1996); R Geyer, *Exploring European Social Policy* (Cambridge, Polity, 2000) pp 164–71.

[82] For example, Waddington has shown how the disability lobby exerted its influence on the EU policy-making process, moving from a 'charity-based' to a 'dignity-based' provision; see L Waddington, *Disability, Employment and the European Community* (London, Blackstone Press, 1995).

[83] Gijzen, above n 67, p 47.

[84] A Lyon-Caen, 'Fundamental Social Rights as Benchmarks in the Construction of the EU' in L Betten and D McDevitt (eds), *The Protection of Fundamental Social Rights in the European Union* (The Hague, Kluwer, 1996), p 45.

powers and markets. Some of these are now elaborated with respect to the right to health.

WHAT DIFFERENCE MIGHT A 'RIGHT TO HEALTH' MAKE?

With these possible effects of the social rights recognised in the Charter in mind, three case studies[85] are now considered in which the 'right to health' might make a difference in various areas of EU activity. These have been chosen to represent the breadth of scope of the EU's activities, and as areas where health may be seen as a concern whose importance is significant and stands in danger of being under-recognised. As will be seen, the different roles of rights may have different significance in the area represented by each case study.

Internal Market Litigation

Recent attempts by patients in the EU to utilise the directly effective Treaty provisions on freedom of movement to receive health care goods and services across national borders within the EU have received a great deal of attention.[86] As I have argued elsewhere,[87] such litigation runs the risk of undermining the financial stability and coherence of national health systems within the Member States of the EU. This is particularly so where national health systems have adopted cost containment measures or other measures of resource allocation that have discriminatory effects on grounds of nationality or otherwise infringe the EC Treaty provisions on freedom of movement, for instance by restricting market access.[88]

---

[85] Space precludes elaboration of further examples, for instance whether a right to health might make a difference to the EU's food safety law (eg BSE/CJD, hormones in beef, additives, genetically modified foods); or to the relationship between the EU and its employees; or to the EU's support for medical research.

[86] Case C–120/95 *Decker* [1998] ECR I–1831; Case C–158/96 *Kohll v Union des Caisses de Maladie* [1998] ECR I–1931; Case C–368/98 *Van Braekel* [2001] ECR I–5363; Case C–157/99 *Geraets-Smits and Peerbooms* [2001] ECR I–4821. For comment, see AP Van der Mei, 'Cross-Border Access to Medical Care within the European Union' (1998) 5 *Maastricht Journal of European and Comparative Law* 277; P Cabral, 'Cross-border Medical Care in the EU—Bringing Down a First Wall' (1999) 24 *European Law Review* 387; HDC Roscam Abbing, 'Editorial: Public Health Insurance and Freedom of Movement within the European Union' (1999) 6 *European Journal of Health Law* 1; A Baeyens, 'Free movement of good and services in health care' (1999) 6 *European Journal of Health Law* 373; K Sieveking, 'The Significance of Transborder Utilisation of Health Care Benefits for Migrants' 2 *European Journal of Migration and the Law* (2000) 143; E Mossialos and M McKee, 'Is an European Healthcare Policy Emerging?' *British Medical Journal* 200; 323: 248 (4 August); R Baeten, M McKee and E Mossialos (eds), *European Integration and National Health Care Policy: a Challenge for Social Policy*, (Brussels, PIE Peter Lang, 2002) following Belgian Presidency Conference December 2001.

[87] T Hervey, 'Social Solidarity: a Buttress Against Internal Market Law' in J Shaw (ed), *Social Law and Policy in an Evolving European Union* (Oxford, Hart, 2000) 31–47.

[88] See C Barnard, 'Fitting the Remaining Pieces into the Goods and Persons Jigsaw?' (2001) 26 *European Law Review* 35; C Barnard and S Deakin, 'Market Access and Regulatory Competition' in C Barnard and J Scott (eds), *The Law of the Single European Market: Unpacking the Premises* (Oxford, Hart, 2002) 197–224.

The Court has dealt with this litigation by referring to a notion of 'solidarity', as part of the 'European social model', which in effect grants Member States a justification for a policy that, on its face, breaches the Treaty-based freedom of movement of persons and the free supply and receipt of services. Neither the right to health care, nor the EUCFR was mentioned in any of the Court's rulings on the subject. Might a strongly articulated right to health, based on Article 35 EUCFR, make a difference to future litigation of this sort?

For example, the British national health service has taken advantage of the rulings on free movement of patients by sending patients to a hospital in Lille,[89] and it appears that there are plans to use hospitals in other Member States, including Germany and Greece.[90] In this context, the rulings thus far have been seen as presenting an opportunity for the British public authorities to alleviate pressure on national health provision, in particular the shortage of hospital beds. However, it is not unimaginable that an individual litigious patient might seek to *demand* a 'cross-border' bed, in accordance with her rights in Community law.[91]

The right to health care in Article 35 EUCFR is based on Article 11 ESC. In its preamble, the Charter refers to 'the Social Charters adopted by the Community and by the Council of Europe'. As noted above, it seems clear that the Charter therefore consolidates the position of the ESC and the RevESC as sources of 'general principles' of Community law.[92] Further, it is at least arguable that the references to the ESC and RevESC in the Charter require due notice to be taken of the interpretations of the ESC and RevESC adopted by the institutions of the Council of Europe.[93] The relevant institution in this context is the European Committee of Social Rights (formerly the Committee of Independent Experts), whose task it is to examine the reports of the Member States, and make a legal assessment of the compliance of those states with their obligations under the ESC and RevESC.[94] In effect, the conclusions of the European Committee of Social Rights constitute the (quasi) jurisprudence of the ESC and RevESC.[95]

---

[89] *Times*, 'European beds for NHS Patients by the New Year' 31 August 2001; *Times*, 'English Patients Take French Cure' 19 January 2002.

[90] *Times*, 31 August 2001; *Times*, 19 January 2002; *Times* 20 January 2002.

[91] Indeed, such a case, involving Yvonne Watts, aged 72, awaiting a hip operation, was reported to be under consideration on 11 December 2002. See BBC News online http://www.bbc.co.uk/news.

[92] See also the reference in Art 136 EC.

[93] As noted above, Art 52(3) EUCFR expressly requires such notice, by requiring that 'In so far as this Charter contains rights which correspond to rights guaranteed by the Convention for the Protection of Human Rights and Fundamental Freedoms, the meaning and scope of those rights shall be the same as those laid down by the said Convention.' If the 'indivisibility' of civil and political and economic, social and cultural rights, EUCFR Preamble, recital 2, is taken seriously, this would imply similar status for the meaning and scope of rights laid down by the (Rev)ESC.

[94] See the Amending Protocol of 1991; See N Casey, 'The European Social Charter and Revised European Social Charter' in Costello (ed), above n 1, pp 55–57

[95] See D Harris, *The European Social Charter* (New York, University Press of Virginia, 1984); Casey, above n 94, pp 61–75. The conclusions of the European Committee of Social Rights with respect to state compliance with a particular provision fall into three categories: positive (there is compliance); negative (there is a violation); or deferred (further information is needed).

In January 2001, the European Committee of Social Rights published its conclusions on UK compliance with the ESC.[96] On the matter of access to health care, the Committee noted that waiting lists and times for hospital appointments within the British national health system were increasing. Taking into account the fact that the duration of waiting times is long in absolute terms, that the situation is not improving, and that simultaneously the number of hospital beds continues to decrease, the Committee concluded that 'on the basis of these data, the organisation of health care in the United Kingdom is manifestly not adapted to ensure the right to health for everyone'.[97]

If the Committee's interpretation of the substantive content of the right to health care in the case of provision of hospital beds and waiting times for medical treatment applies in the construction of the substantive content of Article 35 EUCFR, it might therefore be possible to argue that the UK is currently failing to comply not only with its duties under the ESC, but also with Article 35 EUCFR. The Court has applied fundamental rights in judicial review of acts of the Member States derogating from Community law when exercising one of the 'four freedoms', in matters falling 'within the scope of Community law'.[98] If it were accepted that failure to fund a 'cross-border bed' falls sufficiently within the scope of Community law, an argument might then be raised on behalf of an individual litigant, on the basis of a right to health in Community law plus the classic Community law freedom of movement rights, that, if a British NHS Trust fails to take advantage of the possibility of sending its patients abroad for treatment, it is breaching its duties in Community law. The obligations of the NHS Trust would arise from a combination of provisions of the EC Treaty and of general principles of Community law, as expressed in the Charter. The relevant Treaty-based provisions are directly effective, and thus might found an application for judicial review of the Trust's decision. Such an argument, if successful, would be a version of the 'social rights plus' argument, advanced to bolster the justiciability of social rights. In classic international law, the 'plus' element here is a foundational element of human rights, such as dignity or non-discrimination. Given the centrality of the internal market and its realisation through individual rights of free movement to the EU's legal order, freedom of movement might be sufficiently 'foundational' in this context.[99] Were such an argument accepted, a number of issues would arise.

---

[96] Doc c–15–2–en2.

[97] However, rather than adopting a negative conclusion, the Committee deferred its conclusion, requesting further information on criteria for the management of waiting lists and waiting times in health care.

[98] Case 36/75 *Rutili* [1975] ECR 1219; Case 260/89 *ERT* [1991] ECR I–2925; Case C–368/95 *Familiapress* [1997] ECR I–3689. However, the legal position is not entirely clear, see Cases 60 & 61/84 *Cinétheque* [1985] ECR 2605. Article 51 EUCFR refers to 'Member States only when they are implementing Union law', but the Explanatory Document suggests a broader reading, by reference to the *ERT* case. For discussion, see P Craig and G de Búrca, *EU Law: Text, Cases and Materials* (Oxford, OUP, 2002), pp 341–49.

[99] Other 'social rights plus' litigation might be envisaged, for instance concerning the right to health plus the right to non-discrimination on forbidden grounds, such as age or disability. Thanks to Lisa Waddington for this suggestion.

The articulation of a right to health in Community law in this context might increase the chances of a judicial intervention in what is essentially a matter of policy; the proper disbursement of resources available in the British national health service. In the free movement of patients case law to date, the Court has conceptualised the matter as essentially one of spheres of competence, stressing that the organisation and financing of social security systems, including health care systems, is a matter for Member States, and that, consequently, a risk of seriously undermining the financial balance of a social security system justifies a barrier to the freedom to provide services.[100] However, were a fundamental right to be at stake, the Court might be less inclined to grant such broad discretion to national authorities. Justification would have to be sufficient to offset not simply the political choices of a Member State in terms of the financial organisation of its health service, but the possible breach of a right regarded as fundamental in the EU's legal order. Mere financial arrangements rarely outweigh the requirement of respect for human rights. The British national health system has systemic waiting lists for hospital treatment, because of the system of access to hospital care, and in particular the system of national health service funding. The financial arrangements of the national health service within a Member State are a matter for political resolution, by the relevant electorate. The intervention of a justiciable 'right to health' in Community law might, on this construction, therefore, constitute an inappropriate proxy for appropriate political debate leading to the proper allocation of socio-economic resources (here hospital beds), and might in fact bring about a substantively unjust result in terms of their allocation. To take the point further, a strongly articulated individual right to health, if applied to entitlement to 'cross-border beds', might actually destabilise the financial arrangements for health care within the UK. If this were to occur, it would be at least arguable that the health protection and promotion of the health of the citizens of the UK had actually been *undermined* by a notion of a right to health.

However, on closer inspection, such a 'doomsday' scenario is unlikely to arise. The context in which the Court might hear such 'cross border beds' litigation is the preliminary ruling under Article 234 EC. Here, the final resolution of the case is a matter for the national court. Provided that the Trust had considered the fundamental right to health, such a court would be unlikely to interfere in a policy decision such as whether or not to allow a patient to travel to another Member State for treatment. Although both the national court and the Court (as protector of fundamental rights in the EU's legal order) might be required to consider explicitly the substantive issues concerned, framed in terms of a right to health, the right to health could be found to be respected, by reference to the right to health of others, whose health needs would not be met were cross-border beds to be made available, as the resources available are not

---

[100] Case C–158/96 *Kohll v Union des Caisses de Maladie* [1998] ECR I–1931, para 41; Case C–368/98 *Van Braekel* [2001] ECR I–5363, para 47.

infinite. So long as the Trust had considered this matter, and had not reached a disproportionate decision, it would be unlikely to be overturned by the application of Community law.[101] Overall then, a 'right to health' might make a difference in terms of the *discourse* available to judicial bodies to resolve what are effectively matters of resource allocation, but in the final analysis would be unlikely to make a difference in the *substantive outcome* of any litigation.

The example considered above would require a court to support a 'positive' social right (to health care) in the sense of a claim on the state. Even if such a 'social rights plus' argument were not accepted, it is possible to imagine a 'social rights plus' argument in the context of a 'negative' 'freedom from' type claim to the right to health care. Again a hypothetical example based on the UK provides illustration. Concerns about a possible link between autism and bowel disorders in children and the combined measles, mumps and rubella (MMR) vaccine have led to a significant decline in the take-up of this vaccine among infants in the UK.[102] Single vaccines for measles, mumps and rubella are not licensed within the UK, and the UK Medicines Control Agency has restricted the importation of these unlicensed vaccines, on the basis that a safe and effective licensed alternative is available.[103] However, importation of unlicensed single vaccines is permitted where it meets the special needs of an individual patient, and the doctor takes personal responsibility for this. It has been reported that many parents have availed themselves of this option.[104] Thus far, the UK authorities have not sought to prevent this. But there are concerns that the separate vaccinations are

---

[101] From its earlier fundamental rights jurisprudence, the Court has recognised that rights may be limited by other public interests; see, eg Case 4/73 *Nold* [1974] ECR 491, para 14. As various commentators have pointed out, the actual impact of the Court's recognition of fundamental rights has, in many cases, been rather minimal, see Craig and de Búrca, above n 98, p 331; J Coppel and A O'Neill, 'The European Court of Justice: Taking Rights Seriously?' (1992) 29 *Common Market Law Review* 669.

[102] The original study, undertaken at the Royal Free Hospital, London, that prompted the concerns is published as Wakefield et al, 'Ileal-lymphoid-nodular hyperplasm, non-specific colitis and pervasive developmental disorder in children' (1998) *Lancet* 351 pp 637–41. See also the news report, BBC News, 'Child vaccine linked to autism', 27 February 1998, http://www.news.bbc.co.uk/hi/english/health/newsid_60000/60510.stm. Subsequent research, both in the UK and elsewhere, has cast doubt on these findings, see the studies cited on the UK Department of Health website, http://www.doh.gov.uk/mmr/. A study on take-up, following the media coverage of Wakefield's report, is reported in Thomas et al, 'Rates of first measles-mumps-rubella immunisation in Wales (UK)' *Lancet* 351 (1998) p 1927.

[103] For an accessible explanation of the roles of the relevant UK authorities, and the situation governing import of single MMR vaccines, see the Scottish Executive Publications online, *Report of the MMR Expert Group*, 2002, http://www.scotland.gov.uk/library5/health/rmmr-06.asp.

[104] A quick websearch (using Google) in May 2002 revealed both NGOs and private companies who advertise the availability of single vaccines, and advise parents how to persuade their GP to prescribe single vaccinations on a special needs basis, and to explain to pharmacists how to import the vaccines. Private clinics also advertise the availability of single vaccines. See http://www.singlevaccines.com/gp.htm; http://www.singlevaccines.com/single.htm; http://www.singlevaccines.com/thepharmacy.htm; http://www.dh2.co.uk/mmr.htm; http://www.jabs.org.uk. A number of parents have also taken their children to France for separate measles and rubella vaccinations; see BBC News, 'Parents take children abroad for vaccine' 18 October 1999, http://www.news.bbc.co.uk/hi/english/health/newsid_478000/478338.stm.

not as effective, and in particular that the levels of take-up may be jeopardised by the use of separate vaccines.[105] With this in mind, it is not inconceivable that the UK public health authorities might take the view that the separate vaccinations should not be permitted within the UK, even for individual patients. The Medicines Control Agency has already taken action to prevent a pharmaceutical imports company, IDIS, from importing batches of single vaccines.[106] In response to an argument that this breached the principle of freedom of movement of goods, the authorities might point to the public health risks as justification. Were a national court or the Court to be faced with litigation on this question, might a notion of the right to health care, as articulated in the Charter, make a difference? The right to health care here is conceptualised as a negative 'freedom from' state interference, which might bolster its chances of being found justiciable. Again, the discourse of rights might involve the courts in resolution of difficult issues, in this context in particular the proper balance between the rights of individuals (to choose separate vaccines) and the good of the collectivity (provided by 'herd immunity'). A collective notion of the right to health in Community law might help tip the balance in favour of the collective public health, prevention approach. Again, although the discourse of dispute resolution might be altered, the substantive outcome is likely to remain unchanged.

These examples must be seen in the context of the on-going debate about the 'social identity' of the European Union. As Maduro has argued persuasively, it is no longer possible for the EU to avoid a discussion on its socio-political orientation.[107] The interactions between Community internal market law and the national social policies of the Member States, in the context of a multilevel system of governance within which directly effective Community-level law is supreme, are creating a situation of instability in European social policies, including health systems. Add to this the uncertainties posed by globalisation, changing demographics, changes to family and working patterns, and so on, and the Member States of the EU are facing significant threats to the 'European social model'. The articulation of various social rights in the Charter may help to underscore these elements of the European social model as *values* fundamental to the EU and its Member States. On the other hand, as social policies within the EU undergo necessary changes, social rights as articulated in the Charter

[105] The WHO recommends vaccination rates of 95% to eradicate the targeted diseases; see BBC News, 'MMR's Global Success' 6 February 2002, http://www.news.bbc.co.uk/hi/english/health/newsid_1804000/1804509.stm. The Welsh study showed take-up rates falling from 83.1% in 1997 to 69.6% in 1998, see BBC News, 'Drop in MMR jabs blamed on media scare' 26 June 1998, http://www.news.bbc.co.uk/hi/english/health/newsid_120000/120277.stm.

[106] See Editorial, 'MCA Restricts Imports of Single Antigen MMR Vaccines' *The Pharmaceutical Journal* Vol 263 No 7061, p 336, 4 September 1999. The MCA confirmed that imports where the patient has a special need, such as an allergic reaction, were still permitted.

[107] M Poiares Maduro, 'Europe's Social Self: The "Sickness Unto Death"', in Shaw (ed), *Social Law and Policy in an Evolving European Union* (Oxford, Hart, 2000); M Poiares Maduro, 'Europe and the Constitution: What if This is as Good as it Gets?' in J Weiler and M Wind (eds), *Rethinking European Constitutionalism* (Cambridge, CUP, *forthcoming*).

might form the bulwark of reactionary forces seeking to avoid such changes. Strongly articulated social rights, such as the 'right to health' might alter the terms of the discourse of internal market litigation. However, ultimately, the scope for the notion of, say, a 'right to health' to change the substantive outcome of such litigation is severely limited.

External Relations: Development Policy

It seems clear that the Charter applies to the external relations of the Community and EU.[108] The external human rights policy of the EU manifests itself in a number of ways. The EU issues various foreign policy instruments;[109] it imposes human rights clauses in its bilateral and multilateral cooperation and trade agreements, including those with candidate countries; it seeks to promote its own human rights 'image' within the framework of international organisations;[110] and it provides assistance and support, through financial, trade or other means.[111]

Article 177 (2) EC provides that in such development cooperation, Community policy must contribute to 'the general objective of developing and consolidating democracy and the rule of law, and to that of respecting human rights and fundamental freedoms'.[112] The Treaty of Nice imposes an identical obligation with respect to Community policy in adopting economic, financial and technical cooperation measures with third countries.[113]

The right to health, especially in Toebes' minimalist international definition, is fundamental for citizens of developing countries.[114] One concern is with the

---

[108] The Charter is not explicit on the matter, but see Art 51(1) EUCFR; see also a number of provisions such as abolition of death penalty, which have already been achieved within the Member States of the EU, thus implying external application; see Von Bogdandy, above n 11, at 1309; J Wouters, 'Editorial' (2001) 8 *Maastricht Journal of European and Comparative Law* 3–10, p 4; see also Commission's External Relations Website http://www.europa.eu.int/comm/external_relations/human_rights/intro 'The Commission's action in the field of external relations will be guided by compliance with the rights and principles contained in the EU Charter . . . since this will promote coherence between the EU's internal and external approaches'.

[109] Declarations, *démarches*, common positions and joint actions; see Nowak, 'Human Rights Conditionality in the EU' in Alston (ed), *The EU and Human Rights* (Oxford, OUP, 1999), p 688.

[110] Especially the UN and OSCE.

[111] Rosas, in Eide, Krause and Rosas, above n 3, p 481; Nowak, above n 109, p 688.

[112] In addition, Art 11 TEU provides that one of the objectives of the common foreign and security policy is 'to develop and consolidate democracy and the rule of law, and respect for human rights and fundamental freedoms'.

[113] New Art 181a(1) EC. Technical and financial cooperation programmes of the EC do not list human rights activities as such. The notion of 'human rights' may often be subsumed by 'democracy' or 'good governance'; see B Simma, J Aschenbrenner, and C Schulte, 'Human Rights Considerations in Development Cooperation Activities of the EC', in P Alston (ed), above n 109, p 577.

[114] See, eg the World Health Reports of the WHO, available from http://www.who.int/; the UNICEF Report on child mortality, Hill, Rohini, Mahy, and Jones, *Trends in Child Mortality in the Developing World: 1960 to 1996* (New York, UNICEF, 1999); research on general mortality by the United States Census Bureau, international database available at http://www.census.gov/ipc/www/idbnew.html and the UN Population Division 2000 demographic assessment, *World Population Prospects: the 2000 Revision* (New York, United Nations, 2001).

proportion of available resources governments devote to health; and to what types of health protection or promotion activities resources are devoted.[115] As the UN Development Programme, Human Development Report, 1990,[116] explains,

> Governments can also do much to improve the efficiency of social spending by creating a policy and budgetary framework that would achieve a more desirable mix between various social expenditures, particularly by reallocating resources:
> —from curative medical facilities to primary health care programmes,
> —from highly trained doctors to paramedical personnel,
> —from urban to rural services,

The EU might have a role to play, along with others in the international and national communities, in encouraging governments of developing countries to respect, promote and fulfil the right to health in these ways.

Human rights clauses in trade and cooperation agreements,[117] including the Europe Agreements, Mediterranean Agreements and the Cotonou Agreement,[118] have two main functions. They reaffirm commonly shared values and principles, and they express the notion of 'conditionality'.[119] The significance of human rights clauses is not limited to the extreme penalty of treaty suspension,[120] but the threat of use might be sufficient to ensure compliance in the diplomatic phase

[115] Toebes, above n 2, pp 333–34; 338.

[116] Cited in Steiner and Alston, above n 4, p 303.

[117] Such clauses began to appear in the early 1990s, and were included more systematically from 1995, when the Council adopted a model human rights clause, see COM(95) 216 final; Rosas, in Eide, Krause and Rosas, above n 3, p 484; M Cremona, 'Human Rights and Democracy Clauses in the EC's Trade Agreements' in N Emiliou and D O'Keeffe, *The European Union and World Trade Law* (Wiley, Chichester, 1996), p 62; E Riedel and M Will, 'Human Rights Clauses in External Agreements of the EC' in Alston (ed), above n 109; B Brandtner and A Rosas, 'Trade Preferences and Human Rights', in Alston (ed), above n 109; D Napoli, 'The EU's Foreign Policy and Human Rights' in N Neuwahl and A Rosas (eds), *The European Union and Human Rights* (The Hague, Martinus Nijhoff Publishers, 1995).

[118] Formerly the Lomé Conventions.

[119] In other words, human rights clauses in international agreements spell out the suspension rights of parties to the agreement in the event of non-respect for these values and principles in the context of human rights clauses in international agreements. The notion of 'conditionality' of trade preferences and other trade measures on respect for human rights is controversial in the WTO context (see Article XX GATT), as it is seen as potential protectionism; see Riedel and Will, in Alston (ed), above n 117, p 745. In the context of social rights, the 'social clause' or 'labour standards clause' discussed at Singapore 9–13 December 1996 and mentioned in the Ministerial Declaration at Doha 14 November 2001, is regarded by some as a legitimate means of linking core labour standards (if not other social rights) to trade sanctions. However, the WTO's formal position is that the ILO, not the WTO, is the competent body to oversee labour standards. See V Leary, 'The WTO and the Social Clause: Post-Singapore' (1997) 8 *European Journal of International Law* 118–22; C Thomas, 'Trade-Related Labor and Environmental Agreements?' (2002) 5 *Journal of International Economic Law* 791–819.

[120] Suspension would not be undertaken lightly, not least because of the implications of economic sanctions for the economic and social rights of the population of the targeted state, Brandtner and Rosas, in Alston (ed), above n 117, p 699; see also Rosas, in Eide, Krause and Rosas, above n 3, p 487.

prior to its application.[121] Other possible penalty measures[122] might also be used or threatened. Probably more significant than the possible penalty measures for failure to comply with human rights clauses in external relations treaties[123] is the use of such clauses to promote a positive approach that stimulates respect for human rights, by creating an environment conducive to such respect.[124] This involves EU support for human rights initiatives through open and constructive dialogue with governments of other states, and increased support for states supporting human rights. Indeed such a 'carrot' (rather than 'stick') approach may be more appropriate for promotion of social rights.[125] However, the list of positive measures promulgated by the Council in 1991 does not include any specific reference to promotion of social rights.[126] It seems clear from the EU's practice that, in terms of pressure on governments of other states, human rights clauses may at least in theory provide opportunities in terms of promoting civil and political rights,[127] but, at least as yet, have not been seen as a useful mechanism for promoting social rights. This is for a number of reasons, including the fear (or excuse) of cultural imperialism and related concerns about interfering in resource allocation, and all that that means in terms of democratic processes, in states with relatively few resources.

At present then, the notion of a 'right to health', along with other social rights, as a mechanism for imposing pressure on governments of developing

---

[121] Riedel and Will, in Alston (ed), above n 117, p 751.

[122] Such as 'confidential or public *démarches*; a change in the content of cooperation programmes or the channels used; deferment of decisions needed to implement cooperation; reduction of cultural, scientific or technical cooperation programmes; deferment of joint committee meetings; suspension of high-level bilateral contact; postponement of new projects; refusal to act on partner's initiatives; and trade embargoes' COM(94) 42 final, cited in Cremona in Emiliou and O'Keeffe, above n 117, p 64.

[123] For discussion of the drawbacks of sanctions and benefits of 'positive measures', see Simma, Aschenbrenner, and Schulte, above n 113, pp 579–82.

[124] Simma, Aschenbrenner, and Schulte, above n 113, p 578; Brandtner and Rosas, above n 117, p 711, using the example of EU cooperation with the countries formally in the Republic of Yugoslavia, show how the concept of 'conditionality' has been used by the EU in its trade relations not just as a 'stick' in terms of non-compliance with human rights standards, but also as a 'carrot' by introducing 'a clear link between these countries' performance as regards, inter alia, democracy, the rule of law and higher standards of human and minority rights (in line with some of these countries' commitments under the Dayton Peace Agreements), and the Community's willingness not only to grant autonomous trade measures, but also economic and financial cooperation, and even to enter into new contractual relations'. Compliance is promoted by a reporting system, undertaken by the Commission.

[125] Brandtner and Rosas, above n 117, p 701.

[126] Positive measures include (28 November 1991 Council Resolution) 1 support for countries attempting to institute democracy and improve their human rights performance; 2 holding of elections, setting up of new democratic institutions, strengthening the rule of law; 3 strengthening of administration of justice, crime prevention, and treatment of offenders; 4 promoting the role of NGOs and other institutions necessary for a pluralist society; 5 adoption of decentralised approach to cooperation; 6 ensuring equal opportunities for all.

[127] Although even these are limited in practice, see Riedel and Will, above n 117, p 739, 742 'As far as can be ascertained, not a single suspension case exists today which was decided solely and entirely on the basis of a human rights clause'. 'Yet its theoretical potential is in conspicuous contrast to its utilisation in practice'.

states, stands little chance of being promoted through human rights clauses in the EU's external relations. If it were, would it make a difference? Riedel and Will implicitly think so, and argue that the EU should follow a 'bottom-up approach' and emphasise the idea that any human rights clause also embraces social rights. This would imply actively applying the existing clause to situations in other states with whom the EU has treaty relations, where such social rights are systematically and seriously violated. They also suggest a system of regular country reports about the human rights situation in all states with which the EU has concluded an agreement with a human rights clause.[128] In the context of a right to health, this would mean the EU promoting 'maternal and child care, including family planning; immunisation against the major infectious diseases; appropriate treatment of common diseases and injuries; and provision of essential drugs'; along with an 'adequate supply of safe water and basic sanitation; and freedom from serious environmental health threats', the core content of the right to health. Riedel and Will's 'bottom-up approach' would mean that the general clause should first be applied to 'flagrant breaches of the most important and undisputed social rights', and subsequently extended to other social rights and standards.[129] It might be possible to argue that the right to health would fall within the category of 'most important' social rights, but it would be difficult to maintain the position that it is 'undisputed' as a social *right*.

In contrast, Von Bogdandy[130] suggests that the inclusion of social rights such as the right to health in the EU's external relations would make a *detrimental* difference. Von Bogdandy argues that the standard of human rights protection to be applied by the EU to foreign states in its conduct of foreign policy should be limited to countering only grave civil and political human rights violations. This is to avoid Western imperialism and to respect the principle of non-intervention, as well as avoiding conflict with the law of the WTO. On this perspective, if the EU tried to enforce the social standards of the Charter, including the right to health, on a third state, in particular on developing states, that could easily lead to a counter-productive response such as aggressive protectionism.[131]

In addition to the possible effects that the recognition of a right to health might have in terms of pressure on national governments of recipient or partner states in EU development policy, we should also consider whether a right to health might make a difference in terms of the content or focus of the EU's development aid policy. Regulations 975/99/EC and 976/99/EC[132] provide the legal

---

[128] This should also explain what actions the Community has taken in response to the situation. The benefits would include a more coherent and transparent human rights policy for EU external relations; a single institutional focus within the Commission; interactions with NGOs would enhance the Community's understanding; the publicity of the stigma might be enough to change the activities of the offending state; the Community might become more consistent and non discriminatory in its implementation of the human rights clauses; and the objectivity of reports would enhance Community human rights credibility. See Riedel and Will, above n 117, pp 749–51.

[129] Riedel and Will, above n 117, p 745.

[130] Above n 11.

[131] Von Bogdandy, above n 11, p 1319.

[132] OJ 1999 L 120/1; 120/8.

basis for human rights activities and appropriate procedures for technical and financial assistance for operations which 'contribute to the general objective of developing rights and fundamental freedoms'. These provide a legal basis for human rights activities under Budget Line B7–70.[133] There is an identical Article 2 in each Regulation, which provides, in line with the notion of indivisibility of human rights[134] that assistance should aim at promotion and protection of both civil and political rights and economic, social and cultural rights.[135]

However, the EU's practice has not matched its rhetoric in terms of commitment to social rights in this respect.[136] To simplify, in its earlier phases, EU development policy considered that human rights were only relevant in respect of humanitarian relief; a 'basic needs' or 'charity' approach, rather than a 'rights' or 'entitlements' approach.[137] The tendency in the EU's external relations has been to focus on 'social protection' and combating 'social exclusion', rather than 'social rights'.[138] Beginning in the early 1990s, the focus changed, and human rights per se were explicitly included as an aim of development policy.[139] Because of the de facto 'higher' status of civil and political as opposed to social rights, this may have effectively resulted in a demotion of the status of social rights in development policy. Budget Line B7–70 has not been used for social rights policies[140] and projects in the field of social rights are funded from other budget allocations.[141]

What difference might it make to have a 'right to health' included in this budget line, or as the focus of EU development policy? The EU does support health projects through its development policy,[142] but these have not been conceptu-

---

[133] This budget line was created by an initiative of the European Parliament in 1994, which brought together a series of budget headings specifically dealing with the promotion of human rights.

[134] First EU Annual Report on Human Rights, adopted Council 1999, p 8 'the Union subscribes to the interdependence and indivisibility of all human rights and rejects efforts to limit the enjoyment of one set of rights on the pretext that priority attention must be given to another'; cited Rosas, in Eide, Krause and Rosas, above n 3, p 483.

[135] Rosas, in Eide, Krause and Rosas, above n 3, p 481.

[136] Alston and Weiler, 'An "Ever Close Union" in Need of a Human Rights policy: The European Union and Human Rights', in Alston (ed), p 31.

[137] Simma, Aschenbrenner and Schulte, above n 113, p 576.

[138] Alston and Weiler, in Alston (ed), above n 136, p 31.

[139] Contrast Lomé IV 1989 which has various provisions on economic and social rights, 'probably because the drafters perceived these rights as more closely related to 'economic development', with Council Resolution of 28 November 1991—the starting point for the human rights approach—which 'explicitly puts equal emphasis on economic, social and cultural rights and civil and political rights'. Simma, Aschenbrenner and Schulte, above n 113, p 576.

[140] 'Despite the fact that economic and social rights are of vital importance to the well-being of many of the stated priority target groups, including women, children, minorities and indigenous peoples' Alston and Weiler, in Alston, ed, above n 136, p 33.

[141] COM(95) 191 final, at 3. As Simma, Aschenbrenner and Schulte, above n 113, p 605, point out, this does not bear out the notion of the 'indivisibility' of rights.

[142] Simma, Aschenbrenner and Schulte, above n 113, pp 595–614 give examples, including support for vulnerable groups such as women, younger generations, certain social groups, refugees, victims of torture and prisoners. For instance, the Community has provided victims of torture with concrete medical and psychological care in specialised centres in Chile and Argentina.

alised as pertaining to human rights.[143] Does this really matter? Simma, Aschenbrenner and Schulte suggest that it does, arguing that the EU should recognise that promoting social rights requires an approach that does more than simply tackle poverty defined as a factual lack of resources such as nutrition, clean water and health care.[144] Simma, Aschenbrenner and Schulte are also critical of the actual levels of provision made in this respect, implying that a rights-based approach might command more resources.[145]

What differences might a 'rights-based/entitlement' approach, as opposed to a 'needs-based/charity' approach, make to health promotion in EU development policy? At a national level, the main difference is in take-up of provision; where social protections such as health care are available as a matter of right, take up is much higher than where a petition has to be made on the basis of charity.[146] This difference seems unlikely to apply in the context of international development provision. It is possible that the deliverers of the relevant programmes might have a different attitude to the beneficiaries of the relevant health care provisions, if the provision is made on the basis of the recipients' *right* to health. But again, it also seems unlikely that such policy-orientation would have a significant effect on programme delivery on the ground. It might be that a rights-based approach would affect the EU's evaluation of its development policies, in that the 'value for money' equation may be different if it is a *right* that is being assessed, rather than simply a charitable donation. It is also possible that conceptualising health provision in EU development policy as a human right might serve to further entrench such provision as essential activity of the EU institutions, preventing withdrawal of a commitment to promote and support the right to health through development policy. It might even be arguable that the EU has a (possibly enforceable) conservative duty to refrain from removing the means for enjoyment of a right to health, once given.

Overall, then in terms of external relations, the 'right to health' might make some difference in terms of focus, assessment or commitment of the EU to health protection, but such difference appears likely to be relatively marginal, given that many key elements of health promotion have already found a place in the EU's development policy.

Security and Criminal Justice: Asylum Policy

Breaches of a minimalist, international law-based right to health (Toebes' approach) *within* the EU are rare. In the main, the Member States of the EU

---

[143] However, the current proposal for a Regulation on aid for policies and actions on reproductive and sexual health and rights in developing countries COM (2002) 120 final explicitly refers to Art 35 EUCFR in its preamble, recital 4.

[144] Above n 113, p 604.

[145] Simma, Aschenbrenner and Schulte, above n 113, p 608.

[146] See N Harris, *Social Security Law in Context* (Oxford, OUP, 2000), pp 35–37, and the literature cited therein.

guarantee such rights to those within their borders. However, even within the EU, there are instances of individuals, particularly those in vulnerable groups, whose rights—even in such a basic sense—to health and health care are not guaranteed. Such vulnerable groups include various migrants and immigrants.

According to the EC and EU Treaties, the EU and Community respect human rights when exercising their (limited) competencies in the area of 'security and criminal justice', including the rules on external border control with respect to movements of people. However, the EU has come under criticism in this respect, both in terms of the thrust of its policy, and when the details of its law and policy on migration and immigration are analysed.[147] Particular criticism has focused on the status of refugees under the evolving EU law and policy, with suggestions that the Member States might, for instance, be failing to comply with their duties under the Geneva Convention.[148] Thus far, however, the focus has tended to be on civil and political rights, especially relating to deprivation of liberty and due process rights. There seems to be little explicit criticism, on the basis of rights discourse, of failure to respect social rights of refugees seeking to enter the EU.

Nevertheless, the Charter as a whole, including its social rights, such as the right to health care, applies to the EU's security and criminal justice policy. Elements of the right to health may be found reflected in some measures of Community law. For instance, Directive 2001/55/EC[149] on the minimum standards for giving temporary protection in the event of a mass influx of displaced persons provides that the Member States are to make provision for persons enjoying temporary protection under the Directive to receive 'necessary assistance in terms of social welfare and means of subsistence, if they do not have sufficient resources, as well as for medical care'.[150] Member States are obliged to provide,

> necessary medical . . . assistance to persons enjoying temporary protection who have special needs, such as unaccompanied minors or persons who have undergone torture, rape or other serious forms of psychological, physical or sexual violence.[151]

---

[147] See eg J Weiler, 'Thou Shalt Not Oppress a Stranger: On the Judicial Protection of the Human Rights of Non-EC Nationals' (1992) 3 *European Journal of International Law* (1992) 65; J Rex, 'Race and Ethnicity in Europe' in J Bailey (ed) *Social Europe* (Longman, London, 1992); M Spencer, *States of Injustice: A Guide to Human Rights and Civil Liberties in the European Union* (London, Pluto Press, 1995); A Geddes, 'Immigrants, Ethnic Minorities and the EU's Democratic Deficit' (1995) 33 *Journal of Common Market Studies* 197; C Gearty, 'Racism, Religious Intolerance and Xenophobia' in Alston (ed), above n 109; G Noll and J Vedsted-Hansen, 'Non-communitarians: Refugees and Asylum Policy' in Alston (ed) above n 109; S Peers, *EU Justice and Home Affairs Law* (London, Longman, 2000); M Bell, 'Mainstreaming Equality Norms into EU Asylum Law' (2001) 26 *European Law Review* 20–34.

[148] See, eg Peers, above n 147, ch 6; P Twomey, 'Constructing a Secure Space: the Area of Freedom, Security and Justice', in D O'Keeffe and P Twomey, *Legal Issues of the Amsterdam Treaty* (Oxford, Hart, 1999); G Goodwin-Gill, 'The Individual Refugee, the 1951 Convention and the Treaty of Amsterdam' in E Guild and C Harlow (eds), *Implementing Amsterdam: Immigration and Asylum Rights in EC Law* (Oxford, Hart, 2001).

[149] OJ 2001 L 212/12.

[150] Art 13(2).

[151] Art 13(4).

However, apart from that especially vulnerable group, the obligation on Member States to provide medical care to persons enjoying temporary protection under the Directive extends only to 'emergency medical care and essential treatment of illness'.[152] Such emergency and essential treatment is usually understood to exclude health care for pre-existing and chronic conditions, on the basis that the burden on the host state would be too great if these were included. 'Essential treatment of illness' is unlikely to include 'maternal and childcare, including family planning' (except, presumably, medical assistance at birth), or 'immunisation against the major infectious diseases', yet these are elements of Toebes' minimalist right to health. If the right to health care in Article 35 EUCFR (everyone has the right of access to preventive health care and the right to benefit from medical treatment under the conditions established by national laws and practices) covers such provision, it might be arguable that failure to guarantee such a right to persons enjoying temporary protection under the Directive is a failure to respect their human rights. On that basis, arguments about the burdens on host states in meeting health needs, or the lack of responsibility of host states towards displaced persons, are more difficult to maintain. A judicial review of the Directive on this basis, at the suit of an institution or Member State might therefore be conceivable. In combination with the non-discrimination principle and/or the right to dignity, one might even imagine a successful challenge brought by an individual, via the Article 234 EC reference procedure, on the basis that the Charter applies to Member States when implementing their duties under Community law. Although discrimination on grounds of nationality is not explicitly mentioned in Article 12 EUCFR, it covers discrimination 'on any ground *such as*', implying a wider list than those explicitly mentioned, and includes 'ethnic or social origin', and so arguably might include discrimination on grounds of citizenship or nationality. Of course, any court considering such an application for judicial review might take the view that the 'claw-back clause' ('under the conditions established by natonal laws and practices') means that no obligations further to those already in place under national legal regimes are imposed upon Member States by the Charter. However, the Charter provision would apparently be meaningless were this the case.[153]

Health care also features in a number of security and criminal justice measures currently in the pipeline.[154] For instance, the original proposal for a Directive laying down minimum standards on the reception of applicants for asylum in Member States[155] includes a duty on Member States to:

---

[152] Art 13(2).

[153] Craven, in Costello ed, above n 1. See also M Bell, in this collection, who is critical of the exclusion of nationality from the list in Art 21(1) EUCFR, at pp 98–99.

[154] See, for instance Commission Proposal for a Council Directive concerning the status of third-country nationals who are long-term residents COM (2001) 127 final.

[155] COM (2001) 181 final, agreed in principle JHA Council, 25/26 April 2002; adopted Council 19 December 2002.

make provisions on material reception conditions to ensure a standard of living adequate for the health and well-being of applicants and their accompanying family members as well as the protection of their fundamental rights.

Such a formulation clearly suggests that the standard of living provision is not a 'fundamental right' of asylum seekers, presumably on the basis that 'fundamental' rights are only civil and political rights. Further, this was modified to a requirement only to ensure 'health and subsistence', dropping the reference to fundamental rights altogether.[156] This part of the proposed Directive therefore does not adopt a rights-based approach to health. An articulation of such measures along the lines of a 'right to health' might therefore make a difference in terms of the status of such entitlements. For instance, this might affect their interpretation, in terms of assessment by national courts or the Court of the direct effect (and thus enforceability) or the scope of the provisions of the Directive. It might also alter the possibilities for the work of non-governmental organisations or other human rights advocacy work, and provide another point of access to criticism of Member States who fail to meet such requirements.

For instance, Human Rights Watch has highlighted human rights violations, which could be constructed as violations of a right to health, with respect to migrants and asylum seekers in the Canary Islands, in terms of over-crowding, poor sanitation, and lack of access to health care and medication.[157] Human Rights Watch has also highlighted breaches of the rights of unaccompanied migrant children in the Spanish cities of Ceuta and Mellila.[158] These include many failings on the part of the city authorities and the Spanish government that could be constructed as violations of the right to health, such as lack of access to health care (procedures for granting unaccompanied minors the national health card (*tarjeta sanitaria*), necessary for access to health services, were inadequate), and inadequate food (on the basis of a right to health plus freedom from religious discrimination, as many of the meals provided contained pork). Concerns have also been raised by the Greek immigration law, which denies undocumented migrants access to public health facilities except in emergencies.[159] A recognition of a right to health in Community law would allow these criticisms to be made in terms of rights, rather than humanitarian notions of charity, which might lend potency to the positions of relevant human rights or health non-governmental organisations within the EU policy-making process.

---

[156] See S Peers, 'European Update: June 2002', *Statewatch Monitor* http://www.statewatch.org; Commission press release Memo/02/300, 19 December 2002.

[157] Human Rights Watch, *Spain: The Other Face of the Canary Islands* February 2002, http://www.hrw.org/reports/2002/Spain0202.pdf.

[158] Human Rights Watch, *Nowhere to Turn: State Abuses of Unaccompanied Migrant Children by Spain and Morocco* May 2002, http://www.hrw.org/reports/2002/Spain-Morocco/spnmorc0502.pdf.

[159] Human Rights Watch, 'Rights Group Concerned about Greek Immigration Bill' 16 November 2000. http://www.hrw.org/press/2000/11/greece1116.htm. See also A Skordas, 'The New Refugee Legislation in Greece' 11 (1999) 4 *International Journal of Refugee Law* 678–701.

The recognition of a right to health might even provide a basis for judicial review of this Directive. The European Council on Refugees and Exiles has criticised the original proposal for failing to provide access to primary health care throughout all procedures until a final decision is notified, pointing out that mere access to emergency health care for applicants during some procedures does not meet the frequently complex health needs of asylum seekers and refugees, in particular by excluding treatment for chronic conditions.[160] On the basis of a right to health plus dignity or non-discrimination, as discussed above, it might be argued that the proposal is invalid as not complying with general principles of Community law. The exclusion of the minority group of asylum seekers from the treatment of chronic conditions granted to nationals might be regarded as unjustified, were the entitlement characterised as a human right, inhering in individuals on the basis of their humanity, rather than their status.

The proposal on minimum reception conditions for asylum applicants also provides for health and psychological care for refugees.[161] During 'regular procedures', up to certain specified points in the procedure, asylum applicants and their accompanying family members are to have 'access to primary health care provided by a general practitioner, psychological care and health care that cannot be postponed'.[162] Again vulnerable groups are singled out for special provision: such vulnerable groups include minors, unaccompanied minors, mentally ill persons, disabled persons, elderly persons, pregnant women, single women subject, in their country of origin, to substantial legal gender-related discrimination and victims of rape, sexual abuse, exploitation or other forms of gender related violence.[163] However, access to 'health care that prevents aggravation of existing illness' (that is, chronic health care) is to be subject to conditions laid down by the Member States.[164] In particular, Member States may require applicants who can afford to do so to cover or contribute to the costs of their health care.[165] Again possible inconsistency with the Charter might be present, if national policies in this respect reveal discrimination between the treatment of nationals, or even lawful residents, and asylum seekers.

---

[160] ECRE, *Position on the Reception of Asylum Seekers* November 2001, paras 43–47, http://www.ecre.org/positions/receptio.shlml. The amended version removed the differentiation in reception conditions based on the stage reached in the procedure. The current proposal provides only for 'emergency care and essential treatment', which excludes core elements of the 'right to health', see above.

[161] See ch IV of the proposal.

[162] Proposed Art 20(1).

[163] Proposed Arts 20(2) ('Member States shall meet the special needs of applicants and their accompanying family members who are pregnant women, minors, mentally ill persons, disabled persons, or victims of rape or other forms of gender related violence'); 23 ('Member States shall take into account the specific situation of persons who have special needs . . . in the national legislation implementing the provisions of chs III, IV and V relating to material reception conditions, psychological and health care; 24(2) (minors); 26 (victims of torture and organised violence).

[164] Proposed Art 20(3).

[165] Proposed Art 20(4).

A fundamental role of human rights is to protect vulnerable minorities. The very notion of *human* rights implies entitlement as a human being, regardless of status, in particular regardless of formal relationship with the relevant state or non-state polity. A recognition of a right to health within the EU's legal order would therefore imply a significant shift of emphasis in terms of protection of the health of those who are not citizens of the European Union, or even permanent residents of one of its Member States. Health protection could no longer be conceptualised as a humanitarian, charity-based entitlement for these vulnerable individuals, but would have to be seen as something enjoyed on an equal basis with 'insiders'. There is scope for the EU to play an important leadership and standard-setting role here, as, compared to the governments of its Member States, it is relatively insulated from populist pressure to exclude 'the other', and thus perhaps better placed to promote fundamental rights of minorities than its Member States.[166]

CONCLUSIONS

This paper is highly conjectural, considering whether, if it were articulated strongly within the EU's legal order, a 'right to health' might make a difference to various EU policies and activities. Overall, it would seem that a rights-based approach to health might make a difference within certain elements of EU law and policy with respect to the protection of human health. In some contexts, such as development policy, it would seem that the 'right to health' would make very little difference in terms of focus, assessment or commitment of the EU to health protection. In the context of internal market litigation, although a 'right to health' might alter the discourse of dispute resolution, it would be unlikely to make a significant change in terms of substantive outcome. In other contexts, such as asylum policy, the difference might be beneficial in terms of promoting the health status of some of the most vulnerable persons within the territory of the EU.

---

[166] See Weiler, above n 147; Von Bogdandy, above n 11, p 1317. For criticism that the EU has singularly failed to do this, see for instance T Hervey, 'Putting Europe's House in Order' in D O'Keeffe and P Twomey, *Legal Issues of the Amsterdam Treaty* (Oxford, Hart, 1999) 329–49 and the literature cited therein.

10

Education, Multiculturalism and the Charter of Fundamental Rights of the European Union

CHLOË WALLACE and JO SHAW[*]

INTRODUCTION

TRADITIONALLY, QUESTIONS OF education and culture have frequently been excluded from human rights instruments, because of the difficulties of definition, scope of protection and means of protection, which are so commonly associated with social rights. Of course, the inclusion of economic and social rights in the Charter, alongside more traditional civil liberties and indeed political rights, was regarded as one of the great victories for the Charter and the process whereby it was elaborated—the now infamous Convention. Even so, the specific provisions on education and culture are hardly the most dynamic examples of the codificatory approach to drafting which lay at the heart of the Charter's evolutionary process and of the intention to promote the indivisibility of the universal values of human dignity, freedom, equality and solidarity.

The provisions on education are a slightly odd little *pot pourri*. There is, first, the 'right to education' itself, but with the link made between education and economic development in the crudest possible way through the addition of the right of access to vocational and continuing training (Article 14(1) EUCFR). This provides the most concrete linkage between these provisions and the current provisions of the EC Treaty on the promotion of policies on vocational training and education (Articles 149–50 EC). In addition, there is the requirement that the right must include the 'possibility' of receiving free compulsory education (a strange phrasing in English) (Article 14(2) EUCFR), and finally explicit recognition of respect for the freedom to found educational establishments, including a reference to the religious, philosophical and pedagogical

* Centre for the Study of Law and Policy in Europe, University of Leeds; and Professor and Jean Monnet Chair of European Law, University of Manchester; Senior Research Fellow at the Federal Trust for Education and Research, London, respectively. Many thanks to Tamara Hervey and Robert McCorquodale for helpful comments on the draft presented at the Nottingham Workshop: *Economic and Social Rights under the EU Charter of Fundamental Rights: A Legal Perspective*, June 2002.

convictions of parents (Article 14(3) EUCFR). This seems to guarantee, for example, the right to establish faith schools. These provisions should be read in the light of Article 10 EUCFR (freedom of thought, conscience and religion) and Article 24 EUCFR (rights of the child). In contrast, there is only one provision on culture in the Charter. Article 22 EUCFR sets out a guarantee of respect by the EU for cultural diversity, along with linguistic and religious diversity, and it is located, for reasons that might require a little elaboration, in the Equality Chapter.

Yet despite those cautionary words of introduction, we find something positive in the very presence of provisions on education and culture in the Charter. Even though the Charter is declaratory, it does not in any way develop Community competence, and has very uncertain effects vis-à-vis the Member States which have declined even to proclaim it as a formal instrument. These provisions are, in our view, none the less an important symbol of a developing awareness of issues such as multiculturalism and positive respect for diversity at the transnational and supranational levels, as well as the economic and cultural importance of education in modern societies.

However, when we come to muse upon these provisions and the possible interpretations which could be placed upon them as the EU gradually develops an enhanced human rights culture, we find a dark shadow has been cast over them by a conjunction of recent events and trends. We can name these events and trends quite easily; it would be much more challenging to try to unpick their consequences and effects, and to do so is beyond the scope of this paper. We can only hint at the background conditions under which any discussion of social rights pertaining to education and culture must proceed. These include the shadows of the terrorist attacks of 11 September 2001, the securitisation agenda which has been taken up by the USA and other states in the putative 'war on terrorism', as well as the more general reappraisal of policies towards foreigners, immigrants and ethnic minorities which has occurred in many western liberal states. Securitisation policies have proved, in many respects, popular vote winners, and appear to chime with a widespread fear of immigration and its consequences in terms of the creation of increasingly multicultural societies. To promote policies of multiculturalism, especially those which promote a critical perspective upon immigrant integration and assimilation, apparently fails to respond to a popular wave of hostility towards outsiders and the fear that they take jobs, cause unemployment and 'swamp' supposedly monocultural and monoethnic societies (the latter being, in general of course, a myth maintained for the purposes of sustaining a concept of national identity). Yet since there is also widespread recognition that some economic migration is necessary because of labour market gaps in many Western countries, the discourse has shifted towards drawing an increasingly sharp distinction between legal and illegal immigration. Politicians' rhetoric now focuses on the differences between legitimate mobility for the purposes of serving globalisation by ensuring that skilled human resources move to where the demand for them is greatest, and illegitimate 'bogus' mobility on the part of those who 'claim' to be asylum seekers or refugees, but who are actually trying to get access to the relatively privileged informal 'grey' labour markets of the western capitalist economies where there are large numbers of undocumented workers. Such rhetorics are widely thought to feed the attempts by far right political forces to foster hostility towards immigration, and to suggest that successful multicultural societies are simply a chimera.

The electoral success and even entry of far right populist parties into some level of government, whether national, regional and local, in almost every Member State of the European Union has shocked much mainstream political opinion. Most of these parties operate on platforms which are anti-immigration and anti-foreigner, and they are often specifically hostile towards Islam and Muslims in particular. Interestingly, while the more centrist parties seem generally agreed that the EU—in policy-making terms—is part of the solution to resolving the problems and challenges of immigration in an increasingly globalised world, more extremist forces on both the left and the right tend to see it as part of the problem, destroying the capacity of the nation state to resist destructive global forces such as unwanted population movements and to build either authentic 'national' futures (the right) or to check the onward march of global capital (the left). In both cases, it is the deregulatory agendas which the EU is said to promote which are put under the microscope.

It is impossible, in sum, to ignore the apparent dissonance or state of contradiction between on the one hand the assumed contribution which the proclamation of a Charter of Rights for the European Union ought to offer in terms of enhanced awareness of the promises and challenges of a human rights culture and of a policy of multiculturalism, and the current state of politics as sketched in the last few paragraphs. The pressing question before us in this chapter is whether there is a way out of this state of contradiction.

PREMISES AND FRAMEWORK OF THE CHAPTER

Aims of the Chapter

In this chapter, we concentrate on the possible problem-solving or conflict-reduction capacity of an instrument such as the Charter in relation to some specific cases which can be linked to our general diagnosis of 'malaise' or worse in the heart of European societies, a malaise which appears to undermine the 'promise' of multiculturalism. To take the argument further, we need to define a number of crucial terms.

The Promise of Multiculturalism

Multiculturalism has become something of a political battleground. One of the themes underlying some of the political developments sketched out here has been an increasing questioning of the liberal acceptance of multiculturalism within a number of European societies—notably the United Kingdom and the Netherlands—as the most constructive and morally sustainable way for public policy to engage with the challenges posed by mass immigration especially since the second world war. Coincidentally, even in states such as France and Germany, where there has been no 'official' policy of multiculturalism, in practice there has been a convergence in many fields of public policy towards the types of measures (eg on housing, welfare or education) which would in other states such as the UK, the Netherlands or Canada, be recognised as fostering multiculturalism. In all these states, multiculturalism is encountering opposition. In the most extreme cases, this involves the assertion that multicultural societies are inherently wrong, because they lead to the 'dilution' of the majority 'race' (which is usually perceived as superior). More subtle versions of this argument present multiculturalism, not as bad, but rather as impossible, and argue that attempting to achieve this impossible goal leads to a fragmented society, lacking in patriotism and cohesion, and ultimately giving rise to serious conflict. Within this climate, we consider it essential to reaffirm the nature and goals of multiculturalism. Whilst, as shall be seen, it may not be possible to propose an ultimate solution to the challenges which a multicultural society creates, it is nevertheless important to assert the inherent value in such a society, and consequently the urgency of continuing to search for such a solution.

The discourse of multiculturalism is a relatively new arrival on the social, political and legal scene, at least in Europe.[1] As a consequence, it is easy to forget, and must then be reasserted, that the facts to which multiculturalism is a response are not in themselves new. Since the Roman Empire at least, governments and society have had to grapple with the question of how to ensure social stability in a situation where a population is made up of more than one cultural grouping. At this stage, it is important to specify what we mean by culture. Within the discourse of multiculturalism, cultural groups are defined solely by ethnic or religious identity or affiliation. Within contemporary cultural theory, however, a culture can be based on many types of common characteristics: gender, profession, class, political affiliation, interests and enthusiasms, and much more besides. On this second understanding, we all belong to a number of different cultures and are ourselves multicultural beings, whereas, in the culture of multiculturalism, most people (although not everyone) can be said to belong to only one culture. Within the context of this piece, the narrower meaning is used.

---

[1] In Canada, multiculturalism has been 'official' policy at least since 1971, when the word was introduced into national political discourse by Pierre Trudeau, if not earlier.

However, the insight that we are all part of a number of different cultures is a useful one to bear in mind, as an antidote to the kind of thinking that sees ethnic and religious groups as clearly defined, discrete and completely determinative of human behaviour. We therefore reject essentialist thinking about human identity and human behaviour. In particular, we reject the tendency, sometimes evident in perceptions of multiculturalism, to reify ethnic identity by reducing individual identity to membership of one culture and by perceiving that culture as hermetically sealed from outside influences. In a multicultural society more than any other kind of society, individual identity is often affected by connections with a number of different cultural groups, as well as by factors which can only be equated with culture through a tenuous stretching of the meaning of that term.

If the co-existence of cultures is a long-standing fact of human society, what, then, is the novelty of multiculturalism? One, narrow, view of multiculturalism would see it as policy or a set of rights which a state enacts in order to respond to the co-existence of cultures within the national territory. A multicultural policy gives specific claims and status to different cultural groups within the society, in order to ensure that they continue as distinct cultural groups rather than being assimilated into a dominant culture.[2] In this paper, however, we want to take a wider view than that. Raz has described multiculturalism as, in part, 'a heightened awareness of certain issues and certain needs people encounter in today's political reality.'[3] Rather than being a discrete political theory, it is an indication of a new respect being given to diversity within society, which is itself perceived as a moral virtue. This respect given to diversity can express itself through the granting of rights or the creation of multicultural policies. However, those rights and policies are tools of multiculturalism, rather than multiculturalism itself. The distinguishing feature of multiculturalism is that the recognition of diverse cultures is seen as a good in itself, either because of the inherent value of those cultures and their existence, or, perhaps more persuasively, because respect for human dignity requires an understanding of the fact that belonging to a culture is an important part of being human.[4]

Our rejection of essentialism, however, should lead us to emphasise that this is only one part of being human. A criticism that can be made of multiculturalism as a political project is that it runs the risk of minimising the common humanity which individuals share, as well as the consequent possibilities of cross-cultural communication.[5] This criticism is linked with that which would argue that multiculturalism, in allowing for differential treatment of people according to their identification with different cultural communities, is inherently inimical to

---

[2] See eg, W Kymlicka, *Multicultural Citizenship* (Oxford, Clarendon Press, 1995).

[3] J Raz, 'Multiculturalism' (1998) 11 *Ratio Juris* 193–205 at p 197.

[4] For this view of culture, see eg C Geertz, 'The Impact of the Concept of Culture on the Concept of Mind' in *The Interpretation of Cultures: Selected Essays* (London, Fontana Press, 1993); JM Balkin, *Cultural Software* (New Haven, Yale University Press, 1998).

[5] See A Kuper, *Culture: the anthropologist's account* (Cambridge, Mass, Harvard University Press, 1999).

individual equality. Answering this criticism would seem to require a lengthy discussion about the concept of equality and how it is achieved; a discussion for which there is no space here.[6] Nevertheless, it can be observed that equality is not equivalent to sameness and that even traditional, Aristotelian conceptions of equality allow for different treatment insofar as differences exist. Whether the fact that, in the EU's Charter, Article 22 EUCFR is found in the section entitled 'Equality' means that its drafters saw the respect for diversity as an essential part of equality, rather than opposed to it, is unclear. The implication that cultural diversity involves just another equality claim is unfortunate, but it certainly dovetails neatly with the decision to locate the 'culture' provision of the Charter in the Equality Chapter.

Here, a comparison with the Canadian context is instructive. The debates in Canada around the question of multiculturalism have been focused, to a large extent, on the question whether the protection of minorities is best served through the application of traditional rights and a rigid concept of equality, or through a more complex embrace of diversity, not necessarily based on rights discourse.[7] One of the significant problems that arise when a rights-based approach is used is the risk of clashes between different, competing rights. Looking at the list of rights contained within the Equality Chapter of the Charter, potential clashes can be identified between respect for cultural groups and the non-discrimination principles concerning gender,[8] sexual orientation, disability,[9] children[10] and race.[11] Consequently, any strategy for promoting respect for cultural diversity must be able to negotiate these clashes.

Many of the debates surrounding this problem are concerned with the situation where certain groups have a level of autonomy within the State and claim that their cultural values do not allow them to respect the rights claims of some of their members: groups such as the indigenous peoples of Canada[12] and the US,[13] and, in some contexts, religious groups in Israel and India.[14] In general,

---

[6] See M Bell, in this volume, first section, and the references therein.

[7] See JC Bakan and M Smith, 'Rights, Nationalism and Social Movements in Canadian Constitutional Politics' (1995) 4 *Social and Legal Studies* 367–90 for a discussion of the limits of rights strategies in this context.

[8] The literature on this is substantial, and we draw on it for much of this analysis. The specific issue of the relationship between gender equality and cultural diversity is discussed in more detail in Costello's contribution to this volume.

[9] For example, Islamic attitudes towards dogs can have an impact on guide dog users. We are indebted to Anna Lawson for this point.

[10] For example, is it always in the child's best interests to be educated according to a set of strict religiousand/or cultural values?

[11] Particularly in the education context, the desire of a cultural group to educate their children separately can be construed as racially discriminatory.

[12] See M Deveaux, 'Conflicting Equalities? Cultural Group Rights and Sex Equality' (2000) 48 *Political Studies* 522–39.

[13] A Shachar, 'Group Identity and Women's Rights in Family Law: The Perils of Multicultural Accommodation' (1998) 6 *Journal of Political Philosophy* 285–305; J Spinner-Halev 'Feminism, Multiculturalism, Oppression, and the State' (2001) 112 *Ethics* 84–113.

[14] *Ibid.*

this situation does not pose a significant problem within the EU context, in that those groups or nations with autonomy claims are not ones that are likely to reject rights-based claims on cultural grounds. It is, however, an important issue to consider in the context of education, where the right to educate within a particular cultural context and/or, perhaps more crucially, according to a particular set of religious beliefs, may carry with it a claim for a degree of autonomy on the part of the school. May a faith school refuse to admit children from outside the faith, even when to do so would be indirectly racially discriminatory? May it teach different subjects to boys and girls? May it teach that homosexual behaviour is sinful, to the potential detriment to pupils who are coming to terms with their own sexuality?

A number of proposals have been made as to how to mediate these conflicting rights claims. One argument, typified by the work of Kymlicka, would be to take an individualist approach, arguing that self-government must always be limited by the basic rights of individuals, and that consequently cultural diversity may not be used as a justification for discriminatory policies.[15] At the other extreme, some writers have argued that autonomous groups must be given full rights of self-governance, even if this means them violating the fundamental rights of their members.[16] Both of these approaches involve automatic prioritisation of one or the other set of rights; in the first case, individual rights, and in the second, rights to group autonomy. Shachar has taken a more subtle approach, propounding an 'intersectionist joint governance approach', which would allow groups the right to define their own membership (and thus exclude people on the grounds, for example, of parentage or dogma), but require them to respect the non-discrimination rights of people acknowledged as members.[17] This approach, however, constitutes an uneasy compromise between competing rights, and does not always reach satisfactory results. On the one hand, it is unfortunate, to say the least, not to enforce the often hard-won rights of individuals simply because it is cultural norms, as articulated by the leadership of the cultural group, who are denying them, rather than the State. On the other hand, cultural groups who are breaking free from oppression and marginalisation can perceive the imposition of individual rights claims as further oppression. As Mernissi suggests, in the context of women in the Islamic world, any grant of women's rights can be characterised as 'concessions to the coloniser' and dismissed as cultural imperialism.[18]

Spinner-Halev suggests that the issue of oppression may hold the key to the problem.[19] The reason why multicultural policy is important, he argues, is because of the role it had in freeing cultural groups from state oppression.

---

[15] Above, n 2.

[16] C Kukathas, 'Are There Any Cultural Rights? (1992) 20 *Political Theory* 105–39; A Margalit and M Halbertal 'Liberalism and the Right to Culture' (1994) 61 *Social Research* 491–510.

[17] Shachar, above n 133.

[18] F Mernissi, *Beyond the Veil: Male-Female Dynamics in a Modern Muslim Society* (Cambridge, Mass., Shenkman Publishing Company, 1975) at p vii.

[19] Above, n 133.

Therefore, any policy, which is adopted, must not serve to perpetuate that oppression. Oppression of an individual can take the form of a denial of individual rights, either by the State or by cultural groups. However, it can also take the form of oppression of the culture of which that individual is part. Both forms of oppression are detrimental to the individual; neither is acceptable. This complexity of individual identity is used by Eisenberg to formulate her difference approach to adjudicating cases where a respect for diversity appears to clash with individual equality. Eisenberg argues that such cases should not be dealt with in the form of a clash of rights, but rather by assessing the identity-related impact of the different claims, and choosing the claim which has the least impact on identity as a whole (understood as encompassing a broad range of characteristics including culture, gender, religion and language).[20] In other words, the decision is made which is least oppressive of an individual's identity.

A legal model, which facilitates this idea, is that of the Canadian Charter of Rights and Freedoms, which approaches cultural diversity, not as a requirement of equality, or a non-discrimination right, but rather as a general principle according to which the rest of the Canadian Charter must be interpreted.[21] A similar clause within the EU Charter would mean that other key rights within the Charter, such as freedom of association, freedom of speech, freedom of conscience, freedom of religion, the right to fair and just working conditions and, as we shall suggest here, crucially, the right to education, must be interpreted in a way which respects the multicultural nature of the EU.

This approach is effective for two reasons. Firstly, as Eisenberg suggests, it avoids the difficulties and conflicts inherent in mediating a clash of rights. Secondly, it recognises that multiculturalism should only require different treatment in situations where it is necessary to avoid oppression. As Kuper reminds us, the politics of difference represented in multiculturalism can give rise to extreme separatist—and consequently discriminatory and oppressive—policies, such as apartheid.[22] Further, it is at least arguable that, even in the West, fundamental rights claims were often originally counter-cultural in nature, in that they gave rights to groups which had traditionally not had those rights. While genuine cultural difference should be respected, it is essential that it is not used as a mask for conservative resistance to reform, and individual rights must continue to be available to members of all cultures as a weapon against oppression, whatever its source. In this way, multiculturalism at its best can reflect our common humanity, not only through the respect of fundamental rights for all, but also through the acknowledgement that cultures are part of our common humanity. Further, multiculturalism can, at its best, facilitate cross-cultural

---

[20] A Eisenberg, 'Diversity and Equality: Three Approaches to Cultural and Sexual Difference' Constitutionalism Web-Papers, ConWEB 1/2001 http://les1.man.ac.uk/conweb/.

[21] Art 27: This Charter shall be interpreted in a manner consistent with the preservation and enhancement of the multicultural heritage of Canadians.

[22] Above n 5.

communication and co-operation by providing the context of an informed understanding of and respect for the different cultures concerned.[23]

Multiculturalism and EU Policy

Most discussion and theorising about multiculturalism assumes the existence of a state of some kind, whether unitary or federal, which has to accommodate cultural pluralism within its boundaries. Questions then arise as to the place which a policy of multiculturalism may have within the EU, that is, within an entity which cannot be equated with a state but which has political authority. The argument that the EU ought actively, for specific as well as general reasons, to foster multiculturalism will be put forward in some detail later on; for now, however, it can be assumed that we believe that the case for multiculturalism is just as persuasive, if not more so, for the EU as for states. However, there are important questions concerning the way in which multiculturalism is to be promoted within the EU, given its particular nature. In the first instance, the thorny issue of competence and the principle of subsidiarity in Article 5 EC are relevant here. While Article 13 EC gives explicit (but shared) competence to the Community to legislate against racial discrimination (inter alia), this is only a very small part of what is necessary for the purposes of a full range of policies fostering multiculturalism, and there are no further obvious existing competences within the Treaties. Even beyond that, to what extent is it possible to argue that the goals of multiculturalism can only be sufficiently achieved at Community level rather than the national level, as the principle of subsidiarity would seem to require? Each Member State has a different cultural make-up and history and, it could be argued, requires a different approach to ensure effective cultural pluralism. In particular, given the important role which education plays within a wider multicultural policy, the fact that Member States continue to be protective about their sovereignty in the field of primary and secondary education has to be significant. However, the important point about policy-making in areas such as rights policy or education policy where competence is shared between the Member States and the EU—and indeed where EU competence might be thought only to be complementary to that of the Member States[24]—is to acknowledge that an appropriate policy mix may require some goals to be set at the EU level, while the bulk of implementation measures must be carefully tailored to domestic circumstances. Even goal-setting itself may need to be flexible to take account of differing national traditions and heritages. This could be

---

[23] This constitutes a general defence of multiculturalism. As we will argue later, there are specific reasons why multicultural policies are necessary within the EU.

[24] See the careful note prepared by the Secretariat to the Convention on the Future of the Union, *Delimitation of competence between the European Union and the Member States—Existing system, problems and avenues to be explored*, Conv 47/02 15 May 2002 which explores these issues in detail.

where the so-called 'Open Method of Co-ordination' and other 'new governance' instruments might usefully be invoked as flexible means for encouraging the sharing of best practice between Member States and requiring the benchmarking of national policies against each other.[25]

Secondly, it has traditionally been the case that, within its cultural policy and its foundational frameworks, the EU has been committed, not to the respect of all the cultures which exist within the territory of the EU, but primarily to the respect of the national identities of Member States (see, for example, Article 6(3) TEU). This has to be one aspect of multiculturalism within the EU, but it is by no means the only aspect. An EU policy of multiculturalism would require not only that the EU itself respect the minority cultures within Member States, but also that the EU encourage and require that Member States respect those cultures within their own territory.

These questions about competence, and about the extent to which the EU can interfere in the cultural policy of Member States, render problematic the possibility of a comprehensive EU policy on multiculturalism. *Legally*, it may well be difficult for the EU to justify action in that area. *Politically*, sufficient consensus for such action may be difficult to achieve. *Constitutionally*, however, we would argue that multiculturalism is an imperative for the development of an inclusive and internally and externally responsible Euro-polity.[26] We would therefore argue that, while the current provisions of the Charter of Rights are perhaps inadequate, the Charter itself is a useful tool for introducing a policy of multiculturalism into the EU legal order. In particular, Article 27 of the Canadian Charter of Rights and Freedoms, referred to above, which takes the form, not of a positive rule but rather of a principle according to which other, more individualistic, rights should be interpreted, could form a useful model for development of the EU Charter. In this context, it is important to consider in more detail the use to which the Charter can be put in the search for a EU policy of multiculturalism.

What Use is a Charter of Rights?

We have begun by arguing that the recognition of cultural diversity and the promotion of a multi-cultural Europe is not only a moral good in its own right, but is also an important aspect in the development of European identity and citizenship as aspects of EU polity-building and constitutionalisation. It is now time to move back to the subject matter of this project and to consider the role that the Charter can play in this process. Apart from instruments in the field of

---

[25] See generally J Scott and D Trubek, 'Mind the Gap: Law and New Approaches to Governance in the European Union' (2002) 8 *European Law Journal* 1–18.

[26] J Shaw, 'Process, Responsibility and Inclusion in EU constitutionalism' (2003) 9 European Law Journal 45–68.

external relations and enlargement (which will be returned to), the Charter is perhaps the strongest EU document in which a requirement for the respect of cultural diversity is found.[27] To this extent, the Charter can be contrasted with the much more limited Community Charter of the Fundamental Social Rights of Workers 1989, now effectively enshrined in the EC Treaty since the Treaty of Amsterdam, which failed to address the question of diversity in any way. The question remains, however, whether the Charter under scrutiny is indeed capable of offering a solution to the challenges to multiculturalism, which we have identified, and of ensuring sufficient respect for diversity to provide a basis for unity within the EU.

Very obviously, the Charter has significant limitations. Its provisions are only addressed to the EU, and thus cannot affect the behaviour of Member States unless they are implementing provisions of EU law. It cannot itself extend the scope of Community or EU competence. Thus, for example, any Member State pursuing policies which are sympathetic to the securitisation agenda, or to a general hostility towards 'foreigners', cannot be prevented by the Charter from doing so unless there are specific provisions of EU law which they are implementing (although of course they might fall foul of Article 7 TEU if there were persistent breaches of fundamental rights). Even within the context of the EU, the Charter is not legally binding and thus cannot affect the normative framework of laws and legal institutions, although it has been used by the Advocates General in the European Court of Justice[28] and by some national courts[29] as part of their general human rights jurisprudence or heritage. In a technical legal sense, then, the Charter has very little power and very little potential for achieving anything.

Nevertheless, the Charter can provide a useful starting point from which the EU can proceed. Its utility derives from two factors. First, the Charter was put together through a process which many have seen as highly positive, being open, deliberative and consensus driven. The Convention which compiled the Charter was relatively representative of the different political interests involved even

---

[27] Art 151(4) EC does require the Community to take cultural aspects into account in its action, in particular in order to respect and protect diversity. However, Art 151(1) EC requires the Community to 'bring the common cultural heritage to the fore'; a statement which would seem significantly to dilute the impact of Art 151(4).

[28] See the opinion of A-G Tizzano in Case C–173/99 *R v Secretary of State for Trade and Industry ex parte BECTU* [2001] ECR I–4881. Although the use of the Charter has usually been restricted to Advocates-General, it was referred to by the Court of First Instance in Case T–54/99 *max.mobil Telekommunication v Commission* [2002] ECR II–313.

[29] In the English courts, for example, the Charter was referred to by the Administrative Court in *R v Wakefield MDC* [2002] 2 WLR 889 (QBD (Admin Ct)), where Maurice Kay J stated that the Charter was not a source of law in the strict sense, but could be used to interpret, and in this case, using Art 8, the data protection provision, update the ECHR. It was also referred to by the Court of Appeal in *Sepet v Secretary of State for the Home Department* [2001] Imm AR 452, where it was used as part of a long list of evidence for the existence of a fundamental international right of conscientious objection. See also the references to decisions of the Spanish and Italian constitutional courts, cited in M Poiares Maduro, in this volume, at p 293.

though human rights lawyers did predominate amongst its members, and, while the involvement of civil society was not perfectly managed, there was some consultation with various representative groups.[30] Subsequently, it was in effect agreed to by all the Member States, in the sense that they actively supported its formal and solemn 'proclamation' by the Presidents of the three political institutions (ie European Parliament, Commission and Council—the latter representing the Member States) at the Nice IGC in December 2000.[31] At a very basic level, this will give it moral authority in circumstances where the EU or the Member States are in violation of its principles. Neil Walker describes the Charter process as maintaining a significant momentum, even after the disappointment to some of its proclamation in declaratory form at Nice.[32] More broadly, its very existence as an agreed set of human rights principles and thus an expression of common values may well prove to be a springboard for discussion about the way in which those rights are to be put into practice. A dialogue which takes place on the basis of an agreed set of principles and values is more likely to be productive than one where a principled starting point has not been reached. Most fundamental rights adjudication is based around a balancing of different interests, and this will still need to be negotiated. However, the existence of agreed principles according to which this process should be carried out gives it an invaluable head start. Further, strategic questions, such as those concerning problem solving through the extension of Community or EU competence into particular areas, can also be debated on the basis of these agreed principles. As in Canada, a statement of principle within the Charter can be supported and filled out by further legislation and policy developments,[33] although, unlike Canada, such a development would require a specific extension of the competence of the EU.

Secondly, as de Búrca points out, the initial mandate for the Charter suggested that it was aimed primarily at the citizens, rather than at the EU or Member States.[34] It was an exercise in consciousness-raising, even an attempt to engage in political education—to use a very old-fashioned phrase in these days of 'spin'—and in making the EU's commitment to rights more visible to citizens. As such, the very existence of provisions making evident a commitment to cultural diversity, particularly within education, may prove to be a first step along the road of unity through diversity, which we have discussed. If multicultural-

---

[30] See G de Búrca, 'The Drafting of the European Union Charter of Fundamental Rights' (2001) 26 *European Law Review* 126–38; F Deloche-Gaudez, 'The Convention on a Charter of Fundamental Rights: a method for the future', Notre Europe Research and Policy Paper No 15, November 2001 http://www.notre-europe.asso.fr/fichiers/Etud15-en.

[31] OJ 2000 C364/1.

[32] N Walker, 'Human Rights in a Postnational Order: Reconciling Political and Constitutional Pluralism', in T Campbell, KD Ewing and A Tomkins (eds), *Sceptical Essays on Human Rights* (Oxford, Oxford University Press, 2001) 119 at p 120.

[33] Such as the Canadian Multiculturalism Act 1988, which makes multiculturalism the official policy of the government of Canada and grants specific enforcement powers.

[34] Above n 300.

ism is less a concrete situation and more a state of mind which is sensitive to certain issues, in principle, the demonstration of that sensitivity through the inclusion of those issues in a major document such as the Charter should, in itself, be a positive move.

CASES UNDER THE MICROSCOPE

The Charter, then, has potentially some role to play in mediating the dialogue necessary in order to move towards that unity through diversity which is an explicit goal of the EU. Some of its strengths and limitations have been outlined, in general terms, in the previous section. Here, it is time to look at the specific rights to education and to cultural diversity contained within the Charter, to see what they can and cannot achieve.

The Right to Education

The declaration of a right to education in Article 14 EUCFR has its source in the constitutional traditions of the Member States and Article 2 of the First Protocol of the ECHR. However, the right to education is also contained within a number of international human rights agreements, most notably Article 26 of the Universal Declaration of Human Rights (UDHR), Article 13 of the International Covenant for Economic, Social and Cultural Rights (ICESCR) and, within their specific contexts, Article 10 of the Convention to Eliminate Discrimination against Women (CEDAW) and Articles 28–30 of the Convention on the Rights of the Child (CRC). The first thing that becomes apparent on comparing the Charter provision with these provisions is that the international provisions tend to be much broader. It is common to find a general recital as to the purpose and value of education, based on Article 26(2) of the UDHR:

> Education shall be directed to the full development of the human personality and to the strengthening of respect for human rights and fundamental freedoms. It shall promote understanding, tolerance and friendship among all nations, racial or religious groups, and shall further the activities of the United Nations for the maintenance of peace.

These recitals incorporate reference to relations between cultural groups. Indeed, Article 29(1)(c) CRC states that one goal of education is:

> The development of respect for . . . his or her own cultural identity, language and values, for the national values of the country in which the child is living, the country from which he or she may originate, and for civilizations different from his or her own.

This is, to a large extent, to be assured by allowing parents the right to have their children educated according to their convictions or culture. However, a number of international agreements contain more specific provision for the education of minority cultural and linguistic groups.[35] In addition, the ICESCR is ambitious in its aims to secure, eventually, free education at primary, secondary and tertiary level.

In contrast, the Charter, not unlike Protocol 1, Article 2 of the ECHR, is relatively laconic. It declares a general right to education and, unlike the ECHR, includes within this vocational and continuing education. It also improves on the ECHR, in that paragraph 2 of Article 14 EUCFR explicitly lays down the principle of free compulsory education which, the explanatory notes tell us, only implies that each child in compulsory education should have the right to attend a school free of charge. This express inclusion of free compulsory education may be taken to imply that there is no right to free non-compulsory education, whether that be a continuation of compulsory education into higher levels of school, college or university, or free access to vocational and continuing training. Thus, while a right to education framed in this way can be understood as giving an entitlement to access to education, it does not give a right to equal access to education: the right to non-compulsory education may be restricted to those who can pay for it, and, even in compulsory education, those who can pay may be afforded more choice as to where their child is educated. While the latter question is not addressed by international human rights instruments, Articles 13(2)(b) and (c) ICESCR require the progressive introduction of free education, notably at tertiary level. To that extent, the Charter is narrower in scope in terms of guaranteeing accessibility; presumably, at least in part, because of the political hot potato of tuition fees in the UK.

This point is particularly significant in the context of vocational and continuing education. While, as we shall discuss later, education policy has a particular identity-forming role within the EU,[36] it is also deeply rooted in the goal of economic development. There is an increasing emphasis within policy making on the development of a dynamic knowledge-based economy, which requires a highly trained workforce, hence the emphasis on vocational training and lifelong learning. More recently, it has also been linked to the development of the information society and the knowledge economy.[37] However, the failure to grant anything more than a basic right of access to such training has significant potential to exclude. This might particularly affect people historically excluded from the workforce, such as those with little previous education, or people with disabilities, who may not be in a position to pay for training, and for whom training may not be seen to be 'cost-effective' by employers or potential

---

[35] Such as, for example, Art 5(1)(c) Convention against Discrimination in Education; Art 30 CRC.

[36] On the background of EU education law see B de Witte (ed), *European Community Law of Education* (Baden-Baden, Nomos, 1989).

[37] J Shaw, 'From the Margins to the Centre: Education and Training Law and Policy' in P Craig and G de Búrca (eds), *The Evolution of EU Law* (Oxford, Oxford University Press, 1999) 555 at p 582 *et seq*.

employers.[38] For such people, the right to education has a particular significance, as it provides a way into the employment market. However, equally, that right needs to be backed up by practical policies facilitating access.

Further, the Charter contains neither recitals as to the purpose of education or the reasons why such a right is important, nor a right to any particular type of education. Article 14(3) EUCFR, while focused on the question of providing an education in conformity with the religious, philosophical and pedagogical convictions of the parents, does not confer such a right on parents (although it seems to be inferred, and is contained within the ECHR as well as within other international agreements) but rather grants the freedom to found education establishments, thus allowing for the foundation of schools using particular teaching methods, or teaching according to a specific religious or philosophical agenda. In the context of the ECHR rights, the European Court of Human Rights has held that this right can be guaranteed merely by permitting the existence of private schools, and that the right does not permit interference with the defined curriculum within a school, provided it is delivered objectively and there is no indoctrination.[39] There is a concordance between this freedom, and the (single market) freedom to provide education services and to establish educational establishments guaranteed under Articles 43 and 49 EC.[40] However, none of this confers a right on individuals to receive an education which conforms to their particular convictions or the convictions of their parents. That right could only be effectively exercised in situations where such an education is available, and available without charge; a situation which may prove unattainable in states with a commitment to a secular identity, such as France. As Dunbar points out, such a right granted with no guarantee of State support is a 'hollow right at best'.[41] Further, neither the Charter nor the ECHR provide any rights or protections for those who wish to educate their children in a particular cultural, or linguistic, context. The European Court of Human Rights has made it clear that what is protected by Protocol 1, Article 2 is the religious or philosophical convictions of the parents, rather than their culture or language; beliefs, in other words, rather than identity.[42] In particular, in the *Belgian Linguistic* case, the Court stated that the Convention grants no right to education in a minority language, given that the State has an interest in preserving linguistic unity.[43]

---

[38] Art 5 of the Equal Treatment Dir 2000/78/EC OJ 2000 L 303/16, requiring reasonable accommodation for disabled persons might apply here, although it is open to question whether bearing the costs of training would impose a disproportionate burden on the employer.

[39] *Kjeldsen, Busk Madsen and Pedersen v Denmark* Series A No 23 (1979–80) 1 EHRR 711.

[40] This is implicit from Case 305/87 *Commission v Greece* [1989] ECR 1461 in which the Court held that the rights of non-nationals to own property were guaranteed under what were then Arts 48, 52 and 59 EEC.

[41] R Dunbar, 'Minority Language Rights in International Law' (2001) 50 *International and Comparative Law Quarterly* 90–120, at p 110.

[42] *Campbell and Cosans v United Kingdom* Series A No 60 (1991) 13 EHRR 441.

[43] *Belgian Linguistic Case* Series A No 6 (1979–80) 1 EHRR 252.

As it stands, therefore, the Charter seems to provide a very basic, and limited, right to education. However, the right to education has a much broader scope than this. In its General Comment on the Right to Education, the UN Committee on Economic, Social and Cultural Rights outlined the basic features which need to be assured in order to give meaning to any declaration of that right.[44] The comment begins with an important statement of the nature of education rights:

> Education is both a human right in itself and an indispensable means of realising other human rights. As an empowerment right, education is the primary vehicle by which economically and socially marginalised adults and children can lift themselves out of poverty and obtain the means to participate fully in their communities. Education has a vital role in empowering women, safeguarding children from exploitative and hazardous labour and sexual exploitation, promoting human rights and democracy, protecting the environment, and controlling population growth. Increasingly, education is recognised as one of the best financial investments States can make. But the importance of education is not just practical: a well-educated, enlightened and active mind, able to wander freely and widely, is one of the joys and rewards of human existence.

This statement clarifies the central role which education must have in society, and, importantly, its relationship with other rights. Education is the means of empowering individuals and groups to make full use of their rights and participate within society. However, according to the General Comment, education rights are also dependent on other factors. For education rights to be sufficiently guaranteed, they must be available, accessible to all (physically, economically and in a non-discriminatory way), acceptable (relevant, culturally appropriate and of good quality) and adaptable to diverse social and cultural settings. Thus, while education can be instrumental in making declared rights effective within societies, education rights for all can only be *fully* operationalised in the context of wider rights of non-discrimination and of the recognition of cultural and social diversity.

Looking at it this way, a number of weaknesses can be identified, not only within Article 14 EUCFR itself, but within the wider context of the Charter. Economic accessibility is limited by the failure of the Charter to make any statement about free non-compulsory or vocational education, despite the implication within the ICESCR that wealthier signatory states should be able to assure free education at all levels. Acceptability and adaptability are also compromised by the failure of the Charter explicitly to recognise any right to an education within a specific cultural or linguistic context. It is this second point which is the focus of this piece.

---

[44] *The right to education: Article 13.* E/C.12/99/10, CESCR General Comment 13.

The Link Between Education and Culture

The connection between education and culture made in this piece mirrors the fact that both areas are dealt with by the same Directorate-General in the Commission. It is important, however, to consider why that might be the case. There are important reasons why we are following this institutional lead, which are related to the interconnectedness of, and clashes between, cultural rights and educational rights.

Despite sharing a Directorate-General and indeed a common website on the *Europa* server, an examination of the latter would suggest the links between the two elements are not carried further than the Directorate-General's mission statement. That statement has recently been rewritten, and currently gives little help in the search for common ground between the two policy areas, linking them by a mission to 'bring people together to foster respect and understanding'. A previous mission statement was more explicit about how this goal is part of both education and cultural policy. The keyword here is identity:

> Education and culture in the broad sense . . . [are] not only deeply rooted in national identities but also vectors of globalisation, from the most scholarly level to the daily realities of the supermarket, the cinema and the Saturday football match.

Thus, this statement connotes recognition that education and culture are areas where national sensitivities are particularly apparent. However, it is also noted that, as 'vectors of globalisation', education and culture are ways in which a European identity can be fostered—almost as a counterculture. Using education and culture to add a European dimension to individual identity, through policies such as educational mobility, promotion of language learning, the support of cultural co-operation projects with a European dimension, the designation of European Capitals of Culture, and the establishment of a common market in broadcasting is an important policy theme. This somewhat impoverished view of cultural policy can have significant consequences. If cultural policy is seen as a vehicle for promoting European integration and a European identity, rather than as a valid goal in itself, it is surely likely that such policy runs real dangers of emphasising the common ground that Europeans share at the expense of the differences and, in particular, of excluding from cultural consideration those groups which do not have a long history of European identity.[45]

This emphasis on identity forms part of the link between education and culture. Just as education and culture are vectors of globalisation, so education can be understood as a vector for the transmission of culture. EU policy sees educational mobility not only as a way of helping individuals learn more about different EU countries, but more generally as a way of introducing a European dimension to the identities of those participating in such schemes. This is

---

[45] For discussion, in the context of citizenship and cultural policy, see NW Barber, 'Citizenship, Nationalism and the European Union' (2002) 27 *European Law Review* 241–59.

because education, particularly education for children and young people, is a prime means of transmitting wider culture. The type of school or university attended can have an important effect on the cultural background of an individual, either confirming or, in some cases, competing with, the culture absorbed through family background. Most schools, whether state-run or private, will have a role in transmitting the majority national culture, in the form of underlying values and attitudes. This will be particularly the case in states where some form of citizenship education is on the curriculum, but will happen even without such conscious motivation. Thus, in a multi-nation or immigrant state, if the minority cultures are to be respected, some way must be found of recognising those cultures within the education system.[46] This can be done through multicultural policies, which try to ensure that schools do not focus solely on the majority national culture, or through the existence of separate schools.[47] Multicultural education policy is, as Raz points out, one of the most significant concrete policies of multiculturalism as a whole.[48]

This point is recognised to some extent in the EU by its provisions on the education of migrant children.[49] However, as Cullen points out, the Directive on migrants' children is marked by policy ambivalence and limitations. First, the issue of competence referred to above means that the application of the Directive is limited to the children of migrants from other Community countries and requires Member States to take measures to promote the culture of the country of origin of the child; i.e. the dominant national culture, rather than any minority culture. Secondly, as well as promoting the language and culture of the country of origin—in order to facilitate re-integration when the parents return to their country of origin—the Directive requires measures to be taken to enable the child to integrate into the host state. There is thus a lack of clarity as to whether the goal of the Directive is to foster integration, or to encourage the preservation of the child's national (rather than cultural) identity.[50]

As well as being linked by the complementarity of focus on identity and education as a transmitter of culture, educational and cultural rights can often limit each other. On the one hand, education policies can affect cultural rights. Generally speaking, as General Comment 13 makes clear, education rights can be understood as empowerment rights, and one of the things which education can give people is knowledge of and confidence in their cultural identity. For

---

[46] See generally A-G Gagnon and J Tully (eds), *Multinational Democracies* (Cambridge, Cambridge University Press, 2001).

[47] See, for example, Art 12 of the Framework Convention for the Protection of National Minorities, which requires States to 'take measures in the fields of education and research to foster knowledge of the culture, history, language and religion of their national minorities and of the majority' and Art 13, which gives groups the right to set up and manage private educational and training establishments (without implying a commitment on the part of the State to finance this).

[48] Above n 3.

[49] Dir 77/486/EEC on the education of the children of migrant workers OJ 1977 L 199/32.

[50] H Cullen, 'From Migrants to Citizens? European Community Policy on Intercultural Education' (1996) 45 *International and Comparative Law Quarterly* 109.

example, education through the medium of a minority language encourages the continuity and growth of that language and, through that, of the cultural identity expressed through that language. Education in the context of and/or which is respectful of particular cultural identity has the effect of encouraging children to feel confident within their culture and see their culture validated, rather than marginalised. On the other hand, cultural identity can affect the exercise of education rights. A good example here is the clash of rights which surround the existence of 'faith schools'. Proponents of such schools argue that, as a religion is a fundamental part of cultural identity, it should be a right of parents to educate their children in the context of their religious faith. However, a number of other rights must also be considered. In the first place, do faith schools have the right to exclude children from a different religious background, or no religious background? This problem is particularly acute, given the connection between some religions (eg Islam) and particular ethnic groups. Secondly, what of the rights of the children themselves? Education rights are almost always conceptualised as parental rights, with childrens' rights being limited to certain aspects of their experience within education. However, as the Convention on the Rights of the Child suggests, the right to education can be seen as a childrens' right, as can the right to a particular approach to education or type of education. Do faith schools limit the right of children to choose not to follow the religion of their parents; a right which, in a liberal society, must be maintained? Are faith schools, which insist on teaching certain subjects and refusing to teach others, violating the rights of their pupils to a reasonable and broad education?[51]

Specific Cases

These general debates are reflected in any number of policy issues arising right across Europe. However, current and future developments, as well as providing possible space for increased cultural conflict within the EU, also offer the potential for future developments, using the Charter provisions as a springboard.

Minority Rights, Language, Education and Enlargement

Minority rights have not traditionally had a place within EU rights discourse. As Schwellnus has pointed out, if any move towards minority rights can be detected, it is very recent and, to a large extent, a response to the challenges of enlargement.[52] This state of affairs is not atypical: within the Council of Europe,

---

[51] This issue has been brought to the fore in recent debates over the right of a Christian school to teach creationism as a scientific perspective, and continues to be visible in the issue of sex education in schools (see, for example, the case of *Kjeldsen* et al, above n 39, which concerned parental wishes that their children not be given sex education in school).

[52] G Schwellnus, '"Much Ado About Nothing?" Minority Protection and the EU Charter of Fundamental Rights' Constitutionalism Web-Papers, ConWEB 5/2001 http://les1.man.ac.uk/conweb/.

for example, minority rights are not included within the ECHR (except within the context of Article 2 of the First Protocol) and the Framework Convention for National Minorities was only signed in 1995.[53] However, these more recent moves within the Council of Europe towards the protection of minorities have not really been duplicated at EU level. Given the multi-national and multi-cultural nature of the EU itself, some consideration of minority rights would be helpful.

This state of affairs is all the more puzzling when we consider the extent to which the protection by accession states of minority rights has been under the microscope during the enlargement process. The 1993 Copenhagen criteria explicitly require that candidate countries should achieve 'stability of institutions . . . guaranteeing respect for and protection of minorities'. The enforcement of this principle has been a significant theme of negotiations with a number of candidate States: the treatment of Roma has been and continues to be a cause for concern in several states, as has been the position of the Turkish minority in Bulgaria and the Russian-speaking minorities in Estonia and Latvia. Provision in all states for the protection of minorities, particularly in the context of education and language rights, has been closely scrutinised under the enlargement process. This scrutiny suggests that the EU places value on minority rights, and considers them to be an essential part of the standards of democracy required of Member States of the EU.

However, once candidate states become Member States, as EU law currently stands, that scrutiny will come to an end—barring an application of Article 7 TEU, which the Member States purported, in a somewhat skewed way, to invoke against Austria's new government incorporating Haider's Freedom Party in 2000 and which has been significantly widened in relation to its procedures by the Treaty of Nice. The current state of law would prevent discrimination on the grounds of race, and there is some EU action combating racism and xenophobia, but there are, as yet, no binding provisions requiring states to take positive measures to ensure and support multicultural policies. Article 7 TEU could never be used to push for positive policies of this nature. Given the complex ethnic make-up of some candidate states, and the deep-rooted divisions which can be found to exist, this inability to continue to police the situation may exacerbate problems—even though it can be anticipated that scrutiny will continue under the aegis of international institutions including the Council of Europe, the Organisation for Security and Co-operation in Europe and the Council of the Baltic States. Further, existing Member States are not, and never have been, subject to the same scrutiny as accession states. Whether this apparent double standard is based on an assumption that the same issues do not exist within existing Member States is not clear, but such an assumption cannot be borne out. Further, the EU itself must guard against the violation of minority rights and, particularly, language rights. As more national and ethnic

---

[53] This was preceded by the 1992 European Charter for Regional and Minority Languages.

groups enter the EU, more concerns are likely to arise, both in terms of the maintenance of their national identity, and also in terms of their ability to participate politically within the processes of governance. Ensuring that new states alone comply with minority rights standards is an inadequate way of asserting the value of such standards.

On this basis, stronger protection of minority rights would seem to be an essential part of the development of the EU as a multi-national and multicultural polity. Schwellnus has argued that the existence of Article 22 EUCFR, within the context of EU cultural policy, could provide one of the bases of a more developed and coherent minority rights policy.[54] The same can be said about Article 14(3) EUCFR. In some ways, it is unfortunate that more specific minority rights were not included within the Charter; Article 22 EUCFR is a rather weak provision, which appears to confer positive rights neither on individuals nor groups. Article 14(3) EUCFR only grants rights to education providers, rather than the recipients of that education and is, as we have already suggested, limited to groups with a common belief, rather than a common identity. Nevertheless, particularly when combined with the recent development of legislation outlawing race discrimination and a broadening policy on the elimination of racism and xenophobia,[55] Articles 14 and 22 EUCFR could be a way of opening a dialogue which could lead to the creation of positive rights for minorities.

Education, Culture and Citizenship

A second area to be considered is the eternal question of citizenship. If citizenship is understood as having two aspects—a citizenship of identity, and a citizenship of political rights—education and culture have central roles to play in both of those aspects. In terms of identity, we have already argued that education has an important role to play in the developing of common cultural identity. However, the question of European identity remains contested. One of the explicit roles of EU education and cultural policy is to help in the development of that European identity, through, by and large, initiatives which promote that which is common amongst Europeans, rather than that which divides us. It could be argued, indeed, that this aspect of EU cultural policy tends towards the assimilation of the different national cultures into an abstract ideal of what it is to be European, at the expense of their individual cultural identities.

If this is the case, it has wide implications. Cultural pluralism does not always follow the same model. A distinction needs to be made between a multi-nation polity, which is comprised of a number of complete historical communities within one state (examples include the United States, Canada and Australia

---

[54] Above n 522.
[55] For the connection between race legislation and minority protection, see D Chalmers, 'The Mistakes of the Good European?' in S Fredman (ed), *Discrimination and Human Rights. The Case of Racism* (Oxford, Oxford University Press, 2001).

(where indigenous nations were colonised and conquered by the now dominant nation) and Belgium (where federalism was a much later development) and Switzerland (formed from a more or less voluntary act of federation)), and pluralism caused by individual or familial immigration, where the developing immigrant communities often continue to have links with the country of origin of themselves or their ancestors. Kymlicka argues that these types of cultural pluralism need to be understood separately, as they can give rise to different challenges.[56] The EU, of course, is a multi-nation polity. However, it is important not to forget that immigration forms another aspect of its pluralistic character.[57] An emphasis within cultural policy on common European characteristics, based on a historical perception of a common European identity, can serve to exclude immigrant communities, who do not share in the whole of that history. One effect of this can perhaps be seen in the Culture 2000 project, where the scarcity of projects originating from immigrant communities which are given funding is noticeable. This latter, exclusionary tendency should be of particular concern in the light of recent events, and more broadly what has been argued to be a significant incidence of racism throughout the EU.[58]

The political side of citizenship also poses challenges. The development of a cohesive, consensus-based and democratic polity is precisely what is required in order to support a multicultural citizenship in Europe. Attempts to form, or identify, a sufficiently strong European identity upon which to base citizenship would seem doomed to failure. European unity itself is, to a great extent, based on diversity, as the European Parliament has recognised.[59] Kymlicka argues that, in general, it is extremely difficult to identify sources of unity such as to form the basis of a common citizenship in a multicultural society.[60] The only way for any multicultural polity to work is to value the diversity of the people within it. Raz takes this further, arguing that respect for cultural groups is essen-

---

[56] Above n 2. This distinction has been criticised. See, eg Y Abu-Laban, 'The Future and the Legacy: Globalization and the Canadian Settler-State' (2001) 35 *Journal of Canadian Studies* 262–76, who argues that the distinction between colonisers and immigrants is less clear than Kymlicka would seem to suggest. Further, as Kymlicka himself acknowledges, this framework does not allow for groups, such as the Roma, who fit in neither of these categories: W Kymlicka, 'Do We Need A Liberal Theory of Minority Rights? Reply to Carens, Young, Parekh and Frost' in *Politics and the Vernacular: Nationalism, Multiculturalism and Citizenship* (Oxford, Oxford University Press, 2001). Nevertheless, for the purposes of our discussion, it is important to distinguish between immigrant and national minority groups within Europe, in order to give both types of group prominence.

[57] Within the specific field of language rights, this fact is often not recognised: see Dunbar, above n 411. This has been criticised: see P Keller, 'Re-thinking Ethnic and Cultural Rights in Europe' (1998) 18 *Oxford Journal of Legal Studies* 29.

[58] See CA Gearty, 'The Internal and External 'Other' in the Union Legal Order: Racism, Religious Intolerance and Xenophobia in Europe' in P Alston (ed), *The EU and Human Rights* (Oxford, Oxford University Press, 1999) 327.

[59] European Parliament Resolution on cultural cooperation in the European Union, OJ 2002 C 72E/142. See also M McDonald, 'Unity in Diversities: Some Tensions in the Construction of Europe' (1996) 4 *Social Anthropology* 47.

[60] Above n 2.

tial to ensure the identification of members of those groups with the wider polity.[61] The recognition of and respect for diversity can be the source of unity of a multicultural polity. The idea of unity through diversity is the way forward.

Respect for the rights of cultural groups, however, needs to be based on something other than identity politics. The challenges to multiculturalism based on the practical impossibility of the unity of diverse cultures into one must be taken seriously. It is definitely the case that, as Walzer puts it, 'the solid lines on the old cultural and political maps are turned into dotted lines.'[62] Cultures are being seen as less rigidly defined and exclusive. In multicultural societies, the language, customs and eating habits of each culture are being influenced by those of the others. Even within less pluralist societies, the influences of a global mass media, tourism, and returning *émigrés* have led to a blurring of the lines between local and more alien cultures. Nevertheless, distinct cultural groupings and identities continue to play an important part in the way in which individuals see themselves and their loyalties.

Canada again provides a useful point for discussion here. While the search for a distinctive Canadian identity has not been absent from Canadian constitutional debates, perhaps because of the tensions between the English-speaking and French-speaking populations, that identity has necessarily had to be looser in nature. Helly goes so far as to argue that multiculturalism has become part of Canada's founding ideology,[63] and it is certainly the case that the unity of the Canadian state is not based on a monocultural identity. In this context, ethnos and demos appear to have been uncoupled; the solution which according to Lehning, is the only way to found a European identity which cannot be based on ethno-cultural characteristics.[64] Lehning goes on to suggest that it is the rights and opportunities for participation within the democratic process which can form the basis of a common European identity. In a wider context, Wheatley argues that rights of political participation are essential to ensure the inclusion of minority groups within the polity.[65] This view is supported by the work of Tully, who argues that a sense of belonging within a multicultural society can be engendered by the participation of different cultural groups in dialogue and deliberation about the constitutional development of that society. Such participation is important because it marks an acknowledgement of the existence and needs of minority groups, and also allows society as a whole to respond to

---

[61] Above n 3. Raz's argument seems to based on the idea of a number of smaller cultures being part of one wider culture. The complexity of culture may mean that a rather more fluid, multi-level model needs to be used. Nonetheless, the basic point still seems valid.

[62] M Walzer, 'The Politics of Difference: Statehood and Toleration in a Multicultural World' (1997) 10 *Ratio Juris* 165–76 at p 176.

[63] D Helly, 'The Political Regulation of Cultural Plurality: Foundations and Principles' (1993) 25 *Canadian Ethnic Studies* 15–35.

[64] PB Lehning, 'European Citizenship: Towards a European Identity?' (2001) 20 *Law and Philosophy* 239–82.

[65] S Wheatley, 'Minority Rights and Political Accommodation in the 'New' Europe' (1997) 22 *European Law Review* Supp HRS 63–81.

the dynamic identities of different groups, rather than to a reified stereotype.[66] This needs to form part of the wider democratisation of the EU. However, education policy also has a role to play. It is through education that citizens can be taught about their citizenship and can be made aware of their rights and their identity as members of specific cultural groups who need to be heard. An education policy which is sensitive to diversity and promotes multiculturalism as a moral good, but which also embraces the need to teach how political citizenship can contribute towards wider participation of minority groups.

Here, however, we can also return to the Charter. The ideals of participation of civil society in the decision-making process and of consensus politics rather than majority decision-making are ideals, which can facilitate the political integration of minority groups. They are also the ideals which informed, to a great extent, the process of drafting the Charter. It has been suggested that this process, which has been hailed as a great success, could be used for future decision-making—particularly the Convention on the Future of Europe. It may be that the biggest contribution which the Charter can make to inclusive citizenship within Europe is not the rights which it contains, but the process by which it was decided.

CONCLUSION

This paper has begun the process of exploring the intersections between the ideals or 'promise' of multiculturalism, as a response to the challenges of diversity within modern society, and the EU's concerns regarding policies on education and culture, both in the context of the current Treaty framework and, specifically, the innovations provided by the Charter of Fundamental Rights of the European Union 2000. Quite apart from the inherent challenges in developing policies of multiculturalism within any polity, it is clear from the analysis above that there are particular difficulties attaching to any attempt to match multicultural policies to the EU's limited goals and competences. Yet as a supranational governance structure, the EU constitutes a potentially powerful venue within which the values of tolerance and diversity awareness could be effectively articulated, should the political will be present. This can be achieved, using techniques of 'new governance' without unnecessarily constraining or interfering with the autonomy of the Member States.

---

[66] J Tully, *Strange Multiplicity: Constitutionalism in an Age of Diversity* (Cambridge, Cambridge University Press, 1995). The importance of dialogue is also referred to by Abu-Laban above n 56.

11

A 'New Governance' Approach to Economic, Social and Cultural Rights in the EU

NICHOLAS BERNARD*

INTRODUCTION

IS A LEGALLY binding, judicially enforceable Charter of Fundamental Rights of the European Union something we should aspire to? The question of whether, and if so how, the Charter should be integrated in the EU legal order was left open when the Charter was proclaimed in Nice in December 2000. Most non-governmental organisations that participated in the Convention regarded a legally binding Charter as a desirable outcome. Some of the contributions in this book express reservations about the contents of the Charter with respect to specific rights.[1] However, many would equally argue that, with a properly designed package of rights, a legally binding Charter could make a positive difference for the protection of fundamental socio-economic rights in the EU. There is little doubt that the status of the Charter has symbolic importance. By refusing to make the Charter binding, the EU and its Member States may signal that their commitment to fundamental rights in the EU is at best half-hearted[2] and they may thereby deprive the Charter of its potential 'totemic force.'[3] Beyond this, however, would the possibility of invoking the Charter in the courts make a substantial difference?

This is far from self-evident in a multi-level legal environment such as that of the EU. The idea of a Charter of Fundamental Rights, understood as catalogue of justiciable rights enforceable in the courts, is conspicuously at odds with current trends in EU governance. It seems to constitute an attempt to return to the

* Queen's University Belfast. I would like to thank Kenneth Armstrong and David Harris as well as other workshop participants for their comments on a previous version of this Chapter.

[1] For example, see the chapters by J Hunt, B Ryan, M Bell, C Costello, M Barbera, C Wallace and J Shaw and J Tooze.

[2] See JHH Weiler, 'Editorial comments: Does the European Union Truly Need a Charter of Rights?' (2000) 6 *European Law Journal* 95.

[3] The phrase is borrowed from D Chalmers, 'Post-nationalism and the Quest for Constitutional Substitutes' (2000) *Journal of Law and Society* 178 at 179.

values of the integration-through-law school, with its resolute faith in the capacity of law and judicial processes to push forward the integration agenda through uniform, 'hard' rules at EU level. By contrast, 'new governance' insists on power-sharing, diversity and decentralisation, flexible instruments and a re-assertion of the primacy of political processes over legal ones.[4]

Admittedly, the rhetoric of rights has played an important role in the development of the Community legal order. However, the language of rights was then a means to strengthen the Community *vis-à-vis* its Member States and facilitate the achievement of its core objective, viz economic integration. A similar strategy is unlikely to work in the context of social and cultural rights. Charters of rights are normally designed to impose obligations on states. They assume both responsibility and power on the part of the state to adopt the necessary measures to observe, protect and fulfil the rights that they contain. The EU, however, is not a state. It has neither general responsibility nor general competence to ensure the well-being of EU citizens in all fields. EU competences in the social and cultural fields are carefully circumscribed and available means of intervention are essentially of the 'new governance' type.[5] The failure of the Charter to engage with new governance and, more generally, with the specificity of the EU as a non-state presents us with the danger that it may promise more than it can deliver. Even if one were to assume a sympathetic judiciary, that judiciary may simply not be in a position to make much of the Charter.

However, judicial enforcement is not the only way to make use of the Charter. The thesis underlying this Chapter is that we have more to gain by engaging with new modes of governance and using the opportunities that they offer than we have by relying on judicial means of enforcement. The chapter will be divided in three sections. In the first section, I will highlight how rights discourse in the EU has been used to the detriment of fundamental social rights, preventing the emergence of an autonomous sphere of national competence immune from the economic logic of the internal market. In the second section, the inappropriateness of judicial control mechanisms to the changing forms of EU governance will be considered. The third and final section will propose an alternative mechanism to the development of fundamental socio-economic rights, based on an Open Method of Co-ordination (OMC) process in preference to judicial enforcement.

---

[4] See J Scott and DM Trubek, 'Mind the Gap: Law and New Approaches to Governance in the European Union' (2002) 8 *European Law Journal* 1 esp at 5–6.

[5] On the 'quiet revolution' in social policy, see E Szyszczak, 'The Evolving European Employment Strategy' in J Shaw (ed), *Social Law and Policy in an Evolving European Union* (Oxford, Hart Publishing, 2000) 197.

THE CHARTER AND OLD GOVERNANCE: RIGHTS TALK AND EU COMPETENCE

Among the many narratives of European integration, integration as the vindi-
cation of individual rights has been particularly popular with lawyers. In this
story, the hero is the European Court of Justice (the Court) protecting the inno-
cent (individuals) from the evil of protectionist-minded Member States. Heroic
deeds include the development of the doctrine of direct effect, under which
Community law is recognised as intended to confer rights on individuals, which
the national courts must protect, and its application to the fundamental freedoms of the internal market.

In this story, however, not all rights have equal value. The championing of the
individual's economic (market) rights has not been paralleled by a comparable
development of social rights. Seen from a competence perspective, both sets are
liable to produce rather different effects. Given the division of tasks between the
Community and the Member States, social protection falls primarily within
the competence of the Member States whereas the completion of the internal
market falls within that of the Community. Market rights have been invoked in
an offensive mode against measures adopted by Member States susceptible of
hindering the realisation of the internal market. By way of contrast, social rights
have primarily been invoked in a defensive mode, to protect national competence from Community law incursions likely to have a negative impact on
national systems of social protection.[6] However, attempts at removing spheres
of activity from the scope of internal market law on the ground that they fulfil
social functions have, on the whole, enjoyed limited success.

Social Rights and Internal Market Jurisprudence

In theory, internal market rules should not apply in the absence of an economic
activity. In some cases, the Court has shown willingness to accept that non-
commercial public services would indeed escape the application of internal market rules. In *Gravier* and in *Humbel*,[7] the Court considered that free, public
secondary and third level education fell outside the scope of the provisions on
freedom to provide services on the ground that they were not 'normally
provided against remuneration.' Under Article 90 [now 86] EC the Court held
in *Eurocontrol* that the provision of air navigation services to airlines by
Eurocontrol[8] did not constitute an economic activity notwithstanding the payment of fees by the airlines for the service, on the ground that Eurocontrol's
activities were 'connected with the exercise of powers relating to the control and

---

[6] See especially the chapters by M Poiares Maduro, and S Deakin and J Browne in this collection.
[7] See cases 293/83 *Gravier v City of Liège* [1985] ECR 593 and 263/86 *Belgium v Humbel* [1988]
ECR 5365.
[8] Eurocontrol is an international organisation created by a Treaty between a number of
European states and entrusted with various tasks related to air traffic control.

supervision of air space which are typically those of a public authority.'[9] In order to conclude that the fees paid by the airlines did not amount to remuneration for a service, the Court noted that 'Eurocontrol acts in that capacity on behalf of the Contracting States without really having any influence over the amount of the route charges.'[10] In the field of social security, the Court considered in *Poucet and Pistre*[11] that a body entrusted with the management of a compulsory social security scheme could not be regarded as involved in an economic activity. This was justified on the ground that,

> sickness funds, and the organizations involved in the management of the public social security system, fulfil an exclusively social function. That activity is based on the principle of national solidarity and is entirely non-profit-making. The benefits paid are statutory benefits bearing no relation to the amount of the contributions.[12]

The tendency, however, has been towards a tightening of the Court's approach to the notion of economic activity justifying the application of the internal market rules. Notwithstanding *Gravier* and *Humbel*, the Court decided in *Macrotron*[13] that public employment agencies, which provide employment placement services free of charge, were to be regarded as engaging in an economic activity. It is difficult to reconcile these cases. What exactly is this 'economic activity' that public employment placement agencies engage in which is not a 'service', according to *Gravier* and *Humbel*? *Macrotron* does not even fit with the essentialist approach in *Eurocontrol* of tasks which are 'typically those of a public authority,' given that free employment placement is undoubtedly a task typically undertaken by public authorities.[14] The approach taken by the Court in *Geraets-Smits*[15] is also hard to reconcile with *Gravier* and *Eurocontrol*. Here, the Court considered that a 'free-at-the-point-of-delivery' system of medical care financed from social security contributions by patients to a sickness insurance fund to which they are affiliated would not necessarily be regarded as falling outside the scope of freedom to provide services. The Court explicitly rejected the argument that the fact that the patient does not pay for the service is a relevant consideration. The Court regarded the payments made by the sickness fund to the medical services provider (hospital), on the basis of a pre-set scale of fees determined in national legislation as consideration for the medical services provided. How can this be reconciled with the finding in

---

[9] Case C–364/92 *SAT Fluggesellschaft v Eurocontrol* [1994] ECR I–43 at para 30.

[10] *Ibid* at para 29.

[11] Joined Cases C–159/91 and C–160/91 *Poucet and Pistre* [1993] ECR I–637.

[12] At para 18.

[13] Case C–41/90 *Klaus Höfner and Fritz Elser v Macrotron GmbH* [1991] ECR I–1979.

[14] But see the remark of the Court in Case C–55/96 *Job Centre* [1997] ECR I–7119 at para 22: 'the fact that the placement of employees is normally entrusted to public offices cannot affect the economic nature of such activities. Placement of employees has not always been, and is not necessarily, carried out by public entities.' The Charter Convention did not have the same expectation as the court in *Job Centre* as to what public authorities typically do: Art 29 EUCFR stipulates that 'everyone shall have the right of access to a free placement service.'

[15] Case C–157/99, *Geraets-Smits and Peerbooms* [2001] ECR I–5473.

Eurocontrol that the fact that Eurocontrol had no control over the amount of charges for services and was bound to apply a set formula determined by the Contracting States was deemed a relevant consideration to conclude that no economic activity took place? Does it not follow from *Geraets-Smits* that payments by the State to universities on account of the number of students they teach constitute remuneration and university education, therefore, is a service, contrary to what was held in *Gravier*?[16] *Poucet and Pistre* have not been left untouched either. If anybody thought that solidarity-based social security systems were outside the scope of internal market law altogether as a result of *Poucet and Pistre*, the rulings of the Court in *Sodemare* (under Article 49 EC) *FFSA* and *Albany* [17] (under Article 86 EC) made it clear that such is not the case. The full implications of the *Poucet*, *FFSA* and *Albany* line of cases are not altogether clear. It is submitted, however, that it is, at most, only those pensions and sickness funds which are carrying out activities which could manifestly not be undertaken in any circumstances by the private sector which are likely to be regarded as falling outside the scope of internal market law altogether.[18]

The key findings on which the Court relied in *Albany* were that the pension fund in question operated on the principle of capitalisation rather than redistribution and that it was free to determine the amount of contributions it required and the benefits it paid. The fact that it pursued an essential social function, that affiliation was compulsory, that the fund was non-profit making and that it was organised on a principle of solidarity reflected in various other rules was not considered by the Court sufficient to remove it from the scope of competition law, as an undertaking engaging in an economic activity.

It has therefore become increasingly difficult for non-commercial public services to escape the reach of internal market law altogether.[19] On the other hand,

---

[16] Interestingly, *Geraets-Smits* seems to depart from *Gravier* on another point. In *Gravier*, the Court rejected the argument that Miss Gravier was a recipient of services since she paid a substantial fee (the Minerval then charged by Belgian universities to foreign students) on the ground that what mattered was whether the services were 'normally' provided against remuneration. By contrast, the Court noted in *Geraets-Smits* that Ms Geraets-Smits had in fact paid for the treatment without considering the issue whether the hospital normally provided the service without remuneration from the patient.

[17] Cases C–70/95 *Sodemare and Others v Regione Lombardia* [1997] ECR I–3395, C–244/94 *Fédération Française des Sociétés d'Assurance and Others v Ministère de l'Agriculture et de la Pêche* [1995] ECR I–4013, and C–67/96 *Albany International v Stichting Bedrijfspensioenfonds Textielindustrie* [1999] ECR I–5751.

[18] As Advocate-General Jacobs noted at para 330 of his Opinion in *Albany*, 'it is clear from the general case-law on the concept of an undertaking . . . that the decisive factor is whether the activity is *necessarily carried out by public entities or their agents*' (emphasis added). It is also significant that the Court seems to attach a great deal of importance on the mode of financing of pension schemes, viz. whether by capitalisation or by contributions from current members to finance the pensions of retired members: see *Poucet* at para 11, *FFSA* at para 17 and *Albany* at para 81.

[19] *Quaere* whether the wide concept of undertaking in the context of non-economic public services is intellectually coherent with the *Meng* case law on the non-applicability of Arts 10 and 81 EC to state measures that lessen the competitiveness of the environment by removing the possibility of competition. On this case law, see N Reich, 'The "November Revolution" of the European Court of Justice: *Keck, Meng and Audi* revisited' (1994) 31 *Common Market Law Review* 459.

the Court has been fairly receptive to arguments aimed not at placing activities altogether outside the scope of internal market law but at justifying some accommodation of internal market principles to take into account the specific characteristics and objectives of public services.

In *Geraets-Smits*, the Court found that hospital treatment could fall within the scope of freedom to provide services but also accepted that the provision of adequate medical facilities in a Member State may require planning and control of the supply of hospital facilities and types of treatment available and that a Member State may derogate from the rules on free movement for that purpose.[20]

In *Albany*, the Court considered that the sectoral pension fund at stake constituted an undertaking for the purposes of Article 86 [now 82] EC but it also held that compulsory affiliation to the pension fund was justified under Article 90(2) [now 86(2)] EC as a necessary condition for the fulfilment of its essential social purpose.[21]

Albany follows the line developed by the Court in *Corbeau*[22] in which it accepted that universal service considerations may justify restrictions on competition so as to avoid 'cream-skimming' of the more profitable segments of the market, making it difficult or impossible for the universal service provider to sustain its financial equilibrium.

Although the language of fundamental rights is conspicuously absent from these cases, they can nevertheless be read as consistent with a concern about the protection of fundamental social rights. In *Geraets-Smits*, *Albany* and *Corbeau*, the determining factor was whether the application of internal market law would lead the service provider to be unable to fulfil its function of guaranteeing the right to medical care and an adequate standard of living, in the form of pension entitlements and basic facilities such as the postal service, to all. One could also justify the solution reached in *Macrotron* on this basis. The monopoly of public placement agencies over employment procurement cannot find a justification in upholding the right of everybody to access to a free placement service, as provided for in Article 29 EUCFR, if those agencies are manifestly unable to satisfy the demand for such placement services.[23]

Social Rights and Internal Market Legislation

The picture that emerges from secondary legislation is very similar to the one from the case law. Fundamental rights considerations do not constitute per se a

---

[20]   Paras 72–82 of the judgment.

[21]   Paras 108–110 of the judgment.

[22]   Case C–320/91 *Criminal proceedings against Paul Corbeau* [1993] ECR I–2533.

[23]   On the other hand, one may wonder whether the acceptance as axiomatic in *Job Centre* (n 14 above) that public placement agencies are unable to satisfy the demand for employment procurement is sound. Then again, it is unclear how the need to ensure a right of access to placement agencies to all can justify a monopoly.

ground to halt the progress of the internal market and specifically the policy of liberalisation in a number of sectors with obvious social welfare implications, such as telecommunications, postal services, transport or energy. Again, the language of fundamental rights is absent from key instruments, as least as far as 'hard law' is concerned. Here too, however, fundamental rights concerns in terms, in particular, of universal access at a reasonable cost to basic services is obvious in a number of provisions. The techniques used vary. In electronic telecommunications and postal services, the principle is that of imposition on the Member States of universal service obligations.[24] In energy and transport, the preferred approach is to allow Member States to impose public service obligations on providers, without, however, requiring them to do so nor explicitly requiring them to ensure universal service provision.[25]

Impact of the Charter

Two characteristics of the case law and legislation concerning the relationship between the internal market and social policy have been brought to the fore in this section. Firstly, social policy is not, as a rule, regarded as a distinct sphere of activity immune to the discipline of the internal market. Secondly, although social considerations are taken into account in the interpretation or design of internal market rules, these are not conceptualised as rights, but rather as derogations from (economic) rights. As such, this places social considerations in a more fragile position since derogations from fundamental internal market freedoms are to be interpreted narrowly according to the case law of the Court.

It is doubtful that the Charter would necessarily imply a substantial departure from this. Nothing in the conceptualisation of social issues as fundamental rights would imply the creation of a special sphere of immunity from internal market law. What the Charter could conceivably do, however, is lead to a re-conceptualisation of the issue not as one of derogation from a fundamental economic right but rather as one of conflict between an economic freedom and a social right.[26] In theory, if both rights are fundamental, there is no a priori reason to decide that one set should be superior to the other and therefore to give priority to market rights by requiring a narrow construction of social rights. In many cases, however, the opposition will be between an individual market right

---

[24] See Dir 2002/22/EC of the European Parliament and of the Council of 7 March 2002 on universal service and users' rights relating to electronic communications networks and services (Universal Service Directive) OJ 2002 L108/51 and Dir 97/67/EC of the European Parliament and of the Council of 15 December 1997 on common rules for the development of the internal market of Community postal services and the improvement of quality of service OJ 1998 L15/14.

[25] For example, electricity: Article 3(2) of Dir 96/92/EC of the European Parliament and of the Council of 19 December 1996 concerning common rules for the internal market in electricity OJ 1997 L27/20; air transport: Art 4(1)(a) of Reg 2408/92/EEC on access for Community air carriers to intra-Community air routes, OJ 1992 L240/8.

[26] See the contribution of M Poiares Maduro in this collection at pp 284–6.

and a collective social right. Thus *Geraet-Smits* can be construed as a conflict between an individual right to seek medical services in another Member State versus a collective right to health in the state of origin, implying a capacity for the Member State to organise its hospital system in a way that enables it to satisfy that right to health.[27]

Whether a court steeped in a culture of individual rights would be willing to place such a collective right on an equal footing with individual market rights is open to question. The Court's case law on affirmative action in the context of gender discrimination would suggest a preference for individualistic interpretations of fundamental rights.[28] While, despite some initial reluctance, the Court now admits that recruitment and promotions policies giving preference to women in tie-break situations are acceptable, it will not accept priority to be given over and above individual 'merit'.[29]

While the Charter may induce marginal changes of interpretation in specific situations, it is unlikely that it will lead to any fundamental rethink of the approach to the balance between economic and social rights in the internal market.

THE CHARTER AND NEW GOVERNANCE: WITHER THE COURT?

Morison once criticised the package of constitutional reforms put forward by the first Blair government[30] for being outdated,

> bring[ing] the United Kingdom into line with other constitutions that were founded in the eighteenth and nineteenth centuries and are now beginning to feel their age.[31]

For Morison, the constitutional reform package failed to take into account the fundamental reconstitution of public power that the shift from the language of government to that of governance signifies. Does the Charter fall into the same trap?

EU law and governance have changed. Dissatisfaction with command-and-control modes of regulation have led to a move away from the traditional 'Community method' in favour of techniques of governance relying on softer and more flexible instruments. There are multiple reasons for this, which one

---

[27] On the right to health, see the ch in this collection by TK Hervey.

[28] See Case C–450/93, *Kalanke v Freie Hansestadt Bremen* [1995] ECR I–3051. For discussion see C Costello in this collection at pp 122–28.

[29] See Case C–409/95 *Marschall v Land Nordrhein-Westfalen* [1997] ECR I–6363 and Case C–158/97 *Badeck and others v Hessischer Ministerpräsident* [2000] ECR I–1875.

[30] J Morison, 'The Case Against Constitutional Reform' (1998) 25 *Journal of Law and Society* 510. Such as, the adoption of a Human Rights Act, devolution for Scotland and Wales, an elected authority for London, freedom of information legislation and House of Lords reform.

[31] *Ibid* at p 512.

could subsume under two broad headings: complexity and legitimacy.[32] Neither is specific to the EU but they affect it with particular acuity.

Firstly, the complexity of the problems that the EU is called upon to address makes them less amenable to treatment by means of general, abstract rules. Norms have to be constantly tested, evaluated and adapted to particular circumstances and evolving conditions. They therefore need to be flexible and the distinction between rules and their application becomes blurred.[33] The diversity of conditions in the EU[34] increases the degree of complexity compared to regulation in the context of an individual Member State.

Secondly, weak legitimacy means that the authority of EU institutions to unilaterally impose binding norms is open to contestation. From such a perspective, power to enact binding norms is to be seen as the least attractive and therefore a last resort option, to be used when alternatives appear grossly inadequate to tackle the issue. This weak legitimacy may be reflected in the refusal to grant independent powers to the EU in sensitive areas or, where such powers exist, in the preference for alternative tools to binding legislation where suitable.

As a consequence, less emphasis is placed on imposing outcomes through binding rules and more on securing the active co-operation of all those involved throughout the regulatory chain. Firstly, soft instruments may be preferred over binding ones and self-regulation, or at least participation by stakeholders in decision-making, over traditional command-and-control. The Open Method of Co-ordination and the social dialogue constitute examples of this trend. Secondly, where traditional types of instruments are used, such as directives, they may be more concerned about prescribing procedural requirements than substantive outcomes and leave wide areas of discretion to the Member States. It is questionable whether a distinction between implementation of Community law and exercise by a Member State of its own independent decision-making powers can remain meaningful when the Community instruments are so open-ended. Thirdly, regulatory activity ceases to be the sole responsibility of public authorities and is distributed to a multiplicity of bodies whose status may be public, private or anything in-between. Is a judicially enforceable Charter of Rights a useful instrument in the context of governance techniques based on soft law instruments, not clearly delineating norms from their implementation and relying on regulatory activity by bodies across the public-private divide? Each of these issues will be considered in turn.

---

[32] J Scott and D Trubek (above n 4) identify six causes for the increase in the use of new governance methods: complexity, diversity, new approaches in public administration, legitimacy, competence creep and subsidiarity. Arguably, the last two are particular manifestations of the legitimacy problem and the second is an aspect of complexity.

[33] See K-H Ladeur, 'Towards a Legal Theory of Supranationality—the Viability of the Network Concept' (1997) 3 *European Law Journal* 33.

[34] Such as, for instance, different labour markets or different regulatory cultures.

The Charter and Soft Law

New governance techniques make use of a rich palette of instruments such as, for instance, guidelines, codes of conduct, indicators and benchmarks, recommendations, memoranda of understanding and declarations of intent.

Lack of binding effect does not necessarily mean lack of legal effect. Recommendations, for instance, may not be binding but produce a legal effect, in the sense that there may be a duty on the Member States to take them into account.[35] In this vein, guidelines adopted by the Council under Articles 99(2) and 128(2) EC, in the context of the Open Method of Co-ordination in the fields of economic policy and employment, have to be taken into account by the Member States in formulating their economic and social policies. However, the existence of a specific (political) process to evaluate compliance with the guidelines clearly excludes the existence of a concurrent judicial process of enforcement. In the case of the economic policy co-ordination, the fact that the Treaty specifies that the guidelines shall be adopted by means of a Council recommendation makes their legally unenforceable character even more obvious.

The Charter does not explicitly state that it is concerned with violations of fundamental rights arising out of binding acts of the institutions. It simply states that it is 'addressed to the institutions.' Nonetheless, if the Charter were to be a binding instrument, remedies available for its enforcement would become a crucial issue and avenues of redress for violations of fundamental rights contained in non-binding acts are far more limited.

The most obvious route to challenge the validity of an act violating fundamental rights is the action for annulment under Article 230 EC. The explicit exclusion of recommendations and opinions from acts subject to review under Article 230 EC, however, would suggest that only binding measures come within its scope. This has indeed been confirmed by the case law of the Court. While the Court is ready to go beyond the label and declare actions in annulment in principle admissible against any kind of act whatever its nature and form, this is on the condition that the measure is legally binding.[36] Thus, the Court has been prepared to review the legality of interpretative communications from the Commission when such communications go beyond merely interpreting existing Community law but seek to impose additional obligations on their addressees.[37]

This would seem to rule out the possibility of challenging the legality of soft law under Article 230 EC on grounds of violation of fundamental rights. It is doubtful that the Article 234 EC route could be used either. Admittedly, the Court has pointedly referred to the difference of wording between Articles 230

---

[35] See Case C–322/88 *Grimaldi v Fonds des Maladies Professionnelles* [1989] ECR I–4407.

[36] See, among many others, Cases 22/70 *Commission v Council (Re ERTA)* [1971] ECR 263 and 60/81 *IBM v Commission* [1981] ECR 2639.

[37] See, inter alia, case C–57/95 *France v Commission (re: Pension Funds Communication)* [1997] ECR I–1627.

and 234 EC to establish its jurisdiction to interpret non-binding acts adopted by the institutions in the context of the preliminary ruling procedure.[38] Rulings on validity, however, are a different matter and it would be difficult to understand why a particular category of act is open to challenge under Article 234 EC but not under Article 230 EC.

This leaves us with the action for damages under Article 288 EC. Chances of success here are slim. For one thing, most of the acts at stake are likely to be concerned with the exercise of wide discretion and it is likely that the restrictive *Schöppenstedt* test, requiring a 'sufficiently flagrant violation of a superior rule of law for the protection of the individual,'[39] will apply. For another, the lack of binding effect may create substantial difficulties with regard to causation.

Thus, the capacity of EU judicial processes to apprehend soft measures is extremely limited. One should not regard this as irrelevant simply because the measures concerned are non-binding. Soft instruments, especially broad policy documents and reports, provide cognitive maps in which certain topics are constructed as policy issues. While they do not necessarily close the policy space, in the sense that they cannot preclude the emergence of other ideas, one should not underestimate the degree to which they shape that space and provide a worldview in which certain solutions may be regarded as possible and others not and yet others be utterly unthinkable. It would be difficult for economic and social rights to prosper in a policy space in which labour market 'rigidity' and excessive public spending are regarded as key problems to solve. Nor should we underestimate the power of extra-judicial means of inducing compliance. The broad economic policy guidelines may not be binding but the will to avoid a negative Council recommendation constitutes a non-negligible incentive to address the guidelines seriously.

Addressing compliance with fundamental rights at the tail end of the policy process through actions in annulment directed at implementing measures may therefore be rather ineffective. Even that, however, may prove problematic.

The Charter and the Implementation of Community Policies

Taking its cues from the case law of the Court,[40] Article 51(1) EUCFR states that the Charter is addressed to,

> institutions and bodies of the Union with due regard to the principles of subsidiarity and to the Member States only when they are implementing Union law.

The Charter thus assumes a distinction between the state acting in an autonomous capacity and the state acting as implementer of Community law. This distinction, however, is becoming increasingly blurred.

---

[38] See *Grimaldi*, above n 35, at para 8.
[39] Case 5/71 *Aktien-Zuckerfabrik Schöppenstedt v Council* [1971] ECR 975, at para 11.
[40] See cases 5/88 *Wachauf v Germany* [1989] ECR 2609 and C–260/89 *ERT* [1991] ECR I–2925.

Where a Member State simply carries out obligations imposed on it by a provision of Community law, one can safely say that it falls within the scope of the Charter. To this, the case law of the Court adds that a Member State is bound by general principles of law concerning the protection of fundamental rights when a Member State seeks to rely on a derogation from basic Treaty rules.[41] While Article 51(1) EUCFR does not explicitly refer to this addition and adopts a somewhat narrower phrase,[42] it should perhaps be interpreted as implicitly including it.[43]

Beyond this, however, does the Charter apply to action by Member States? Where on a subject-matter which is (partly) regulated by Community law, a Member State adopts measures which are neither required nor prohibited by Community law, is the Member State still acting within the field of 'Union law'? Does it make a difference whether the discretion enjoyed by the Member State arises by implication from the silence and the non-regulation of an aspect of the issue by Community law or, on the contrary, Community law expressly refers to the issue and expressly grants discretion to the Member State? When a Member State elects to enforce a Community law obligation on individuals by criminal sanctions, does the whole prosecution and trial process fall within the scope of the Charter?[44]

Thus far, I have assumed problems of delimitation of the scope of the Charter in relation to implementation of binding Community law. Should the taking into account or the giving effect to non-binding Community law be regarded as falling within the concept of 'implementation' of 'Union law'? A positive answer might perhaps be defensible in relation to a specific recommendation.[45] It is, however, more difficult to sustain in relation to policy guidelines in such contexts as that of the Open Method of Co-ordination.

Third Parties and the Charter

If the Charter is only addressed to EU institutions and bodies and, in certain circumstances, the Member States, the question arises of the effect of the Charter on all other entities involved in European governance.

The EU relies increasingly on bodies and entities outside the formal institutional framework of both the Union and the Member States for the pursuit and implementation of its policies. Among other examples, one could cite the role of

---

[41]   See Case C–260/89 *ERT*, *ibid*.

[42]   It speaks of Member States 'implementing' Union law, rather than acting in the context of Union law.

[43]   For further discussion of the scope of this provision see M Poiares Maduro in this collection at pp 289–92.

[44]   It is possible to read case C–144/95 *Maurin* [1996] ECR I–2909 as implying a positive answer to that question.

[45]   Such as the recommendations at issue in the *Grimaldi* case (above n 35).

the social partners in the 'social dialogue' under Article 139 EC or that of stand-ardisation bodies such as CEN and CENELEC under the new approach to tech-nical harmonisation. Should a binding Charter also be directly binding on those bodies or, if not, are there indirect ways to make such bodies comply with the terms of the Charter?

Article 51(1) EUCFR states that the Charter is addressed to the 'institutions *and bodies* of the Union.'[46] The Charter does not specifically define the expres-sion 'bodies of the Union.' Arguably, some entities involved in the implementa-tion of EU policies could fall within the concept of a 'Union' body. The window, however, is small. The term suggests a body, which is created by the EU itself.[47] This would not include the social partners or standardisation bodies.

The problem is neither new nor specific to the EU. Human rights lawyers are familiar with the problematics of 'human rights in the private sphere'[48] and the 'horizontal' application[49] of human rights norms between private parties. In international human rights law, the problem has been to some extent resolved, or side-stepped, by establishing obligations on states of not just 'observing' human rights but 'protecting' individuals against interference with their rights by non-state actors.[50] This, however, assumes that the state has competence to impose human rights obligations on those non-state actors. This is not a prob-lem for the states given their legal omnipotence. It is however more of an issue for the EU.

Under the terms of its Article 51(2) EUCFR, the Charter does not establish any new power or task for the Community or the Union, or modify powers and tasks defined by the Treaties. Thus, the EC/EU has neither more nor less com-petence to impose human rights obligations on third parties than it had before the Charter. The Court made its view clear in *Opinion 2/94*,[51] on a putative accession of the Community to the European Convention for the protection of Human Rights, that the Community enjoys a very limited competence in the human rights field. In particular, the Court held that Community institutions do not have at their disposal a 'general power to enact rules on human rights or to conclude international conventions in this field.'[52] For the Court, respect for human rights is not so much a basis for Community action as such but rather a 'condition of the lawfulness of Community acts.'[53] The case law of the Court on

---

[46] Emphasis added.

[47] Such seems to be the interpretation of the Council itself, in its explanatory notes on the Charter: see Council of the EU, *Charter of Fundamental Rights of the European Union—Explanations relating to the complete text of the Charter*, (Office for Official Publications of the European Communities, Luxembourg, 2001) at 24.

[48] See A Clapham, *Human Rights in the Private Sphere* (Oxford, Clarendon Press, 1993).

[49] Viz application between non-governmental actors.

[50] For a similar logic in the context of Art 28 EC, see case C–265/95 *Commission v France* [1997] ECR I–6959.

[51] [1996] ECR I–1759.

[52] At para 27 of the Opinion.

[53] At para 34 of the Opinion.

the powers of the Community in this field is not limpid and probably raises more questions than it answers. Nonetheless, a reasonable interpretation of that body of law may be that human rights can be taken into account as a modality in the exercise of powers enjoyed by the Community even though it could not found a competence on its own.[54] The only two areas where the Community enjoys wider powers to impose fundamental rights obligations are in the field of discrimination, under Articles 12 and 13 EC,[55] and certain aspects of work and employment under Article 137 EC. In other fields of importance for economic, social and cultural rights, such as health or education, the powers of the EC are extremely limited.[56]

On this basis, it would seem difficult for the EC to adopt legislation specifically requiring the social partners or CEN and CENELEC to observe fundamental rights. On the other hand, it should be possible for the Community to attach human rights considerations and, in particular observance of the Charter, to acts founded on other competences. For instance, in deciding whether to adopt a Community act to implement an agreement between the social partners under Article 139 EC, it would be proper for the Council to consider whether the agreement complies with the Charter. Similarly, when formally mandating CEN or CENELEC to adopt standards to implement Community directives, it would be appropriate to include human rights clauses in the contract, where relevant.

This route, however, will normally only be suitable when formal acts are adopted and formal legal relationships established between the institutions and the non-governmental actors. If the relationship is less formal, perhaps based on a 'memorandum of understanding' or a (non-legally binding) 'code of good practice', there may be nothing on which to anchor an obligation on the non-governmental partner to observe fundamental rights. If, for instance, the Community were to rely on the initiative of standardisation bodies to adopt standards in implementation of directives rather than formally mandating them and if the standardisation bodies were to adopt standards that discriminate against persons with disabilities,[57] the Community institutions will not be in a position to sanction this breach of fundamental rights. Similarly, if the social partners, under Article 139 EC, decide to 'go their own way' and implement their agreement 'in accordance with the procedures and practices specific to management and labour and the Member States' rather than requesting the

---

[54] This would seem consistent with Case C–268/94 *Portugal v Council* [1996] ECR I–6177, in which the Court upheld the validity of a Council Decision concluding a Co-operation Agreement with India, noting that respect for human rights formed the background of the agreement rather than constituting a specific field of co-operation within it. It must be said, however, that Art 177 EC specifically states that Community policy in the field of development co-operation 'shall contribute to the general objective of [. . .] respecting human rights and fundamental freedoms.'

[55] See further the ch by M Bell in this collection.

[56] See the chs by Hervey, and Wallace and Shaw in this collection.

[57] This example assumes that discrimination on grounds of disability constitutes a breach of the Charter, which is far from obvious given the cautious wording of Art 26 of the Charter.

Council to adopt a decision, there is again no act on which to anchor a fundamental rights obligation.

Technical harmonisation and conditions of employment are areas in which the Community enjoys fairly general legislative powers. Protection of fundamental rights could therefore be ensured by the Community legislating directly rather than relying on third parties to complement the general measures that it adopts. The problem of lack of 'horizontal' application of fundamental rights provisions could therefore be avoided in this way in at least some cases. Still, this would mean having to renounce the new forms of governance. Those new forms of governance are here for a reason. Their 'irresistible rise'[58] is linked to the inability of the Community to regulate, whether for practical reasons linked to the complexity of the issues to regulate or out of legitimacy concerns.[59] From this perspective, it would have been preferable for the Charter to engage with new governance rather than attempt to suppress it.

Even where the EU institutions can impose human rights obligations on non-governmental actors, it is still not clear the extent to which a binding Charter would impose a duty on them to do so. If the Charter, explicitly or implicitly, requires the EU to 'protect' the fundamental rights of individuals, this would seem *prima facie* to impose on the institutions a duty to act when such rights are at risk of being infringed by non-state actors. Yet, this might prove more difficult than it seems. In the first place, the wording of the Charter does not always lend itself to the discovery of an obligation to protect rather than a simple obligation to observe. Secondly, the Court has generally recognised a wide legislative discretion to the institutions and, to that extent, has been reluctant to find legally binding obligations to act.[60] For instance, even though Article 141(3) EC would seem to require the institutions to take measures to '*ensure* the application of the principle of equal opportunities and equal treatment of men and women in matters of employment and occupation,'[61] it is doubtful that it would be interpreted by the Court as imposing a duty to act enforceable under Article 232 EC. Similarly, even though the Community has wide powers under Articles 12–13 EC in the field of discrimination law, it is doubtful that the Charter would have the effect of requiring us to read a duty to act under these provisions. Indeed, Article 51(2) EUCFR expressly states that the Charter does not 'modify powers and tasks defined by the Treaties.'

---

[58] To paraphrase Joerges's comment on the 'irresistible rise of the committee system': C Joerges, 'Bureaucratic Nightmare, Technocratic Regime and the Dream of Good Transnational Governance' in C Joerges and E Vos (eds), *EU Committees: Social Regulation, Law and Politics* (Oxford, Hart Publishing, 1999) 3–17 at 3.

[59] See above n 32 and related text. See also the discussion in N Bernard, *Multilevel Governance in the European Union* (The Hague, London, Kluwer Law International, 2002) at 234 *et seq.*

[60] But see case C–68/95 *T Port GmbH & Co KG v Bundesanstalt für Landwirtschaft und Ernährung* [1996] ECR I–6065, in which the Court suggested that the institutions might be under a duty to act where failure to do so would result in a breach of fundamental rights. This, however, was in the context of a legal regime established by Community law and concerned the application of supplementary, transitional measures.

[61] Emphasis added.

Furthermore, an applicant seeking to enforce a duty on the institutions to act to protect fundamental rights, or, for that matter, seeking the annulment of a measure taken by the institutions violating fundamental rights, would still have to face the stringent *locus standi* requirements of Articles 230 and 232 EC. In particular, the individual would have to establish that (s)he is directly and individually concerned by the act under challenge or the act whose adoption is requested. In *Jégo-Quéré*,[62] the Court of First Instance (CFI) was willing to relax somewhat the current restrictive regime on *locus standi* and allow an applicant whose legal position is affected by the measure 'in a manner which is both definite and immediate, by restricting his rights or by imposing obligations on him.'[63] The CFI was concerned that the strict application of current criteria on the notion of individual concern could result in a breach of the right to an effective remedy, enshrined in the ECHR and enforced in the Community legal order as a general principle of law, and 'reaffirmed Article 47 of the Charter of Fundamental Rights of the European Union.'[64] In doing so, the CFI was following the lead of Advocate General Jacobs in *UPA*,[65] who had also suggested a relaxation of the individual concern test.[66] The Court of Justice, on the other hand, was more reticent in its judgment in *UPA*. While admitting in principle that the concept of individual concern should be interpreted in the light of the principle of effective judicial protection, 'such an interpretation cannot have the effect of setting aside the condition in question.'[67] The Court firmly indicated that it did not see itself as having the power to amend the system of remedies in a more liberal way and that it was for the Member States to do so through an amendment to the Treaty if they so wished.[68]

The judgment of the Court in *UPA* is also important in another respect. When discussing the implications of the right to an effective remedy, the Court stressed the primary role played by the legal system of Member States in protecting the rights of individuals. If there is some deficiency in the system of remedies, 'it is for the Member States to establish a system of legal remedies and procedures which ensure respect for the right to effective judicial protection.'[69] Thus, the Court is unwilling to draw consequences for Community norms from fundamental rights standards when competence falls primarily in the hands of the Member States. This is potentially of great relevance for socio-economic rights, where formal competence also falls primarily in the hands of the Member States.

---

[62] Case T–177/01 *Jégo-Quéré v Commission* [2002] ECR II–2365.
[63] At para 51 of the judgment.
[64] At para 42.
[65] Case C–50/00 *Unión de Pequeños Agricultores v Council* [2002] ECR I–6677.
[66] The AG suggested that a person should be regarded as individually concerned by a Community measure 'where, by reason of his particular circumstances, the measure has, or is liable to have, a substantial adverse effect on his interests.' (see para 103 of the opinion)
[67] At para 44 of the judgment.
[68] See para 45 of the judgment.
[69] See paras 40–41 of the judgment.

The judicial route to enforcement of socio-economic rights contained in the Charter thus appears paved with obstacles. Other strategies than judicial enforcement are, however, conceivable. In the previous section, new modes of governance were approached as an object over which to project the standards of the Charter and we have seen that this presented us with major difficulties. However, the approach can be reversed and new methods of governance, in particular the Open Method of Co-ordination, be used as a vehicle for the pursuit of a social and cultural rights agenda.

In principle, there are several advantages in approaching social and cultural rights from the perspective of the Open Method of Co-ordination rather than a judicial route: (i) it takes the sting out of the competence issue; (ii) it is arguably better suited to the complexity of social and economic rights than a judicial approach and (iii) it potentially affords a more involved participation of disadvantaged groups in the definition of policy. Each of these issues will be considered in turn.

Competence

That Community competence and interference with Member States powers remains a sensitive issue is obvious from the Charter itself. Not only does Article 51(1) EUCFR specify that the Charter is addressed to EU institutions and *not* Member States, except when implementing EU law, but it was also felt necessary to confirm that the Charter cannot constitute the legal basis for Community action and neither confers any new power on the EU nor modifies any existing one.

If the Community is to go beyond merely respecting fundamental social and cultural rights and is expected to engage in protecting and fulfilling those rights, one would be forced to conclude prima facie that, outside the labour law field,[70] it does not have the competence to do so.

However, in terms of determining key priorities, formal competence has lost much of its significance. The Open Method of Co-ordination has now become the instrument of choice for overall policy orientation. Notwithstanding the possibilities opened by the Social Chapter since Maastricht/Amsterdam, OMC-style co-ordination under the Employment Title of the EC Treaty is the mainstay of social policy.[71] Even the traditional core area of the internal market has

---

[70] But see the contributions of J Kenner and B Ryan in this collection.

[71] See the Commission Communication on the Social Policy Agenda for 2000–2005: 'the new Social Policy Agenda does not seek to harmonise social policies. It seeks to work towards common European objectives and increase co-ordination of social policies in the context of the internal market and the single currency.' COM(2000) 379 at 7.

ceased to be an area of policy in its own right to become subsumed in the wider context of an economic policy the parameters of which are defined through OMC methods.[72]

The Open Method of Co-ordination softens the edges of the competence debate. Based on soft instruments, it makes little demands in terms of hard powers for the EC/EU. Primarily oriented towards exchanging views and experiences and promoting 'best practice', it is able to reach sensitive areas of policy where harmonisation or other hard measures are excluded. Yet, the experience acquired in those areas where it has been operating for a number of years, such as employment and economic policy, indicates that OMC processes can shape the frame of reference and belief system within which domestic policies are conceived and implemented.[73]

As Weiler has argued, what the Community needs is not so much a Charter of Rights as a *human rights policy*.[74] The usefulness of the Open Method lies in its ability to constitute a vehicle for the EU to develop such a policy on social and cultural rights in a situation of limited competence. In this respect, the use of the Open Method in the field of social exclusion shows the way forward.

Complexity

Economic and social rights sceptics often distinguish these from civil and political rights on the ground that the former impose positive obligations on states with substantial resource implications whereas the latter impose negative obligations and are cost-free. Their opponents are quick to point out the lack of foundation of the argument and, indeed, the artificiality of a purported distinction between both categories of rights on such a ground. Civil and political rights can also impose positive obligations and have a cost. Ensuring humane conditions of detention for prisoners, for instance, has a cost. The fact that the implementation of a right has resource implications can affect how the issue is approached by courts and the kind of remedy available for breach of the right. It is not, however, an obstacle to justiciability per se. Indeed, courts in a number of jurisdictions have developed an elaborate jurisprudence on the enforcement of socio-economic rights.[75]

---

[72] See N Bernard, 'Flexibility in the European Single Market' in C Barnard and J Scott (eds), *The Law of the Single Market—Unpacking the Premises* (Oxford, Hart Publishing, 2002) 101–22 at 114 *et seq*.

[73] See C de la Porte, 'Is the Open Method of Co-ordination Appropriate for Organising Activities at European Level in Sensitive Policy Areas?' (2002) 8 *European Law Journal* 38.

[74] See JHH Weiler, 'Editorial comments: Does the European Union Truly Need a Charter of Rights?' (2000) 6 *European Law Journal* 95 at 96.

[75] See, for instance, the judgment of the Supreme Court of India in *Olga Tellis v Bombay Municipal Corporation*, (1986) AIR SC 18. For a discussion of the justiciability of socio-economic rights in the South African Constitution, see the *Certification* judgment of the South African Constitutional Court: *Ex Parte Chairperson of the Constitutional Assembly: In re Certification of the Constitution of the Republic of South Africa, 1996* 1996 (4) SA 744 (CC); 1996 (10) BCLR 1253 (CC) para 78.

Economic and social rights, however, create difficulties for courts because of the high degree of complexity of the issues they usually raise. The legal system would put its credibility in jeopardy by imposing obligations, which cannot be satisfied by those to whom they are addressed. This is reflected in the tendency of courts to recognise, when determining the scope of socio-economic rights, that public authorities are entitled to take into account available resources and prioritise actions on this basis.[76] 'Available resources', however, is but a short-hand to signify the variety of ways in which socio-economic deprivation can be addressed and the absence of any privileged route to tackle these issues.

It is worth noting, in this respect, that national constitutional courts often refer to the social and historical context of bills of rights and constitutions to provide them with the frame of reference within which their provisions be understood. Thus, the Supreme Court of India in *Samity*[77] drew from the fact that the Constitution envisaged the establishment of a welfare state at the federal level implications as to the extent to which the State was obliged to provide free medical treatment in public hospitals. Similarly, the South African Supreme Court repeatedly referred to the need to place socio-economic rights within the Constitution in the context of the 'difficulty confronting the state in the light of our history in addressing issues concerned with the basic needs of people.'[78] In Canada, the Supreme Court referred to the constitutional history of the development of the Canadian Federation to extract key Constitutional principles on which to evaluate whether Québec could lawfully unilaterally secede from Canada.[79]

From this perspective, the historical and social context of the Charter would offer the courts little room for manoeuvre. The EU does not have a coherent economic and social 'model' which could serve as the bedrock for the development of a socio-economic rights jurisprudence. While the phrase 'European Social Model' has been much in use by the Commission in the last decade, such a model is only discernible, Hervey notes, at a high level of abstraction.[80] For Padraig Flynn, former EU Social Affairs Commissioner, it is a 'system steeped in plurality and diversity—reflecting our richness of culture, tradition and political development . . . conceived and applied in many different ways, by many agents,' the essential idea of which consists in the balancing of two principles: competition on the one hand and solidarity between citizens on the other.[81]

---

[76] See, eg the judgment of the South African Constitutional Court in *Minister of Health and others v Treatment Action Campaign (TAC) and others*, CCT 8/02 (5 July 2002).

[77] *Paschim Banga Khet Mazdoor Samity and others v State of West Bengal and another* (1996) AIR SC 2426.

[78] *Minister of Health v TAC*, above n 76 at para 24, referring the the Court's previous judgment in *Government of the Republic of South Africa and Others v Grootboom and Others* 2001 (1) SA 46 (CC); 2000 (11) BCLR 1169 (CC) at paras 93–94.

[79] *Reference re Secession of Quebec* [1998] 2 SCR 217.

[80] T Hervey, 'Social Solidarity: A Buttress Against Internal Market Law?' in J Shaw (ed), *Social Law and Policy in an evolving European Union* (Oxford, Hart Publishing, 2000) 31–47 at 43.

[81] Speech for the conference 'Visions for European Governance' held at Harvard University, 2 March 1999, cited in T Hervey, *ibid*.

The Charter itself, notably through its frequent reference to 'national law and practices' qualifying the contents of many socio-economic rights,[82] is anchored in a vision characterised by diversity of practices and approaches to fundamental socio-economic rights rather than uniformity.

Judicial enforcement is not impossible in such a context, but it is bound to be very limited if it is to leave room for diverse approaches. A reasonableness test might be suitable for these purposes. However, a reasonableness test coupled with the fact that competence in the field is pre-eminently in the hands of the Member States and that the Charter does not apply to autonomous action by the Member States is likely to make the socio-economic rights contained in the Charter an irrelevance from a judicial perspective. A more promising route would consist of using the Charter as a springboard for the development of standards from which compliance with the Charter can be assessed, albeit not necessarily in a judicial context. The UN Committee on Economic, Social and Cultural rights has advocated the development of benchmarks as an appropriate tool for evaluating compliance with the International Covenant on Economic, Social and Cultural Rights (ICESCR) in a context of diversity.[83] There is much to be said for such an approach to be adopted in the EU. Developing benchmarks, however, is not a task that can effectively be undertaken in a judicial environment. The Open Method of Co-ordination constitutes the most obvious vehicle for the development of such benchmarks and assessment of Member States compliance with them. The central question with the OMC, however, is whether it can be structured in such a way as to allow for meaningful participation.

Participation

Courts are sometimes viewed as mechanisms to increase participation in decision-making by giving voice to those who have difficulties in making themselves heard through political processes, for instance where they are excluded from the political process altogether or where, in the context of a majority process, they are part of a structural minority. It is however, a mode of participation, which has severe limitations.

One of the most stringent limitations is that claims and arguments have to be framed within legal language and modes of reasoning. In particular, arguments have to be structured alongside the lawful/unlawful dichotomy, on the basis of categories provided for by the legal system. As Armstrong notes, law projects its substantive rules and normative visions onto social struggles and removes them

---

[82] The limited competence of the Community in the field and the non-applicability of the Charter to autonomous Member State action are also of relevance here.

[83] See P Alston, 'Making Economic and Social Rights Count: A Strategy for the Future' (1997) 68 *Political Quarterly* 188 at 191–93.

from their social context.[84] Admittedly, any system or forum imposes its own language and code of what counts as a valid or invalid, effective or ineffective utterance. This is true of political processes just as much as legal ones. However, legal processes are arguably especially constraining. Secondly, participation through the legal process is haphazard and fragmented. It depends on the identification of an appropriate case to act as a vehicle for the argument[85] and participants will be limited to the parties to the case rather than a broad-based dialogue involving all relevant interests.

The Open Method does not suffer from the same shortcomings and, as such, it constitutes an attractive alternative to the judicial enforcement route. In principle, the very concept of OMC is premised on the participation of all stakeholders throughout the policy chain and the agenda is not restricted to the narrow code of legality/illegality. This being said, one should remain aware of the limitations of the format in any likely implementation.

From this perspective, one cannot ignore the institutional embedding of the dominance of EMU and economic co-ordination processes over social policy and fundamental rights considerations. At the Lisbon European Council in March 2000, it was decided that the opinion of different formations of the Council should be taken into account in the formulation of the Broad Economic Policy Guidelines. While this could, in theory, signal a more balanced approach and a diminution of the hegemony of ECOFIN, one can doubt the extent to which this would suffice to 'upgrade' social policy considerations in EU economic policy formation.[86]

The Open Method is premised on a consensual approach, which does not lend itself well to direct challenges to firmly established policies. For this reason, some NGOs may prefer to stay aloof from any process of this kind and opt for direct confrontation. From their perspective, a legally binding Charter which could be used to challenge EU economic policy could, in principle, be seen as prima facie more useful. However, since such a strategy would pre-suppose challenging either Member State autonomous action in the social and economic field or 'soft' EU processes, neither of which can easily be reached through judicial enforcement of the Charter, the benefits to be expected here are extremely limited. An OMC process for the purpose of implementing the Charter, offering the perspective of a public debate on National Action Plans for Fundamental Rights followed by exchange of views in the Council would seem a more promising way to introduce into EU decision-making processes a fundamental rights discourse which is at present virtually absent.

---

[84] K Armstrong, 'Legal integration: Theorizing the Legal Dimension of European Integration' (1998) 36 *Journal of Common Market Studies* 155 at 166.
[85] Neither should we forget that it requires sufficient resources to finance the litigation.
[86] See C de la Porte, above n 73 at 44.

CONCLUSION

Judicial enforcement and the Open Method of Co-ordination are not mutually exclusive means of carrying forward a fundamental economic, social and cultural rights agenda. Clearly, there will be situations where a judicially enforceable Charter could be useful, as the examples given in some contributions to this volume show. In terms of significance, however, judicial enforcement is likely to remain limited. If political capital has to be spent, my contention is that it is better used arguing for the development of an OMC process for the purposes of developing and reviewing compliance with the Charter than relying on courts to do so. An OMC process would allow the Charter to be considered where, as far as socio-economic and cultural policies are concerned, it matters most, most specifically in the context of *national* social and cultural policies. It would allow for greater adaptation of the Charter to the circumstances of each Member State and, as such, would be likely to enjoy more support from the Member States governments and their citizens. It would be the starting point for the development of a European discourse on fundamental social and cultural rights, something which is absent even in areas where fundamental rights seem prima facie highly relevant, such as social exclusion. Crucially, it could provide the framework for what, as some commentators have argued,[87] the EU needs more than a catalogue of rights: a fundamental rights *policy*.

---

[87] P Alston and JHH Weiler, 'An "Ever Closer Union" in Need of a Human Rights Policy: The European Union and Human Rights' (1998) 4 *European Journal of International Law* 658.

12

The Double Constitutional Life of the Charter of Fundamental Rights of the European Union

MIGUEL POIARES MADURO*

L ET ME START with a cliché: the Charter of Fundamental Rights of the European Union represents a constitutional paradox. It reflects an emerging trend to agree on the use of the language of constitutionalism in European integration without agreeing on the conception of constitutionalism underlying such language. For some, the Charter is the foundation upon which to build a true constitutional project for the European Union. It will promote the construction of a European political identity and mobilise European citizens around it. For others, the Charter is simply a constitutional guarantee that the European Union will not threaten the constitutional values of the Member States. It is a constitutional limit to the process of European integration. The Charter reflects this tension between its conception as a constitutional instrument for polity building and its conception as a simple consolidation of the previous fundamental rights *acquis* aimed at guaranteeing regime legitimacy.[1] These two conceptions confronted each other in the drafting of the Charter[2] and are reflected in many of its provisions. It is thus difficult to clearly establish the nature of the relationship between the Charter and European Constitutionalism. Much will depend on which of those two constitutional conceptions becomes the dominant constitutional discourse on the Charter.

---

* New University of Lisbon. This chapter stems from a paper prepared for a workshop on the Charter at the University of Nottingham in June 2002. I would like to thank the participants at the workshop (in particular the commentator, Joanne Scott). I would also like to thank the participants at conferences organised by the Instituto Ortega y Gasset (Madrid) and the Universidad de Zaragoza for comments on earlier versions.

[1] On the notion of regime legitimacy see below.

[2] See further, G de Búrca, 'The Drafting of the European Union Charter of Fundamental Rights' (2001) 26 *European Law Review* 126. It was also reflected in the different justifications advanced to justify the need for an EU Charter of Fundamental Rights. As stated by McCrudden: 'these justifications often point to entirely different models of a human rights Charter', see *The Future of the EU Charter of Fundamental Rights*, Jean Monnet Paper No 10/01, including contributions by C McCrudden, G de Burca and J Dutheil de la Rochèle, available at http://www.jeanmonnetprogram.org/papers/papers01.html; at 9.

In this chapter I will review the impact of the Charter on European Constitutionalism, identifying and taking into account the underlying tension between those constitutional conceptions of the Charter. They are not linked, however, to a particular position on the legal value that ought to be given to the Charter. As a consequence, the analysis undertaken in this chapter is not dominated by the debate on the binding legal value of the Charter. In some cases, the impact of the Charter on the European Constitution will be largely independent of its legal value. In other cases, however, that impact may vary depending on whether or not the Charter will have binding legal value.[3] Thus, in some instances I will assume that the Charter will be given some form of binding legal value as the work of the current Convention on the Future of Europe appears to indicate.[4] But I will also highlight current instances in which the discussion on the legal value to be given to the Charter identifies different perceptions of its constitutional impact.

The discussion on the constitutional dimensions of the Charter will also be linked to the current constitutional debate on the future of Europe. It now appears clear that both the Convention and the Inter-governmental Conference of 2004 will adopt some form of constitutional document for the EU. But this agreement on constitutional language may hide two different conceptions on the role of constitutionalism in the EU. Such conceptions are already identifiable in the Charter. In this way, the analysis of the Charter gains added importance in the discussion of the constitutional future of the EU.

I will begin by discussing how the Charter affects the constitutionalisation of the EU; how it constitutes a different form of constitution-making in the EU; and what are and/or ought to be the consequences for the current constitutional debates on the Future of Europe. Following that, I will review the impact of the Charter on the *acquis communautaire* and the current constitutional model of the EU regarding both its institutional balances and its constitutional values. I will address issues such as the impact of the Charter on the role of the Community courts, the scope of application of EU fundamental rights and the balance between the different constitutional values of the EU. Here, the scope

---

[3] For further discussion see the chapters by N Bernard and J Kenner in this collection. For Vitorino, the Commission representative at the Convention on the Charter and now responsible for the working group on the Charter in the current Convention, there is no doubt that the Charter will have binding legal effect, the only question is when and how. See A Vitorino, *The Charter of Fundamental Rights as a Foundation for the Area of Freedom Security and Justice*, Exeter Paper in European Law No 4, available at http://www.uaces.org/RP-1-CM.pdf_. For an analysis of the different possible forms of legal effect of the Charter independently from an express attribution of binding legal value, see: A Menéndez, 'Chartering Europe: Legal Status and Policy Implications of the Charter of Fundamental Rights of the European Union' (2002) 40 *Journal of Common Market Studies*, 471 at 472 ff.

[4] The European Council's Laeken Declaration of December 2001 establishes this as one of the key issues to be dealt with by the Convention on the Future of Europe. Available at: http://europa.eu.int/council/off/conclu/. The forms through which the Charter may acquire some form of binding legal value vary and they have already been identified in the Convention.

for the Charter's social rights to correct the 'social deficit' in the EU's constitutional values will be discussed. Next, I will discuss the polity building value of such a constitutional document: will it help in forming a European political community and legitimising the process of European integration? Finally, I will review the impact of the Charter on the relationship between the EU legal order and national constitutions, notably on the issue of ultimate legal and political authority.

THE CHARTER AND CONSTITUTION-MAKING IN THE EUROPEAN UNION

The process of constitutionalisation of the European Communities[5] has been mainly a functional development from a set of Treaty rules centred on the promotion of a common market. Europe's constitutional dimension has, therefore, been closely linked with the logic of economic integration. Europe assumed a constitutional body without a constitutional soul: it lacked a process of truly constitutional deliberation. In some respects, the process of constitutionalisation was an unintended consequence of an inter-governmental bargaining among states, albeit later ratified by the political practice of those states. As is well known, those constitutional consequences were mainly a product of the European Court of Justice (the Court). In this way, some perceive the process of constitutionalisation as an illegitimate expansion of the ambitions of the European integration project. Others accept and favour such constitutionalisation but see it as lacking a full constitutional expression backed by a classic process of constitutional deliberation. The Charter reflects these two perspectives. It marks a departure from the traditional way of 'doing constitutional business' in Europe and it does so by embracing a process of deliberation much closer to the traditional forms of constitutional deliberation. But the way in which such a process is embarked upon reflects two different constitutional perspectives. There are those that accepted the idea of a Charter of Fundamental Rights because they saw it mainly as a process of codification of EU fundamental rights which had already been recognised in the Treaties, legislation or the case law of the Court. The Charter would both reinforce the limits on EU powers and reinstate the States' control over the process of constitutionalisation. There are others, instead, who perceived the Charter as the starting point of a truly constitutional deliberative process and the construction of a European political identity. The role attributed to the Convention, its composition and its decision-making process reflected elements from these two perspectives.

As is now well known, it was decided at the Cologne European Council of June 1999 'to establish a Charter of fundamental rights in order to make their

---

[5] I dispense myself from citing the numerous works on the process of European Constitutionalisation. For all, see JHH Weiler, *The Constitution of Europe* (Cambridge, Cambridge University Press, 1999).

overriding importance and relevance more visible to the Union's citizens'.[6] This aim limited the ambitions of the Charter: the proclaimed goal was to make the protection of fundamental rights already provided for in the EU more visible to its citizens and not to change the nature and scope of that protection. This was reinforced by the attribution to the Charter of a mere role of consolidating the fundamental rights already recognised in the EU legal order. Seen in this light, the Charter would mainly serve as an additional instrument of constitutional control over the EU and not of constitutional building of its polity. It would reassure that the EU would not threaten the national constitutional values identified with the protection of fundamental rights, and, by making these rights clearer for European citizens, it would increase the degree of review of the powers exercised by the EU. Furthermore, it would reinstate political control over the EU catalogue of fundamental rights which, so far, had been mainly determined by the case law of the Court.

But the Council also agreed on an innovative process to draft the Charter. A body, that came to be known as the Convention, was set up to prepare the draft. It was composed of representatives of the Heads of State and Government and of the President of the Commission as well as of members of the European Parliament and national parliaments.[7] Its specific composition and working methods were established by the Tampere Council.[8] Though the legal status to be assumed by the Charter was left open,[9] the Convention decided to work on the assumption that the Charter would ultimately be given binding legal effect. Though such a process also presented elements reflecting the narrower constitutional discourse on the Charter (the role attributed to national parliaments may be seen as ascertaining that Europe's constitution-making can only proceed through national polities), it constituted, in many other respects, a constitutional breakthrough for those that argue in favour of the adoption of a real process of constitutional deliberation in the EU.[10] It may not to be an overstatement to say that the most important constitutional dimension of the Charter stems from its process of deliberation. Though ultimately adopted simply as a declaration from the EU institutions, the Charter was the result of a drafting process that constituted a kind of constitution-making experiment for

---

[6] Cologne European Council 3–4 June 1999, Presidency Conclusions, paras 44–45 and Annex IV. Available at: http://europa.eu.int/council/off/conclu/.

[7] *Ibid* Annex IV.

[8] Tampere European Council 15–16 October 1999, Presidency Conclusions, Annex on the Composition, Method of Work and Practical Arrangements for the Body to Elaborate a Draft EU Charter of Fundamental Rights. Available at: http://europa.eu.int/council/off/conclu/.

[9] 'The European Council will propose to the European Parliament and the Commission that, together with the Council, they should solemnly proclaim on the basis of the draft document a European Charter of Fundamental Rights. It will then have to be considered whether and, if so, how the Charter should be integrated into the treaties. The European Council mandates the General Affairs Council to take the necessary steps prior to the Tampere European Council'. *Ibid* Annex IV.

[10] On the issue of constitutional deliberation in the EU see EO Eriksen and JE Fossum (eds), *Democracy in the European Union—Integration Through Deliberation?* (London, Routledge, 2000).

the EU. Instead of being subject to the traditional inter-governmental process, the drafting of the Charter was the product of a different kind of process: the Convention. The proclaimed success of such a method led to a similar method being adopted in the context of the current constitutional process on the Future of Europe. In this sense, the Convention on the Charter consisted of an experiment in constitution-making that spilled over into the current Convention on the Future of Europe. Therefore, the extent to which this method truly has a constitutional character and the impact it may have in the outcome of the current debates can, at least in part, be assessed by looking at the convention method of the Charter.

But what makes such process more 'constitutional'? And how does it impact on the constitutional outcome? Usually, the stress is placed on the broader scope of representation entailed in such a method. As stated, the Convention was composed of representatives of the EU institutions, national parliaments and national governments. It also promoted a broader participation from the so-called civil society (though the extent to which it did so successfully is a cause of dispute).[11] However, its constitutional characterisation can also be linked to other elements. The constitutional character of this process must be discussed not only in the light of its scope of representation, but also by taking into account the character of its deliberative process and the balance between the political and judicial roles in the constitutionalisation of the EU. The convention method presents, with regard to these three aspects, a major departure from the two traditional methods of constitutional development in the EU: the inter-governmental process and judicial activism.

The Scope of Representation

As stated, the Convention drew its participants from a much broader pool of institutions. In particular, the role played by national parliaments and the European Parliament was aimed at expressing a more direct link with European citizens. These institutions (notably, national parliaments) are seen as providing a form of direct representation that national governments lack. In this sense, the convention method, by comparison with the inter-governmental method, appears closer to a constitutional convention with direct representatives of the people reflecting different social interests. But also the representatives of the national governments reflected a pattern of representation different from the classical inter-governmental process. In some cases, though not in all, they were independent personalities selected in view of their technical and/or political experience and not as representatives of the state. This might also have been the case because national governments did not fully grasp the potential impact of

---

[11] See de Búrca, above n 2 at 132 and JB Liisberg, 'Does the EU Charter of Fundamental Rights Threaten the Supremacy of Community Law' (2001) 38 *Common Market Law Review* 1171 at 1182.

the Convention. It was forecasted by some mainly as an intellectual exercise that would then be subject to the political impact of the inter-governmental process. Yet, once again, the 'being' escaped the control of its creator and it is now clear that, whatever the legal status that will ultimately be accorded to the Charter, its content will essentially, if not fully, correspond to that agreed at the Convention.[12]

The approximation to a constitutional model of deliberation 'by the people' was also promoted by the added legitimacy that the Convention attempted to draw from the broader participation of individuals and social groups whose contributions were asked for and stimulated (albeit not always taken into account).[13] At least theoretically, civil society's participation was furthered and a strong emphasis was placed on making the debates more transparent for public opinion. This mirrors an idea of constitutional deliberation for Europe: constitutional moments are identified with a much broader mobilisation of society and a higher degree of direct participation from citizens.[14] The deliberative process on the Charter would enhance Europe's constitutionalisation by promoting such broad involvement and, at the same time, would help legitimise it.

The Character of Deliberation

The second major difference brought in by the convention method relates to the way deliberation is expected to take place and the nature of the contract arising thereof. Inter-governmental conferences have as their purpose the production of an agreement between states. A forum of inter-governmental bargaining is expected to reduce information and transaction costs between states facilitating the adoption of co-operative decisions. Each state departs from a pre-definition of the national interest that it attempts to promote and harmonise with the interests of the other states. This inter-governmental bargaining is quite different from the nature of the deliberative process usually identified with the framing of constitutions. In the latter, the vision of a social contract appears with its

---

[12] This explains why some national governments decided to appoint national ministers or other public officials as their representatives in the current Convention on the Future of Europe. This has been reinforced in the recent past by the changes undertaken by some States in their representation. Many States now perceive the Convention as potentially more important than the 2004 IGC in shaping the future of the EU. This inter-governmentalisation of the Convention may, however, undermine some of the constitutional aspects of its deliberation.

[13] Liisberg notes that 'even if the Charter process was extraordinarily open, the drafting history of individual provisions is far from transparent. In some ways, tracking provisions of human rights conventions drawn up at diplomatic conferences under the auspices of the United Nations is easier. The uniquely pluralistic and diverse process for the drafting has much to be said for it, in terms of popular participation and legitimacy, especially as compared to the traditional very secretive treaty-making process of the EU. But such a process may also enhance and disguise the power of the draftsmen who lurk behind the piles of drafts and amendments, and may thus paradoxically produce less, rather than more, accountability and transparency'. Above n 11 at 1182.

[14] For an in depth analysis see B Ackerman, *We The People, Vol I: Foundations* (Cambridge, Harvard University Press, 1991).

universal underpinnings. Deliberation is seen as an agreement among individuals on the basis of universally constructed rules under a hypothetic veil of ignorance. The framers of a constitution are seen as rational actors in search of universal rules that can best satisfy everyone's future interests.

This form of constitutional deliberation is substantially different from inter-governmental bargaining even when we realise that every constitutional deliberation is shaped and influenced by the specific interests of the participants and the contexts from which and within which they deliberate. The difference arises from four elements that the convention method expresses, albeit in an imperfect manner. First, the expectation is that an overall political contract will be produced and not simply a particular negotiation on certain opposing interests; this helps to detach participants from their contextual standpoints and to take an overall long term perspective that is more conducive to the universal rules typical of a constitutional contract. Second, the creation of a forum of stable long-term deliberation, instead of the short-term highly concentrated (though previously prepared) inter-governmental conferences, shifts the attitude of participants towards the process of deliberation itself and promotes higher mutual trust, stronger involvement and a more rational engagement between the participants. Thirdly, the participants in the convention are expected to consist of more independent individuals, more committed to certain rational conceptions of the common good than to pre-established assertions of the national interest. Even when that is not the case, because, for example, national governments appoint public officials as their representatives in the convention, the convention method still promotes a more open deliberation on the part of the participants. This is due to the circumstance that the 'national interest' is not represented by a particular single representative at the process of negotiation. The variety of national participants both releases them from being the individual guardians of a pre-defined national interest and challenges their respective notions of that national interest. The fourth and final element of constitutional differentiation of the convention deliberative method regards its potential higher transparency. The subjection of the deliberative process to higher transparency requires arguments to be put forward in terms of universal rules of a social contract and not as a defence of the national interest. This change in the character of the arguments that participants can use will end up reflecting itself in the agreements that they will reach.

It is wrong, however, to adopt an idealist perspective of the convention method. On the one hand, this process entrusts a great degree of authority to those that shape the agenda and provide the technical expertise and legal drafting required. The 'independence' and lack of in-depth expertise of many of the participants make them much more dependent on the EU technocracy.[15] At the same time, in such a large scale and comprehensive project, the Praesidium and Secretariat assume a key role in setting the agenda, processing the different

---

[15] De Búrca, above n 2 and Liisberg, above n 11 at 1178.

amendment proposals and drafting final versions. This is visible in the process of drafting the Charter, and in particular in the tremendous impact that the EU technocracy and the Praesidium had on the final versions of the more contentious provisions, particularly when compared with the degree of incorporation of the amendments proposed by other participants at the Convention and civil society.[16]

The Politicisation of Europe's Constitutionalisation

The third constitutional change introduced by the Convention method on Europe's constitution-making was a reinstatement of political control over the constitutional development of European integration. As said above, it is well known that the constitutionalisation of Community law has been a judicially driven process. The introduction of fundamental rights protection was a key example of the role of the Court in that constitutionalisation. It was the Court that introduced a system of fundamental rights protection in the European Communities and it was the Court that controlled such a catalogue through the criteria it itself developed.[17] In this instance, the political process ended up simply ratifying the constitution-making of the Court by restating it in Article 6(2) TEU. The drafting of a Charter of Fundamental Rights constitutes in this light a challenge to the role of the Court in the constitutionalisation of the EU. It is the political process taking back into its own hands the definition of the system and catalogue of fundamental rights in the EU. There are important consequences that can be expected in the outcomes arising from these two different processes, as both representation and the form of deliberation differ between them. It also impacts on the sources of law and its process of discovery that have dominated the European Constitution. In the absence of a written constitution, the Court has constitutionalised the European Communities (now the EU) by reference to the constitutional principles of its Member States. The European Constitution becomes, in this light, mainly a product of both the EU Treaties and national constitutions, and it is upon these sources that the constitutional values of the emerging polity are to be found by the Court. Once the EU political process takes over, EU constitutional values become a product of a transnational political deliberative process that takes place at EU level. The dynamics of this new constitutional political arena are bound to determine a different set of constitutional values. It is this that explains some of the substantive constitutional changes introduced by the Charter even if, in theory, it was not supposed to be more than a simple consolidation of the pre-existent fundamental rights.

---

[16] See Liisberg, above n 11 at 1178 and de Búrca, above n 3.

[17] For a presentation of such process see B de Witte, 'The Past and Future Role of the European Court of Justice in the Protection of Human Rights' in Alston (ed) *The EU and Human Rights* (Oxford, Oxford University Press, 1999) pp 859–97 at 863–69.

THE CHARTER AND THE CONSTITUTION

The Charter was officially proclaimed to be nothing more than an exercise in codification and consolidation of the rights that were already recognised in the Treaties, the Court's case law and Community legislation. The aim was not to alter the substance of fundamental rights protection in the EU but to make that protection clearer for European citizens. That was expected to promote a more effective application of those rights and, at the same time, reinforce the legitimacy of the integration process. It is this that also explains why the attribution of binding legal effect was not considered to be a priority. However, the final product is much more complex. The duplicity of constitutional discourses on the Charter also comes to light in its catalogue of rights that is broader than what would simply result from the consolidation of previous Community legislation, Treaty provisions and the Court's case law. In fact, the Charter constitutes the most comprehensive catalogue of rights adopted in many years.[18] On the other hand, the scope of application of these rights is substantially limited in its horizontal provisions. This expresses once again the dual constitutional conceptions of the Charter identified above. Its reading as a novel and ambitious constitutional document or as a simple consolidation of the previous fundamental rights *acquis* will ultimately determine the degree of its impact on the content of the European Constitution. And the Charter can, in effect, produce important changes in the values and institutional balances of the European Constitution. Even if seen as a simple dogmatic restatement of the pre-existent rights in EU law it is bound to impact on the constitutional conception of the rights affirmed in the Treaties, case law and legislation. It is sufficient to read some of the rights developed in the Charter to see that its content is altered, albeit in a context of restatement of a previously existent right (the wording of the right to property,[19] for example, is closer to the case law of the European Court of Human Rights than of the European Court of Justice). Consider also how the systematic placing of the rights may alter their future interpretation and the balance with conflicting rights and values. The legal dogmatic reconstruction of an existent landscape of rights will inevitably change that landscape. But the extent to which it will do so and the sense in which the change will take place will depend on which constitutional conception of the Charter will become dominant. The following are a few important examples of possible constitutional impacts and of their interaction with the alternative constitutional conceptions of the Charter.

---

[18] G Sacerdoti, 'The European Charter of Fundamental Rights: From a Nation State Europe to a Citizens Europe' (2002) *Columbia Journal of European Law* 37 at 43.
[19] Art 17 EUCFR.

The Standard of Fundamental Rights Protection

What impact may the Charter have on the standard of fundamental rights protection guaranteed by the Court? For those that believe that the Court 'has not taken fundamental rights seriously',[20] the Charter may be seen as requiring from the Court a more sophisticated and more clearly articulated approach in this area of the law. German scholarship, in particular, has expressed some degree of concern with the level of fundamental rights protection accorded by the Court and, as a result, has tended to see in the Charter an attempt to promote the adoption of a higher standard of fundamental rights protection by the Court.[21] One author has remarked that the Charter,

> by convincing the ECJ of the overall importance of the protection of fundamental rights it can lead the ECJ to accept that this is the principal mission it has to accomplish.[22]

Yet, though some specific problems may at times have been highlighted in the Court's approach,[23] there has never been any sustained widespread challenge to the decisions of the Court in the area of fundamental rights; and neither have those decisions been effectively linked to the problems of political and social legitimacy faced by the EU.[24] Moreover, it is often difficult to determine what constitutes the highest level of fundamental rights protection.[25] Mainly, it

[20] This refers to the title of an article that became famous because of its very harsh critique of the Court's approach to fundamental rights: J Coppel and A O'Neill, 'The European Court of Justice: Taking Rights Seriously' (1992) 29 *Common Market Law Review* 669. No less famous became an article by Weiler and Lockart challenging that reading of the Court's case law: JHH Weiler and N Lockhart, ' "Taking Rights Seriously" Seriously: The European Court and Its Fundamental Rights Jurisprudence' (1995) 32 *Common Market Law Review* 51 and 574.

[21] See T von Danwitz, 'The Charter of Fundamental Rights Between Political Symbolism and Legal Realism' (2001) *Denver Journal of International Law and Policy* 289 at 293–94; and, for a general review of German scholarship, A von Bogdandy, 'The European Union as a Human Rights Organization? Human Rights and the Core of the European Union' (2000) *Common Market Law Review* 1307 at 1309 ff 1312 and 1320 ff.

[22] Von Danwitz, *ibid* at 294–95.

[23] See, for moderate critiques highlighting some shortcomings on the Court's case law: A Clapham, 'A Human Rights Policy for the European Community' (1990) *Yearbook of European Law* 309; and de Witte, above n 17. Perhaps the only case where a Court's judgment on fundamental rights has been seriously under challenge has been the decision on the Bananas regulation. See Case C–280/93 *Germany v Council* [1994] ECR I–4973, and the harsh opposition to it by Everling, 'Will Europe Slip on Bananas?' (1996) *Common Market Law Review* 401. The possible collision with German courts was, nevertheless, prevented by subsequent decisions of both the Court and the German Constitutional Court (Case C–68/95 *T Port v Bundesanstalt für Lanwirtschaft und Ernährung* [1996] ECR I–6065 and the Bundesverfassungericht's 'Bananas' decision of 7 June 2000. For an analysis see von Bogdandy, above n 21 at 1322–23.

[24] In this sense see JHH Weiler, Editorial: 'Does the European Union Truly Need a Charter of Rights?' 6 (2000) European *Law Journal* 95, von Bogdandy, above n 21 at 1322.

[25] This is so because often what the courts are presented with is a collision of fundamental rights. It would be possible to say that the highest standard is that which always accords the maximum protection to the individual against the state in each specific case, but that will ignore that the State's interest may correspond, in practice, to other individuals interests also worth of protection. See JHH Weiler, 'Eurocracy and Distrust: Some Questions Concerning the Role of the European Court

cannot honestly be said that the distrust of citizens in the EU is linked to the degree of fundamental rights protection accorded by the Court. It can be contested whether the level of protection accorded by the Court effectively embodies the best fundamental rights theory for the EU but it cannot be contested that it has so far proved sufficient to prevent any widespread challenge to the legitimacy of the EU on that basis. The best evidence of this is the respect that the Court has enjoyed from national constitutional courts. It is well known that some national constitutional courts have always claimed to have constitutional authority over EU acts if they violate in a systematic or particularly serious manner national fundamental rights without proper protection being provided by the Court.[26] Yet, the fact that they have never exercised these threats constitutes, in reality, a sign of trust in the way in which the Court has protected fundamental rights in the EU legal order.

Even if given binding legal value, the Charter will probably not produce any dramatic changes in the standard of fundamental rights protection in place in the EU legal order. Article 52 (1) EUCFR, for example, does not appear to be particularly stringent in the definition of the restrictions that can be authorised to fundamental rights. The choice of a horizontal provision to regulate in general terms the admissibility of restrictions to fundamental rights deviates, itself, from the system in place in most national constitutions and the European Convention on Human Rights 1950 (ECHR) where exceptions are regulated with respect to each fundamental right. In itself, Article 52 (1) EUCFR seems to reproduce the criteria that have been affirmed by the Court:[27] restrictions must be proportional and necessary to the pursuit of general interests recognised by the EU or the protection of the rights and freedoms of others and they must not affect the essence of the rights and freedoms at stake. The reference to general interests, in particular, can continue to raise some concerns due to its potentially broad and undetermined character that may not totally fit the standards in place in some national constitutions.[28]

---

of Justice in the Protection of Fundamental Human Rights Within the Legal Order of the European Communities' (1986) *Washington Law Review* 1103 at 1127 ff. For a contrasting view, see L Besselink, 'Entrapped by the Maximum Standard: On Fundamental Rights, Pluralism and Subsidiarity in the European Union' (1998) 35 *Common Market Law Review* 629.

[26] That has been particularly the case with the German and Italian constitutional courts. See their decisions (with nuances on the approaches of both courts) in, among others: Decision of the Bundesverfassungsgericht in '*Solange II*' [1987] 3 CMLR 225, Decision 170 of the Italian Constitutional Court of 8 June 1984, *Granital v Amministrazione delle Finanze*, unofficially translated at (1984) 21 *Common Market Law Review* 756, and Decision 232 of the Italian Constitutional Court of 21 April 1989, *Spa Fragd v Amministrazione delle Finanze* [1989] 72 RDI.

[27] See Case 4–73 *Nold v Commission* [1974] ECR 491 para 14, and Case 5/88 *Wachauf v Germany* [1989] ECR 2609 para. 18.

[28] That is the case with national constitutions that regulate with regard to each fundamental right the possible grounds for exceptions, but it is also the case when compared with an horizontal provision such as that included in the Portuguese Constitution that exceptions to fundamental rights are only permitted to the extent necessary to safeguard other rights and interests constitutionally protected (Art 18(2)).

The framework created by the Charter may, however, help the Court in developing a more structured and coherent fundamental rights theory for the EU.[29] This will be particularly important to provide a better theoretical and dogmatic explanation for the different degrees of judicial activism adopted by the Court in different circumstances. Often the Court is criticised not so much by reason of the criteria it uses to review EU acts in light of fundamental rights, but by reason of a perceived lighter standard than the one used in the review of Member States' acts under similar EU rules and principles. In reality, different proportionality tests, for example, may in fact be required in different circumstances depending on the institutions under review, the affected rights and the regulated groups. This is nothing peculiar to the EU legal order. It is well known that in any system of constitutional judicial review, courts have developed more or less stringent tests depending on the character and type of the measures under review, the interests they affect and the institutions that enact them. Such tests may be based, for example, on particular categories affected by legislation.[30] They may also be based on a perception of higher or lower risks of political malfunction in the institutions whose decisions are subject to judicial review in different sets of circumstances.[31] What appears to be lacking in the case law of the Court is a coherent theoretical and dogmatic explanation of the variations in the standards it uses. The Charter may help the Court in developing a more appropriate framework for its different degrees of judicial activism. This will be so because it provides the Court with both a more solid and complete fundamental rights framework and a reinforced legitimacy in addressing the actions of other institutions in the light of fundamental rights. One area where this can refocus the role of the Court in the protection of fundamental rights concerns review of actions of the Council. Though it is possible to find several instances where the Court has struck down acts of the Commission in light of fundamental rights, it is more rare to find such instances with regard to the Council when acting as Community legislator. This could be explained by both the way in which the Council decides and its different legitimacy. The Council has often acted unanimously or with a particularly qualified majority. This provides its decisions with an added legitimacy. To this legitimacy the Court could only oppose the limited legitimacy of a judicially developed catalogue of rights. It would thus make sense for the Court to concentrate its fundamental rights jurisprudence in the review of the acts of a bureaucratic body such as the Commission that enjoys a very limited degree of democratic legitimacy and is often perceived as subject to a lower political accountability. A formal catalogue of fundamental rights, such as that of a legally binding Charter of Fundamental

---

[29] See the contribution of C Costello in this collection at pp 122–24.

[30] The US Supreme Court is usually considered, for example, to use only a reasonableness test in reviewing legislation in general, but to apply a much more strict form of judicial review where such legislation affects particular categories (such as those determined by race).

[31] For an example, see below the debate on the tests that can be adopted under the free movement of goods.

Rights, can both help to dogmatically reconstruct these differences in approach by the Court and, at the same time, reinforce the legitimacy of the Court in reviewing the acts of the Council in the light of fundamental rights. Such a development will be particularly welcome in the context of the current trend towards majoritarian decision-making in the EU. To a more majoritarian political system, the Court should answer with a more active role in the review of EU legislation for the protection of individual rights and minorities.

Institutional Consequences and the Issue of the Charter's Legal Value

The question of the standard of protection is linked with a broader issue: the definition of the role of the Court in the EU system of fundamental rights protection and, broadly, on the constitutionalisation of the EU. In particular, this concerns the way in which the Charter affects or may affect the institutional balance between the judiciary and the EU political institutions. On the one hand, the existence of a catalogue of fundamental rights will limit the ability of the Community courts to 'recognise' other rights as fundamental rights of the EU or to give particular interpretations to such rights and their scope of application and protection. It is the politically developed catalogue that becomes the predominant source of law in the definition of EU fundamental rights, replacing the sources previously identified by the Court: international human rights documents subscribed to by the Member States (in particular the ECHR) and their common constitutional traditions. The latter constitute an open and undetermined concept whose definition was mainly a dominion of the Court. As a consequence of the Charter, the Court will have its role on the definition of the EU catalogue of fundamental rights limited. This will also be the case with regard to the scope of application and protection of these rights. As stated above, with the drafting of the Charter, the political process regained control over that area of Europe's constitutionalism. This is so even if the Charter does not proclaim to be a complete exposition of the rights that the EU must protect and therefore does not prevent, in theory, the Court from developing further rights.[32] But, in particular, if the Charter becomes legally binding, the Court will be bound to recognise and apply all its rights and, moreover, will face a much higher burden if it seeks to establish rights not proclaimed therein. The discourse on EU fundamental rights will be framed by the Charter and no longer by the sources of the Court's traditional case law.

On the other hand, a broader and clearer catalogue of fundamental rights may promote greater judicial activism in the review of legislative and administrative acts of the EU institutions. At the infra-constitutional level, the Charter may have the opposite effect of empowering the Court with regard to the political

---

[32] L Betten, 'The EU Charter of Fundamental Rights: a Trojan Horse or a Mouse?' (2001) 17 *International Journal of Comparative Labour Law and Industrial Relations* 151 at 161.

system. In the first place, the Charter reinforces the legitimacy of the Court in the review of the acts of EU institutions. In the second place, the higher transparency and better knowledge of EU individual rights promoted by a written catalogue such as the Charter may increase litigation against EU acts on the basis of fundamental rights. The Charter will lower the information and transaction costs for individuals in litigating in this area of the law and it will increase public awareness of their rights to challenge the actions of EU institutions and Member States when implementing EU law. In the same way, it will allow a greater variety of legal arguments to be brought before the Court. This will both enhance the Court's legitimacy and possibly feed activism into the Court's fundamental rights case law.

To summarise, the Charter has two possible opposite effects with respect to the relationship between the EU's political process and its judiciary. The Charter will reduce the freedom of the Court in developing the EU catalogue and system of fundamental rights protection. But it will enhance the Court's activism in the review of acts of the EU institutions. The Charter brings higher political control over the process of constitutionalisation but, in turn, empowers the judiciary in the review of the acts of political institutions. These two contrasting effects may, in part, help to explain the current different attitudes of the European Court of Justice and the Court of First Instance (CFI) with regard to the Charter.

One might expect the Charter to acquire an indirect binding legal effect through its judicial use, in particular to interpret the common constitutional traditions of the Member States. What better evidence could there be that a certain fundamental right constitutes part of the common constitutional traditions of the Member States than its inclusion in the Charter? This view, hinted at by the Commission even before the adoption of the Charter,[33] appears to have been largely endorsed by the Advocates General of the Court[34] and by the CFI, which

---

[33] 'It is reasonable to assume that the Charter will produce all its effects, legal and others, whatever its nature. As the Commission said in the European Parliament on 3 October 2000 . . . it is clear that it would be difficult for the Council and the Commission, who are to proclaim it solemnly, to ignore in the future, in their legislative function, an instrument prepared at the request of the European Council by the full range of sources of national and European legitimacy acting in concert . . . [and] it is highly likely that the Court of Justice will seek inspiration in it, as it already does in other fundamental rights instruments. It can reasonably be expected that the Charter will become mandatory through the Court's interpretation of it as belonging to the general principles of Community law.' Communication from the Commission on the legal nature of the Charter of fundamental rights of the European Union COM(2000) 644, para 10.

[34] The most important are: Opinion of Advocate General Tizzano in Case C–173/99 *The Queen v Secretary of State for Trade and Industry, ex parte Broadcasting, Entertainment, Cinematographic and Theatre Union (BECTU)* [2001] ECR I–4881; Opinion of Advocate General Mischo in Cases C–20 and 64/00 *Booker Aquaculture*, delivered on 20 September 2001, not yet reported, mainly para 126; Opinion of Advocate General Léger, Case C–353/99 *Council v Hautala* [2001] ECR I–9565, mainly paras 80–83; Opinion of Advocate General Colomer in Case C–466/00 *Arben Kaba v Secretary of State for the Home Department*, delivered on 11 July 2002, not yet reported. For a detailed analysis of the early judicial references to the Charter see: J Morijn, 'Judicial Reference to the EU Fundamental Rights Charter—First Experiences and Possible Prospects', Working Paper No 1 of the Ius Gentium Conimbrigae Institute (Human Rights Centre), available

has already referred to the Charter in more than one instance. In the recent *Jégo-Quéré* decision the CFI referred to the Charter to support a new interpretation of Article 230 (4) EC and to extend individuals access to the Community courts in the review of the legality of acts of EU institutions.[35] The CFI appears therefore to be ready to draw legal effects from the Charter even in the absence of formal binding legal value. In contrast, the European Court of Justice has so far refused the many 'invitations' by its Advocates General to make a reference to the Charter. Its scepticism towards the Charter also became particularly clear when in *UPA*, a decision where the Court had to decide a question substantially similar to that decided by the CFI in *Jégo-Quéré*, not only did it not support the decision of the CFI, but it also did so without any reference to the Charter provision on access to justice that had been referred to by the CFI.[36]

There are two readings that can be made of the Court's reluctance to accord any weight to the Charter. One is a cynical reading: it is to see in this attitude of the Court an attempt to preserve its dominion over the fundamental rights discourse in the EU, that is, its control over the process of constitutionalisation. The Charter would challenge the Court's creative role and discretionary power in that area and it would be this that would explain the neglect of the Court in this regard. But a quite different reading is also possible. It is to perceive, in the reaction of the Court, a message to the EU political process: the Court is, contrary to the previous view, no longer ready to assume the constitutional leadership of the EU and believes that the next steps must be taken by the political process and follow a much more classical form of constitution-making. The Court considers that it is no longer its appropriate role to step into the shoes of the political process and decide itself what binding legal value the Charter ought to have.[37] Its refusal to refer to the Charter would, in this case, be aimed at forcing the political process to address, in a complete and appropriate manner, this constitutional issue.[38]

This issue can also be approached from the perspective of the political process. The reluctance to accord binding legal value to the Charter may be explained by three reasons: first, the empowerment that the Charter may give over to the judiciary control of acts of the political process; second, to preserve the development and the application of the Charter in the dominion of the political process (it can

at: http://www.fd.uc.pt/hrc/working_papers; AJ Menéndez, 'Chartering Europe: The Charter of Fundamental Rights of the European Union', F Lucas Pires Working Papers on European Constitutionalism', WP 2001/03, available at: http://www.fd.unl.pt/je/wpflp03a.doc; and AJ Menéndez, 'Exporting rights: The Charter of Fundamental Rights, Membership and Foreign Policy of the European Union', ARENA Working Papers, WP 02/18, available at: http://www.arena.uio.no/publications/wp02_18.htm.

[35] Case T–177/01 *Jégo-Quéré v Commission*, [2002] ECR II–2365, esp paras 41–47.

[36] Case C–50/00 *Unión de Pequeños Agricultores*, [2002] ECR I–6677.

[37] McCrudden refers to this as a possible path to decide on the legal value of the Charter (above n 2 at 14).

[38] I owe this point to a comment by Montserrat Pí Lloréns.

therefore have legal effects,[39] only those will be primarily determined by political institutions instead of being opposed to them); and third, the fear on the part of some Member States that the Charter can be used to promote a further political and constitutional growth of the EU. Not all of these reasons are shared by the same actors. Moreover, the same occurs in the explanation for the emerging agreement at the current Convention on the Future of Europe to give some form of binding legal value to the Charter. There are those that envision such binding legal value as necessary for the Charter to effectively constrain EU powers and the constitutional role of the Court; there are others who aspire to the Charter having such legal binding value (and, particularly, an effective incorporation into the 'Constitutional Treaty')[40] as the best way to promote the political and constitutional spill-over that they foresee in many of its rights. Once again, the competing constitutional conceptions of the Charter come to life and the one that prevails will not be dependent on a simple definition of the Charter's legal status.

Constitutional Values (Economic Freedom vs Social Rights)

One of the areas where the Charter is expected to have a significant impact is on the balance between economic freedoms and social rights in the European Constitution. Many have noted that social rights have occupied a secondary position in the fundamental rights regime of the EU contrary to the values of economic freedom that are promoted by market integration.[41] The core of the European Constitution has lain in market integration. It is mainly under this legitimacy and through the rules provided in the Treaties to its achievement, that the Court has developed the very notion of a European Constitution. Though the EC Treaty also contains social provisions (notably, Articles 39–42 EC on free movement of workers and Articles 136–145 EC), at the core of market integration are the free movement provisions promoting access to the different national markets. The Court has defined these free movement provisions as 'fundamental freedoms'. The fundamental rights character granted to the free movement provisions and the widening of their scope of action in order to extend EU supervision over national regulation, and to support the constitutionalisation of Community law, has led to a spill-over of market integration

---

[39] See AJ Menéndez, 'Chartering Europe: Legal Status and Policy Implications of the Charter of Fundamental Rights of the European Union' (2000) 40 *Journal of Common Market Studies* 471. The Charter may also come to play a particularly important role in soft law areas such as the Open Method of Co-ordination to measure both the targets set and the progress in achieving them. See further, N Bernard in this collection.

[40] Its textual inclusion in the 'Constitutional Treaty' will reinforce its more ambitious constitutional dimension: its catalogue of rights as a comprehensive political document of fundamental rights to be assured to any European citizen. In this sense, see F Rubio Llorente, 'Mostrar Los Derechos Sin Destruir la Unión' (2002) *Revista Española de Derecho Constitucional* 13 at 50–51.

[41] I have made a more in depth analysis of this issue in M Poiares Maduro, 'Striking the Elusive Balance Between Economic Freedom and Social Rights in the EU' in Alston, above n 17, 449–72. For different perspectives see S Deakin and J Browne, and N Bernard in this collection.

rules into virtually all areas of national law. Indeed, it has led some to argue that they should be conceived as fundamental economic freedoms limiting public power and safeguarding competition in the free market. This dynamic has been reinforced by the patterns of litigation in EU law and has been expressed in the fundamental rights discourse of the Court. Most cases on fundamental rights decided by the Court under the doctrine now enshrined in Article 6 (2) TEU addressed economic rights and freedoms such as the right to property and freedom of economic activity.

At the same time, the status of social rights in the Treaties appeared to be in a subsidiary position. Article 136 EC is the Treaty provision that refers to fundamental social rights, in particular the European Social Charter, 1961, and Community Social Charter, 1989. Such a systematic position in the Treaties appears to distinguish them from the fundamental rights referred to in Article 6 (2) TEU. Other fundamental social rights can be found in Community legislation and the Treaties (such as equality between men and women) or have resulted from the interpretation of the Court in certain areas (including free movement rules).[42] These references have, however, been limited and rarely has the Court affirmed, as general principles of Community law, some fundamental social rights. Furthermore, many of the developments that took place in the area of social rights were also closely linked to the objectives of a well-functioning common market. They appeared to be mainly aimed at preventing distortion of competition and not to pursue the social values in themselves.[43] The constitutional justification for the social action of the EU has often been dependent on the values of market integration and not on social values that the EU would be constitutionally commanded to promote.[44] In many respects, this rationale still dominates the 'genetic code' of EU social rights even after the development of an EU social policy. Even social lawyers tend to argue for EU social rights in light of the need to guarantee a common level playing field that will prevent a race to the bottom of national social rights and policies.[45] EU social rights are not conceived as rights corresponding to social entitlements that EU citizens can claim with regard to the European polity. They are conceived, instead, either as an instrument of undistorted competition or as a guarantee that such competition will not affect the level of social protection afforded by the Member States.

This status quo has had three main consequences: first, social rights have had a lower impact on the fundamental rights discourse developed by the Court; second, many national social rights and policies have been challenged under the

---

[42] Consider how the *Bosman* decision (Case 415/93 *Union Royale de Belge des Sociétés de Football Association ASBL et al v Bosman* [1995] ECR I–4921) on free movement of workers indirectly affirms a right to work and to freely choose a job and employment.

[43] It is well known that such was the origin of the principle of equal pay between men and women already inserted in the original version of the Treaty of Rome (Art 141 EC, previously 119 EC). This principle was enshrined in the Treaty to prevent the distortion of competition that would arise from different national rules in this regard.

[44] For a more developed analysis see Poiares Maduro, above n 41.

[45] *Ibid.*

free movement provisions, since the balance between economic freedom and social rights in the European Constitution was largely defined by the balance between market integration and national social rights; and, third, social values have never fully assumed the status of independent goals for an emerging European polity.

The Charter attempts to correct this social deficit in the EU's constitutional discourse by eliminating the uncertainty regarding the status and position of fundamental social rights in the EU's legal order. Social rights are given an important role in the context of the Charter and they are systematically placed in an equivalent position to other economic rights. Naturally, some of the social rights affirmed by the Charter are immediately effective and judicially enforceable, while others are rights of a programmatic character expressing goals which are to be attained on a gradual basis. The qualification of social rights as 'real rights' (enforceable in courts) or goals will, no doubt, be an issue of contention in the interpretation of the Charter, reinforced by the distinction it makes between rights and principles which, in turn, it does not really identify or define.[46] But that is not particular to the Charter and has, for a long time, constituted a topic of heated debate surrounding national constitutions. What is more important, in the light of the past EU fundamental rights context, is that, be it as rights, principles or goals, social values are effectively incorporated in the EU fundamental rights discourse. Once again, however, the extent of their impact on the European Constitution will depend on the dominant constitutional conception of the Charter. For some, their growing importance will reflect in their political mainstreaming, the promotion of a more active judicial review of EU acts in the light of fundamental social rights and, mainly, in providing Member States with possible exceptions to free movement rules and their possible deregulatory impact on national social policies.[47] For others, however, such social rights should also legitimise new claims of social entitlements from European citizens with regard to the European polity. This is so even if Article 51(2) EUCFR attempts to limit the expansionist effect of fundamental rights by stating that they may not give rise to a new power or task for the Community or the Union. EU citizens can still claim new social entitlements from the EU on the basis of fundamental social rights so long as those claims can be satisfied through the exercise of an existing competence.

---

[46] Rubio Llorente, above n 40 at 37–39. The Spanish Constitution, for example, distinguishes between basic rights (Arts 15–29), rights and duties of citizens (Arts 30–38) and guiding principles of economic and social policy (Arts 39–52). See also J Kenner in this collection at p 16.

[47] The Court has admitted that fundamental rights can, in some circumstances, justify restrictions on free movement rules. See, notably, Case C–368/95 *Vereinigte Familiapress v Heirich Bauer Verlag* [1997] ECR I–3689.

European Citizenship

It could be expected that the consolidation character of the Charter would determine that it would have no relevant impact on the status of EU citizenship. The Charter chapter on citizenship in effect merely includes the rights already present in the Treaties (though, in some cases, they are stated in the Charter in accordance with what resulted from jurisprudential and legislative developments). Article 51(1) EUCFR even appears to make the reference to citizenship rights totally irrelevant in the context of the Charter. It states that the provisions of the Charter, 'are addressed to the institutions and bodies of the Union with due regard for the principle of subsidiarity and to the Member States only when they are implementing Union law'. It happens that most of the rights inserted in the Chapter on Citizens' Rights are primarily directed to the Member States. In order not to make an entire chapter highly irrelevant, it is necessary to consider that all cases where Member States can restrict a citizenship right or are bound to give it effect are situations where they are implementing 'Union law' for the purposes of Article 51(1) EUCFR.[48] A further limitation on citizenship rights could be derived from Article 51(2) EUCFR that makes clear that fundamental rights declared in the Charter that correspond to Treaty rights are subject to the limits and conditions established therein. Thus, for example, the general right of freedom of movement and residence proclaimed in the Charter would be subject to the conditions and limits to which it is subject in Article 18(1) EC and, indirectly, the Community legislation to which the Treaty provision refers.[49] This reflects a basic constraint to which EU fundamental rights have been subject: many of such rights proclaimed in the legislation or the EC Treaty are often seen as fully dependent on the content that is given to them by the Community legislative process. They are not seen as fundamental rights flowing from a constitutional source. This can be presented as the result of the absence of a true fundamental rights policy.[50] Fundamental rights have not assumed in the EU the

[48] Such a reading of Art 51(1) EUCFR will also be important in order to maintain the current degree of incorporation of EU fundamental rights in national legal orders as developed by the Court. See below.

[49] Even if given direct effect, Art 18(1) EC still limits the general right of free movement of persons in accordance with the existent legislation referred to therein (even if such legislation would have to be interpreted in light of fundamental rights). This appears to be, in effect, the interpretation of the Court. See Case C–413/99 *Baumbast and another v Secretary of State for the Home Department*, judgment of 17 September 2002, not yet reported, where the Court held, at para 94 that: 'a citizen of the European Union who no longer enjoys a right of residence as a migrant worker in the host Member State can, as a citizen of the Union, enjoy there a right of residence by direct application of Article 18(1) EC. The exercise of that right is subject to the limitations and conditions referred to in that provision, but the competent authorities and, where necessary, the national courts must ensure that those limitations and conditions are applied in compliance with the general principles of Community law and, in particular, the principle of proportionality'.

[50] The absence of such a policy and its impact on the overall status of fundamental rights in the EU have been highlighted by P Alston and JHH Weiler, 'An 'Ever Closer Union' in Need of a Human Rights Policy: The European Union and Human Rights' in Alston, above n 17, pp 3–66.

role of constitutional values that ought not only to control but also to promote and direct its actions. As a consequence, many of the rights the Charter now treats as fundamental have existed in the EU legal order as mere rights whose content and even existence was dependent on the ordinary political process. This is also the result of the difficulty of differentiating between the *legislature constituent* and the *legislature ordinaire* in the EU. This creates a tendency to mix the constitutional and legislative tracks in the EU and, as a consequence, for the Court to be judicially deferent towards the EU political process (in particular, its legislative process). A further consequence for those rights is that legislative acts that set the conditions for their exercise are not seen as restrictions on fundamental rights but as the instruments of their effective determination. Even though, as we will see, some of the Charter's horizontal provisions appear to embody a similar conception, the simple recognition of such rights as fundamental rights can however have a tremendous impact on the conception of such rights, in particular citizenship rights.

As explained earlier, Article 51(2) EUCFR appears to maintain a restrictive understanding of citizenship rights by stating that the 'rights recognised by this Charter which are based on the Community Treaties or the Treaty on European Union shall be exercised under the conditions and within the limits defined by those Treaties'. Can the limits defined by those Treaties include any limits set by legislation if the Treaties so state? If that were the case, such provisions would in fact challenge the nature of such rights as fundamental rights recognised by the Charter. It would de facto derogate from the constitutional protection assured to these rights by Article 51(1) EUCFR which enshrines the idea that fundamental rights have a hard core that cannot be dependent on or challenged by any other exercise of power:

> Any limitation on the exercise of the rights and freedoms recognised by this Charter must be provided for by law and respect the essence of those rights and freedoms. Subject to the principle of proportionality, limitations may be made only if they are necessary and genuinely meet the objectives of general interest recognised by the Union or the need to protect the rights and freedoms of others.

What if the conditions and limits defined by the Treaties or the legislation referred to therein do not meet these requirements? A true fundamental rights conception of citizenship rights will impose an epistemological shift in their process of discovery and application: it will be those rights that ought to serve as criteria to judge the admissibility of the legislation that develops or restricts them and no longer the legislation that serves as criteria to determine the existence and extent of such rights. If this seems abstract, it is sufficient to look at one of the most relevant citizenship provisions to envisage the impact of their conception as true fundamental rights that must be embraced by a full constitutional reading of the Charter. The free movement of persons is proclaimed in the EC Treaty and restated in the Charter as a fundamental right.[51] Is it not the case

---

[51] See Art 18 EC and Art 45(1) EUCFR.

that the exclusion of some people from this right of residence arising from the conditions imposed by current EC legislation affects the essence of the freedom of movement and residence? Does the essence of that right not entail the free movement of persons without discrimination on the basis of their economic status? If that is the case, then the Charter will both require a new interpretation of Article 18 EC and call into question the lawfulness of some of the conditions currently imposed by Community legislation on the free movement of persons.

The Scope of EU Law: Incorporation and Competences

A major area of debate surrounding both the drafting of the Charter and its current and future constitutional status regards its possible impact on the extent of powers granted to the EU. This question involves, in reality, two issues: one regards the extent to which the Charter could be used to further broaden the scope of Community competences or, instead, to restrict and limit the use of those competences; the other concerns the impact of the Charter on the review of acts of the Member States for compliance with EU fundamental rights. The Charter appears again compatible with quite different constitutional discourses in this respect.

The issue of competences appears to be disposed in a quite restrictive and definitive manner by Article 51(2) EUCFR. This provision establishes that the rights ascertained in the Charter cannot constitute the basis for new Community competences and was clearly drafted to quiet the concerns of those that feared that the Charter, with its breadth of goals and rights, could constitute a new source of growth for Community competences. However, the creation of new legal grounds of competences is one thing; the other, quite different, but potentially much more relevant in the current EU context, is the provision of reasons for the exercise of competences that the Community already has. It is well known that the Community already has the legal authority to exercise an enormous array of competences (some argue almost any competence). There is nothing to prevent the Charter from providing a basis for claims for new Community actions or legislation on areas where the current Treaty rules already provide a sufficient legal basis. This effect of the Charter will not even be dependent upon its binding legal value since it derives its legitimacy mainly from its binding character on the political institutions that proclaimed it.

The paradoxical attitude of the Charter towards the issue of competences is particularly noticeable when we contrast Article 51(2) EUCFR with some of the rights enshrined in the Charter. In effect, many of the rights stated in the Charter make little sense in the light of the current competences of the Community and the Union. Article 2 EUCFR is an example. It states:

1. Everyone has the right to life
2. No one shall be condemned to the death penalty, or executed.

If there is something that we can safely say the EU currently has no competence to do, that is to impose the death penalty! The explanation for the presence of this provision is, first of all, the ambition of totality involved in the project of a Charter of Fundamental Rights. The intellectual and political project was to write a Charter of Fundamental Rights and not simply a document with the set of rights necessary for the protection of individuals vis à vis the powers of the EU. Yet, many of the horizontal provisions, and one of the competing constitutional readings of the Charter, limit its role to the second function. This explains the tension expressed in the Charter by proclaiming certain rights with which its latter provisions then tell us we cannot exercise. But, being a lawyer, I must move beyond what I believe truly explains such contradictions to, in legal dogmatic terms, an attempt to reconcile them. How can this be done? In two ways: first, it is possible to argue that the rights that currently are inapplicable are in the Charter to anticipate any future competences of the Community and the Union; second, it is also possible to say that the current broad catalogue will play a role in the review of Member States' or applicant countries' fundamental rights policies even if purely in the context of Articles 7 and 49 TEU.[52]

This last point can be related to the second issue, which affects the balance of powers between the EU and the Member States: the extent to which EU fundamental rights can be used to review acts of the Member States. It is an issue that is traditionally referred to as the 'incorporation' of EU fundamental rights in national legal orders. This makes allusion to the process through which the US Supreme Court incorporated the Bill of Rights of the US Constitution[53] (which was only directed at the federal government) into the due process clause directed at the individual states. This, de facto, made the Bill of Rights applicable to the states even in their pure domestic arenas. No such fully-fledged incorporation has yet occurred in EU law. However, it is well known that the Court has extended the initial reach of EU fundamental rights to also cover Member State actions that fall within the scope of application of Community law, notably when they either implement Community law or derogate from it.[54] In this regard, Article 51(1) EUCFR appears to restrict that scope since (at least in the English version)[55] it determines that the provisions of the Charter are only applicable to the Member States 'when they are implementing Union law'. This appears to limit the more extensive scope of application recognised in the case law of the Court. In the latter, as stated, EU fundamental rights may also be applied to Member State acts that derogate from Community rules. If inter-

---

[52] Von Danwitz, above n 21 at 304, even argues that such broad set of rights must be intended to provide the Court with the framework necessary to extend its review of national measures in the field of fundamental rights.

[53] The Bill of Rights corresponds to the first 10 amendments of the US Constitution.

[54] See: Case 5/88 *Wachauf* [1989] ECR 2609; and Case C–260/89 *Elliniki Radiophonia Tileorassi AE v Domitiki Etairia Pliroforissis and Sotiris Kouvelas* [1991] ECR I–2925.

[55] Some of the other language versions of this provision are more open. For further discussion see, for example, the contributions by J Hunt, N Bernard, M Bell and J Kenner in this collection.

preted literally, Article 51(1) EUCFR could thus lead to a more restrictive scope of application of EU fundamental rights. It would be a reading that would particularly fit with the constitutional conception of the Charter as an instrument of control over what some foresee as an excessive constitutionalisation of the EU.

However, a literal reading of Article 51(1) EUCFR[56] will prove too much where it would also make meaningless the presence in the Charter of many rights whose main scope of application regards precisely the Member States. Most of the rights on European citizenship, for example, are primarily directed at the Member States and their actions. To make full sense of the inclusion of such rights in the Charter it is necessary to read the allusion in Article 51(1) EUCFR to Member States implementing 'Union law' as referring to all actions of the Member States that fall within the scope of application of EU law (either by acting under the authority or control of such rules or derogating from them).

The question of the scope of application of EU fundamental rights is one of the most important questions in determining the role of human rights in the context of European integration. If the rights of the Charter are only applicable to acts of the EU institutions, the tendency is to see human rights as having a prevailing defensive function with regard to European integration.[57] The same is true if they are not foreseen as giving rise to new actions from the EU. Instead, if they were also applicable to acts of national institutions (in other words, incorporated in domestic legal orders), the tendency would be to conceive the promotion of human rights as a primary goal of European integration, justifying the expansion of its reach into the domestic orders of the Member States. A similar ambitious vision of the role of fundamental rights in the EU would be linked to their use for justifying new actions and policies from the EU. The Charter's horizontal provisions clearly embrace the first alternative: the protection of fundamental rights continues to be mainly a condition that EU institutions must fulfil in order to legitimately pursue other policies. But it remains to be seen how these provisions will interact with the much more ambitious constitutional dynamics imprinted on the rights proclaimed in the Charter and its vision of reflecting the common political values of Europe that it will be the role of the EU to guarantee to its citizens.[58]

---

[56] This provision also ignores that, in effect, several of the rights contained in the Charter can also produce horizontal effects. In other words, they can also be applicable to private entities such as companies and individuals. That is the case, for example, of the principle of equality between men and women (Art 23), in particular in the areas already covered by the EC Treaty and legislation (that the Charter was supposed to simply consolidate).

[57] This is not totally correct, however, because some of those rights (in particular social rights) may generate claims for action from EU institutions.

[58] Garcia notes that both the nature of the catalogue of rights included in the Charter and the growing stress on European citizenship are conducive to an extension of the Community's judicial control over Member States' actions and, therefore, opposes a restrictive interpretation of Art 51(1) EUCFR. See RA Garcia, 'Las Clausulas Horizontales de la Carta de Los Derechos Fundamentales de la Unión Europea' in E Garcia de Enterría and RA Garcia (ed), *La Encrucijada Constitucional de la Unión Europea* (Madrid, Civitas, 2002) 151 at 157–58.

What this debate demonstrates, once again, is the tension between the constitutional conception of the Charter as the bill of rights of a political community (a constitutional document that is part of a complete political contract among citizens and that therefore legitimises new claims and an increased incorporation at state level) and the constitutional conception of the Charter as a mere instrument to guarantee the conformity of the increased powers of a supranational entity with the fundamental rights of its founding states (an instrument that will therefore limit and not expand the powers of the supranational entity).

THE CHARTER AND POLITICAL IDENTITY

The third constitutional dimension of the Charter regards its possible role in forming a European political identity, in other words, its potential for polity building in the EU. Many of the issues previously dealt with in this Chapter will determine that potential. In this section, I will address this question from a more general perspective albeit touching again upon issues previously mentioned. The polity-building ambition of the Charter is well described by McCrudden:[59]

> The function of a Charter of Rights is partly constitutional in that, like other modern national constitutions, it attempts to identify the basic values that Europe is committed to. Recognising a common set of rights in a document that all can commit to, at least in part, is seen as an important element in building a new political society, providing the possibility of common identification by all with a basic set of values if not with the institutions of the Community.

Will the Charter promote a common European political identity capable of sustaining and reinforcing the process of European integration? Moreover, what is important in assessing the polity-building perspectives generated by the Charter?

The same author notes that the broader and more legally binding the set of rights to be included in the Charter, the higher will be its potential for building political identity in Europe.[60] But even here, one can find opposite perspectives noting that the Charter, in its consolidation process of a wide variety of legal sources of different ranking, may be seen as compiling both fundamental rights and other rights of a non-fundamental character that could undermine instead of support its constitutional power.[61] One author has defined the Charter, in such a context, as a 'complex (pre-) constitutional document'.[62] Either way, the Charter does appear to reflect an overarching consensus on what are common European political values. This assumption of the Charter as reflecting values

---

[59] McCrudden, above n 2 at 21.

[60] He notes that 'a broad-based list of rights can thus enable a set of common values to be identified that transcends the Member State, offering an alternative vision of the future', *ibid.*

[61] Von Bogdandy, above n 21 at 1317.

[62] A Rainer, 'A Fundamental Rights Charter for the European Union' 15 *Tulane European and Civil Law Forum* (2000–2001) 43 at 47.

that are common to all EU Member States has already expressed itself in references made by two national constitutional courts. The Spanish Constitutional Court was, in effect, the first judicial body to refer to the Charter.[63] More recently also, the Italian Constitutional Court has showed its adherence to the Charter.[64] But is it sufficient for the Charter to be seen as expressing a set of common European political values for it to have true polity-building potential? How can those common political values be transformed into building blocks of an emerging European political community?

In this respect, I believe it is important to distinguish between two different sets of rights that a Charter of Fundamental Rights could promote in the EU. These are rights that European citizens may have to protect themselves from the EU institutions and rights that they can claim from the European polity. This does not correspond to the traditional distinction between negative and positive rights since the rights that European citizens can claim from European polity may regard their protection vis à vis the powers of national institutions. The first set of rights simply guarantees that European citizens will not see their sphere of personal autonomy (in civil, political but also social and economic terms) diminished by the powers granted' to EU institutions. It guarantees the national status quo of fundamental rights protection. The second set of rights concerns, instead, any new rights that European citizens may claim from EU institutions or from Member States through EU law. They may include the expansion of the scope of political and civic rights with regard to Member States (for example, electoral rights, non-discrimination on the basis of nationality or, in some respects, the free movement of persons) or even new instruments for their protection (EU review of national acts with regard to fundamental rights). But they also include new social, cultural and economic entitlements that European citizens may claim from EU institutions (for example, free movement rules and their link to economic freedom or emerging social rights such as those regarding working conditions and, possibly in the future, even distributive justice in the EU).

The relevance of distinguishing between these two sets of rights lies in their relation to the development of a political community in the EU. Rights given to EU citizens to protect them from EU institutions are aimed at providing regime legitimacy.[65] They guarantee that the actions of those institutions will not

---

[63] Even before the Charter had been adopted: Sentencia 292/2000 of 30 November 2000, available in: http://www.tribunalconstitucional.es/STC2000/STC2000–292.htm.

[64] Sentencia 135/2002 of 11 April 2002, para 2.1, available at: http://www.cortecostituzionale.it/pron/rp_m/pr_02/pr_02_m/pron_h_02.htm.

[65] The distinction between regime legitimacy and polity legitimacy (see below) was advanced by Bellamy and Castiglione (see R Bellamy and D Castiglione, 'Normative Theory and the European Union: Legitimising the Euro-Polity and its Regime' in L Tragardh (ed), *After National Democracy: Rights, Law and Power in the New Europe* (Oxford, Hart, 2003, forthcoming), and recently also used by N Walker, 'The White Paper in a Constitutional Context', part of the Jean Monnet Chair Working Paper 6/01 (available at: http://www.jeanmonnetprogram.org/papers/01/011001.rtf). The meaning in which these expressions will be used here does not totally coincide with the meanings attributed to these authors.

threaten the degree of fundamental rights protection that is accorded to European citizens by their Member States. EU institutions will act in accordance with the fundamental rights that are inherent in any constitutionally democratic system. Further, the recognition of economic and social rights, in this context, is simply aimed at preserving the social and economic status that citizens are granted by their States. The first set of rights will not have a substantial effect in terms of polity-building. They do not justify the need for a new polity; they simply assure that such a new polity will not threaten the fundamental rights linked to the states. The building of polity legitimacy requires the second type of rights: rights derived from the European polity and not opposed to it. It is in these new rights that citizens can find the added value of European integration with regard to their national polities. But it is in this respect that the Charter is more disappointing. This is so because this second dimension would require the discussion of much more contentious issues regarding what ought to be the fundamental rights policy of the EU or even if there ought to be such a policy.

The debate on the elevation of fundamental rights into commanding principles of the *telos* of the EU is not really solved by the Charter. The proposal of Alston and Weiler to raise human rights into the status of a proper EU policy[66] and a dominant goal of its activities has not been heard at either the Charter Convention or the EU political process. This is not unexpected since that step will involve possible present and future consequences on the political characterisation of the EU that some simply refuse and others fear.[67] Even if in their specific proposals Alston and Weiler try to present the creation of an EU fundamental rights policy as not requiring substantial changes in the law and balances of power of the EU, the simple raising of human rights into the status of the *telos* of European integration will change its entire constitutional dynamics. That status would lead to the exploration of the full potential of the EU as a new political community entrusted with the promotion of fundamental rights. That would, in turn, ignite the debates which are linked with the second type of rights mentioned above. These debates would have to address quite contentious issues such as the content of European citizenship and the incorporation of EU fundamental rights in the domestic order of the Member States. In this respect, the Charter strictly followed its mandate of mere consolidation of the previous status quo. That means, however, that it does not really elevate fundamental rights to a dominant policy for the EU.[68] Whether or not its ambitious catalogue can promote a discourse on fundamental rights that will later be conducive to the creation of such policy remains to be seen.

---

[66] Alston and Weiler, above n 50.

[67] Von Bogdandy (above n 21) has recently made a powerful defence of the current system, and opposing the raising of human rights into the status of a primary goal of European integration. His article is put forward, in this respect, as a reply to Weiler and Alston.

[68] See the analysis of Von Bogdandy, above n 21.

THE CHARTER, CONSTITUTIONAL AUTHORITY AND THE CHARACTER OF
EUROPEAN CONSTITUTIONALISM

The fourth and final area of constitutional impact of the Charter will be the relationship between the EU legal order and national constitutions. This is the question of ultimate legal and political authority in Europe, or, if you prefer, the
question of sovereignty. In this respect, it has become common to characterise
the relationship between European and national constitutionalism as a form of
legal pluralism.[69] This is so, because both national and EU constitutional law
continue to assume, in the internal logic of their respective legal systems, the role
of higher law. According to the internal conception of the Community legal
order developed by the Court, Community primary law will be the 'higher law'
of the EU, the criterion of validity of secondary rules and decisions as well as
that of all national legal rules and decisions within its scope. Moreover, the
Court is the higher court of this legal system. However, a different perspective
is taken by national legal orders and national constitutions. Here, Community
law owes its supremacy to its reception by a higher national law (normally constitutions). The higher law remains, in the national legal orders, the national
constitution and the ultimate power of legal adjudication belongs to national
constitutional courts. In this way, the question of ultimate legal authority has
different answers in the EU and national legal orders.

Possibilities of conflict have therefore always been present in the relationship
between EU law and national constitutions and one of the areas most susceptible to conflict as regards fundamental rights. One the one hand, it is well
known that the development of a system of fundamental rights protection in the
European Communities was, in part, linked to the potential challenges arising
from the German and Italian constitutional courts to the supremacy of
Community law in cases of possible fundamental rights violations.[70] Following
the Court's recognition of fundamental rights as general principles of
Community law to which all EU acts ought to conform, those national courts
have partially retracted from their claim to review the validity of EU acts in the
light of national fundamental rights. But they have continued to affirm that

---

[69] See, for example: N MacCormick, , 'Beyond the Sovereign State' (1993) 56 *Modern Law Review*
1 (the foundation article in this respect); C Richmond, 'Preserving the Identity Crisis: Autonomy,
System and Sovereignty in European Law' (1997) 16 *Law and Philosophy* 377; M Kumm, 'Who Is the
Final Arbiter of Constitutionality in Europe?' Harvard Jean Monnet Chair Working Papers 10/98,
available at: www.law.harvard.edu/Programs/JeanMonnet/papers/98/98–10–.html; N Walker 'The
Idea of Constitutional Pluralism (2002) 65 *Modern Law Review* 317 (only pp 319–33); N Walker
'Postnational Constitutionalism and the Problem of Translation' in JHH Weiler and M Wind (ed),
European Constitutionalism Beyond the State (Cambridge, Cambridge University Press, 2003, forth-
coming), M Poiares Maduro, 'The Heterenonyms of European Law', (1999) 3 *European Law Journal*
160, and M Poiares Maduro, 'Contrapunctual Law: Europe's Constitutional Pluralism in Action' in
N Walker (ed), *Sovereignty in Transition* (Oxford, Hart Publishing, 2003, forthcoming).
[70] For all, see B de Witte, 'Community Law and National Constitutional Values' (1991/2) *Legal
Issues of European Integration*, 1–22.

hypothesis in the case of either systematic fundamental rights violations or particularly serious violations.[71] On the other hand, the Court has always affirmed, without exceptions, the absolute supremacy of Community law even in the face of national fundamental rights or constitutional norms.[72] This state of affairs has always been presented as a clear example of the form of legal pluralism upon which the relationship between EU law and national constitutions has been built. When viewed from a perspective outside the internal hierarchical conceptions of national and EU legal orders, the characterisation of such a relationship requires a conception of the law which is no longer dependent upon a hierarchical construction and a conception of sovereignty as single and indivisible. Such a conception of sovereignty has been under challenge by notions such as shared sovereignty, but what the relationship between the EU and national legal orders brings is an even more challenging notion: that of competitive sovereignty. We can talk of constitutional pluralism to describe these competing claims of legal and political authority that relate between themselves in a non-hierarchical discourse. Does the Charter impact on this European constitutional pluralism? Does it alter the current equilibrium of constitutional authority between the EU and national constitutions in which fundamental rights have played a major role? Again, there are two possible readings of the Charter in this respect that can, in turn, be linked to the two broader constitutional discourses that have been identified.

A first reading, and a matter of great concern for some, is drawn from Article 53 EUCFR. On its face, it appears to recognise the supremacy of national constitutions over EU law in the area of fundamental rights. In fact, it states that:

> Nothing in this Charter shall be interpreted as restricting or adversely affecting human rights and fundamental freedoms as recognised, in their respective fields of application . . . by Member States' constitutions.

Such a provision might indicate that, where national constitutions would provide a more extensive protection in the area of fundamental rights, their provisions would prevail over EU norms. It would therefore reinstate the authority of national constitutions over EU law in certain circumstances. Article 53 EUCFR restricts such supremacy of national fundamental rights to 'their respective fields of application' but it is difficult to conceive this as referring to its exclusive application to national acts. This is so because Article 51 EUCFR already fulfils that function. The latter provision is aimed precisely at protecting the field of application of national fundamental rights by excluding national acts from the jurisdiction of the Charter. That being the case, Article 53 EUCFR would be superfluous if applicable only to national acts.[73] Yet, the drafting history of the

---

[71] For developments see Poiares Maduro, 'Contrapunctual Law', above n 69.

[72] This has been clearly affirmed by the Court since Case 11–70 *Internationale Handelsgesellschaft mbH v Einfuhr- und Vorratsstelle für Getreide und Futtermittel* [1970] ECR 112.

[73] In this sense, see also Liisberg, above n 11 at 1191–92.

provision[74] and all the weight of the Community law *acquis* oppose any interpretation that might risk undermining the uniform application of Community law. It cannot be expected that Community law will implode its own foundations.[75] It may be that some national constitutional courts will attempt to rely on that provision to support some challenges to the absolute supremacy of Community law but it does not appear that the provision ought to be interpreted as such from the point of view of the EU legal order. That would constitute a complete legal revolution in the internal conception of the EU legal order and its sources of law. This would constitute a revolution that the Charter was not supposed to undertake and that, in the absence of any further evidence, cannot be assumed to have undertaken. It is sufficient to interpret Article 53 EUCFR literally to prevent any recognition of national constitutional supremacy over EU acts even if that may make it superfluous in the light of Article 51 EUCFR.[76] It is not uncommon for legislators to repeat themselves.

In a totally different sense from the threat to supremacy feared by some, it has also been argued that the Charter will, instead, strengthen the supremacy of Community law. This is so because it will remove any reason for national constitutional courts to make the application of Community law dependent on national fundamental rights.[77] In this second light, the Charter becomes an instrument to reinforce the authority of European constitutionalism vis à vis national constitutions. It relieves the European constitution from its dependence on national constitutions and it gives it, instead, independent constitutional authority. Again, we have a different constitutional discourse taking precedence: the Charter further constitutionalises the EU and, in so doing, reinforces its constitutional authority vis à vis national constitutional orders.

There is a further issue whereby, albeit in a less obvious and less discussed manner, the Charter may end up having a much more profound impact on the nature of European constitutionalism. Traditionally, Europe's constitutionalism has been built in a bottom-up sense. It is national constitutional sources that shape the European Constitution and not vice versa. This was a consequence of the dependence of the process of constitutionalisation on national legal orders and national courts. The legitimacy of the constitutional reading undertaken by the Court was supported by the reference to national constitutions and their common legal principles. At the same time, the Court was also aware of the potential for national constitutional control over Community law and, as a consequence, tried to adapt Community law to national constitutions. In this respect, the EU legal order constitutes a quite different federal legal order: both

---

[74] See, for a detailed analysis, Liisberg, above n 11 at 1181 ff.

[75] See Rubio Llorente, above n 40 at 43–44, which argues that it would be so even if it were upon the ECJ to determine and apply the level of protection afforded by the national constitutions. In a different sense see: R Alonso Garcia, above n 57 at 179–81.

[76] Even more strongly Rubio Llorente talks of a an empty or plain wrong provision! Above n 39 at 44.

[77] G Sacerdoti, above n 18 at 48.

constitutional authority and constitutional values are installed from the smaller units into the federal entity and not the opposite. The European Constitution appears, in this light, as a result of a permanent learning process inspired from national constitutions that constitute both its ultimate source of legitimacy and its constitutional laboratory.

In one sense, the Charter can be seen as challenging both the discursive and bottom-up character of European constitutionalism. The creation of an independent constitutional source from national constitutions and the formalisation of European constitutionalism it entails both appear to threaten those two trademarks of European constitutionalism. Weiler has strongly criticised the formalisation of European constitutionalism inherent in the Charter as changing one of the highest added values of European constitutionalism: its ongoing development by the Court from constitutional principles derived from national constitutions.[78] Others, instead, argue that the best way to pursue such constitutional pluralism is through the Charter and the constitutional dialogues it will promote albeit with a lower degree of judicial dominance. This view stresses a less court-oriented vision of the European Constitution that is seen as the product of a broader set of institutions and reflecting a broader political consensus. The Charter, in turn, is seen as an instrument for future development and updating of such political consensus and not as an arrival point that crystallises the current fundamental rights *acquis*.[79]

CONCLUSION

All that has been said about what the Charter is or will be depends very much on which 'constitutional life' will be adopted for the EU. There are two very different charters in the current document depending on the constitutional discourses used for its legal dogmatic reconstruction. One discourse places the Charter at the centre of the political building of Europe and foresees it as a dynamic element for further constitutionalisation. Another presents the Charter as a limit to the political growth of Europe and conceives it as a tool for the protection of national constitutional values. To determine which one of these discourses ought to dominate the reading of the Charter will be, at least, as important as determining the formal legal value to be given to it. There is nothing dramatic about this. It is common for constitutional agreements to be made on the basis of what Sunstein has called incompletely theorised agreements.[80] In these instances, constitutional norms and constitutional principles do not offer solutions, but simply regulate the constitutional discourse by setting their

---

[78] See Weiler, above n 24.
[79] This appears to be the view, for example, of Menéndez, n 34 above. See also C McCrudden, above n 2 at 6–7 and 10.
[80] CR Sunstein, 'Incompletely Theorized Agreements' (1995) 108 *Harvard Law Review* 1733.

margins and the acceptable arguments. This means that the Charter will be as much a product of its text as of its discourse and the institutions that will dominate it. In this respect, intentions and outcomes may differ greatly. It is sufficient to recall that in the United States, the insertion into the Constitution of a catalogue of fundamental rights was mainly argued by those that *opposed* the powers of the federation. Yet, the Bill of Rights ended up constituting one of the most important elements of federal control over the states.

In the EU, the political ambitions of the more ambitious constitutional discourse on the Charter appear to be constrained by the fears of some Member States. The Convention itself, with its focus on institutional questions and regime legitimacy, also appears to limit the constitutional promise of the Charter. But, as always in the process of European integration, the non-formalised constitutional dynamics may determine a constitutional future for the Charter that will be much more 'glamorous' than the limited dimension that currently appears to be prevailing. The masters of the Treaties may again find themselves in the position of the theatre producer in Mel Brooks play and film *The Producers*, who ends up with an unintended hit on his hands: 'How could this happen? I was so careful. I picked the wrong play, the wrong director, the wrong cast. Where did I go right?'

Bibliography

ABU-LABAN Y, 'The Future and the Legacy: Globalization and the Canadian Settler-State' (2001) 35 *Journal of Canadian Studies* 262

ACKERMAN B, *We The People, Vol I: Foundations* (Cambridge: Harvard University Press, 1991)

ADDO K, 'The Correlation between Labour Standards and International Trade: Which Way Forward' (2002) 36 *Journal of World Trade* 285

AHMED L, *Women and Gender in Islam: Historical Roots of Modern Debate* (New Haven: Yale University Press, 1992)

ALSTON P and STEINER H, *International Human Rights in Context: Law, Politics, Morals: Text and Materials*, 2nd ed (Oxford: OUP, 2000)

ALSTON P and WEILER J, 'An 'Ever Close Union' in Need of a Human Rights Policy: The European Union and Human Rights' in Alston P (ed) *The EU and Human Rights* (Oxford: OUP, 1999) 3–66

ALSTON P, 'Making Economic and Social Rights Count: A Strategy for the Future' (1997) 68 *Political Quarterly* 188

——, (ed) *The Best Interests of the Child: Reconciling Culture and Human Rights* (Oxford: Clarendon Press, 1994)

ANDREASSEN B, 'Article 22' in Alfredsson G and Eide A (eds) *The Universal Declaration of Human Rights. A Common Standard of Achievement* (London: Martinus Nijhoff Publishers, 1999) 453

ARAMBULO K, *Strengthening the Supervision of the International Covenant on Economic, Social and Cultural Rights. Theoretical and Procedural Aspects* (Oxford: Intersentia-Hart, 1999)

ARMSTRONG K, 'Legal Integration: Theorizing the Legal Dimension of European Integration' (1998) 36 *Journal of Common Market Studies* 154

ARNULL A, 'What shall we do on Sunday' (1991) 16 *European Law Review* 112

BAETEN R, MCKEE M and MOSSIALOS E (eds) *European Integration and National Health Care Policy: a Challenge for Social Policy*, (Brussels: PIE Peter Lang, 2002)

BAEYENS A, 'Free Movement of Goods and Services in Health Care' (1999) 6 *European Journal of Health Law* 373

BAKAN J and SMITH M, 'Rights, Nationalism and Social Movements in Canadian Constitutional Politics' (1995) 4 *Social and Legal Studies* 367

BALKIN J, *Cultural Software* (New Haven, Yale University Press, 1998)

BALL S, 'The European Employment Strategy: The Will But Not the Way?' (2001) 30 *Industrial Law Journal* 353

BARBER N, ' Citizenship, Nationalism and the European Union' (2002) 27 *European Law Review* 241

BARBERA M, 'Not the Same? The Judicial Role in the New Community Anti-discrimination Law Context' (2002) 31 *Industrial Law Journal* 82

——, *Dopo Amsterdam. I Nuovi Confini del Diritto Sociale Comunitario* (Brescia: Promodis, 2000)

BARKER C, *The Health Care Policy Process* (London: Sage, 1992)

BARLETT K, 'Feminist Legal Method' (1990) 103 *Harvard Law Review* 829

BARNARD C and HEPPLE B, 'Indirect Discrimination: Interpreting *Seymour-Smith*' (1999) 58 *Cambridge Law Journal* 399

BARNARD C and DEAKIN S, 'Costituzionalizzare il diritto del lavoro. L'esperienza britannica' (2000) *Lavoro e diritto* 575

—— and ——, 'Market Access and Regulatory Competition' in Barnard C and Scott J (eds) *The Law of the Single European Market: Unpacking the Premises* (Oxford: Hart, 2002) 197–224

BARNARD C, 'The Social Partners and the Governance Agenda' (2002) 8 *European Law Journal* 80

——, 'Fitting the Remaining Pieces into the Goods and Persons Jigsaw?' (2001) 26 *European Law Review* 35

——, 'The Changing Scope of the Fundamental Principle of Equality?' (2001) 46 *McGill Law Journal* 955

——, *EC Employment Law*, 2nd ed (Oxford: OUP, 2000)

——, 'Social Dumping and the Race to the Bottom: Some Lessons for the European Union from Delaware?' (2000) 25 *European Law Review* 57

——, 'Gender Equality in the EU: A Balance Sheet' in Alston P (ed) *The European Union and Human Rights* (Oxford: OUP, 1999) 215–79

——, 'The Economic Origins of Article 119 EEC' in Hervey T and O'Keeffe D (eds) *Sex Equality Law in the European Union* (Chichester: Wiley, 1996) 321–34

BARRY B, 'The Muddles of Multiculturalism' (2001) *New Left Review* 56

——, *Culture and Equality: An Egalitarian Critique of Multiculturalism* (Cambridge: Polity Press, 2001)

BAUBÉROT J, *Histoire de la laïcité française* (Paris: Que sais-je, 2000)

BEETHAM D, 'What Future for Economic and Social Rights?' (1995) 43 *Political Studies* 41

BELL M, 'Mainstreaming Equality Norms into EU Asylum Law' (2001) 26 *European Law Review* 20

BELLACE J, 'The ILO Declaration of Fundamental Principles and Rights at Work' (2001) 17 *International Journal of Comparative Labour Law and Industrial Relations* 269

BELLAMY R and CASTIGLIONE D, 'Normative Theory and the European Union: Legitimising the Euro-Polity and its Regime' in Tragardh L (ed) *After National Democracy: Rights, Law and Power in the New Europe* (Oxford: Hart, 2003, forthcoming)

BELLAMY R, 'Constitutive Citizenship versus Constitutional Rights: Republican Reflections on the EU Charter and the Human Rights Act' in Campbell T, Ewing K and Tomkins A (eds) *Sceptical Essays on Human Rights* (Oxford: OUP, 2001) 15–39

BEN-ISRAEL R, 'The Rise, Fall and Resurrection of Social Dignity' in R Blanpain (ed) *Labour Law, Human Rights and Social Justice: Liber Amicorum in Honour of Ruth Ben-Israel* (The Hague: Kluwer, 2001) 1–8

BERCUSSON B, 'A European Agenda?' in Ewing K (ed) *Employment Rights at Work* (London: Institute of Employment Rights, 2001) 159–87

——, 'Democratic Legitimacy and European Labour Law' (1999) 28 *Industrial Law Journal* 153

——, 'Fundamental Social and Economic Rights in the European Community' in Cassesse A, Clapham A and Weiler J (eds) *Human Rights and the European Community: Methods of Protection* (Baden-Baden: Nomos, 1991) 195–291

BERENSTEIN A, 'Economic and Social Rights: Their Inclusion in the European Convention on Human Rights, Problems of Formulation and Interpretation' (1981) 2 *Human Rights Law Journal* 257

BERNARD N, 'Flexibility in the European Single Market' in Barnard C and Scott J (eds) *The Law of the Single European Market: Unpacking the Premises* (Oxford: Hart, 2002) 101–22

——, *Multilevel Governance in the European Union* (The Hague: Kluwer, 2002)

——, 'Legitimising EU Law: Is the Social Dialogue the Way Forward? Some Reflections around the *UEAPME* Case' in Shaw J (ed) *Social Law and Policy in an Evolving European Union* (Oxford: Hart, 2000) 279–302

——, 'What are the Purposes of EC Discrimination Law?' in Dine J and Watt B (eds) *Discrimination Law—Concepts, Limitations, and Justifications* (London, Longman, 1996)

BESSELINK L, 'Entrapped by the Maximum Standard: On Fundamental Rights, Pluralism and Subsidiarity in the European Union' (1998) 35 *Common Market Law Review* 629

BETTEN L, 'The EU Charter on Fundamental Rights: a Trojan Horse or a Mouse?' (2001) 17 *International Journal of Comparative Labour Law and Industrial Relations* 151

——, 'New Equality Provisions in European Law: Some Thoughts on the Fundamental Value of Equality as a Legal Principle' in Economides K, Betten L, Bridge J, Tettenborn A and Shrubsall V (eds) *Fundamental Values* (Oxford: Hart Publishing, 2000) 69–84

——, 'The Democratic Deficit of Participatory Democracy in Community Social Policy' (1998) 23 *European Law Review* 20

BETTEN L and GRIEF N, *EU Law and Human Rights* (Harlow: Longman, 1998)

BEVERIDGE F, NOTT S and STEPHEN K, 'Addressing Gender in National and Community Law and Policy-Making' in Shaw J (ed) *Social Law and Policy in an Evolving Union* (Oxford: Hart Publishing, 2000) 139–54

——, —— and —— (eds), *Making Women Count: Integrating Gender into Law and Policy-Making* (Aldershot: Ashgate, 2000)

BIFULCO R, CARTABIA M, CELOTTO A, 'Introduzione' in Bifulco R, Cartabia M and Celotto A (eds) *L'Europa dei diritti. Commento alla Carta dei diritti fondamentali dell'Unione Europea* (Bologna, il Mulino 2001) 11

BIN R, 'La famiglia: Alla Radice di un Ossimoro' (2001) *Lavoro e Diritto* 9

BLOM J, FITZPATRICK B, GREGORY J, KNEGT R and O'HARE U, *The Utilisation of Sex Equality Litigation in the Member States of the European Community*, V/782/96-EN (Report to the Equal Opportunities Unit of DG V, 1995) 2

BOBBIO N, *L'età dei Diritti* (Torino: Einaudi, 1990)

BOUSSINESC J, *La laïcité française, mémento juridique* (Paris: Seuil, 1994)

BRAIDOTTI R, 'On the Female Feminist Subject' in Bock G and James S (eds) *Beyond Equality and Difference. Citizenship, Feminist Politics and Female Subjectivity* (London: Routledge, 1992) 177–92

BRANDTNER B and ROSAS A, 'Trade Preferences and Human Rights' in Alston P (ed) *The EU and Human Rights* (Oxford: OUP, 1999) 699–722

BRAZIER M, 'Rights and Health Care' in Blackburn R (ed), *Rights of Citizenship* (London: Mansell, 1993) 56–74

BROWNE J, DEAKIN S and WILKINSON F, 'Capabilities, Social Rights and European Market Integration' Centre for Business Research Working Paper No 253 (Cambridge: University of Cambridge, 2002)

BRUNING G and PLANTENGA J, 'Parental Leave and Equal Opportunities: Experiences in Eight European Countries' (1999) 9 *Journal of European Social Policy* 195

Cabral P, 'Cross-border Medical Care in the EU—Bringing Down a First Wall' (1999) 24 *European Law Review* 387

CALAFÀ L, 'La Prestazione di Lavoro tra Assenze e (Dis)equilibri Familiari' (2001) *Lavoro e Diritto* 143

CARACCIOLO DI TORELLA E and MASSELOT A, 'Pregnancy, Maternity and the Organisation of Family Life: An Attempt to Classify the Case Law of the Court of Justice' (2001) 26 *European Law Review* 239

CARUSO D, 'Limits of the Classic Method: Positive Action in the European Union after the New Equality Directives' Jean Monnet Working Paper 10/02, <*http://www.jeanmonnetprogram.org/papers/02/021001.pdf*>

CASSESE A, LALUMIERE C, ROBINSON M, LEUPRECHT P, *Leading by Example: A Human Rights Agenda for the European Union for the Year 2000* (Florence: EUI, 2000)

CASEY N, 'The European Social Charter and Revised European Social Charter' in Costello C (ed), *Fundamental Social Rights: Current Legal Protection and the Challenge of the EU Charter of Fundamental Rights* (Dublin: Irish Centre for European Law, 2001) 55–75

——, *The Right to Organise and Bargain Collectively: Protection within the European Social Charter* (Strasbourg: Council of Europe, 1996)

CHALMERS D, 'The Mistakes of the Good European?' in Fredman S (ed) *Discrimination and Human Rights. The Case of Racism* (Oxford: OUP, 2001) 193–249

——, 'Post-nationalism and the Quest for Constitutional Substitutes' (2000) 27 *Journal of Law and Society* 178

CHAPMAN A, *Exploring a Human Rights Approach to Health Care Reform* (Washington DC: American Association for the Advancement of Science, 1993).

CHARPENTIER L, 'The European Court of Justice and the Rhetoric of Affirmative Action' (1998) 4 *European Law Journal* 167

CLAPHAM A, 'A Human Rights Policy for the European Community' (1990) 10 *Yearbook of European Law* 309

CLARK B, 'The Vienna Convention Reservations Regime and the Convention on Discrimination Against Women' (1991) 85 *American Journal of International Law* 281

COLEMAN D, 'Individualizing Justice though Multiculturalism: The Liberal's Dilemma' (1996) *Columbia Law Review* 1093

COOK R, 'Reservations to the Convention on the Elimination of All Forms of Discrimination Against Women' (1990) 30 *Virginia Journal of International Law* 643.

COPPEL J and O'NEILL A, 'The European Court of Justice: Taking Rights Seriously?' (1992) 29 *Common Market Law Review* 669

COSTELLO C, 'The Legal Status and Legal Effect of the Charter of Fundamental Rights of the European Union' in Costello C (ed) *Fundamental Social Rights: Current Legal Protection and the Challenge of the EU Charter of Fundamental Rights* (Dublin: Irish Centre for European Law, 2001) 127–50

——, 'The Court' in *IGC 2000: Issues, Options and Implications* (Dublin: Institute of European Affairs, November 2000)

——, 'The Preliminary Reference Procedure and the 2000 Intergovermental Conference' (1999) *Dublin University Law Journal* 40

Council of Europe, *Conditions of Employment in the European Social Charter, Human Rights*, Social Charter Monographs No 6, 2nd ed (Strasbourg: Council of Europe, 2000)

——, *Equality Between Women and Men in the European Social Charter*, Social Charter Monograph No. 2 (Strasbourg: Council of Europe, 1999)

——, *Social Protection in the European Social Charter* (Strasbourg: Council of Europe, 1999)

——, *Gender Mainstreaming: Conceptual Framework, Methodology and Presentation of Good Practices: Final Report of Activities of the Group of Specialists on Mainstreaming* (EG-S-MS (98)) (Strasbourg: Council of Europe, 1998)

CRAIG C, RUBERY J, TARLING R, and WILKINSON F, *Labour Market Structure, Industrial Organisation and Low Pay* (Cambridge: Cambridge University Press, 1982)

CRAIG P and DE BURCA G, *EU Law—Text, Cases and Materials*, 3rd ed (Oxford: OUP, 2002)

CRAIG P, 'The jurisdiction of the Community Courts reconsidered' in Weiler J & De Búrca G (eds) *The European Court of Justice* (Oxford: OUP, 2001) 177

CRAM L, *Policy-making in the EU: Conceptual Lenses and the Integration Process* (London: Routledge, 1997)

CRANSTON M, *What are Human Rights?* (London: Bodley Head, 1973)

CRAVEN M, 'A View from Elsewhere: Social Rights, International Covenant and the EU Charter of Fundamental Rights' in Costello C (ed) *Fundamental Social Rights: Current European Legal Protection and the Challenge of the EU Charter on Fundamental Rights* (Dublin: Irish Centre for European Law, 2001) 77–93

——, 'The Justiciability of Economic, Social and Cultural Rights' in Burchill R, Harris DJ and Owers A (eds) *Economic, Social and Cultural Rights: Their Implementation in United Kingdom Law* (Nottingham: University of Nottingham Human Rights Law Centre, 1999) 1–13

——, *The International Covenant on Economic, Social and Cultural Rights* (Oxford: Clarendon Press, 1995)

CREMONA M, 'Human Rights and Democracy Clauses in the EC's Trade Agreements' in Emiliou N and O'Keeffe D (eds) *The European Union and World Trade Law* (Wiley: Chichester, 1996) 62–77

CROMPTON R and HARRIS F, 'Employment, Careers, and Families: The Significance of Choice and Constraints in Women's Life' in Crompton R (ed), *Restructuring Gender Relations and Employment. The Decline of the Male Breadwinner* (Oxford: OUP, 1999) 128–49

CULLEN H, 'From Migrants to Citizens? European Community Policy on Intercultural Education' (1996) 45 *International and Comparative Law Quarterly* 109

DANKWA E, 'Working Paper on Article 2(3) of the International Covenant on Economic, Social and Cultural Rights' (1987) 9 *Human Rights Quarterly* 230

DAVIES P 'Market Integration and Social Policy in the Court of Justice' (1995) 24 *Industrial Law Journal* 49

DE BÚRCA G, 'Human Rights: The Charter and Beyond' in *Europe 2004 Le Grand Debat: Setting the Agenda and Outlining the Options,* Proceedings of European Commission Symposium (Brussels: European Commission, 2001)

——, 'The Drafting of the European Union Charter of Fundamental Rights' (2001) 26 *European Law Review* 126

——, 'The Role of Equality in European Community Law' in Dashwood A and O'Leary S (eds) *The Principle of Equal Treatment in European Community Law* (London: Sweet and Maxwell, 1997) 13–34

DE BÚRCA G, , 'The Quest for Legitimacy in the European Union' (1996) 59 *Modern Law Review* 349

——, 'The Language of Rights and European Integration' in Shaw J and More G (eds) *New Legal Dynamics of European Union* (Oxford: Clarendon Press, 1995) 29-54

DE LA PORTE C, 'Is the Open Method of Co-ordination Appropriate for Organising Activities at European Level in Sensitive Policy Areas?' (2002) 8 *European Law Journal* 38

DE SCHUTTER O, LEBESSIS N and PATERSON J (eds) *Governance in the European Union* (Luxembourg: OOPEC, 2001)

DE SIERVO U, 'L'ambigua redazione della Carta dei diritti fondamentali nel processo di costituzionalizzazione dell'Unione Europea' (2001) *Diritto Pubblico* 33

DE VOS P, '*Grootboom*, the Right of Access to Housing and Substantive Equality as Contextual Fairness' (2001) 17 *South African Journal of Human Rights* 258

DE WITTE B, 'The Legal Status of the Charter: Vital Question or Non-Issue?' (2001) 8 *Maastricht Journal of European and Comparative Law* 81

——, 'The Past and Future Role of the European Court of Justice in the Protection of Human Rights' in Alston P (ed) *The EU and Human Rights* (Oxford: OUP, 1999) 859-97

——, 'Community Law and National Constitutional Values' (1991/2) *Legal Issues of European Integration* 1

—— (ed), *European Community Law of Education* (Baden-Baden: Nomos, 1989)

DEAKIN S, 'Labour Law as Market Regulation: the Economic Foundations of European Social Policy' in Davies P, Lyon-Caen A, Sciarra S and Simitis S (eds) *European Community Labour Law: Principles and Perspectives* (Oxford: Clarendon Press, 1996) 62-93

DEAKIN S and WILKINSON F, 'Labour Law, Social Security and Economic Inequality' (1991) 15 *Cambridge Journal of Economics* 125

DEL PUNTA R, *Commentario al Codice civile, sub artt. 2110, 2111* (Milano: Giuffrè, 1992)

DELL'OLIO M, 'Sospensione del rapporto di lavoro' (1999) *Digesto Italiano IV*, vol XV, 22

DELOCHE-GAUDEZ F, 'The Convention on a Charter of Fundamental Rights: a method for the future', Notre Europe Research and Policy Paper No 15, November 2001, http://www.notre-europe.asso.fr/fichiers/Etud15-en

DEN EXTER A and HERMANS H (eds) *The Right to Health Care in Several European Countries*, proceedings of a conference held in Rotterdam, the Netherlands, 1998 (1999) *Studies in Social Policy* No 5

DEVEAUX M, 'Conflicting Equalities? Cultural Group Rights and Sex Equality' (2000) 48 *Political Studies* 522

DIEBALL H and SCHIEK D, 'Vereinbarkeit einer sog. Quotenregelung mit dem Gemeinschaftsrecht', *Informationsdienst Europäisches Arbeits- und Sozialrecht* 11/1995, 183-9

DINE J and WATT B, 'Sexual Harassment: Moving Away from Discrimination' (1995) 58 *Modern Law Review* 343

DOCKSEY C, 'The Principle of Equality between Women and Men as a Fundamental Right under Community Law' (1991) 20 *Industrial Law Journal* 258

DONNER L A, 'Gender Bias in Drafting International Discrimination Conventions: The 1979 Women's Convention Compared with the 1965 Racial Convention' (1994) 24 *California Western International Law Journal* 241

DUNBAR R, 'Minority Language Rights in International Law' (2001) 50 *International and Comparative Law Quarterly* 90

DUNCAN N, 'Croson Revisited: A Legacy of Uncertainty in the Application of Strict Scrutiny' (1995) 26 *Columbia Human Rights Law Review* 679

Dunning Report *Choices in Health Care: A Report by the Government Committee on Choices in Health Care, the Netherlands* (Rijswijk: Minister of Welfare, Health and Cultural Affairs, 1992)

ECONOMIDES K and WEILER J, 'Accession of the Communities to the European Convention on Human Rights: Commission Memorandum' (1979) 42 *Modern Law Review* 683

EICKE T, 'The European Charter of Fundamental Rights—Unique Opportunity or Unwelcome Distraction' (2000) *European Human Rights Law Review* 280

EIDE A, 'Economic, Social and Cultural Rights as Human Rights' in Eide A, Krause C, and Rosas A (eds) *Economic, Social and Cultural Rights: A Textbook*, 2nd ed (The Hague: Kluwer, 2001) 9–28

——, 'Realisation of Social-Economic Rights and the Minimum Threshold Approach' (1989) 10 *Human Rights Law Journal* 35

EISENBERG A, 'Diversity and Equality: Three Approaches to Cultural and Sexual Difference' Constitutionalism Web-Papers, ConWEB 1/2001, http://les1.man.ac.uk/conweb/

ERIKSEN E and FOSSUM J (eds) *Democracy in the European Union—Integration Through Deliberation?* (London: Routledge, 2000).

European Commission, *Handbook on Equal Treatment for Women and Men in the European Union,* 2nd ed (Brussels: European Commission, 1999)

——, *Affirming Fundamental Rights in the European Union—Time to Act* (Brussels: European Commission, 1999)

European Communities, *For a Europe of Civic and Social Rights* (Luxembourg: Office for Official Publications of the European Communities, 1996).

European Parliament Working Paper *Fundamental Social Rights in Europe* (Brussels: European Parliament, 1999)

European Trade Union Institute, *A Legal Framework for European Industrial Relations* (Brussels: European Trade Union Institute, 1999)

European Union, Secretariat to the Convention on the Future of the Union, *Delimitation of competence between the European Union and the Member States—Existing system, problems and avenues to be explored,* Conv 47/02 (15 May 2002)

European Union, Council, *Explanations Relating to the complete text of the Charter* (Luxembourg: Office for Official Publications of the European Communities, 2001)

European Union, *Charter of Fundamental Rights of the European Union: Explanations relating to the complete text of the Charter* (Luxembourg: Office for Official Publications of the European Communities, 2001)

EVERLING, 'Will Europe Slip on Bananas?' (1996) 33 *Common Market Law Review* 401

EVERSON M, 'The Legacy of the Market Citizen' in Shaw J and More G (eds) *New Legal Dynamics of European Union* (Oxford: Clarendon Press, 1995) 73–90

EVJU J, 'Collective Agreements and Competition Law. The *Albany* Puzzle and *Van der Woude*' (2001) 17 *International Journal of Comparative Labour Law and Industrial Relations* 165

EWING K, *The EU Charter of Fundamental Rights: Waste of Time or Wasted Opportunity?* (London: Institute of Employment Rights, 2002)

EWING K, 'Social Rights and Human Rights: Britain and the Social Charter—the Conservative Legacy' [2000] *European Human Rights Law Review* 91

——, 'Social Rights and Constitutional Law' [1999] *Public Law* 104

——, ' The Human Rights Act and Labour Law' (1998) 27 *Industrial Law Journal* 275

FENWICK H and HERVEY T, 'Sex Equality in the Single Market: New Directions for the European Court of Justice' (1995) 32 *Common Market Law Review* 443

FENWICK H, 'Perpetuating Inequality in the Name of Equal Treatment' (1996) 18 *Journal of Social Welfare and Family Law* 263

FITZPATRICK B, 'European Union Law and the Council of Europe Conventions' in Costello C (ed) *Fundamental Social Rights: Current European Legal Protection and the Challenge of the EU Charter on Fundamental Rights* (Dublin: Irish Centre for European Law, 2001)

FLYNN L, 'The Implications of Article 13 EC—After Amsterdam, Will Some Forms of Discrimination be More Equal than Others?' (1999) 36 *Common Market Law Review* 1127

FORDE M, 'The "Closed Shop" Case' (1982) 11 *Industrial Law Journal* 1

FREDMAN S, 'Combating Racism with Human Rights: the Right to Equality' in Fredman S (ed) *Discrimination and Human Rights—the Case of Racism* (Oxford: OUP, 2001) 20

——, 'Equality: a new generation?' (2001) 30 *Industrial Law Journal* 145

——, 'Scepticism under Scrutiny: Labour Law and Human Rights' in Campbell T, Ewing K and Tomkins A (eds) *Sceptical Essays on Human Rights* (Oxford: OUP, 2001) 197–213

——, *Discrimination Law* (Oxford: Clarendon Press, 2002)

——, 'Affirmative Action and the Court of Justice: A Critical Analysis' in Shaw J (ed) *Social Law and Policy in an Evolving European Union* (Oxford: Hart, 2000) 171–95

——, 'After Kalanke and Marschall: Affirming Affirmative Action' [1998] *Cambridge Yearbook of European Legal Studies* 199

——, 'Social Law in the European Union: The Impact of the Lawmaking Process' in Craig P and Harlow C (eds) *Lawmaking in the European Union* (Deventer: Kluwer, 1998) 405–11

——, 'A Difference with Distinction: Pregnancy and Parenthood Reassessed' (1994) 110 *Law Quarterly Review* 106

FREDMAN S, McCrudden C and FREEDLAND M, 'An EU Charter of Fundamental Rights' [2000] *Public Law* 178

FREEDLAND M, 'Employment Policy' in Davies P, Lyon-Caen A, Sciarra S and Simitis S (eds) *European Community Labour Law: Principles and Perspectiva, Liber Amicorum Lord Wedderburn,* (Oxford: OUP, 1996) 287

FREEMAN R, *The Politics of Health in Europe* (Manchester: MUP, 2000)

FUDGE J, 'Lessons from Canada: the Impact of the Charter of Rights and Freedoms on Labour and Employment Law' in K Ewing (ed) *Human Rights at Work* (London: Institute of Employment Rights, 2000)

GAGNON A and TULLY J (eds) *Multinational Democracies* (Cambridge: CUP, 2001)

GALOTTO J, 'Strict Scrutiny for Gender, via *Croson*' (1993) 99 *Columbia Law Review* 508

GARCIA R, 'Las Clausulas Horizontales de la Carta de Los Derechos Fundamentales de la Unión Europea' in Garcia de Enterría E and Garcia R (eds) *La Encrucijada Constitucional de la Unión Europea* (Madrid: Civitas, 2002) 151

GARDE A, 'Recent Developments in the Law Relating to Transfers of Undertakings' (2002) 39 *Common Market Law Review* 523

GEARTY C, 'The Internal and External "Other" in the Union Legal Order: Racism, Religious Intolerance and Xenophobia in Europe' in Alston P (ed) *The EU and Human Rights* (Oxford: OUP, 1999) 327–58

GEDDES A, 'Immigrants, Ethnic Minorities and the EU's Democratic Deficit' (1995) 33 *Journal of Common Market Studies* 197

GEERTZ C, 'The Impact of the Concept of Culture on the Concept of Mind' in Geertz (ed) *The Interpretation of Cultures: Selected Essays* (London: Fontana Press, 1993) 33–54

GERMANOTTA P and NOVITZ T, 'Globalisation and the Right to Strike: The Case for European-Level Protection of Secondary Action' (2002) 18 *International Journal of Comparative Labour Law and Industrial Relations* 67

GERNIGON B, ODERO A and GUIDO H, 'ILO Principles Concerning Collective Bargaining' (2000) 139 *International Labour Review* 33

——, —— and ——, 'ILO Principles Concerning the Right to Strike' (1998) 137 *International Labour Review* 441

GEYER R, *Exploring European Social Policy* (Cambridge: Polity, 2000)

GIJZEN M, 'The Charter: A Milestone for Social Protection in Europe?' (2001) 8 *Maastricht Journal of European and Comparative Law* 33

GIORGIS A, 'Art. 33. Vita familiare e professionale' in Bifulco R, Cartabia M, Celotto A (eds), *L'Europa dei diritti. Commento alla Carta dei diritti fondamentali dell'Unione Europea* (Bologna: il Mulino 2001) 237

GOLDSMITH LORD, 'A Charter of Rights, Freedoms and Principles' (2001) 38 *Common Market Law Review* 1201

GOODWIN-GILL G, 'The Individual Refugee, the 1951 Convention and the Treaty of Amsterdam' in Guild E and Harlow C (eds) *Implementing Amsterdam: Immigration and Asylum Rights in EC Law* (Oxford: Hart, 2001)

GOTTARDI D, 'Lavoro di Cura. Spunti di Riflessioni' (2001) *Lavoro e Diritto* 121

GUTTO S, 'Beyond Justiciability: Challenges of Implementing/Enforcing Socio-Economic Rights in South Africa' (1998) 4 *Buffalo Human Rights Law Review* 79

HARRIS DJ, *The European Social Charter*, 2nd ed (New York, Transnational Publishers Inc, 2001)

HARRIS DJ, O'BOYLE M and WARBRICK C, *Law of the European Convention on Human Rights* (London: Butterworths, 1995)

HARRIS N, *Social Security Law in Context* (Oxford: OUP, 2000)

HAYEK F, *Law, Legislation and Liberty. A New Statement of the Liberal Principles of Justice and Political Economy* (London: Routledge, 1980)

——, *The Political Order of a Free People* (London: Routledge, 1979)

——, *The Mirage of Social Justice* (London: Routledge, 1976)

——, *Rules and Order* (London: Routledge, 1973)

HELLY D, 'The Political Regulation of Cultural Plurality: Foundations and Principles' (1993) 25 *Canadian Ethnic Studies* 15

HEPPLE B, 'The EU Charter of Fundamental Rights' (2001) 30 *Industrial Law Journal* 225

——, 'Social Values in European Law' (1995) 48 *Current Legal Problems* 39

——, 'The Implementation of the Community Charter of Fundamental Social Rights' (1990) 53 *Modern Law Review* 643

HEPPLE B and BARNARD C, 'Substantive Equality' (2000) 59 *Cambridge Law Journal* 562

HERINGA A and VERHEY L, 'The EU Charter: Text and Structure' (2001) 8 *Maastricht Journal of European and Comparative Law* 11

HERRMANN C, 'Common Commercial Policy after Nice: Sisyphus Would Have Done a Better Job' (2002) 39 *Common Market Law Review* 7

HERVEY T, 'Social solidarity: a Buttress Against Internal Market Law' in Shaw J (ed) *Social Law and Policy in an Evolving European Union* (Oxford: Hart, 2000) 31–47

——, 'Putting Europe's House in Order' in O'Keeffe D and Twomey P (eds) *Legal Issues of the Amsterdam Treaty* (Oxford: Hart, 1999) 329–49

——, 'Sex Equality as Substantive Justice' (1999) 62 *Modern Law Review* 614

——, *European Social Law and Policy* (London: Longman, 1998)

——, *Justifications for Sex Discrimination in Employment* (London: Butterworths, 1993)

——, 'Justification of Indirect Discrimination in Employment: European Community Law and United Kingdom Law Compared' (1991) *International and Comparative Law Quarterly* 807

HERVEY T and SHAW J, 'Women, Work and Care: Women's Dual Role and Double Burden in EC Sex Equality Law' (1998) 8 *Journal of European Social Policy* 43

HOFFMAN L, 'Fatal in Fact: An Analysis of the Application of the Compelling Governmental Interest Leg of Strict Scrutiny in *City of Richmond v JA Croson*' (1990) *B U L Review* 889

HOQ L, 'The Women's Convention and Its Optional Protocol: Empowering Women to Claim Their Internationally Protected Rights' (2001) 32 *Columbia Human Rights Law Review* 677

HOSKYNS C, 'Encapsulating Feminism' (1996) 1 *European Law Journal* 1

——, *Integrating Gender—Women, Law and Politics in the European Union* (London: Verso, 1996)

HUNT J, 'The European Union: Promoting a Framework for Corporate Social Responsibility?' in Macmillan F (ed), *International Corporate Law: Vol 2* (Oxford: Hart, 2003, forthcoming)

——, 'The Court of Justice as a Policy Actor: The Case of the Acquired Rights Directive' (1998) 18 *Legal Studies* 336

HUNTER A, 'Between the Domestic and the International: The Role of the European Union in Providing Protection for Unaccompanied Refugee Children in the United Kingdom' (2001) 3 *European Journal of Migration and Law* 383

ICHINO A and ICHINO P, (1998) 'A chi serve il diritto del lavoro? Riflessioni interdisciplinari sulla funzione economica e la giustificazione costituzionale dell'inderogabilità delle norme giuslavoristiche', in Amendola A (ed) *Istituzione e mercato del lavoro* (Rome, Edizione Scientifiche Italiane, 1998)

ICHINO P, *Il Tempo Della Prestazione nel Rapporto di Lavoro* (Milano: Giuffrè, 1984)

JACOBS A, 'Towards Community Action on Strike Law?' (1978) 15 *Common Market Law Review* 133

JACOBS F, 'The Extension of the European Convention on Human Rights to Include Economic, Social and Cultural Rights' (1978) 3 *Human Rights Review* 166

JOERGES C, 'Bureaucratic Nightmare, Technocratic Regime and the Dream of Good Transnational Governance' in Joerges C and Vos E (eds) *EU Committees: Social Regulation, Law and Politics* (Oxford: Hart, 1999) 3–17

JOWELL J, 'Is Equality a Constitutional Principle?' (1994) 47 *Current Legal Problems* 1

KAHN-FREUND O, 'The European Social Charter' in Jacobs F (ed) *European Law and the Individual* (North-Holland: Amsterdam, 1976) 181–211

——, 'Labour Law and Social Security' in Stein E and Nicholson T (eds) *American Enterprise in the European Common Market: A Legal Profile, Vol.1* (Ann Arbor: University of Michigan Press, 1960) 297–458

KELLER P, 'Re-thinking Ethnic and Cultural Rights in Europe' (1998) 18 *Oxford Journal of Legal Studies* 29

KENNER J, *EU Employment Law: From Rome to Amsterdam and Beyond* (Oxford: Hart, 2003)

——, 'The EC Employment Title and the "Third Way": Making Soft Law Work' (1999) 15 *International Journal of Comparative Labour Law and Industrial Relations* 33

——, 'A Distinctive Legal Base for Social Policy?—The Court of Justice Answers a "Delicate Question"' (1997) 22 *European Law Review* 579

KILKELLY U, *The Child and the European Convention on Human Rights* (Aldershot: Ashgate, 1999)

KIM N, 'The Cultural Defense and the Problems of Cultural Preemption: A Framework for Analysis' (1997) 27 *New Mexico Law Review* 101

KLEINMAN M and PIACHAUD D, 'European Social Policy: Conceptions and Choices' (1993) 3 *Journal of European Social Policy* 1

KLERK Y, 'Working Paper on Article 2(2) and Article 3 of the International Covenant on Economic, Social and Cultural Rights' (1987) 9 *Human Rights Quarterly* 250

KUKATHAS C, 'Are There Any Cultural Rights? (1992) 20 *Political Theory* 105

KUMM M, 'Who Is the Final Arbiter of Constitutionality in Europe?' Harvard Jean Monnet Chair Working Papers 10/98, www.law.harvard.edu/Programs/JeanMonnet/papers/98/98-10-.html

KUPER A, *Culture: the Anthropologist's Account* (Cambridge, Mass.: Harvard University Press, 1999)

KYMLICKA W, 'An Update from the Multiculturalism Wars: Commentary on Schachar and Spinner-Halev' in Lukes S and Joppke C (eds), *Multicultural Questions*, (Oxford: OUP, 1999) 112

——, *Multicultural Citizenship; A Liberal Theory of Minority Rights* (Oxford: OUP, 1995)

LADEUR K-H, 'Towards a Legal Theory of Supranationality—the Viability of the Network Concept' (1997) 3 *European Law Journal* 33

LEARY V, 'The WTO and the Social Clause: Post- Singapore' (1997) 8 *European Journal of International Law* 118

——, 'Justiciability and Beyond, Complaint Procedures and the Right to Health' (1995) 55 *International Commission of Jurists: The Review* 105

——, 'The Right to Health in International Human Rights Law' (1994) 1 *Health and Human Rights* 3

LECKIE N, 'The Justiciability of Housing Rights' in F Coomans and G Van Hoof (eds) *The Right to Complain and Economic, Social and Cultural Rights* (Netherlands: Studie— en Informatiecentrum Mensenrechten, 1995) 35

LEFORT C, *Democracy and Political Theory* (Cambridge: Polity Press, 1988)

LEHNING P, European Citizenship: Towards a European Identity?' (2001) 20 *Law and Philosophy* 239

LEIBFRIED S and PIERSON P, 'Prospects for Social Europe' (1992) 20 *Politics & Society* 333

LENAERTS K and FOUBERT P, 'Social Rights in the Case-Law of the European Court of Justice' (2001) 28 *Legal Issues of Economic Integration* 267

LENAERTS K and DE SMIJTER E, 'A "Bill of Rights" for the European Union' (2001) 38 *Common Market Law Review* 273

LENAERTS K, *Le Juge et la Constitution aux Etas-Unis d'Amerique and dans l'ordre iuridique européen* (Brussels: Bruylant, 1998)

LIEBENBERG S, 'The Protection of Economic and Social Rights in Domestic Legal Systems' in Eide A, Krause C, and Rosas A (eds) *Economic, Social and Cultural Rights : A Textbook*, 2nd ed (The Hague: Kluwer, 2001) 82

——, 'The Right to Social Assistance: the Implications of *Grootboom* for Policy Reform in South Africa' (2001) 17 *South African Journal of Human Rights* 232

LIISBERG J, 'Does the EU Charter of Fundamental Rights Threaten the Supremacy of Community Law?' (2001) 38 *Common Market Law Review* 1171

LO FARO A, *Regulating Social Europe. Reality and Myth of Collective Bargaining in the EC Legal Order* (Oxford: Hart, 2000)

——, *Funzioni e Finzioni Della Contrattazione Collettiva Comunitaria* (Milano: Giuffrè, 1999)

LOENEN T, 'Indirect Discrimination: Oscillating Between Containment and Revolution' in Loenen T and Rodrigues P (eds), *Non-discrimination Law: Comparative Perspectives* (The Hague: Kluwer, 1999) 195–211

LOENEN T and VELDMAN A, 'Preferential Treatment in the Labour Market after *Kalanke*: Some Comparative Perspectives' (1996) *International Journal of Comparative Labour Law and Industrial Relations* 48

LOI P, *La sicurezza. Diritto e fondamento dei diritti nel rapporto di lavoro,* (Torino, Giappichelli, 2000) 160

LOPEZ J, 'Famiglia e Condivisione dei Ruoli in Spagna' (2001) *Lavoro e Diritto* 163

LYON-CAEN A, 'The Legal Efficacy and Significance of Fundamental Social Rights: Lessons from the European Experience' in Hepple B (ed) *Social and Labour Rights in a Global Context* (Cambridge: CUP, 2002) 182–91

——, 'Fundamental Social Rights as Benchmarks in the Construction of the EU' in Betten L and McDevitt D (eds) *The Protection of Fundamental Social Rights in the European Union* (The Hague: Kluwer, 1996) 43–6

MACCORMICK N, 'Beyond the Sovereign State' (1993) 56 *Modern Law Review* 1

MACMILLAN F (ed), *International Corporate Law: Vol 2* (Oxford: Hart, 2003, forthcoming)

MANCINI F and O'LEARY S, 'The New Frontiers of Sex Equality Law in the European Union' (1999) 24 *European Law Review* 331

MARGALIT A and HALBERTAL M, 'Liberalism and the Right to Culture' (1994) 61 *Social Research* 491

MAZEY S, 'The Development of EU Gender Policies: Towards the Recognition of Difference' (2002) 15 *European Union Studies Association Review* 3

MCCRUDDEN C, 'Theorising European Equality Law' in Costello C and Barry E (eds) *Equality in Diversity: The New EC Equality Directives* (Dublin, Irish Centre for European Law, 2003, forthcoming)

——, 'The Future of the EU Charter of Fundamental Rights' Harvard Jean Monnet Working Paper No.10/01, <http://www.jeanmonnetprogram.org/papers/01/013001.html>

——, 'International and European Norms Regarding National Legal Remedies for Racial Inequality' in Fredman S (ed) *Discrimination and Human Rights—The Case of Racism* (Oxford: OUP, 2001) 251–307

MCCRUDDEN C and DAVIES A, 'A Perspective on Trade and Labour Rights' (2000) 3 *Journal of International Economic Law* 43

McDONALD M, 'Unity in Diversities: Some Tensions in the Construction of Europe' (1996) 4 *Social Anthropology* 47

McGLYNN C, 'Rights for Children? The Potential Impact of the European Union Charter of Fundamental Rights' (2002) *European Public Law* 387

——, 'Reclaiming a Feminist Vision: the Reconciliation of Paid Work and Family Life in European Union Law and Policy' (2001) 7 *Columbia Journal of European Law* 241

——, 'Families and the European Union Charter of Fundamental Rights: Progressive Change or Entrenching the Status Quo?' (2001) 26 *European Law Review* 582

——, 'The Europeanisation of Family Law' (2001) 13 *Child and Family Law Quarterly* 35

——, 'Pregnancy, Parenthood and the Court of Justice in *Abdoulaye*' (2000) 25 *European Law Review* 654

McHALE J, 'Enforcing Health Care Rights in the English Courts' in Burchill R, Harris DJ and Owers A (eds), *Economic, Social and Cultural Rights: Their Implementation in United Kingdom Law* (Nottingham: University of Nottingham Human Rights Law Centre, 1999) 66–87

MENÉNDEZ A J, 'Chartering Europe: Legal Status and Policy Implications of the Charter of Fundamental Rights of the European Union' (2000) *Journal of Common Market Studies* 471

——, 'Exporting rights: The Charter of Fundamental Rights, Membership and Foreign Policy of the European Union', ARENA Working Papers, WP 02/18, http://www.arena.uio.no/publications/wp02_18.htm

MERNISSI F, *Beyond the Veil: Male-Female Dynamics in a Modern Muslim Society* (Cambridge Mass., Shenkman Publishing Company, 1975)

MILLAR J 'Obligations and Autonomy in Social Welfare', in Crompton R (ed) *Restructuring Gender Relations and Employment. The Decline of the Male Breadwinner* (Oxford: OUP, 1999) 26–39

MINOR J, 'An Analysis of Structural Weaknesses in the Convention on the Elimination of All Forms of Discrimination Against Women' (1994) 24 *Georgia Journal of International and Comparative Law* 137

MINOW M, Anderson K and Mandler M, *Economic and Social Rights and the Right to Health*, Human Rights Program, Harvard Law School and François-Xavier Bagnoud Center for Health and Human Rights Workshop, September 1993, www.law.harvard.edu/programs/HRP/Publications/economic1.html

MOLLER OKIN S and respondents, *Is Multiculturalism Bad for Women?* (Princeton: Princeton University Press, 1999).

——, 'Feminism and Multiculturalism: Some Tensions' (1998) *Ethics* 108

MONTGOMERY J, *Health Care Law* (Oxford: OUP, 1997)

——, 'Recognising a Right to Health' in Beddard R and Hill D (eds) *Economic, Social and Cultural Rights: Progress and Achievement* (Basingstoke: Macmillan, 1992) 188–92

MOON G, 'Substantive Rights and Equal Treatment in Respect of Religion and Belief: Towards a Better Understanding of the Rights, and their Implications' [2000] *European Human Rights Law Review* 580

——, 'The Draft Discrimination Protocol to the European Convention on Human Rights: A Progress Report' [2000] *European Human Rights Law Review* 49

MOORE S, 'Nothing Positive from the Court of Justice' (1996) 21 *European Law Review* 156

MOORMAN Y 'Integration of ILO Core Standards into the WTO' (2001) 39 *Columbia Journal of Transnational Law* 555

MORE G, 'The Principle of Equal Treatment: From Market Unifier to Fundamental Right' in Craig P and de Búrca G (eds) *The Evolution of EU Law* (Oxford, OUP, 1999) 517–53

——, 'Equality of Treatment in European Community Law: the Limits of Market Equality' in Bottomley A (ed) *Feminist Perspectives on the Foundational Subjects of Law* (London: Cavendish, 1996) 261–78

MORIJN J, 'Judicial Reference to the EU Fundamental Rights Charter—First Experiences and Possible Prospects', Working Paper N° 1 of the Ius Gentium Conimbrigae Institute (Human Rights Centre, http://www.fd.uc.pt/hrc/working_papers)

MORISON J, 'The Case Against Constitutional Reform' (1998) 25 *Journal of Law and Society* 1 Murray J, *Transnational Labour Regulation: The ILO and EC Compared* (The Hague: Kluwer, 2001)

MUYLLE K, 'Angry Farmers and Passive Policemen: Private Conduct and the Free Movement of Goods' (1998) 23 *European Law Review* 467

NAPOLI D, 'The EU's Foreign Policy and Human Rights' in Neuwahl N and Rosas A (eds) *The European Union and Human Rights* (The Hague: Martinus Nijhoff Publishers, 1995).

NARAYAN U, *Dis/locating Cultures/Identitites, Traditions, and Third World Feminism* (London: Routledge, 1997).

NEAL A (ed), *Fundamental Social Rights at Work in the European Community* (Aldershot: Ashgate, 1999)

NOLL G and VEDSTED-HANSEN J, 'Non-communitarians: Refugees and Asylum Policy' in Alston P (ed), *The EU and Human Rights* (Oxford: OUP, 1999) 359–410

NOVITZ T, '"A Human Face" for the Union or More Cosmetic Surgery? EU Competence in Global Social Governance and Promotion of Core Labour Standards' (2002) 9 *Maastricht Journal of European and Comparative Law* 231

——, 'Are Social Rights Necessarily Collective Rights? A Critical Analysis of the Collective Complaints Protocol to the European Social Charter' [2002] *European Human Rights Law Review* 50

——, 'Remedies for Violation of Social Rights within the Council of Europe' in Kilpatrick C, Novitz T and Skidmore P (eds) *The Future of Remedies in Europe* (Oxford: Hart, 2000) 231–51

NOWAK M, 'Human Rights Conditionality in the EU' in Alston P (ed), *The EU and Human Rights* (Oxford: OUP, 1999) 687–98

O'HARE U, 'The Future of Positive Action in the European Union: The *Marschall* Case' (1998) 49 *Northern Ireland Legal Quarterly* 426

O'HIGGINS P, 'Labour is Not a Commodity'—an Irish Contribution to International Labour Law' (1997) 29 *Industrial Law Journal* 225

ORLANDINI G, 'The Free Movement of Goods as a Possible "Community" Limitation on Industrial Conflict' (2000) 6 *European Law Journal* 341

PAREKH B, *Rethinking Multiculturalism: Cultural Diversity and Political Theory* (London: Palgrave Press, 2000)

SPINNER-HALEV J, *Surviving Diversity: Religion and Democratic Citizenship* (Baltimore: Johns Hopkins University Press, 2000)

PEERS S, *EU Justice and Home Affairs Law* (London: Longman, 2000)

PETERS A, *Women, Quotas and Constitutions: A Comparative Study of Affirmative Action for Women under American, German, European Community and International Law* (The Hague: Kluwer, 1999)

Pfau Effinger B, 'The Modernization of Family and Motherhood in Western Europe' in Crompton R (ed) *Restructuring Gender Relations and Employment. The Decline of the Male Breadwinner* (Oxford: OUP, 1999) 60–79

Plant R, *Can There be a Right to Health Care?* (Southampton, Institute for Health Policy Studies, 1989)

Poiares Maduro M, 'Contrapunctual Law: Europe's Constitutional Pluralism in Action' in Walker N (ed) *Sovereignty in Transition* (Oxford: Hart Publishing, 2003, forthcoming)

——, 'Europe and the Constitution: What if this is as Good as it Gets?' in Weiler J and Wind M (eds) *Rethinking European Constitutionalism* (Cambridge: CUP, 2003, forthcoming)

——, 'Europe's Social Self: The "Sickness Unto Death"' in Shaw J (ed) *Social Law and Policy in an Evolving European Union* (Oxford: Hart, 2000) 325–49

——, 'Striking the Elusive Balance Between Economic Freedom and Social Rights in the EU' in Alston P (ed) *The EU and Human Rights* (Oxford: OUP, 1999) 449–72

——, 'The Heterenonyms of European Law' (1999) 3 *European Law Journal* 160

——, *We the Court, The European Court of Justice and the European Economic Constitution* (Oxford: Hart, 1998)

Pollitt K, 'Whose Culture?' in Moller Okin S and respondents, *Is Multiculturalism Bad for Women?* (New Jersey: Princeton University Press, 1999) 27–34

Poulter S, 'Muslim headscarves in school: contrasting legal approaches in England and France' (1997) *Oxford Journal of Legal Studies* 43.

Rainer A, 'A Fundamental Rights Charter for the European Union' 15 *Tulane European and Civil Law Forum* (2000–2001) 43

Raz J, 'Multiculturalism' (1998) 11 *Ratio Juris* 193

Reich N, 'The "November Revolution" of the European Court of Justice: *Keck, Meng and Audi* revisited' (1994) 31 *Common Market Law Review* 459

Rex J, 'Race and Ethnicity in Europe' in Bailey J (ed) *Social Europe* (Longman: London, 1992) 106–20

Rich R, 'Right to Development: A Right of Peoples' in Crawford J (ed) *The Rights of Peoples* (Oxford: Clarendon Press, 1988) 39–54

Richmond C, 'Preserving the Identity Crisis: Autonomy, System and Sovereignty in European Law' (1997) 16 *Law and Philosophy* 377

Riedel E and Will M, 'Human Rights Clauses in External Agreements of the EC' in Alston P (ed) *The EU and Human Rights* (Oxford: OUP, 1999) 723–54

Roccella M and Treu T, *Diritto del lavoro della Comunità europea* (Padova: CEDAM, 2002)

Rodríguez-Piñero M, Bravo-Ferrer M and Rodríguez-Piñero Royo M, 'The Principle of Equality in the Labour Market—Reflections in the Spanish Model' (2002) 18 *International Journal of Comparative Labour Law and Industrial Relations* 169

Rogowski R and Wilthagen T (eds) *Reflexive Labour Law* (Deventer: Kluwer, 1994)

Rosas A and Eide A, 'Economic, Social and Cultural Rights: A Universal Challenge' in Eide A, Krause C and Rosas A (eds), *Economic, Cultural and Social Rights* (The Hague: Kluwer, 2001) 15–19

Roscam Abbing H, 'Editorial: Public Health Insurance and Freedom of Movement within the European Union' (1999) 6 *European Journal of Health Law* 1

Rubio Llorente F, 'Mostrar Los Derechos Sin Destruir la Unión' (2002) *Revista Española de Derecho Constitucional* 13

RYAN B, 'Pay, Trade Union Rights and European Community Law' (1997) 13 *International Journal of Comparative Labour Law and Industrial Relations* 305

——, 'The Private Enforcement of European Union Labour Laws' in Kilpatrick C, Novitz T and Skidmore P (eds) *The Future of Remedies in Europe* (Oxford: Hart, 2000) 141–63

SACERDOTI G, 'The European Charter of Fundamental Rights: From a Nation State Europe to a Citizens Europe' (2002) 8 *Columbia Journal of European Law* 37

SACHS A, 'Social and Economic Rights: Can they be made Justiciable?' (2000) 53 *Southern Methodist University Law Review* 1381

SALAIS R, 'Libertés du travail et capacités: une perspective pour une construction européenne?' [1999] *Droit Social* 467

SALTMAN R, 'A Conceptual Overview of Recent Health Care Reforms' (1994) 4 *European Journal of Public Health* 287

SALTMAN R, FIGUERAS J and SAKELLARIDES C (eds) *Critical Challenges for Health Care Reform in Europe* (Buckingham: Open University Press, 1998)

SARACENO C, 'Politiche del lavoro e politiche della famiglia: una alleanza lunga e problematica' (2001) *Lavoro e diritto* 37

——, 'Un'Europa di Donne e di Uomini?' (1999) *il Mulino* 46

SCARPONI S, 'Il Lavoro Delle Donne fra Produzione e Riproduzione' (2001) *Lavoro e Diritto* 97

——, 'Luci ed Ombre Dell'accordo Europeo in Materia di Lavoro a Tempo Parziale' (1999) *Rivista Giuridica del Lavoro* 399

SCHACHAR A, *Multicultural Jurisdictions: Cultural Differences and Women's Rights* (Cambridge: CUP, 2001)

SCHENIN M, 'Economic and Social Rights as Legal Rights' in Eide A, Krause C, and Rosas A (eds) *Economic, Social and Cultural Rights : A Textbook*, 2nd ed (The Hague: Kluwer, 2001) 29–54

SCHIEK D, 'Elements of a New Framework for the Principle of Equal Treatment of Persons' (2002) 8 *European Law Journal* 290

——, 'Torn Between Arithmetic and Substantive Equality? Perspectives on Equality in German Labour Law' (2002) 18 *International Journal of Comparative Labour Law and Industrial Relations* 149

——, 'Sex Equality after *Kalanke* and *Marschall*' (1998) 4 *European Law Journal* 148

SCHMIDT M, 'Parental Leave: Contested Procedure, Creditable Results' (1997) 13 *International Journal of Comparative Labour Law and Industrial Relations* 113

SCHWELLNUS G, '"Much Ado About Nothing?" Minority Protection and the EU Charter of Fundamental Rights' Constitutionalism Web-Papers, ConWEB No 5/2001, http://www.qub.ac.uk/ies/onlinepapers/const.html

SCIARRA S (eds) *Labour Law in the Courts: National Judges and the European Court of Justice* (Oxford: Hart Publishing, 2001)

——, 'The Employment Title in the Amsterdam Treaty. A Multi-language Legal Discourse', in O'Keeffe D and Twomey P (eds) *Legal Issues of the Amsterdam Treaty* (Oxford: Hart, 1999) 157–70

SCOTT C, 'The Interdependence and Permeability of Human Rights Norms: Towards a Partial Fusion of the International Covenants on Human Rights' (1989) 27 *Osgoode Hall Law Journal* 769

SCOTT J and TRUBEK D, 'Mind the Gap: Law and New Approaches to Governance in the European Union' (2002) 8 *European Law Journal* 1

Scottish Executive Publications online, *Report of the MMR Expert Group*, 2002, http://www.scotland.gov.uk/library5/health/rmmr-06.asp

SEN A, *Development as Freedom*, (Oxford: OUP, 1999)

——, *Commodities and Capabilities* (Deventer: North Holland, 1985)

SHACHAR A, 'Group Identity and Women's Rights in Family Law: The Perils of Multicultural Accommodation' (1998) 6 *Journal of Political Philosophy* 285

SHAW J, 'Process, Responsibility and Inclusion in EU constitutionalism: The challenge for the Convention on the Future of the Union' Federal Trust Constitutionalism Online Essays, www.fedtrust.co.uk/eu_constitution, July 2002

——, 'From the Margins to the Centre: Education and Training Law and Policy' in Craig P and de Búrca G (eds) *The Evolution of EU Law* (Oxford: OUP, 1999) 555–95

——, 'The Scope and Content of European Community Social Law: A Review of Progress and a Bibliographical Note' (1992) 14 *Journal of Social Welfare and Family Law* 71

SHUE H, 'The Interdependence of Duties' in Alston P and Tomasevski K, *The Right to Food* (Utrecht: Stichting Studie en Infomatiecentrum Mensenrechten, 1984) 83–95

SIEVEKING K, 'The Significance of Transborder Utilisation of Health Care Benefits for Migrants' 2 *European Journal of Migration and the Law* (2000) 143

SIMMA B, Aschenbrenner J, and Schulte C, 'Human Rights Considerations in Development Cooperation Activities of the EC', in Alston P (ed), *The EU and Human Rights* (Oxford: OUP, 1999) 571–626

——, 'The Implementation of the International Covenant on Economic, Social and Cultural Rights' in Matscher F (ed) *The Implementation of Economic and Social Rights. National, International and Comparative Aspects* (Strasbourg: N.P. Engel Verlag, 1991) 75–94

SKORDAS A, 'The New Refugee Legislation in Greece' (1999) 4 *International Journal of Refugee Law* 678

SPENCER M, *States of Injustice: A Guide to Human Rights and Civil Liberties in the European Union* (London: Pluto Press, 1995)

SPINNER-HALEV J 'Feminism, Multiculturalism, Oppression, and the State' (2001) 112 *Ethics* 84

STALFORD H, 'The Citizenship Status of Children in European Union Law' (2000) 8 *International Journal of Children's Rights* 101.

——, 'The Developing European Agenda on Children's Rights' (2000) 22 *Journal of Social Welfare and Family Law* 229

STEINER H and ALSTON P, *International Human Rights in Context: Law, Politics, Morals* 2nd edn (Oxford: OUP, 2000)

STEINER H, 'Social Rights and Economic Development: Converging Discourses?' (1998) 4 *Buffalo Human Rights Law Review* 25

STREECK W, 'Neo-Voluntarism: A New European Social Policy Regime?' (1995) 1 *European Law Journal* 31

SUNSTEIN C, 'Social and Economic Rights? Lessons from South Africa' (2001) Public Law and Legal Theory Working Paper No 12, The University of Chicago

——, 'Incompletely Theorized Agreements' (1995) 108 *Harvard Law Review* 1733

SUPIOT A, 'Principe d'égalité et Limites du Droit du Travail (en marge de l'arret Stoeckel)' [1992] *Droit Social* 385

——, 'Temps de travail: pour une concordance des temps' [1995] *Droit Social* 947

SWEPSTON L, 'Human Rights Law and Freedom of Association: Development through ILO Supervision' (1998) 137 *International Labour Review* 169

SYRPIS P, 'Smoke without Fire: The Social Policy Agenda and the Internal Market' (2001) 30 *Industrial Law Journal* 271

——, 'Social Democracy and Judicial Review in the Community Order' in Kilpatrick C, Novitz T and Skidmore P (eds) *The Future of Remedies in Europe* (Oxford: Hart, 2000) 253–66

——, 'The Integrationist Rationale for EU Social Policy' in Shaw J (ed) *Social Law and Policy in an Evolving European Union* (Oxford: Hart, 2000) 17–30

SZYSZCZAK E, 'The New Paradigm for Social Policy: A Virtuous Circle?' (2001) 38 *Common Market Law Review* 1125

——, 'The Evolving European Employment Strategy' in Shaw J (ed) *Social Law and Policy in an Evolving European Union* (Oxford, Hart, 2000) 197–217

TAYLOR C, 'The Politics of Recognition' in Gutmann A (ed), *Multiculturalism: Examining the Politics of Recognition* (New Jersey: Princeton University Press, 1994) 25–74

TOEBES B, 'The Right to Health' in Eide A, Krause C and Rosas A (eds) *Economic, Cultural and Social Rights*, 2nd ed (The Hague: Kluwer, 2001) 170

——, *The Right to Health as a Human Right in International Law* (Antwerp: Intersentia/Hart, 1999)

TOOZE J, *Identification and Enforcement of Social Security and Social Assistance Guarantees under the International Covenant on Economic, Social and Cultural Rights* (PhD thesis, University of Nottingham, 2002)

TULLY J, *Strange Multiplicity: Constitutionalism in an Age of Diversity* (Cambridge: CUP, 1995)

TWOMEY P, 'Constructing a Secure Space: the Area of Freedom, Security and Justice' in O'Keeffe D and Twomey P (eds) *Legal Issues of the Amsterdam Treaty* (Oxford: Hart, 1999)

United Kingdom Parliament, House of Lords Select Committee of European Affairs, Eighth Report, *The EU Charter of Fundamental Rights* (16 May 2002)

VALTICOS N, 'International Labour Standards and Human Rights: Approaching the Year 2000' (1998) 137 *International Labour Review* 135

VAN DER MEI A, 'Cross-Border Access to Medical Care within the European Union' (1998) 5 *Maastricht Journal of European and Comparative Law* 277

VAN HOOF G, 'The Legal Nature of Economic, Social and Cultural Rights: A Rebuttal of Some Traditional Views' in Alston P and Tomasevski K (eds) *The Right to Food* (Utrecht: Stichting Studie-en Informatiecentrum Mensenrechten, 1984) 97–110

VANDAMME F, 'The Revision of the European Social Charter' (1994) 133 *International Labour Review* 635

VASAK K, 'A Thirty Year Struggle' *UNESCO Courier* (No 1977) 29

VEGETTI FINZI S, 'Female Identity between Sexuality and Maternity' in Bock G and James S (eds) *Beyond Equality and Difference. Citizenship, Feminist Politics and Female Subjectivity* (London: Routledge, 1992) 126–45

VERSCHUEREN H, 'EC Social Security Coordination Excluding Third Country Nationals: Still in Line with Fundamental Rights after the *Gaygusuz* Judgment?' (1997) 34 *Common Market Law Review* 991

VISSER J, 'The First Part-time Economy in the World: a Model to be Followed?' (2002) *Journal of European Social Policy* 24

VITORINO A, *The Charter of Fundamental Rights as a Foundation for the Area of Freedom Security and Justice*, Exeter Paper in European Law No. 4, http://www.uaces.org/RP-1-CM.pdf

VOLPP L, 'Blaming Culture for Bad Behaviour' (2000) *Yale Journal of Law and the Humanities* 89

VON BOGDANDY A, 'The European Union as a Human Rights Organization? Human Rights and the Core of the European Union' (2000) 37 *Common Market Law Review* 1307

VON DANWITZ T, 'The Charter of Fundamental Rights Between Political Symbolism and Legal Realism' (2001) *Denver Journal of International Law and Policy* 289

VOUSDEN S, '*Albany*, Market Law and Social Exclusion' (2000) 29 *Industrial Law Journal* 181

WADDINGTON L and BELL M, 'More Equal than Others: Distinguishing European Union Equality Directives' (2001) 38 *Common Market Law Review* 587

WADDINGTON L, 'Evolving Disability Policies: From Social Welfare to Human Rights— an International Trend from a European Perspective' (2001) 19 *Netherlands Quarterly of Human Rights* 141

——, *Disability, Employment and the European Community* (London: Blackstone Press, 1995)

WALBY S, *Patriarchy at Work: Patriarchal and Capitalist Relations in Employment* (Cambridge: Polity Press, 1986)

WALDRON J, *Law and Disagreement* (Oxford: OUP, 1999)

WALKER N 'Postnational Constitutionalism and the Problem of Translation' in Weiler J and Wind M (eds) *European Constitutionalism Beyond the State* (Cambridge: CUP, 2003, forthcoming)

——, 'The Idea of Constitutional Pluralism' (2002) 65 *Modern Law Review* 317

——, 'Human Rights in a Postnational Order: Reconciling Political and Constitutional Pluralism' in Campbell T, Ewing K and Tomkins A (eds) *Sceptical Essays on Human Rights* (Oxford: OUP, 2001) 119–41

——, 'The White Paper in a Constitutional Context', Jean Monnet Chair Working Paper 6/01, http://www.jeanmonnetprogram.org/papers/01/011001.rtf

WALZER M, 'The Politics of Difference: Statehood and Toleration in a Multicultural World' (1997) 10 *Ratio Juris* 165

WARD I, 'Beyond Constitutionalism: The Search for a European Political Imagination' (2001) 7 *European Law Journal* 24

——, 'Tempted by Rights: The European Union and its New Charter of Fundamental Rights' (2000–2001) *Constitutional Forum* 112

WEDDERBURN Lord, 'Inderogability, Collective Agreements and Community law' (1992) 21 *Industrial Law Journal* 245

——, 'European Community Law and Workers' Rights: Fact or Fake in 1992?' (1991) 13 *Dublin University Law Journal* 1

WEILER J, 'Epilogue: The Judicial Après Nice' in Weiler J and de Búrca G (eds), *The European Court of Justice* (Oxford: OUP, 2001) 216–26

——, 'Does the European Union Really Need a Charter of Rights?' (2000) 6 *European Law Journal* 95

——, *The Constitution of Europe* (Cambridge: CUP, 1999)

——, 'Thou Shalt Not Oppress a Stranger: On the Judicial Protection of the Human Rights of Non-EC Nationals' (1992) 3 *European Journal of International Law* 65

WEILER J, 'Eurocracy and Distrust: Some Questions Concerning the Role of the European Court of Justice in the Protection of Fundamental Human Rights Within the Legal Order of the European Communities' (1986) 61 *Washington Law Review* 1103

WEILER J and LOCKHART N, ' "Taking Rights Seriously" Seriously: The European Court and Its Fundamental Rights Jurisprudence' (1995) 32 *Common Market Law Review* 51 and 574

WEISS M, 'The Politics of the EU Charter of Fundamental Rights' in Hepple B (ed) *Social and Labour Rights in a Global Context* (Cambridge: CUP, 2003, forthcoming)

WELLENS K and BORCHARDT R, 'Soft Law in European Community Law' (1989) 14 *European Law Review* 267

WENTHOLT K, 'Formal and Substantive Equal Treatment: the Limitations and Potential of the Legal Concept of Equality' in Loenen T and Rodrigues P (eds) *Non-Discrimination Law: Comparative Perspectives* (The Hague: Kluwer, 1999) 53–64

WESTERHÄLL L and PHILLIPS C (eds) *Patients' Rights: Informed Consent, Access and Equality* (Stockholm: Nerenius & Santérus, 1994)

WHEATLEY S, 'Minority Rights and Political Accommodation in the 'New' Europe' (1997) 22 *European Law Review* Supp HRS 63

WHITEFORD E, 'Occupational Pensions and European Law: Clarity at Last?' in Hervey T and O'Keeffe D (eds) *Sex Equality Law in the European Union* (Chichester: Wiley, 1996) 21

WOUTERS J, 'Editorial' (2001) 8 *Maastricht Journal of European and Comparative Law* 3

WYNN M, 'Pregnancy Discrimination: Equality, Protection or Reconciliation?' (1999) 62 *Modern Law Review* 435

YEANDLE S, 'Women, Men, and Non-Standard Employment: Breadwinning and Caregiving in Germany, Italy and the UK' in Crompton R (ed), *Restructuring Gender Relations and Employment. The Decline of the Male Breadwinner* (Oxford: OUP, 1999) 80–104

Index